Developments in the European Union 2

Developments titles available from Palgrave Macmillan

Maria Green Cowles and Desmond Dinan (eds)
DEVELOPMENTS IN THE EUROPEAN UNION 2

Patrick Dunleavy, Andrew Gamble, Richard Heffernan and Gillian Peele (eds)
DEVELOPMENTS IN BRITISH POLITICS 7

Alain Guyomarch, Howard Machin, Peter A. Hall and Jack Hayward (eds)
DEVELOPMENTS IN FRENCH POLITICS 2

Paul Heywood, Erik Jones and Martin Rhodes (eds)
DEVELOPMENTS IN WEST EUROPEAN POLITICS 2

Stephen Padgett, William E. Paterson and Gordon Smith (eds)
DEVELOPMENTS IN GERMAN POLITICS 3

Gillian Peele, Christopher Bailey, Bruce Cain and B. Guy Peters (eds)
DEVELOPMENTS IN AMERICAN POLITICS 4

Stephen White, Judy Batt and Paul G. Lewis (eds)
DEVELOPMENTS IN CENTRAL AND EAST EUROPEAN POLITICS 3

Stephen White, Alex Pravda and Zvi Gitelman (eds)
DEVELOPMENTS IN RUSSIAN POLITICS 5

Of related interest

Ian Holliday, Andrew Gamble and Geraint Parry (eds)
FUNDAMENTALS IN BRITISH POLITICS

If you have any comments or suggestions regarding the above or other possible *Developments titles*, please write to Steven Kennedy, Publishing Director, Palgrave Macmillan, Houndmills, Basingstoke RG21 6XS, UK or e-mail s.kennedy@palgrave.com

Developments in the European Union 2

edited by

Maria Green Cowles
and
Desmond Dinan

Published 2004 by
PALGRAVE MACMILLAN
Houndmills, Basingstoke, Hampshire RG21 6XS and
175 Fifth Avenue, New York, N.Y. 10010
Companies and representatives throughout the world

PALGRAVE MACMILLAN is the global academic imprint of
the Palgrave Macmillan division of St. Martin's Press, LLC and of
Palgrave Macmillan Ltd. Macmillan® is a registered trademark in
the United States, United Kingdom and other countries. Palgrave is a
registered trademark in the European Union and other countries.

ISBN–13 978–0–333–96168–1 hardback
ISBN–1 0 0–333–96168–4 hardback
ISBN–13 978–0–333–96169–8 paperback
ISBN–10 0–333–96169–2 paperback

This book is printed on paper suitable for recycling and made from fully
managed and sustained forest sources.

A catalogue record for this book is available from the British Library.

Library of Congress Cataloging-in-Publication Data

Developments in the European Union 2 / edited by Maria Green Cowles and
    Desmond Dinan.—2nd ed.
        p. cm.
    Rev. ed. of: Developments in the European Union. 1999.
    Includes bibliographical references and index.
    ISBN 0–333–96168–4 (hbk.) —ISBN 0–333–96169–2 (pbk.)
        1. European Union. 2. European Union countries—Politics and government.
    I. Cowles, Maria Green, 1961–   . II. Dinan, Desmond, 1957–   III. Developments
    in the European Union.
    JN30.D48 2004
    341.242´ 2—dc22

                                                                    2004041583

10   9   8   7   6   5   4   3   2
13   12   11   10   09   08   07   06   05

Printed and bound in China

Contents

List of Maps, Tables and Figures

Map

Tables

Figures

Preface

This volume is an all-new replacement for *Developments in the European Union*, edited by Laura Cram, Desmond Dinan and Neill Nugent, and published in 1999. In keeping with the format of the *Developments* series, *Developments in the European Union 2* features a new cast of contributors and a new selection of topics. Our aspiration, however, has remained the same: to provide comprehensive, authoritative and informative assessments of key issues and developments in a rapidly-changing EU.

In order to help readers keep up to date with developments in the EU, especially in light of enlargement and the intergovernmental conference of 2003–2004, Palgrave Macmillan has a website linked to this and related titles. The address is http://www.palgrave.com/politics/eu.

We would like to thank the contributors for their efforts, including their rapid responses to our editorial comments and questions. We are especially grateful to Steven Kennedy, our publisher at Palgrave Macmillan, and to his assistant, Cecily Wilson, for their patience and guidance. Finally, we would like to thank our families for their encouragement and support.

MARIA GREEN COWLES
DESMOND DINAN

Notes on the Contributors

Marios Camhis is a senior official in the European Commission, Brussels. He was a visiting EU Fellow at George Mason Univeristy, Arlington, Virginia, USA, during the 2002–2003 academic year. He has written widely on social policy, urban planning and regional policy.

Maria Green Cowles is Associate Director of the University Honors Program and Scholar in Residence at American University in Washington, DC. Her recent publications include *Transforming Europe*, with James Caporaso and Thomas Risse (Cornell, 2001), and 'Non-State Actors and False Dichotomies' in the *Journal of European Public Policy* (2003).

Stephanie Curtis is an analyst at International Security Management/ TranSecur in Potomac, Maryland, USA.

Desmond Dinan is Jean Monnet Professor and Director of the International Commerce and Policy Program in the School of Public Policy, George Mason University, Arlington, Virginia, USA. His recent publications include *Europe Recast: A History of European Union* (Palgrave Macmillan, 2004), and a new edition of *Ever Closer Union: An Introduction to European Integration* (Palgrave Macmillan, 2005).

Virginie Guiraudon is a research fellow at the National Centre for Scientific Research in Lille, France, and a member of the European Union Studies Association's executive board. Her recent publications include *Controlling a New Migration World*, with Christian Joppke (Routledge, 2001), and 'The Constitution of a European Immigration Policy Domain: A Political Sociology Approach', in the *Journal of European Public Policy* (2003).

Martin Holland is Jean Monnet Professor and Director of the National Centre for Research on Europe at the University of Canterbury, New Zealand. His most recent books are *The European Union and the Third World* (Palgrave Macmillan, 2002) and a new edition of *Common Foreign and Security Policy: The First Decade* (Continuum, 2004).

Robert Ladrech is Senior Lecturer in Politics and Director of the Keele European Research Centre at Keele University, UK. His recent publications include editing a special issue of the journal *Party Politics* on Europeanization and party politics, and contributing a chapter, 'Europeanization of Political Forces', to *Member States and the EU,* edited by Simon Bulmer and Christian Lequesne (Oxford University Press, 2004).

Andrea Lenschow is an assistant professor at the University of Osnabrück. She has published on various aspects of European environmental policy, EU regulatory policy and institutional analysis. She edited and contributed to *Environmental Policy Integration; Greening Sectoral Policies in Europe* (Earthscan, 2002).

Anand Menon is Director of the European Research Institute and Professor of West European Politics in the University of Birmingham, UK. He has published widely, both in academic journals and national newspapers, such as the *Financial Times*. His books include *Governing Europe*, edited with Jack Hayward (Oxford University Press, 2003).

John D. Occhipinti is Associate Professor of Political Science and Director of European Studies at Canisius College in Buffalo, New York, USA. His recent publications include *The Politics of EU Police Cooperation: Toward a European FBI* (Lynne Rienner, 2003), and 'Justice and Home Affairs' in Neill Nugent (ed.), *European Union Enlargement* (Palgrave Macmillan, 2004).

Michael Smith is Professor of European Politics and Jean Monnet Chair in the Department of Politics, International Relations and European Studies at Loughborough University, UK. He has published widely on EU–US relations, and relations between the EU, the USA and Asia-Pacific, as well as on EU external relations and foreign policy. His recent books include *The State of the European Union, Vol. 5: Risks, Reform, Resistance and Revival*, co-edited with Maria Green Cowles (Oxford University Press, 2000). He is currently working on a co-authored text on EU–US relations and a co-edited text on the international relations of the EU (forthcoming 2004).

Aleks Szczerbiak is Senior Lecturer in Contemporary European Studies at the Sussex European Institute, University of Sussex, specializing in Central and East European politics. He is co-convenor of the European Parties Elections and Referendums Network, and Associate/Reviews Editor of *Party Politics*. His publications include *Poles Together? The Emergence and Development of Political Parties in Post-Communist Poland* (Central European University Press, 2001), and, as co-editor with Paul Taggart *Opposing Europe: The Comparative Party Politics of Euroskepticism* (Oxford University Press, 2004).

Paul Taggart is Senior Lecturer in Politics at the Sussex European Institute, University of Sussex, editor of the journal *Politics*, and co-convenor of the European Parties Elections and Referendums Network.

His publications include *Populism* (Open University Press, 2000), and *The New Populism and the New Politics* (Palgrave Macmillan, 1996).

John Van Oudenaren is chief of the European Division at the Library of Congress in Washington, DC. His publications include *Detente in Europe* (Duke University Press, 1991), *Uniting Europe: European Integration and the Post-Cold War World* (Rowman & Littlefield, 2000), and numerous articles, chapters and reports on Europe, Russia and US foreign policy.

Amy Verdun is Jean Monnet Chair and Director of the European Studies Program at the University of Victoria, British Columbia, Canada. Her recent publications include *The Euro: European Integration Theory and Economic and Monetary Union* (Rowman & Littlefield, 2002), *European Responses to Globalization and Financial Market Integration* (Macmillan – now Palgrave Macmillan, 2000), and *Strange Power: Shaping the Parameters of International Relations and International Political Economy*, edited with T. C. Lawton and J. N Rosenau (Ashgate, 2000).

Anthony Wallace is a former Foreign Service officer with the US Department of State, former Deputy Director of International Trade at Westinghouse Electric Corporation, and an adjunct professor in the School of Public Policy at George Mason University, Arlington, Virginia, USA, where he teaches courses in international political economy and the economics of European integration, on which he has published several articles and book chapters.

Alasdair R. Young is a lecturer in the Department of Politics, University of Glasgow, UK, and deputy convenor of the Department's MPhil in International Politics. His recent publications include *Extenting European Co-operation: The European Union and the 'New' International Trade Agenda* (Manchester University Press, 2002), 'Political Transfer and "Trading Up": Transatlantic Trade in Genetically Modified Food and US Politics', in *World Politics* (2003), and 'The Incidental Fortress: The Single European Market and World Trade', in *Journal of Common Market Studies* (2004).

List of Abbreviations

ACP	African, Caribbean and Pacific
APCIMS	Association of Private Client Investment Managers and Stockbrokers
ASEAN	Association of Southeast Asian Nations
ASEM	Asia–Europe Meeting
BEUC	European Bureau of Consumers' Unions
CAP	Common Agricultural Policy
CARDS	Community Assistance for Reconstruction, Development and Stabilization
CBI	Confederation of British Industry
CCP	Common Commercial Policy
CEC	Commission of the European Communities
CEE	Central and Eastern Europeans
CEPOL	The European Police College
CFSP	Common Foreign and Security Policy
CIDSE	International Co-operation for Development and Solidarity
CIS	Customs Information System
COGECA	General Committee for Agricultural Co-operation
COPA	Committee of Agricultural Organizations in Europe
DG	Directorate-General
EAGGF	European Agricultural Guidance and Guarantee Fund
EAPs	Environmental Action Programmes
EBA	Everything But Arms
EBRD	European Bank for Reconstruction and Development
EC	European Community
ECB	European Central Bank
ECHO	European Community Humanitarian Office
ECJ	European Court of Justice
ECRE	European Council for Refugees and Exiles
ECU	European Currency Unit
EEC	European Economic Community
EIA	Environmental Impact Assessment
EIB	European Investment Bank
EIOP	European Integration Online Papers
EIS	Europol Information System
EJN	European Judicial Network

ELOs	European Liaison Officers
EMS	European Monetary System
EMU	Economic and Monetary Union
EP	European Parliament
EPA	Economic Partnership Agreements
EPC	European Political Co-operation
ERDF	European Regional Development Fund
ERM	Exchange Rate Mechanism
ERT	European Round Table of Industrialists
ESCB	European System of Central Banks
ESDP	European Security and Defence Policy
ESF	European Social Fund
ETUC	European Trade Union Confederation
EU	European Union
EUPM	European Union Police Mission
FIFG	Financial Instrument for Fisheries Guidance
FPO	Freedom Party
FSAP	Financial Services Action Plan
GALILEO	EU Global Satellite Navigation System
GATS	General Agreement on Trade in Services
GDP	Gross Domestic Product
GMOS	Genetically Modified Organisms
ICC	International Criminal Court
ICTY	International Criminal Tribunal for the former Yugoslavia
IFOR	Implementation Force
IMPEL	Implementation Network
IMPs	Integrated Mediterranean Programmes
IOM	International Organization for Migration
ISPA	Instrument for Structural Policies for Pre-accession
JHA	Justice and Home Affairs
KEDO	Korean Peninsula Energy Development Organization
LDC	Least Developed Countries
LIFE	Financial Instrument for the Environment in the EU
NATO	North Atlantic Treaty Organization
NGOs	Non-Governmental Organizations
NIS	Newly Independent States
OECD	Organisation for Economic Co-operation and Development
OSCE	Organization for Security and Co-operation in Europe
PCA	Partnership and Co-operation Agreement
PHARE	Poland, Hungary Actions for Economic Reconstruction
QMV	Qualified Majority Voting

RELEX	European Commission's Directorate General for External Relations
SAAs	Stabilization and Association Agreements
SAPARD	Special Accession Programme for Agriculture and Rural Development
SCIFA	Strategic Committee on Immigration, Frontiers and Asylum
SEA	Single European Act
SFOR	Stabilization Force
SGP	Stability and Growth Pact
SIS	Schengen Information System
Synergy	Energy Co-operation
TABD	Transatlantic Business Dialogue
TACIS	Technical Assistance to the Commonwealth of Independent States
TENs	Trans-European Networks
TRACECA	Transport Corridor Europe Caucasus Asia
TRIMs	Trade-Related Investment Measures
TRIPs	Trade-Related Intellectual Property Rights
UK	United Kingdom
UN	United Nations
UNHCR	UN High Commissioner for Refugees
UNICE	Union of Industrial and Employers' Confederations of Europe
UNMIK	United Nations Interim Administration in Kosovo
USA/US	United States
WEU	West European Union
WTO	World Trade Organization

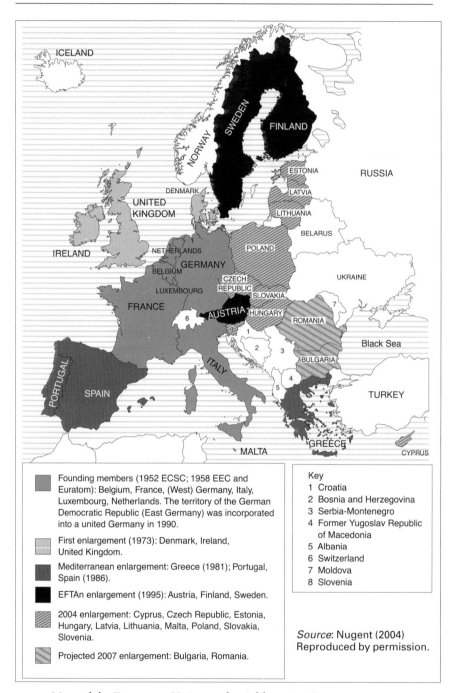

Founding members (1952 ECSC; 1958 EEC and Euratom): Belgium, France, (West) Germany, Italy, Luxembourg, Netherlands. The territory of the German Democratic Republic (East Germany) was incorporated into a united Germany in 1990.

First enlargement (1973): Denmark, Ireland, United Kingdom.

Mediterranean enlargement: Greece (1981); Portugal, Spain (1986).

EFTAn enlargement (1995): Austria, Finland, Sweden.

2004 enlargement: Cyprus, Czech Republic, Estonia, Hungary, Latvia, Lithuania, Malta, Poland, Slovakia, Slovenia.

Projected 2007 enlargement: Bulgaria, Romania.

Key
1 Croatia
2 Bosnia and Herzegovina
3 Serbia-Montenegro
4 Former Yugoslav Republic of Macedonia
5 Albania
6 Switzerland
7 Moldova
8 Slovenia

Source: Nugent (2004)
Reproduced by permission.

Map of the European Union and neighbouring European states

Introduction

MARIA GREEN COWLES AND DESMOND DINAN

Developments in the European Union (EU) since 1999, when this book's predecessor appeared, have been copious and consequential. A number stand out: the onward march of enlargement; negotiation of the Nice Treaty and Irish voters' initial rejection of it; a new aid and trade agreement with the African, Caribbean and Pacific countries; the launch by EU leaders of the so-called Lisbon strategy for economic modernization and reform; the introduction of euro notes and coins; the Convention on the Future of Europe; efforts to tighten rules on immigration and asylum; closer police and judicial co-operation in response to the terrorist attacks on the USA; the impact of the war in Iraq on the EU's fledgling defence and security policy; and the EU's involvement in the faltering Doha Development Round of trade liberalization negotiations in the World Trade Organization.

Enlargement and Economic and Monetary Union (EMU), two of the most prominent developments, had their roots in the late 1980s and early 1990s, in the single market programme and the end of the Cold War. The third, definitive, stage of EMU began in January 1999, when eleven member states (later joined by Greece) fixed their exchange rates irrevocably and followed a common monetary policy managed by the new European Central Bank. Euro notes and coins replaced national currencies three years later, without a hitch (although consumers complained of price rises on the part of opportunistic retailers). The significance of EMU, an objective stretching back to the international financial turmoil of the early 1970s, cannot be overstated. It represented a huge step forward for European integration, brought the EU into the pockets of ordinary Europeans (and visitors to the eurozone), and strengthened the EU's international economic profile.

But, as Amy Verdun points out in Chapter 5, the ultimate success of EMU remains in question. A one-size-fits-all monetary policy is less than ideal for such a disparate economic zone. Who knows how the ECB and national governments would respond to serious asymmetrical shocks? Moreover, EMU was envisioned not as an end in itself, but as a means toward the greater goal of stronger economic growth with more and better jobs. In order to push the EU in that direction, national leaders launched a strategy for economic modernization at the Lisbon summit in

March 2000. The so-called Lisbon strategy, covering an array of policy areas, sought to accelerate economic integration, using novel methods such as benchmarking and best-practice as well as traditional harmonization. Encouraged by major business groups, EU leaders identified a number of targets, including a more flexible labour market and deeper capital markets. As Anthony Wallace shows in Chapter 6, the results have been disappointing, not least because member states are too jealous of their prerogatives and sensitive to domestic political pressures to embrace the many changes called for at the Lisbon summit.

Denmark and Sweden held referendums on whether to adopt the euro; both decided against. The British government promised to hold a referendum once it judged that the time was right (economically) to jettison the pound in favour of the euro. In all three countries, as well as in the eurozone member states, EMU was a pressing political issue. Apart from the import of adopting a new currency, EMU was controversial in the participating countries because of the strictures of the Stability and Growth Pact, an instrument of fiscal rectitude that became a straitjacket during the economic slowdown of the early 2000s. Facing reduced revenues and higher welfare demands, governments chafed at the requirement to limit budget deficits to 3 per cent annually. Germany and France, the political pillars on which EMU rests, complained most about the pact, thereby jeopardizing the credibility of the entire undertaking. Eager to blame Brussels for unpopular domestic developments, national governments unintentionally encouraged a groundswell of public resentment against the EU. As Robert Ladrech argues in Chapter 3, EMU was therefore one of a number of factors contributing to the process of 'Europeanization', the interconnection of EU and domestic politics and policy-making. And as Paul Taggart and Aleks Szczerbiak show in Chapter 4, Europeanization fuelled growing Euroscepticism, the negative evaluations of European integration that many policy-makers and scholars believe contributes to the democratic deficit and therefore also to the EU's purported lack of legitimacy.

Despite its perceived impact on the everyday lives of its citizens, the EU is involved directly in only two redistributive policies: agriculture and cohesion, which account for a half and a third of the EU's expenditure, respectively. As Desmond Dinan and Marios Camhis argue in Chapter 7, the Common Agricultural Policy (CAP) and Cohesion Policy are in urgent need of reform, not least because of enlargement. Without increasing the size of the budget, a politically unpopular move, the EU cannot afford to extend full CAP and cohesion benefits immediately to the new member states of Central and Eastern Europe, which have large agricultural sectors and are economically disadvantaged relative to most other member states. Inevitably, the financial implications of enlargement caused serious difficulties in the accession negotiations and posed a major challenge to the nature of these historic EU policies.

Environmental policy, one of the most significant policy areas in the EU, does not involve the expenditure of EU funds, but imposes considerable costs on member states. In Chapter 8, Andrea Lenschow provides an overview of developments in environmental policy, which has reached a crossroads in the EU. Environmental policy may continue simply to be another EU policy, or may become a pervasive idea that influences all EU policies, internal and external. In recent years, for example, the EU has taken a proactive approach to the governance of environmental issues. Yet enlargement is testing EU environmental policy and governance severely. Economic challenges, massive environmental devastation, poor administrative capacity and EMU-imposed budgetary restraints are making it difficult for the new member states to implement EU environmental law and are slowing down the 'greening' of the region.

Unlike environmental policy, immigration and asylum policy is an area traditionally reserved for the member states. Yet, as Virginie Guiraudon shows in Chapter 9, it is at the core of the EU's 'high politics'. The end of the Cold War, the slowing of the European economy, and the terrorist attacks of September 2001 in the USA pushed immigration and asylum policy to the top of the EU's agenda. Police and judicial co-operation, the other part of the Justice and Home Affairs (JHA) pillar established by the Maastricht Treaty – and the only part still subject to intergovernmental decision-making – also moved to the top of the agenda in the aftermath of the terrorist attacks. John Occhipinti points out in Chapter 10 that the rise of transnational organized crime groups in post-Cold War Europe heightened JHA concerns in the EU. Fears that such groups would use the new Central and Eastern European member states as a launching pad for illegal activities elsewhere in the EU, together with the fallout from the terrorist attacks, generated the political will to push through major legal and institutional changes in the area of police and judicial co-operation. Accordingly, the impact of enlargement and anti-terrorism on internal security matters has prompted changes in Justice and Home Affairs unimaginable a few years earlier.

Enlargement and unrelated external developments have enhanced the EU's international profile, while complicating the EU's ability to be an effective international actor. The EU has long been described as an economic giant and a political dwarf. Although that caricature is obviously out of date, the EU still punches below its weight in the international political ring. Even economically, as Alasdair Young explains in Chapter 11, the EU's dual character as an international organization and an international trade actor constrains the EU's potential. The EU's ability to play both roles is complicated not only by its nascent powers in certain areas, but also by enlargement which, as Young notes, has increased the number and diversity of interests that must be accommodated in order to formulate a cohesive trade policy and is having a major impact in trade-related sectors such as agriculture.

Enlargement has also complicated the EU's efforts to devise an effective common foreign, security and defence policy, efforts already seriously undermined by America's muscular response to the terrorist attacks of September 2001, including the war in Iraq. Long divided on policy towards Iraq, Britain and France – the EU's strongest military players – split over the prospect of outright war. As Anand Menon explains in Chapter 12, that brought the Franco-British initiative for closer defence co-operation, launched in December 1998, to a screeching halt and threw the EU's Common Foreign and Security Policy into disarray. The situation had become so bad at the time of writing that it can only get better. EU leaders endorsed a new security strategy and attempted in the intergovernmental conference on treaty reform to give the EU the procedural means to take a more coherent stand, although the depth of the disagreement over Iraq suggested that member states' foreign policy perspectives and priorities would continue to diverge on key security issues.

The complexity of the EU's international standing and influence are fully apparent in the EU's dealings with the USA and the countries of the Asia-Pacific region, and with Russia, other former Soviet republics, and the Balkans. In Chapter 13, Michael Smith assesses the potential for a trilateral relationship between the EU, the United States and Asia-Pacific. As Smith points out, the outcome depends in part on the EU's ability to manage its growing diversity and increasing member state interests. In Chapter 14, John Van Oudenaren demonstrates the dramatic impact of enlargement on the EU's relations with the Balkans and the newly independent states of the former Soviet Union. Indeed, enlargement inaugurated an era in which the Central and Eastern European countries no longer serve as a buffer zone but as frontline states with these two potentially unstable regions. Challenges such as immigration and asylum, transnational crime and terrorism now oblige the EU to engage more closely than ever before with its new neighbours in Eastern and South-Eastern Europe.

The EU's engagement with the African, Pacific and Caribbean (ACP) countries, a group of approximately eighty developing countries with which the EU has long had a preferential agreement, underwent an important change in 2000, when the EU replaced the venerable Lomé conventions (the first of which was signed in 1975) with the Cotonou Agreement. As Martin Holland explains in Chapter 15, the new direction of Cotonou and the innovative 'Everything But Arms' initiative emerged from the perceived failings of Lomé as well as a broad consensus on the link between global development and political-economic reform. Moreover, the financial demands of enlargement prompted the EU to seek a less costly formal relationship with the ACP countries.

Those external and internal policy developments took place against the background of enlargement, including efforts to reform the EU institutionally in order to cope with the accession of ten new member states. As well as institutional issues, the prospect of enlargement brought a number of related challenges to the fore. The first was governance. How could the enlarging EU, with its single market and monetary union, co-operation on Justice and Home Affairs, and Common Foreign and Security Policy, function effectively in the domestic, European, and international arenas? The second was legitimacy. How could the EU, with its multi-level governance and growing influence in the day-to-day affairs of European citizens, be viewed as legitimate? The third was identity. What identity did the EU have in its relations with European citizens, member states, and other states in the global arena?

The 2001 Nice Treaty failed to deal adequately with the issues of governance, legitimacy and identity, as the Irish electorate's initial rejection of it demonstrated pointedly. Perhaps in another era, the Nice Treaty would not have represented a major debacle. Compared to such notable crises as the failure of the European Defence Community in 1954, for example, or the 'empty chair crisis' of 1965–6, the outcome of the pre-Nice intergovernmental conference was not so bad. After all, the unsatisfactory nature of the treaty did not risk bringing the EU to its knees. Yet the stakes in Nice were high. If governance of the EU was difficult with fifteen member states, how would it work in an EU of twenty-five member states? If legitimacy and the democratic deficit were already a concern, how would the accession of countries whose communist past had stifled their democratic development improve the situation? And if European identity was unclear at the time of Nice, how would it become more distinct with the accession of the Central and Eastern European countries? Moreover, how would the arrival of the countries of the so-called 'New Europe' affect the bitter divisions among Britain, France and Germany that erupted over the war in Iraq?

The inadequacies of the Nice Treaty, in terms of its negotiation and outcome, prompted EU leaders to adopt a new approach to treaty reform and to aim for a more ambitious result. Hence the launch of the Convention on the Future of Europe in February 2002, which produced the draft constitutional treaty in June 2003. As Desmond Dinan argues in Chapter 2, the Convention and the draft treaty are important steps in the constitutionalization of the EU, a process that began with the launch of the original communities in the 1950s. Although far from perfect, the draft constitutional treaty, with which national officials and politicians struggled in the intergovernmental conference at the end of 2003, represented a big step forward in the political development of the EU, especially in the three key areas of governance, legitimacy and identity.

As Maria Green Cowles and Stephanie Curtis show in Chapter 16, scholars of European integration theory, echoing the concerns of policymakers, have also focused in recent years on governance, legitimacy and identity. In doing so, they have introduced new public policy, comparative politics and political economy perspectives into EU scholarship. In addition, scholars have increasingly explored the Europeanization process, first apparent in member states new to the EU, as well as the enlargement process itself. The result, reflected by changes in the literature, is a more dynamic understanding today of the process of European integration.

The Convention and the intergovernmental conference provide the backdrop for this book, as does the road to enlargement that lurked behind them. Enlargement is arguably the most important development in the EU in recent years, more important even than the launch of the third stage of EMU and the introduction of the euro. Apart from providing the underlying *raison d'être* for the Convention on the Future of Europe, enlargement affected – and continues to affect – almost every area of EU activity. Enlargement is both a key development in itself and a powerful force in shaping other developments in the EU. It is, therefore, the obvious starting point for this book.

Chapter 1

The Road to Enlargement

DESMOND DINAN

The road to enlargement is long and seemingly endless. The current round of enlargement, involving the Central and Eastern European countries, plus Cyprus and Malta, began in the early 1990s, following the end of the Cold War. Previous rounds of enlargement have occupied, and sometimes preoccupied, the EU since the early 1960s, shortly after the European Community came into existence. Although episodic in its intensity, especially when the accession negotiations reach a crescendo, enlargement is therefore a major, ongoing EU development, as pervasive as economic modernization, regulatory harmonization, or other key aspects of European integration. This chapter puts enlargement in perspective by asking why countries want to join the EU, and why the EU allows new members to join. It then lays out the road to enlargement for the candidate countries, including Turkey, before assessing the likely impact of enlargement on the EU.

Why join the EU?

Prospective member states want to join the EU for many reasons. Economic advantage is often the most compelling. For example, Britain tried to thwart the European Community (EC) by proposing a rival free trade area in the mid-1950s, but failed either to undermine it or to establish an alternative pole of economic attraction in Europe. Eager for its products to gain unrestricted entry to lucrative continental markets, Britain soon abandoned the European Free Trade Association and applied to join the EC instead. But Britain had a less compelling strategic reason for wanting to join. If and when the EC became an influential global actor, whether in the realm of trade or diplomacy, Britain wanted to be able to shape the EC's orientation from the inside, rather than be marginalized on the outside.

For Britain and Denmark, which applied for EC membership at the same time, there was no question of joining (or rejoining) 'Europe'. The

EC was not then synonymous with Europe in the way in which the EU has later come to be, or projected itself to be. Only for Ireland, the other successful applicant in the first round of enlargement (Norway also applied but eventually decided not to join), did EC membership have a strong 'identity dimension'. Ireland wanted to move out of Britain's shadow and into the European light. EC membership afforded Ireland the economic as well as the political and cultural opportunity to do so. Ireland may not have felt more European for joining the EC, but the country certainly felt less British (despite fifty years of independence) as a result.

For Greece, Portugal and Spain, the next group of candidates, the question of European identity was at the forefront. Here were countries whose 'Europeanness' could hardly be questioned, but which were excluded from participation in the 'New Europe' – the European Community of liberal democracies – because of their dictatorial regimes. Only when they became democracies in the mid-1970s could they apply to join the EC, and thereby rejoin Europe. Prospective and eventual membership in the EC would also help to consolidate their fledgling democracies. The economic rationale for membership was nevertheless uppermost. Apart from consolidating democracy and reconnecting with other European countries, Greece, Portugal and Spain wanted urgently to modernize and become more prosperous.

Austria, Finland and Sweden, which joined in 1995, were already wealthy, democratic and sure of their European identity. All would have applied to join the EC much earlier, in order to gain easier market access and have a voice at the decision-making table, but felt precluded from doing so because of their military neutrality. As long as the Cold War lasted, the European neutrals could not risk compromising their international position by joining a security community, albeit without a military arm, which the Soviet Union perceived as hostile. Precisely because it bordered Russia, Finland greatly appreciated the security implications of EU membership. But for the most part, Austria, Finland and Sweden saw the end of the Cold War as an opportunity finally to participate fully in the EU marketplace, especially at a time of accelerating economic integration as a result of the single market programme.

The newly independent countries of Central and Eastern Europe wanted to join the EU for a range of economic, political and security reasons. Like the earlier Mediterranean candidates, they wanted to consolidate their fledgling democratic norms and institutions. Also like their Mediterranean counterparts, they were no less European for not having joined – or for not having been able to join – the EU at the beginning. Yet because the Cold War had cut off the Central and Eastern European countries so starkly from Western Europe, and because the EU had fifteen member states (by 1995) and was developing a larger political profile, the new candidates spoke openly of wanting to rejoin Europe by joining the EU. For them, or at least for most of their elites, Europeanness and EU membership were synonymous.

Like Finland, only more so, the Central and Eastern European candidates appreciated the security implications of EU membership. As former Soviet satellites or, in the case of Estonia, Latvia and Lithuania, former Soviet republics, they wanted to embed themselves as much as possible in a European security framework. Although their primary security objective was to join NATO, the enhanced security implicit in EU membership offered a valuable insurance policy against Russian revanchism.

Nevertheless, the economic allure of EU membership was particularly powerful. Ruined by forty years of communism, the Central and Eastern European countries struggled in the early 1990s to make the transition to capitalism. For some it was more difficult than others; each chose a slightly different path, and all progressed at varying speeds. But EU assistance and, more important, the prospect of EU membership, was crucial for a successful transition. Investment flowed into Central and Eastern Europe not only because of the abundance of cheap labour, both skilled and unskilled, but also because the countries in question were integrating into a larger, lucrative European marketplace. As relatively poor countries with large agricultural sectors, the Central and Eastern European candidates could look forward to substantial financial transfers from the EU budget through the Common Agricultural Policy and the structural funds (the instruments for implementing cohesion policy).

Yet there were costs associated with EU membership. Meeting EU environmental standards, for example, could be prohibitively expensive, not only because the Central and Eastern European countries were so poor, but also because they suffered enormous environmental damage under their old regimes. Similarly, it would be expensive for them to impose EU social policy directives, notably governing the workplace. As a result, labour costs would rise and foreign direct investment fall. Such calculations had to be balanced against the advantages of environmental improvement and better social policy legislation, a concomitant of economic modernization in democratic countries, regardless of their membership in the EU.

Loss of sovereignty was another, intangible cost, but an important one for countries long controlled by the Soviet Union. Some Central and Eastern European opponents of EU membership argued that, by joining the EU, their countries would be dominated by Brussels or, more pointedly, Berlin, instead of Moscow. Of course, membership of the EU is voluntary: the Central and Eastern European countries could have chosen to stay outside. Yet their sovereignty would still have been constrained by the need to conform, informally or otherwise, to EU rules and regulations in order to increase their global competitiveness. Given that accelerating globalization effectively reduces countries' options and independence, surrendering *de jure* sovereignty in a powerful regional entity that maximizes its members' economic and political opportunities in the global system may, paradoxically, be the best way to protect or even enhance the Central and Eastern European countries' de facto sovereignty.

As small countries, the Central and Eastern European candidates were acutely concerned about the impact of EU membership on national identity and cultural distinctiveness, be it linguistic, artistic or literary. Yet, here again, globalization rather than regionalism would appear to pose a greater potential danger. Despite the emergence of English as the lingua franca of international commerce and pop-culture, however, most countries in the world have managed to retain a distinctly national rather than a global flavour. Within the EU, national traits and characteristics abound. Sensitive to criticism of cultural homogenization, the EU celebrates and supports cultural diversity along national and regional lines. The Central and Eastern European candidates could take comfort from Ireland's experience of EU membership, not only economically, but also culturally. Long in decline, the Irish language is making a comeback as a more prosperous and self-assured people, secure in their new-found Europeanness, unabashedly emphasize their Irishness. For the Central and Eastern European countries, therefore, the cultural costs of EU membership, like the implications for national sovereignty, did not seem excessive.

Why enlarge the EU?

Countries have a choice about whether to apply for EU membership, but the EU has little choice except, eventually, to admit applicants that meet its reasonably clear-cut criteria. One of these, that member states be European countries, is less clear-cut than it seems. Turkey is an obvious example, although the EU has acknowledged Turkey's Europeanness implicitly by granting it candidate status. By contrast, as John van Oudenaren points out in Chapter 14, the Europeanness of many frontier countries to the east and south of today's EU is uncertain for political, geographical and cultural reasons. Morocco, a country that applied in 1987 to join the EC, might seem unequivocally not European. Indeed, the EC decided at the time to reject Morocco's application for that reason. As the geographical definition of Europe becomes increasingly overridden by political and cultural considerations, however, Morocco's claim to European status may not be so far-fetched in the future.

As long as they meet the economic and political criteria for membership, the EU has no grounds for excluding countries that are undeniably European, in the conventional sense of the word. The EU only clarified its membership terms in 1993 with the so-called Copenhagen criteria, when a rush of applications from the Central and Eastern European countries was imminent. These essentially specified what everyone understood already to be that case: that only European countries, with liberal, democratic, free-market systems, would be considered for membership, but not if their membership would be likely to disrupt the process of European integration. A number of observers at the time claimed that the last point was a poke in the eye for the Central and Eastern Europeans, and a warning that even if they met the supposedly objective criteria, the EU could still refuse to admit them. Yet France had kept Britain out of the EC throughout the 1960s precisely because of French fears that British membership would prevent completion of the CAP, a vital French objective and an essential ingredient of deeper European integration. Only after concluding a financial agreement in 1970 that secured the future of the CAP did the French lift their veto on British membership.

Even then, Britain's accession negotiations were arduous. Each side (Britain and the EC) wanted the best budgetary deal, and the British tried to protect their special interests. Eventually, the negotiations ended satisfactorily (although the budgetary agreement became a major bone of contention in Britain's relations with the EC), and the Community enlarged for the first time in 1973, twelve years after Britain applied to join. Despite the difficult negotiations and the long delay, Britain's accession was, for all intents and purposes, unstoppable. Even if they had the support of the other member states, the French could not have kept Britain out indefinitely. After all, the European Community was precisely that: a community of European states. Some of the original six member states might have had misgivings about increasing the EC's membership, but they could not deny the right of Britain, Denmark, Ireland and Norway to join the European club.

The members of the club had serious economic misgivings about admitting Greece, Portugal and Spain, but were once again hoist by their own petard. The rhetoric of European integration was inclusive. As Robert Schuman said in his famous declaration in May 1950, the EC was open to every European country that wanted to participate in it. Thirty years later, Western Europe was in a deep recession and the prospect of admitting three poor countries to the EC did not appeal to most member states. The Greeks deftly played the European card, emphasizing their cultural affinity with the Western European countries. Dismissing the Commission's advice to proceed slowly because of Greece's economic backwardness, the member states followed their hearts rather than their heads and embraced Greece as the cradle of Western civilization. Portugal and Spain, which posed even greater economic problems, had a more difficult time getting into the EC. But they prevailed because they were bound to: how could the EC have excluded two undeniably European countries in need not only of economic support but also of political solidarity?

Yet from the perspective of the original member states, enlargement was a difficult and disruptive process whose drawbacks were obvious and benefits unclear. The first enlargement coincided with a global economic recession and the onset of 'Eurosclerosis'. That was hardly the fault of the new member states, but two of them, Britain and Denmark, brought into the EC a strong streak of Euroscepticism that exacerbated the EC's problems. The government that came to power in Greece soon after the country's EC accession was virulently Eurosceptical, although adept at wringing the greatest economic advantage from membership. The need to fund regional development in Greece, Portugal, Spain, Ireland and parts of Britain – a political as much as an economic imperative – was not particularly popular in the original member states. The economic potential of a large European marketplace seemed more than offset in the early 1980s by the evident costs of enlargement.

The EC's prospects improved greatly in the late 1980s, with the launch of the single market programme during a period of strong economic growth. By that time the EC seemed also to have reached the limits of its potential membership. The Cold War cut off the countries of Central and Eastern Europe, and precluded the European neutrals from applying to join. That changed abruptly after the Berlin Wall came down. Jacques Delors, president of the European Commission, understandably tried to consolidate the single market and complete economic and monetary union before allowing more countries to join. He tried to ward off applications from the European neutrals by offering virtual EC membership via the European Economic Area, and from the Central and Eastern European countries by offering limited market access and other assistance via the Europe Agreements. Both sets of countries were dissatisfied with the Commission's response. They wanted nothing less than full membership, and the EU had little choice but to let them in.

Because of the steady growth of the EC's responsibilities since the 1980s, especially with the launch of the single market programme and the decision to embark on economic and monetary union, the challenges of EU membership became increasingly more formidable for new entrants. Given their advanced economies and membership in the European Economic Area, Austria, Finland and Sweden could cope relatively easily with the rigours of joining the EU. Not so the countries of Central and Eastern Europe, which had a weak administrative and legal infrastructure, suffered from massive environmental degradation, and seemed unable to withstand the pressures of intra-EU competitiveness. Turkey's situation was worse: as well as economic and administrative shortcomings, the country lacked a solid democratic foundation.

Despite the tendency for existing member states to view enlargement uncharitably, the accession of new member states has benefited the EU greatly. Enlargement has added to the EU's economic as well as physical size, and to the EU's share of global trade, therefore allowing the EU to become a major international actor. Enlargement has diversified the EU's interests and obliged it to deal with parts of the world of particular importance to the acceding member states, such as Latin America in the case of Portugal and Spain. Enlargement has also allowed the EU to fill the European space to which its founders and leaders always staked a claim. This is especially true of Central and Eastern European enlargement.

The current round of enlargement also allows the EU to fulfil what some see as its destiny: overcoming the East–West political divide, even though an East–West economic divide will persist for a long time to come. Central and Eastern European enlargement also allows the EU to revive one of its original reasons for existing: to promote stability and enhance security in Europe. The German Question has long been dormant but may have been answered definitively by unification in 1990. But the Central and Eastern European Question – how to modernize and stabilize a region that was chronically insecure in the early twentieth century, and frozen in time for much of the post-war period – can finally be fully addressed. The answer, surely, is to embed Central and Eastern Europe in the EU – a close association of liberal democratic states, bound together by common values and shared sovereignty.

Preparing Central and Eastern Europe for enlargement

So many countries had never before applied at the same time to join the EU (Table 1.1 chronicles the road to enlargement for the Central and Eastern European countries, plus Cyprus and Malta). By Western European standards, all were poor, stunted by forty years of communism. Apart from Poland, all were relatively small. Well before beginning formal accession negotiations, the EU strove to bring the Central and Eastern European countries up to a level of economic performance, political stability and administrative capacity necessary to endure the pressures of membership. The EU's *acquis communautaire* (body of rules and regulations) had grown considerably since the acceleration of European

Table 1.1   Chronology of englargement

Country	Application	Commission opinion	Began negotiations	Accession treaty	Referendum	Membership
Cyprus	3 July 1990	30 June 1993	31 March 1998	16 April 2003	None	1 May 2004
Malta	16 July 1990	30 June 1993	13 October 1999	16 April 2003	8 March 2003	1 May 2004
Hungary	31 March 1994	16 July 1997	31 March 1998	16 April 2003	4 December 2003	1 May 2004
Poland	4 May 1994	16 July 1997	31 March 1998	16 April 2003	7–8 June 2003	1 May 2004
Slovakia	27 June 1995	16 July 1997	13 October 1999	16 April 2003	16–17 May 2003	1 May 2004
Latvia	13 October 1995	16 July 1997	13 October 1999	16 April 2003	20 September 2003	1 May 2004
Estonia	24 November 1995	16 July 1997	31 March 1998	16 April 2003	14 September 2003	1 May 2004
Lithuania	8 December 1995	16 July 1997	13 October 1999	16 April 2003	10–11 May 2003	1 May 2004
Czech Republic	17 January 1996	16 July 1997	31 March 1998	16 April 2003	13–14 June 2003	1 May 2004
Slovenia	10 June 1996	16 July 1997	31 March 1998	16 April 2003	23 March 2003	1 May 2004

integration in the mid-1980s. The EU made a massive addition to it at the time of the Amsterdam Treaty in 1997 by incorporating the so-called Schengen regime on open borders. Starting from a lower base of preparedness than any previous applicants, the Central and Eastern European countries had even more catching up to do.

The EU collectively, and the member states separately, helped, through various programmes, to bring the Central and Eastern European countries along. This amounted to extending the EU by stealth in order to facilitate the success of the accession negotiations at a later date. The challenges were formidable. Concerned about latent irredentism and weak underpinnings for minority rights in Central and Eastern Europe, the EU took one of its first Common Foreign and Security Policy initiatives (the so-called Stability Pact) in the region. The physical infrastructure in most Central and Eastern European countries was in urgent need of repair, as were the administrative and legal foundations. The state of the environment was appalling. Nevertheless, politicians and officials in the region, impatient to join the EU, expressed frustration with the slow pace of the accession process. So did the USA, a champion of rapid enlargement.

The EU treated the candidates equally, yet some were more equal than others. Poland, the largest and most strategically located, was in a category of its own. It was hard to imagine Poland not being among the first countries to join, a presumption that gave the Poles some leverage in their dealings with the EU, and that bothered Poland's fellow candidates. The Czech Republic and Hungary, also strategically located and better off than most of the other candidates, were in a privileged position as well. Germany made no secret of its wish, for geopolitical more than economic reasons, to see these countries in the EU as soon as possible. It was no surprise, therefore, when the Commission announced in 1997, as part of its *Agenda 2000* proposals for enlargement, that Poland, the Czech Republic and Hungary, although not yet ready to join, were at least ready to begin accession negotiations. It was somewhat surprising though, when the Commission included Estonia and Slovenia with them. Those two countries were making reasonably rapid progress, but were not that far ahead of the two other Baltic States (Latvia and Lithuania). The European Council endorsed the Commission's recommendations at the Luxembourg summit in December 1997, paving the way for the opening of accession negotiations with five of the Central and Eastern European applicants in March 1998.

The EU's formal differentiation between the five front runners and the other five applicants was contentious among the member states as well as among the countries concerned. The five countries that did not begin accession negotiations in 1998 feared they would fall further behind.

Some member states, notably Denmark, Finland and Sweden, with close ties to the Baltic states, warned about the possible emergence of a new division between Estonia on the one hand, and Latvia and Lithuania on the other. Emerging from a bleak period of authoritarian rule in the early post-Cold War period, Slovakia needed reassurance rather than rejection from the EU. Bulgaria and Romania, undoubtedly poor performers even by prevailing regional standards, risked remaining for ever beyond the pale of European integration.

The shock of rejection, or of perceived rejection, galvanized the other five applicants to catch up with the rest as soon as possible. Indeed, informal peer pressure between both groups of applicants, and among the applicants as a whole, contributed greatly to the acceleration of the accession process. The Commission conducted a so-called screening exercise with each applicant, a stocktaking of their adoption so far of the *acquis communautaire*. The results were available for all to see. Similarly, the Commission released regular updates on the negotiations, which were organized into about thirty chapters, corresponding to EU policy areas (agriculture, single market, environment and so on). Once negotiations on a particular chapter were completed, the Commission ticked a box on a scorecard that it updated frequently on the World Wide Web. Candidates soon competed among themselves to close the chapters; none wanted to be a laggard.

An impressive performance by the 'other five' applicants, together with the outbreak of war in Kosovo in 1999, which reminded the EU of the danger of instability in South-Eastern Europe and the importance of enlargement as a stabilizing factor, prompted the Commission to recommend, and the European Council to endorse, the opening of accession negotiations with the remaining Central and Eastern European applicants. The new round of negotiations began in February 2000. Thereafter, the EU no longer differentiated officially between the Central and Eastern European applicants, although unofficially the EU and the candidates themselves appreciated that Bulgaria and Romania were unlikely to join at the same time as the others.

Inevitably, the negotiators concluded the easiest chapters first. As more and more check marks appeared on the negotiation scorecards, the most difficult chapters were emphasized. Each applicant had particular issues to address in the negotiations; all had a special interest in chapters involving the redistribution of EU money, notably agriculture and cohesion. All were also concerned about the right of free movement for their citizens in the EU, a basic attribute of the single market, which some member states, fearful of a post-enlargement influx of Central and Eastern Europeans into Western Europe, wanted to limit.

The EU had long been reluctant to set a date for enlargement lest the applicant countries assume that it was their right to join at the appointed time. However, setting a date could hasten the negotiations by encouraging the applicants to conclude the remaining chapters before the appointed time. Visiting EU politicians liked to please their Central and Eastern European hosts by announcing a date for enlargement, much to the irritation of national and EU officials. For example, German Chancellor Helmut Kohl famously announced in Warsaw in 1998 that Poland would be in the EU by 2000. When that date came and went, 2002 became the next presumed year of enlargement. Instead, a consensus emerged in 2002 that if the negotiations ended by December, enlargement could take place in 2004. Successive presidencies, especially the Danish presidency in the second half of 2002, worked closely with the Commission to make that happen. EU leaders decided at their summit in October 2002 that eight of the applicants (excluding Bulgaria and Romania) would be eligible to join in 2004, subject to a resolution of all outstanding issues, notably agriculture, before the end of the year. In a scene reminiscent of previous enlargements, intensive negotiations to conclude the accession agreements continued until the very last minute. Their success made it possible for the European Council, meeting in Copenhagen in December 2002, to give the green light to enlargement. In general, the prospective member states overwhelmingly endorsed EU accession in national referenda held throughout 2003.

The Mediterranean candidates

The Mediterranean candidates – Cyprus, Malta and Turkey – were in a different category from the Central and Eastern European countries, with Malta posing a special challenge. The EU was concerned that Malta, with a population similar in size to that of Luxembourg but without Luxembourg's history of EU involvement, would be unable to fulfil its institutional responsibilities, especially in the Council presidency. That was one of many reasons why the Convention on the Future of Europe proposed moving from a rotating to a 'permanent' presidency. Otherwise Malta was well off economically, and well-developed administratively. The large and influential Labour Party traditionally opposed EU membership and could have become a bastion of Maltese Euroscepticism within the EU, but from the EU's point of view that was a domestic Maltese issue of relatively little import precisely because of Malta's small size.

Cyprus, another small Mediterranean island, posed a special challenge for a different and more important reason. Since 1974, Cyprus has been divided into the self-styled Turkish Republic of Northern Cyprus, an enclave propped up economically, politically and militarily by Turkey,

Table 1.2 *Enlargement referendums on EU accession*

Country	Referendum	Results of referendum		
		Turnout (%)	*Yes (%)*	*No (%)*
Malta	8 March 2003	91.00	53.65	46.35
Slovenia	23 March 2003	60.29	89.61	10.39
Hungary	12 April	45.62	83.76	16.34
Lithuania	10–11 May 2003	63.37	91.07	8.93
Slovakia	16-17 May 16 2003	52.15	92.46	6.20
Poland	7–8 June 2003	58.85	77.45	22.55
Czech Republic	13–14 June 2003	55.21	77.33	22.67
Cyprus	None	Ratified treaty without a referendum		
Estonia	14 September 2003	64.02	66.84	33.16
Latvia	20 September 2003	72.53	67.00	32.30

Source: Europa, Englargement: The Accession Process. Website: http://europa.eu.int/comm/enlargement/negotiations /accession_process.htm

and the Greek-Cypriot south, which enjoyed international recognition as a sovereign state. The EU did not want to acquire a bitterly-divided new member state, but Greece threatened to block enlargement as a whole if the EU discriminated against Cyprus on the basis of its peculiar geopolitical position. The EU duly opened negotiations with Cyprus in March 1998, along with five of the Central and Eastern European candidates.

Rauf Denktash, the hard-line leader of Northern Cyprus, objected strenuously to the Greek-Cypriot government negotiating for the entire island and refused to have anything to do with the accession process. The EU responded by pressing Turkey, which wanted to join the EU, to put pressure on Denktash to come to terms with the Cypriot government and end the division of the island. Denktash proved impervious to such pressure, which some hard-liners in Turkey were in any case unwilling to apply. Denktash's intransigence was matched by that of the Greek Cypriot leadership, despite the opening in April 2003 of the wall separating the two communities. In a UN-sponsored referendum in April 2004, a majority of Turkish Cypriots nevertheless endorsed a plan for reunification, which a large majority of Greek Cypriots rejected. Much to the dismay of many Turkish Cypriots and the international community, the rejectionist Greek Cypriots enjoyed the benefits of EU membership as of May 2004, having condemned the northern part of the island to a state of limbo, outside the EU.

Turkey itself applied to join in 1987, but the EU only took its application seriously a decade later, when the prospect of large-scale Central and Eastern European enlargement made the country's possible accession seem less anomalous. Nevertheless Turkey was in a unique position: apart from being poor and politically volatile, it had a huge population (if it ever joined the EU, Turkey would be the second–largest member state, after Germany) and was predominantly Muslim. Many Europeans doubted that Turkey was European, either geographically or culturally. As the definition of Europeanness grew to be less precise and more inclusive in the post-Cold-War period, however, it seemed churlish to question Turkey's European credentials, especially as Turkey had orientated itself firmly towards the West almost a century earlier. Nevertheless, a deep distrust of Turkey's Muslim heritage accounted in large part for the EU's standoffish approach to the country.

As Samuel Huntington observed in his famous article on the 'clash of civilizations', Turkey is a 'torn country' whose elites want to join the EU, whose population may be indifferent towards membership, and towards which the elites and populations of the existing member states are decidedly indifferent (Huntington, 1993, p. 31). Turkey's trump card is its strategic location on the fault line of East and West, in a chronically unstable region. Turkey wants to join the EU not only for the usual political and economic reasons, but also to shore up secularism against Islamic fundamentalism. The EU strongly opposes Islamic fundamentalism but argues that, as long as Turkey fails to meet the Copenhagen criteria, membership in the EU is not feasible. Nevertheless, in deference to Turkish sensitivity and to US pressure on Turkey's behalf, the EU formally recognized Turkey as a 'candidate' country and agreed at the Copenhagen summit in December 2002 to decide by the end of 2004 whether to open accession negotiations. In order to ensure a favourable outcome, Turkey is undertaking extensive constitutional and political reform. But Turkey has a long way to go economically to meet the Copenhagen criteria, and Turkey's commitment to minority rights and democratic norms and practices remains questionable.

Preparing the EU for enlargement

The EU had insisted that the candidate countries undertake extensive reforms in anticipation of enlargement; reforms that it was in their interests in any case to undertake. Yet, as Desmond Dinan shows in Chapter 2, the EU had avoided undertaking extensive (and necessary) internal reforms in anticipation of enlargement. These reforms were of two kinds: institutional and policy. With each round of enlargement, the EU had increased in size, but its institutional structure had remained largely unchanged. The European Parliament had tried to link enlargement and institutional reform when Austria, Finland and Sweden joined in 1995, but succeeded only in getting the member states to promise to discuss the issue in the next intergovernmental conference, scheduled to begin in 1996. The key questions concerned the size and composition of the Commission, voting weights and the threshold for a qualified majority in the Council of Ministers, and greater use of voting for legislative decision-making. Perhaps because the next round of enlargement was still not imminent, member states ducked these questions at the 1996–7 intergovernmental conference. The only institutional change in the ensuing Amsterdam Treaty relating directly to enlargement was a mechanism to suspend from the EU any member state that violated its citizens' fundamental rights.

Member states agreed in the Amsterdam Treaty to hold another intergovernmental conference closer to the expected date of enlargement, specifically to undertake institutional reform. The Nice Treaty of 2001, which emerged from that conference, was a procedural and public relations disaster. Focused almost exclusively on institutional issues, the conference pitted small against large member states, with the large member states wanting to redress what they saw as an institutional imbalance, and the small member states wanting to preserve what they saw as an institutional balance. The so-called Nice package of institutional reforms, covering the composition of the Commission and the modalities of qualified majority voting, tilted the balance of power in the EU towards the large member states while making the EU's decision-making procedures even more cumbersome and complicated.

The Nice Treaty also included the allocation of votes in the Council and seats in the European Parliament for the candidate countries (apart from Turkey). In previous enlargements, such institutional issues had been included in the accession negotiations. The acceding countries were understandably miffed that the member states decided these issues among themselves, presenting them to the applicants as a fait accompli. Representatives of the applicant countries lobbied furiously at the Nice summit in December 2000, hoping to win an extra vote in the Council or seat in the Parliament. Some, such as Poland, fared well; others, such as Lithuania, were less successful.

The unsatisfactory nature of the intergovernmental conference and treaty change, both procedurally and substantively, prompted a 'post-Nice' debate on the EU's future that began in the pre-Nice period. That was the genesis of the Convention on the Future of Europe, which opened in February 2002 and concluded with the presentation to the European Council of a Draft Constitutional Treaty in June 2003. Representatives of the candidate countries participated in the Convention, although not in a decision-making capacity. Nevertheless, they had as much influence on the proceedings as most other members, given that the leadership (notably Valéry Giscard d'Estaing, the Convention chairman) made the key decisions. The Convention was a good opportunity for the Central and Eastern European politicians, in particular, to meet and mingle with their Western European counterparts, and to immerse themselves in a discussion of the EU's future.

The institutional provisions of the Draft Constitutional Treaty were extremely controversial. They included electing a president of the European Council for a term of up to five years; maintaining member state representation in the Commission, but empowering a core group of fifteen commissioners; and introducing new thresholds for qualified majority voting (a majority of member states representing at least 60 per cent of the population). That set the stage for a bruising intergovernmental conference in 2003, reminiscent of the pre-Nice conference. The soon-to-be member states had different positions on the draft Constitutional Treaty. As a biggish country that fared well in the redistribution of votes in the Nice Treaty, Poland wanted to preserve the Nice package. However, Poland shared the concerns of the other new entrants that the original large member states would dominate the European Council presidency and try to run the EU as if it were their own private fiefdom.

Some of the existing member states had similar concerns. As a result, new alliances emerged between some existing and prospective member states in the run-up to the 2003–04 intergovernmental conference. For example, the Czech government hosted a meeting in Prague in September 2003 of representatives of the so-called 'like-minded' group (Austria, Czech Republic, Denmark, Estonia, Finland, Greece, Hungary, Ireland, Latvia, Lithuania, Poland, Portugal, Slovakia, Slovenia and Sweden) to try to stake out common positions on key institutional issues. The group included all eight Central and Eastern European countries slated to join in May 2004 and all the small member states then in the EU – except the Benelux countries, whose status as original member states put them in an anomalous position.

The 2004 enlargement was unique among EU enlargements in many respects, one of the most important being the extent to which it forced the EU to confront the nagging question of institutional reform. It also obliged the EU to think about policy reform, primarily for financial reasons. How could the EU afford to allocate farm subsidies and structural funds to the Central and Eastern European countries without breaking the bank or taking the politically unpopular step of raising revenue? As Desmond Dinan and Marios Camhis show in Chapter 7, the EU managed to do so during the remainder of the 2000–06 financial perspective (budgetary cycle) by reducing the level of subsidies for Central and Eastern European farmers to much less than that for Western European farmers (about which the Central and Eastern European governments are justifiably aggrieved), and allocating an amount of money for cohesion that fits within the existing financial framework. The inevitable conflict over the financial implications of enlargement, foreshadowed by the *Agenda 2000* negotiations in 1999, broke out over the size and shape of the 2007–13 financial perspective. The new Central and Eastern European member states are participating fully and actively in the budgetary negotiations, which must be resolved before the end of 2006.

The enlarging EU

Although weighty political and economic issues suffuse the enlargement debate, the most immediate practical challenge for the EU is to manage more seats at the table and interpreters' booths in the room. Yet that challenge is easily surmountable. No sooner was the accession treaty signed in Athens, in April 2003, than ministers from the acceding countries began to attend Council meetings as observers. Similarly, parliamentarians from the acceding countries joined the party groups in the European Parliament, also as observers. The Commission began the process of recruiting officials from the acceding countries in order to slot them into positions, allocated according to an unofficial quota of national representation in the EU civil service, once enlargement took place. Central and Eastern European countries lobbied to place their nationals at the highest level in the Eurocracy, in the game of musical chairs that accompanies each round of enlargement. The linguistic challenge did not affect day-to-day operations very much in the institutions, where English and French remained the working languages.

The institutional challenge was greater at the national level which, thanks to the process of Europeanization, as Robert Ladrech points out in Chapter 3, could not be separated neatly from the European level. The most EU-savvy officials from the acceding countries went to Brussels, while those remaining in national capitals and at the regional level were much less familiar with the EU. That compounded the general problem of poor institutional capacity, which manifested itself even before formal enlargement when the Commission tried, with varying levels of success, to negotiate arrangements for the transfer of structural funds to the Central and Eastern European countries. Eligible to receive such funding from January 2004, many of the countries concerned did not have adequate programmes or procedures in place to avail themselves of the amount allocated to them.

Enlargement affected the organizational culture of the EU's institutions. Officials from new member states brought with them new languages, traditions and ways of doing things. They joined existing networks – linguistic, educational and professional – rather than form new ones (apart from the obvious national networks), and their arrival strengthened the prevalence of English over French as the main working language. Less steeped in the EU's history and lore than existing officials, those from the new member states were less deferential toward France and French policy preferences. Linguistically as well as politically, enlargement further undermined French influence in the EU's institutions.

Enlargement exacerbated a major political struggle among the member states over institutional representation and influence. Yet the eventual institutional implications of enlargement would take a long time to work out. The main institutional provisions of the Nice Treaty were planned to come into effect in November 2004, at the time of the swearing in of the new Commission. But the institutional provisions of the Constitutional Treaty, supposed to become effective in November 2009 with the swearing in of the next Commission, would supercede them. It would only be at the end of the first decade of the twenty-first century, by which time Turkey could be much closer to membership, that the institutional impact of enlargement would become fully apparent.

In time, the policy implications of enlargement will become increasingly apparent as well. Even with well-oiled institutional machinery (however unlikely that is in the EU) the involvement of so many more actors is bound to complicate policy-making procedures. Apart from the multiplicity of actors involved, the need to accommodate so many interests and preferences will inevitably affect the substance of EU policy, as many of the contributions in this volume make clear. Overall, the enlarging EU is a more diverse and differentiated place, harder to manage institutionally and politically. With twenty-five member states and other countries queuing up to join, the EU is, ironically, both more European and less united. Accordingly, the key challenges of governance, legitimacy and identity will be uppermost for a long time to come.

Chapter 2

Reconstituting Europe

DESMOND DINAN

In February 2002, the European Union (EU) launched a novel procedure, a Convention of the Future of Europe, to reconstitute itself in fundamental ways. The purpose of the Convention was not, strictly speaking, to revise the treaties, but rather to recommend revisions to the EU's heads of state and government. They, in turn, convened an intergovernmental conference (a conference of national representatives) in October 2003, which alone had the legal authority to change the treaties, subject to ratification by the member states.

Intergovernmental conferences are major events in the history of the EU. The Single European Act (SEA) of 1986 and the Maastricht Treaty of 1992, two epochal episodes in the constitutional development of the EU, were preceded by intensive intergovernmental conferences. The Nice Treaty of 2001, a revision of the EU's founding treaties, emerged from an equally exhaustive conference, but was a severe disappointment. Lacking a big idea such as the single market programme at the time of the SEA, or Economic and Monetary Union (EMU) at the time of Maastricht, the Nice Treaty dealt with highly charged but narrowly focused institutional issues. With the EU facing widespread public disillusionment and about to embark on an unprecedented round of enlargement, the Nice Treaty was a public relations disaster.

Under pressure after the Nice debacle to avoid business as usual, EU leaders decided in December 2001 to precede the next intergovernmental conference with the Convention, consisting of representatives of national and EU institutions, buttressed by a forum through which ordinary Europeans could provide some input. The Convention therefore represented a democratization of the treaty reform process. Although not a decision-making body, the Convention had considerable moral and political suasion.

From the outset, the Convention aimed for a new constitutional treaty, not simply a revision of the existing treaties. While not tantamount to proclaiming a new state, let alone a super-state, the adoption of a constitutional treaty would represent an important development in the political and institutional history of the EU. By emphasizing features that are constitutional and traditionally state-like in nature, the new treaty would take the EU closer to the goal of European political union.

This chapter examines the constitutional character of the EU, with particular focus on the Convention and its outcome. These are best understood in the context of the EU's constitutional development since the launch of the first European Community in the early 1950s. The first part of the chapter therefore reviews institutional adaptation and reform over the course of the last fifty years. The second part outlines how the EU became, by the early 2000s, a constitutional entity of a unique kind, a quasi-federation of sovereign states with a constitutional charter but not a formal constitution. The third part examines the decision to hold the Convention and draft a constitutional treaty, and the fourth assesses the conduct of the Convention itself. The chapter concludes with a reflection on the nature of the reconstituting EU.

Institutional adaptation and reform

What began in the early 1950s as a putative common market for coal and steel changed over the years into the EU, a polity with an ever-wider policy reach and an ever-larger membership. During that time, the EU's institutional architecture remained remarkably stable. The Coal and Steel Community's institutions consisted of a Council representing national governments, a High Authority representing the common interest, an Assembly representing 'the peoples' of the member states, and a supranational Court to ensure the rule of law. The new Communities, and later the EU, adopted the same basic arrangement. The only major changes were the addition in the 1970s of the Court of Auditors, with responsibility for financial accounting, and the European Council, a forum for regular meetings of the heads of state and government and the Commission president. The Court of Auditors was the result of a formal treaty change; the European Council of an informal political agreement.

The Commission

The Commission's role and influence changed over time, depending on political circumstances, national and Commission leadership, and prevailing integration projects. Flushed with the success of the common market's smooth implementation, Walter Hallstein, the Commission's first president, overreached himself in the mid-1960s when he tried to link a new financial agreement for the Common Agricultural Policy with an extension of the Commission and the European Parliament's budgetary powers. French President Charles de Gaulle reacted by withdrawing French representation from the Council, and linking that, in turn, to a demand for limits on the use of qualified majority voting. In the aftermath of the so-called 'empty chair crisis', the Commission retreated politically in the face of more assertive national interests.

The Commission regained its political prominence in the mid-1980s under the leadership of Jacques Delors, its most successful president. As with Hallstein's, Delors's presidency coincided with the launch of a major initiative for deeper economic integration – this time, the completion of the single market. Like Hallstein, Delors also sought to build political union on the back of successful economic integration. But unlike Hallstein, Delors had the support of the powerful French and German leaders. Delors and the Commission rode the wave of the single market programme and became prime movers in the quest for EMU.

However the Commission's remarkable success contained the seeds of its political downfall. Jealous of its increasing assertiveness, national governments clipped the Commission's wings. An unelected and inherently unpopular institution, the Commission suffered grievously from the public backlash against the Maastricht Treaty, and the Commission's political influence waned well before Delors left office in 1995. The Commission's enforced resignation four years later caused further damage, as did growing criticism of the Commission's record of policy implementation.

The Rome Treaty of 1957 gave the Commission two important legislative and executive prerogatives: the exclusive right to initiate legislation, and the authority to implement policy. Based on its claim of impartiality and continuity, the Commission successfully defended its right of legislative initiative in successive intergovernmental conferences. Yet in the Maastricht Treaty, national governments gave the Commission only a shared right of initiative in the politically-sensitive Common Foreign and Security Policy (CFSP), a new area of EU activity, and severely limited the Commission's legislative role in the other new and equally sensitive area of Justice and Home Affairs (JHA). National governments later gave the Commission a prominent legislative role in immigration and asylum policy-making, one part of the JHA portfolio, but kept the Commission at arm's length from judicial and police co-operation, the other part of it.

The Commission fared less well in its defence of executive authority. Soon after the launch of the European Community (EC), national governments established an elaborate committee structure (so-called 'comitology') to oversee the Commission's implementation of EU policy. The Single European Act legitimized the Council's right to encroach on the Commission's executive powers, and the Commission failed in successive intergovernmental conferences to regain its original authority. Critics of the Commission's record of policy implementation are often unaware of the curbs on Commission autonomy imposed by comitology, although criticism of the Commission's managerial performance is generally warranted.

Regardless of the Commission's role and responsibilities, the Commission's composition remained largely unchanged over time. Only in 2000, at the end of the intergovernmental conference that resulted in the Nice Treaty, did EU leaders agree to scrap the old formula whereby large member states appointed two commissioners each, and small member states appointed one each. As part of a deal that redistributed Council votes in their favour, the large member states agreed to appoint only one commissioner each, with the size of the Commission being limited to twenty-five members, beginning in 2005. The Convention presented an ideal opportunity to devise a new formula for appointing the Commission thereafter when, as a result of continuing enlargement, there would be fewer commissioners than member states, while at the same time trying to strengthen the Commission's legitimacy and authority.

The European Parliament

The Parliament of the original Communities consisted of delegates of national parliaments charged with drawing up proposals for direct elections, which the Council was to adopt unanimously and the member states to enact in accordance with their constitutional requirements. Disagreements among member states delayed the holding of the first direct elections until 1979. When they eventually took place, direct elections enhanced the profile and legitimacy of the European Parliament (EP), but not its popularity (the turnout was low and declined in successive five-yearly elections). By virtue of being directly elected, the Parliament staked a claim to greater political power. Earlier, in 1970, a number of sympathetic member states had insisted on granting the EP budgetary power as part of the landmark agreement on the EC's 'own resources' (monies that accrued directly to the EC's coffers).

The original treaties provided for parliamentary involvement in legislative decision-making only through the consultation procedure. The EP could submit an opinion on a legislative proposal, which the Council generally ignored. In an effort to assert its authority at the time of the first direct elections, the EP challenged the validity of a Council directive on the grounds that the Council had acted before receiving the EP's opinion. The Court supported the EP and struck down the directive, proclaiming that the consultation procedure 'reflects at Community level the fundamental principle that the peoples should take part in the exercise of power through the intermediary of an elected assembly' (Corbett, 2001, pp. 119–20).

The Court's ruling emboldened the EP to argue that it was best placed among the EU's institutions to close the democratic deficit, a term first used in the 1970s to describe the apparent gap between the governed and the governing in the EC. The EP therefore demanded a greater role in legislative decision-making. Thanks again to the support of sympathetic member states, Parliament initially won the right, in the SEA, to a second reading of draft legislation under the 'co-operation' procedure.

The EP won another dramatic extension of its legislative role in the Maastricht Treaty. Under the 'codecision' procedure, the EP acquired legislative authority, in certain policy areas, equal to that of the Council. Subsequent treaty amendments tightened up the codecision procedure in the EP's favour and extended its use to new policy areas. As its legislative powers increased, the EP sought a corresponding role in implementing EU policy through the comitology system. Giving Parliament a role in the murky area of comitology would help to eradicate another source of democratic deficit.

Having increased its formal authority progressively, the EP demonstrated its political coming of age dramatically by forcing the Commission's resignation in 1999 over allegations of corruption in the executive body. The EP always had the right to sack the Commission. Only when the Commission was weakened in the post-Maastricht period did the EP feel strong enough to flex its muscles. In the event, the Commission jumped before being pushed. Combined with the EP's recent practice of vetting the Commission president-designate and the other Commission appointees, the resignation crisis greatly strengthened the EP's oversight role.

The Council, qualified majority voting, and national parliaments

The treaties allocated votes among member states, for decision-making in the Council, roughly accordingly to population size. A threshold of about 72 per cent of the total votes constituted a qualified majority, making it relatively easy for member states on the opposing side to form a blocking minority. With each enlargement, small member states became more numerous in the EC, and later the EU. The large member states, concerned about the relative erosion of their voting power as many more small countries joined, insisted during the intergovernmental conference of 2000 on a redistribution of votes in their favour.

The question of voting weights was academic for much of the EC's history as ministers rarely voted in the Council. De Gaulle's challenge to the use of qualified majority voting in 1965–66 ended with the Luxembourg Compromise, a political agreement to refrain from voting when a government claimed that 'very important interests' were at stake. The Luxembourg Compromise legitimized the use of the veto and hampered decision-making until member states agreed, in the SEA, to use qualified majority voting to enact most of the measures listed in the single market programme. Even though decisions were often made 'in the shadow of the vote', without votes actually being cast, the revival of qualified majority voting invigorated the EU.

The greater use of qualified majority voting had the unintended consequence of further marginalizing national parliaments in the EU system. As long as governments could choose to veto in Brussels, national parliaments could hold them accountable for allowing passage of legislation that national parliaments opposed. Once governments could be outvoted in the Council, however, national parliaments could hardly hold them to account for being on the losing side. The extension of the EP's legislative powers compensated at the European level for the loss of parliamentary power at the national level, but that was little consolation for either national parliaments or national electorates, who turned out in low numbers for elections to the EP. Hence the protocol attached to the Amsterdam Treaty on strengthening the role of national parliaments in the EU political system.

The European Council

The greater scope and increasing domestic impact of European integration caused the heads of state and government to become more deeply involved in EU affairs. The European Council, consisting of national leaders and the Commission president, therefore became the key decision-making body for issues ranging from enlargement to treaty reform and multi-annual budget packages. The European Council also found itself striving for political agreement on contentious legislative proposals that became deadlocked in the Council of Ministers. Despite being outside the EU's formal institutional structure, the European Council quickly moved to the centre of the EU system. The emergence of the European Council as the EU's ultimate political arbiter was a key constitutive development in the history of European integration, which the Convention was bound to take into account.

The EU's changing constitutional character

The European Coal and Steel Community was an organization with ambitious political as well as economic objectives. Despite its humble name and pressing purpose, the organization sought 'to create . . . the basis for a broader and deeper community among peoples long divided by bloody conflicts . . . [and] to lay the foundations for institutions which will give direction to a destiny henceforward shared' (Paris Treaty 1951, Preamble). From the outset, therefore, the European project was no ordinary undertaking. Notwithstanding the disappointment of many Euro-enthusiasts and the indifference of most Europeans, the Coal and Steel Community was a singular political entity, far different from other international organizations proliferating at the time (Haas, 1958). The failure of the European Defence Community in 1954, and with it a proposal for a far-reaching European Political Community, refocused European integration on functional economic means and limited political ends. Hence the launch later in the 1950s of the European Atomic Energy Community and the broader-based European Economic Community (EEC), popularly known as the European Community.

The EC reconstituted the European project in a number of important ways. First, its members affirmed in the preamble of the Rome Treaty (1957) their determination 'to lay the foundations for an ever closer union among the peoples of Europe'. Second, the treaty greatly extended the functional scope of European integration. Third, although the Commission of the EC had fewer supranational powers than had its predecessor, the High Authority of the Coal and Steel Community, the Rome Treaty included provisions for extensive use in the Council of qualified majority voting, a supranational instrument. All in all, the establishment of the EC enhanced the political character of European integration.

Two key developments in the 1960s shaped the emerging EC. One, mentioned earlier, was the Luxembourg Compromise, a political agreement that enshrined the national veto in Council decision-making. The other was the elaboration by the European Court of the legal principles on which Community law rests: direct effect and supremacy. In its first landmark ruling, in 1963, the Court declared that, because 'the Community constitutes a new legal order of international law for the benefit of which the [member] states have limited their sovereign rights', the treaty 'produces direct effects and creates individual rights that national courts must protect.' A year later, the Court ruled that, as member states had definitively transferred sovereign rights to the Community, national law could not overrule EC law without the legal basis of the Community itself being called into question. The new legal order survived the scepticism of national governments and, thanks to the complicity of national courts seeking preliminary rulings in cases involving Community law, became firmly entrenched over time (Stein, 1981). Reviewing the nature of the EC in 1991, the Court observed that the Rome Treaty, 'albeit concluded in the form of an international agreement, nonetheless constitutes the constitutional charter of a Community based on the rue of law . . . the

Community treaties established a new legal order for the benefit of which the States have limited their sovereign rights, in ever wide fields, and the subjects of which comprise not only Member States but also their nationals' (Piris, 1999, p. 561).

Beginning in 1973, successive rounds of enlargement radically reconstituted the EC. Having begun with six member states, the EC grew to twelve by the time of the SEA. Three more countries joined in 1995, and the twelve newly independent countries in Central and Eastern Europe submitted membership applications at about the same time. Turkey, Cyprus, and Malta also applied to join. Enlargement changed the character of the EU by bringing into it many more small countries, diversifying member states' policy priorities and institutional preferences, increasing economic and regional disparities, and introducing a strong streak of Euroskeptism. Far from retreating in the face of such challenges, the member states intensified integration despite, and sometimes because of, enlargement. The EC made its first forays into EMU and foreign policy co-operation in the early 1970s, partly in anticipation of the impact of enlargement.

Following an intergovernmental conference in 1970, the EC acquired its own financial resources, but even when augmented later by direct contributions from the member states, the EU budget remained small, amounting to only a fraction of the combined budgets of the member states. The EC never had the right to raise taxes. On the expenditure side, the EU did not have responsibility for big-ticket items such as social welfare and defence. For much of its existence, it allocated most of its budget to agricultural subsidies and price supports, while the development of cohesion policy in the late 1980s introduced a second large item of expenditure. Nevertheless, the EU never acquired a federal budget commensurate with its economic and political weight.

From the Single European Act to the Nice Treaty

The SEA was the first of two major treaty changes that transformed the EC and launched the EU. Article 1 of the SEA declared that the European Communities and European Political Co-operation (co-operation on foreign policy) aimed 'to contribute together to making concrete progress towards European unity'. Of greater practical importance for the EC's constitutional development, the SEA included a number of policy and institutional innovations.

Maastricht was the second major treaty change. Building on the momentum generated by the success of the single market programme and uncertainty surrounding the end of the Cold War, the Maastricht Treaty, with its provisions for EMU, foreign and security policy, and co-operation on JHA, marked a major step towards political union. Aware of its importance and potential public impact, national governments included measures to bring the EU closer to the people. Constitutionally significant in their own right, these ranged from increasing the legislative power of the EP, to enshrining the principle of subsidiarity (whereby member states would act at the EU level only when warranted by the scale and effects of the proposed action), to establishing a Committee of the Regions, and to proclaiming the EU's respect for human rights (the Court had long since established that human rights formed an integral part of the European project).

Despite these ameliorating measures, the treaty triggered a strong public reaction. The Danish electorate's initial rejection of it in June 1992 epitomized widespread concern about the scope and methods of European integration. For Weiler, a leading scholar of EU law,

> the public reaction, frequently and deliciously hostile . . . [was] the most important constitutional 'moment' in the history of the European construct. For four decades European politicians were spoiled by a political class which was mostly supportive and by a population which was conveniently indifferent. That 'moment' has had a transformative impact: public opinion in all Member States is no longer willing to accept the orthodoxies of European integration, in particular the seemingly overriding political imperative which demanded acceptance, come what may, of the dynamics of European evolution. (Weiler, 1999, p. 4)

The democratic deficit, which the Maastricht crisis brought to the fore, continues to overshadow the EU. Although, by any standard, the EU is reasonably representative and accountable (Moravcsik, 2002), there is widespread public disenchantment with its institutions and policies. Whether warranted or not, many Europeans feel that the EU intrudes, as a British minister once said, into the 'nooks and crannies' of everyday life; that EMU costs jobs and stunts growth; that the Commission is unaccountable; and that direct elections for the EP are a waste of time. Ireland's initial rejection of the Nice Treaty, in the June 2001 referendum, demonstrated the extent of public alienation from the EU. The Irish government's response – holding another referendum and threatening that a second 'No' vote would plunge the EU into crisis – reinforced the impression that national governments would do anything to engineer a referendum result to suit their interests.

Although intended primarily to strengthen the EU's foreign and security policy-making capacity, the Amsterdam Treaty of 1997 – a revision of the Rome and Maastricht treaties – included important constitutional provisions. Member states declared in the treaty that the EU 'is founded upon the principles of liberty, democracy, respect for human rights and fundamental freedoms, and the rule of law' (Article 6). With a view to the eventual accession of the newly independent countries of Central and Eastern Europe, member states made EU membership conditional on respect for those principles. In order to ensure continued adherence to them once a country joined the EU, the treaty included a provision whereby the Council could suspend a member state's rights in the event of a 'serious and persistent breach' of the principles outlined in Article 6 (Amsterdam Treaty 1997, Article 7).

Growing interest in the human, political and social rights of EU citizens, together with pressure from Germany for the explicit constitutionalization of the EU, culminated in the convening of a convention and the adoption by the European Council in December 2000 of the Charter of Fundamental Rights. At the same time, the European Council concluded the intergovernmental conference that produced the Nice Treaty. Like Amsterdam before it, Nice amended the Rome and Maastricht treaties (the founding treaties of the EU). But unlike Amsterdam and other treaty reforms, Nice dealt almost exclusively with institutional issues such as the size and composition of the Commission and the weighting of votes in the Council. Although timely, especially in view of enlargement, the institutional changes agreed to in Nice were patently inadequate to facilitate effective decision-making in an enlarging EU.

Towards a constitutional convention

Commenting on the Amsterdam Treaty, Moravcsik and Nicolaïdis observed prophetically that the EU 'stands before a series of ongoing constitutional debates. The focus in the future will be on the construction of a legitimate constitutional order for policy-making responsive to the desires of national governments and their citizens' (Moravcsik and Nicolaïdis, 1998). The Charter of Fundamental Rights was an important part of the emerging constitutional order, but the Nice Treaty failed to address key constitutional questions, including the legal status of the Charter. At a time when momentum in the EU was building for constitutional clarity and reform in order to address mounting concerns about the democratic deficit and the institutional impact of enlargement, the Nice Treaty was a damp squib. Dissatisfied with the narrowness of the pre-Nice intergovernmental conference, German Foreign Minister Joschka Fischer launched what came to be called the post-Nice debate on the future of the EU – fully six months before the European Council concluded the Nice Treaty.

Fischer's famous speech in May 2000, calling for an EU with more federal features, triggered a host of contributions by other leading European politicians on the EU's future shape and character. Public and political reaction against the Nice Treaty emphasized the need for far-reaching constitutional reform. The unprecedented nature of impending enlargement, which the existing member states could no longer ignore, called for an imaginative political response. Under pressure from the Länder (states) in the German federation, which resented the alleged encroachment of the EU into their areas of competence (constitutional authority), German Chancellor Gerhard Schröder suggested attaching to the Nice Treaty a protocol for yet another intergovernmental conference on treaty reform to take place in 2004.

The outcome of the 2000 intergovernmental conference gave little ground for optimism that another conference would produce better results. The EU was in a dilemma: the treaties could be reformed only by means of an intergovernmental conference, but the Nice debacle suggested that yet another conference could be pointless. The EP floated a novel idea: why not organize a convention of representatives of various national and European bodies, similar to the convention that drafted the Charter of Fundamental Rights, to draft a new treaty – possibly even a constitution – for the EU? An intergovernmental conference would still be necessary to adopt the proposed reforms, but the convention could do most of the preparatory work. Some member states resisted, not wanting to lose control of the treaty reform process. Given the pervasive criticism of the Nice Treaty and the intergovernmental conference that preceded it, however, they acquiesced in the Laeken Declaration of December 2001, which called for the launch of a Convention on the Future of Europe early the next year.

The European Council agreed in Laeken on the following allocation of seats in the Convention: one representative for each of the national governments; two representatives for each of the national parliaments; two commissioners; and sixteen members of the EP. The candidate countries (including Turkey) could send representatives of their national governments and parliaments, but only members of the Convention from the current member states had the right to approve (or, more importantly to reject) the final document. The European Council selected three additional members of the Convention: one chair-person and two vice-chairs. French President Jacques Chirac insisted that Valéry Giscard d'Estaing, an old political rival, be appointed chairman. Not only did Giscard reflect traditional French views on the EU, but also, by having him appointed chairman, Chirac removed Giscard from the French political scene during the crucial parliamentary and presidential elections. National governments, national parliaments, the Commission and the EP then chose their representatives. National parliaments and the EP tried to strike a balance in their delegations between politicians in government and opposition; on the left and right; and wanting more or less integration.

The decision to prepare a new round of treaty reform using such a public and prominent method implied that big changes, analogous to those contained in the SEA or the Maastricht Treaty, were in the offing. Unlike those major constitutional events, however, the Convention was not linked to a key policy initiative, such as the completion of the single market, EMU, or closer security and defence co-operation. Instead, the impetus came from widespread disillusionment with the EU and the necessity of preparing for enlargement. Despite efforts to tidy up the treaties in Amsterdam and Nice, the EU was still 'a Europe of bits and pieces' (Curtin, 1993). It remained 'a new kind of polity in the making, not a finished product' (Hueglin, 2000). There was a pervasive desire to clarify the constitutional character of the EU, entrench its basic values, and strengthen its legitimacy by explicating its nature, elucidating its fundamental and organizational principles, and improving its institutional arrangements. As well as strengthening the EU's domestic standing, member states and others engaged in the process hoped that the Convention would enhance the EU's international profile and effectiveness.

The inclusion of the word 'constitution' in the Laeken Declaration, the first time that EU leaders had used the word in such a document, and the ease with which the exercise came to be known as the 'Constitutional Convention', did not mean that its purpose was state building. Certainly, Giscard liked to compare the Brussels Convention to the Philadelphia Convention of 1787, which drafted the constitution of the United States. But he did so in order to raise interest the Convention, especially in the USA. As Giscard well knew, there was no possibility that the Convention would reconstitute the EU as a federation like the USA or a confederation like Switzerland.

Even if member states wanted to reconstitute the EU as a sovereign state, it is difficult to imagine how they would do so. The EU does not have a demos, a single people. It 'lacks the traditional prerequisite for statehood: the Staatsvolk, the people in the political sense of the word' (Rusconi, 1998). Lacking independent sovereignty, the EU derives its power from the sovereignty delegated or attributed to it by the member states. The EU does not have a federal budget, a police force or an army. The plethora of languages in the EU militates against the inculcation of a common European identity. All politics are local, which in the case of the EU means national. There are no European-wide political parties, just collections of national parties and party groups in the EP. Rather than promulgating a fully-fledged constitution, the Convention and the ensuing intergovernmental conference aimed to produce a 'constitutional treaty'. The EU would still rest on an international agreement among sovereign states – but this would be an international agreement of a singular, constitutional kind.

Conduct and outcome of the Convention

The Convention on the Future of Europe was an exceptional political event. The convention that drafted the Charter of Fundamental Rights, on which it was modelled, provided few pointers to the Constitutional Convention's operation or outcome. Whereas the original convention merely catalogued various political, economic and social rights in the EU, the Constitutional Convention sought, among other things, to combine the EU's founding treaties into a single document; delimit the competences of the European level of government; improve the institutions' efficiency, accountability and legitimacy; and enhance the EU's international profile and effectiveness.

The more compelling and consensual the Convention's concluding document, the more likely that the intergovernmental conference would endorse the outcome without much dissent. The worst possible result of the Convention would have been a draft document with lots of square brackets (incomplete text) accompanied by numerous dissents, especially if the dissents came from representatives of the same component group, such as national parliaments or the EP, or the same nationality (for example, the intergovernmental conference would hardly have endorsed a document from which most German conventioneers had dissented).

Whereas only government representatives participate as decision-makers in intergovernmental conferences, national governments, the Commission, the EP and national parliaments were all represented in the Convention, with equal rights. Giscard was not a member of any of the Convention's component groups (although he was a former government minister, a former national parliamentarian, and a former Euro-parliamentarian). Nevertheless, as a former president of France, a country fiercely assertive of its policy and institutional preferences in the EU, he carried considerable political baggage. Moreover, Giscard was the founding father of the European Council, a strongly intergovernmental body, and was notorious during his presidency of France for his irritation with the Commission and the small member states.

Giscard immersed himself in the minutiae of the working groups and the plenary sessions, but remained above the political fray. As the former president of a large country, he had considerable managerial experience and political acumen, which proved useful in dealing with a body as heterogeneous as the Convention. He met the other conventioneers individually and in groups, and frequently met interested parties outside the Convention, such as government ministers and parliamentary committees. He avoided association with particular national, institutional or ideological positions, but seemed most at home at meetings of the European Council, 'his' institution, where he reported on the Convention's work.

Giscard's unapologetic intergovernmentalism irritated the small member states, which were already on the defensive after the pre-Nice intergovernmental conference. Politicians and conventioneers from some small member states accused Giscard of conspiring with their big counterparts to stack the EU's institutional arrangements against them. Giscard made no secret of his opinion that the EU's institutional balance was, in fact, an imbalance in favour of the small member states, which urgently needed redressing. As in the Nice negotiations, the most contentious issues in the Convention therefore revolved around the institutions' composition and decision-making rules.

Procedures, timing and interests

The Laeken Declaration called for the Convention to end in March 2003, but Giscard won an extension until June. Even so, the Convention was not entirely finished by that time. Altogether the Convention lasted nearly eighteen months. It began slowly, with a so-called listening phase, during which it received submissions from interested individuals and groups. This provided an opportunity for the members to familiarize themselves with the Convention method.

As with any major event in the EU, the Convention had to accommodate itself to political developments in the member states. Both France and Germany held general elections in 2002. The French elections resulted in a change of government but not of president; the German elections saw the government narrowly hold on to power. A new president of France or chancellor of Germany might not have altered the political context of the Convention very much, but the Convention could not run at full speed until elections of that magnitude were out of the way. As if to signal their intention to pay more attention to the Convention after the national elections, the French and German leaders appointed their foreign ministers to represent them in the Convention.

The Convention also had to proceed gingerly until after the second referendum in Ireland on the Nice Treaty, in October 2002. In order to ensure a 'Yes' vote this time around, the Irish government argued that the Nice package of institutional reforms was the only deal on offer; that the treaty could not be renegotiated and was essential for enlargement. Yet simultaneously in Brussels, the Convention was meeting precisely because of the unsatisfactory nature of the Nice Treaty. Moreover, the Convention's existence was testimony to the failure of the treaty to meet the challenge of enlargement. The most contentious issue in the Convention subsequently became the Nice agreement on the criteria for a qualified majority vote, which some member states wanted to renegotiate and others to ring-fence. The trick for the Irish and other governments, including the Commission, was to play down the significance of the Convention lest Irish voters decided to reject Nice a second time in the hope that the Convention and subsequent intergovernmental conference would produce a better result.

Only after the referendum in Ireland did the Convention get down to substantive business. By that time it had outgrown its early teething troubles. The presidium met regularly to oversee the work of the Convention as a whole and, as the work progressed, draft the constitutional treaty. Giscard selected John Kerr, a former British permanent representative (most senior official) in Brussels, to head the Convention's small secretariat. Kerr, an intergovernmentalist whose appointment helped to assuage British concerns about the Convention, became Giscard's right-hand man. The Convention met monthly in plenary session. These tended to be unruly occasions, as members vied for attention and rode their favourite personal or institutional hobby horses. The conventioneers performed more creditably in the working groups that the presidium organized to cover the spectrum of agenda items, from economic governance, through the composition and role of the Commission, to JHA. The duration and intensity of the working groups depended on the complexity and contentiousness of the item under discussion.

The Convention's various groups caucused among themselves with greater frequency as the Convention proceeded. The sixteen representatives of the EP had the advantage of working permanently in Brussels, where the Convention met, although they caucused during plenary sessions of the EP, which took place mostly in Strasbourg. Despite their ability to get together relatively often, the Euro-parliamentarians in the Convention represented such diverse views, ranging from the Eurofederal to the Eurosceptical, that they hardly composed a coherent group. Representatives of national governments and parliamentarians had fewer opportunities to caucus, and they also held a range of opinions on the EU's future role and structure.

Only the Commission, with two representatives in the Convention, had a clear-cut position. Nevertheless, the college of the Commission held a number of bruising debates on what that position should be. On one occasion, Chris Patten, the external relations commissioner, castigated his colleagues publicly for suggesting that the position of High

Representative for the CFSP, a Council office, be subsumed entirely into the Commission. Patten argued that such a proposal, anathema to the Council, would merely antagonize the member states. Commission President Romano Prodi ran afoul of the college when he tried to submit a draft treaty on behalf of the Commission without consulting his fellow commissioners adequately. In an embarrassing climb down, Prodi merely released the draft as a Commission 'think piece', on the Internet.

Perhaps more significant than the group caucuses were meetings of the conventioneers in various other configurations. For example, members met under the umbrella of the various political 'families' to which they belonged, notably socialist, Christian democratic, or liberal. Members from small countries, from the candidate countries, from neutral countries and from countries with other common features, met to co-ordinate their positions. As the Convention progressed, conventioneers from the same member state tended to meet more often, in effect developing national positions on key agenda items. Although it was intended to curb the member states' stranglehold of treaty reform, the Convention reflected national preferences and priorities with greater clarity as the deadline for completion approached.

British preferences predominated. That was not because of a strong British caucus in the Convention, but because of sensitivity throughout the EU to the strength of Euroscepticism in Britain. The Convention was loath to challenge entrenched British interests. The most obvious example of this was Giscard's decision to drop the word 'federal' from the draft constitution, and to drop 'United States of Europe' as the new name for the EU. As it was, Eurosceptics in Britain had a field day when the draft constitution appeared, caricaturing it as a blueprint for bureaucratization and centralization.

Germany and France co-ordinated their positions in the Convention, but did not dominate the proceedings. Spain, notoriously assertive in the EU, monitored the Convention closely (the Spanish foreign minister represented the government), and complained at the end about Giscard's efforts to revise the Nice agreement on the composition of a qualified majority vote. Italy was a wild card during the Convention. Silvio Berlusconi, the country's Eurosceptic prime minister, could have played a spoiling role, but restrained himself in the hope of hosting the signing ceremony for the new treaty in Rome.

Key issues

Giscard's bias towards the European Council was apparent in the enthusiasm with which he greeted the call, originally made by the British prime minister, Tony Blair, and the Spanish prime minister, José Aznar, for an elected president of the body, with a mandate of up to five years. Blair and Aznar considered the rotating presidency to be grossly inefficient. They wanted the president of the European Council to enjoy the kind of stature and length in office necessary to impress the EU's international interlocutors, especially the United States. They also imagined themselves holding that office. Chirac, too old to aspire to the position but wanting to strengthen the European Council, supported their proposal. He convinced Schröder to do so as well. The quid pro quo was Chirac's support for Schröder's institutional preference: an elected president of the Commission. Chirac and like-minded leaders had hitherto resisted the idea of an elected Commission president, not wanting to enhance the influence of the office.

These two introductions – an elected president of the European Council and an elected president of the Commission – became the draft constitution's best-known institutional innovations. The Commission proposal was relatively uncontroversial, given that the Convention was supposed to strengthen the institutions' legitimacy. Some conventioneers called for the Commission president to be elected by universal suffrage, but a majority favoured election by the EP. Eager to keep some national control over the process, representatives of national governments succeeded in giving the European Council the right to nominate the candidate for Commission president, whom the EP would then endorse.

Composition of the Commission

The Commission's size was another issue related to legitimacy, but also to national influence and institutional efficiency. The Nice Treaty stipulated that the Commission would continue to have as many members as there were member states until the EU enlarged to twenty-seven countries, at which time the Commission would be reduced radically in size. Small member states generally saw the Commission as a defender of their interests, and wanted to remain represented in it. They therefore mounted a counter-attack and pushed the principle of one commissioner per member state. Because an ever-expanding Commission is inherently inefficient, however, they also agreed to allow the formation of a core group of commissioners. Thus each member state would have the right to nominate a commissioner, but from January 2009 (when, according to the regular five-year tenure, a new Commission is due to take office), only an inner group of fifteen commissioners would have voting rights. Those commissioners would be selected on the basis of strict equality among member states.

A Commission as numerous as the member states, with a decision-making core and an elected president, could be a formidable body. Yet the proposed five-year European Council presidency threatened to undermine the Commission's position. Advocates of the new European Council presidency were not known for their support of the Commission. Moreover, small member states fretted that establishing a 'super-presidency' of the European Council would benefit the big member states unfairly. Their concern seemed excessive, as there was no guarantee that the president would always come from a big country. On the contrary, it was equally conceivable that candidates from small countries would win out when the big member states jostled among themselves to elect a president. Nor was it clear exactly what the new European Council president would do, or how much extra authority the position would carry. Presumably both the Commission and European Council presidents would continue to represent the EU at the biannual summits with the US president. Presumably also the leaders of the big member states would continue to want to meet the US president during an international crisis, regardless of the role of the European Council president.

Qualified majority voting

The trend towards greater use of qualified majority voting since the SEA reflected a long-standing demand for more efficient decision-making. The draft constitution represented another leap forward for the use of qualified majority voting, which would become the rule in the EU, with unanimity being the exception. Of course, the exceptional issues are those that touch on entrenched national interests, such as taxation for Britain and Ireland, or 'cultural exception' for France (in order to safeguard French language films). The unqualified extension of qualified majority voting into foreign and security policy, and JHA, proved impossible to achieve. Nevertheless, the draft constitution abolished the pillar system established by the Maastricht Treaty, which distinguished between supranational and intergovernmental policy areas.

The scope of qualified majority voting was an age-old question in the EU, the criteria for a qualified majority being of more recent vintage. In addition to the original criterion, whereby a qualified majority was about 72 per cent of the total votes in the Council, the Nice Treaty added two more: a majority of member states and a majority of the EU's population. The Nice Treaty also recalculated the number of votes for each member state. At Giscard's insistence, the draft constitution included a simpler system: a majority of member states representing 60 per cent of the EU's population. Spain and other countries that benefited most from the reallocation of votes in the Nice Treaty adamantly oppose the change (Spain got 27 Council votes compared to 29 for Germany, which has twice Spain's population). Inevitably, therefore, the calculation of a qualified majority dominated the ensuing intergovernmental conference.

The European Parliament

Greater recourse to voting in the Council makes the EU more efficient; extending the EP's right to co-decide with the Council makes it more democratic, but arguably less efficient. The record of co-decision, since its introduction in the Maastricht Treaty and reform in the Amsterdam Treaty, suggests that the EP has overcome co-decision's inherent inefficiency by expediting the process as much as possible. The record also shows that Europeans do not necessarily perceive the EU as being more democratic just because co-decision is so prevalent. The Convention called for a major increase in the number of policy areas subject to the co-decision procedure, including areas that some national governments wanted to keep out of the EP's clutches. Not wanting to go too far, however, the Convention did not suggest giving the EP a key decision-making role in either foreign and security policy, or police and judicial co-operation.

Foreign policy and internal security

Foreign and security policy, and JHA, are among the few areas in which many Europeans want to see greater, more effective EU involvement. Accordingly, new provisions on JHA would allow for the establishment of a European Public Prosecutor to fight serious cross-border crimes, which would require extensive harmonization of national criminal law. In order to improve the effectiveness of the foreign and security policy, and end the anomaly that had existed since the implementation of the Amsterdam Treaty, the draft constitution proposed merging the positions of High Representative for the CFSP and commissioner for external relations into the foreign minister of the EU. The foreign minister would straddle both institutions by chairing the external relations Council while also sitting in the Commission. Thus the EU would maximize its diplomatic and external economic clout.

The debate in the Convention on foreign and security policy assumed greater urgency, but also an air of unreality, with the onset of the Iraq crisis in late 2002 and early 2003. Bitter divisions among member states on whether to support the US war effort demonstrated the difficulty of shaping a truly common foreign policy and brought British and French moves to craft an EU defence capability to a screeching halt. It is difficult to imagine that the existence of a European Council 'super-president' and an EU foreign minister would have bridged the differences over Iraq. Nevertheless, the Convention's foreign and security policy provisions testified to the members' determination to put the Iraq crisis behind them and give the EU the institutional framework necessary to formulate and implement a united response, subject to the national governments' willingness to adopt one. The Convention was realistic in its approach to a policy area still characterized by intense national interests. There was no suggestion of obliging Britain or France to give up their permanent seats on the United Nations Security Council, or of creating a single EU diplomatic service to replace the separate national services.

National parliaments and EU competencies

National parliaments agitated successfully in the Convention for a greater role in EU decision-making, although Giscard abandoned his pet proposal for a 'Peoples' Congress' of national and Euro-parliamentarians. Most conventioneers dreaded the prospect of explaining to sceptical constituents the necessity for another European institution, especially as their task was to consolidate and streamline decision-making in the EU. Instead, the Convention built on the declaration in the Amsterdam Treaty on the role of national parliaments by suggesting that meetings between national and Euro-parliamentarians become more frequent and consequential. The Convention also proposed making national parliaments the guardians of subsidiarity. Thus just a third of national parliaments could force the Commission to review and possibly withdraw proposals that seemed unwarranted or disproportionate to the ends envisioned, and could ask the Court to adjudicate in the event of a dispute.

In a related move dealing with a core agenda item, the Convention clarified the division of powers or allocation of competences within the EU. Thus the limits of EU competences are governed by the principle of conferral (competences not conferred on the EU by the member states remain at the national level), with the uses of EU competences being governed by the principles of subsidiarity and proportionality. Under the draft constitution, exclusive competence covers monetary policy, trade policy, the customs union, and part of the common fisheries policy. Areas of shared competence range from the internal market to the Common Agricultural Policy, to economic and social cohesion. In addition, the constitution would give the EU competence to co-ordinate national economic and employment policies, define and implement the CFSP 'including the framing of a common defence policy,' and take supporting, co-ordinating, or complementary action in areas such as industry, culture and civil protection.

Charter of Fundamental Rights

Finally, in another major development, the Convention incorporated the Charter of Fundamental Rights into the draft constitution and recommended that the EU seek accession to the European Convention for the

Protection of Human Rights and Fundamental Freedoms. In deference to British and Irish concerns about the economic costs of enforcing social rights that are not part of national law, the draft constitution acknowledged that the EU's fundamental rights would apply only 'in accordance with Union law and national laws and practices'.

Conclusion

It was remarkable that the Convention produced a single, comprehensive and comprehensible draft constitutional treaty. At times during the Convention it seemed that such a disparate and disputatious body could not possibly reach agreement. To a great extent, the Convention owed its success to Giscard's authoritarian leadership. He wisely avoided taking votes in the Convention, lest opinions harden and the conventioneers find themselves locked into rigid positions. Giscard's preferred method was consensus by acclamation: his acclamation.

In an effort to quell the inevitable Eurosceptical reaction, Britain's representative described the Convention as merely a tidying-up exercise. Certainly, most of the text came from the existing treaties, and from the Charter of Fundamental Rights. Nevertheless, the outcome of the Convention was highly significant. The EU was about to acquire a bill of rights, a feature of many modern constitutions. The draft constitution states unequivocally that the EU is based upon respect for human rights, fundamental freedoms, democratic government and the rule of law. Any European country that subscribes to those principles may apply to join, and any member state that wants to leave may do so. As well as defining the nature of the EU, the draft constitution outlines its organizing principles: conferred powers, subsidiarity, proportionality and loyal co-operation (the obligation for all member states to further the objectives of the EU). In addition, the draft constitution explains the EU's policy scope and institutional arrangements.

The draft constitution is easier to read and understand than the existing treaties, but it is not a lucid document. Critics complain that it is too long and has too much jargon. They may be right, but their criticism belies the singularity and complexity of European integration. The process of pooling or, as Eurosceptics would say, surrendering sovereignty is wrenching and arduous. It requires lengthy negotiations, painful concessions and inelegant compromises. It is a highly political process, and politics is the art of the possible. The fate of 'federalism' proves the point. Because of their negative connotations in certain political circles, the words 'federal' or 'federalism' do not appear anywhere in a quasi-federal constitution. The less-objectionable words 'Community way' are used instead.

The draft constitution alarmed Eurosceptics, but it also disappointed advocates of deeper European integration. A disinterested observer would surely conclude that the Convention and its outcome greatly strengthened the EU's political foundation. The institutional reforms are sub-optimal, decision-making will remain cumbersome, and competences may still be blurred, but the constitution is a marked improvement on the previous treaties and a striking assertion of the EU's coming of age. In the process of producing the constitution, the Convention generated a lengthy public debate about the nature, purpose and scope of European integration. Unfortunately, there was relatively little media coverage of the Convention or public interest in it until the final weeks. Despite their best efforts, the Convention's leaders and rank-and-file members could not excite ordinary Europeans about their endeavours. Although information on the EU is more abundant than ever, general knowledge of the Union remains poor. In that sense, the democratic deficit is as deep as ever.

Near-unanimous support in the Convention for the draft treaty made it difficult for the intergovernmental conference to pick it apart, even if some national representatives were inclined to do so. Nevertheless there were deep disputes in the intergovernmental conference on contentious institutional issues, with diplomats and ministers haggling over the criteria for a qualified majority vote or the composition of the Commission. Indeed, the refusal of the Polish and Spanish prime ministers to give up their hard-won reallocation of Council votes in the Nice Treaty, in favour of the new criteria for calculating a qualified majority contained in the draft constitutional treaty, caused the collapse of the Brussels summit in December 2003, where the intergovernmental conference was to have ended successfully. That caused the conference to drag into 2004, until felicitous changes of government in Poland and Spain facilitated a breakthrough

Regardless of the conduct of the conference, member states would have to ratify the outcome. Successful parliamentary votes and referenda could not be taken for granted. Many Irish voters, for instance, would want to know why the government made such a fuss over Nice when a much more consequential treaty was in the offing. The greatest irony for the EU would be a repeat not of the petty bargaining in the 2000 intergovernmental conference, but of the Irish electorate's initial rejection of the Nice Treaty.

Chapter 3

Europeanization and the Member States

ROBERT LADRECH

In recent years it has become commonplace to speak of the European Union (EU) as a significant actor in the domestic policy-making of its member states. Indeed, the EU has woven itself into member states' domestic politics in fundamental ways. Today, an estimated 60 per cent of domestic policy making must be co-ordinated with Brussels. In many cases this has resulted in the creation of new bodies for national co-ordination of EU policy. For example, many national administrations have created inter-ministerial EU co-ordination agencies to better 'join together' national actors in the executive and legislative processes; devolution and other decentralization reforms in some member states often include liaison offices with the European Commission; and organizational links between national sector producer and consumer bodies with their European level counterpart lobbying organization have increased. This broad engagement of the EU in domestic politics is called Europeanization (Börzel, 1999; Cowles, 2001; Ladrech, 1994; Radaelli, 2000).

The Maastricht Treaty of 1992 was a watershed in the history of European integration, when the EU began to shift from an 'unidentified political object' (Delors, 1985) to a politicized presence in domestic politics. The components of the treaty, especially Economic and Monetary Union (EMU), represented a qualitative leap in supranational power, and in many quarters stimulated a political debate regarding the ceding of national sovereignty to the EU that continues today in some member states. Whether measured in specific public reactions such as the first 'No' in the Danish referendum in June 1992 or the narrow 'Yes' in the French referendum in September 1992; or changes in party politics with the emergence of anti-EU (in addition to anti-Maastricht) parties; or subsequent debates regarding the convergence criteria necessary for membership in the eurozone; the treaty symbolized the beginning of the politicization of European integration on a wide basis.

The purpose of this chapter is to explain why Europeanization has emerged as a significant development in recent years. The short answer is that recent EU initiatives, such as EMU, are clearly unavoidable components of national political and economic life. A more considered response, however, necessitates an investigation of how, in subtle and complex ways, the EU has an impact on domestic political life. The first part of this chapter therefore examines four key issues. First, the way in which the increasing policy scope of the EU engages many more disparate domestic actors than before. Second, that the constraints of the Stability and Growth Pact on the budgets of countries that have adopted the euro are debated beyond the confines of government itself and are reported by the media to a wider audience. Third, that the EU is partly blamed for blurring the difference between centre-left and centre-right politics – that is, between social democracy and Christian democracy/conservatism. Fourth, that as the EU, both in terms of policies and as an issue in itself, becomes increasingly integrated into domestic politics, so too does it become an additional factor in domestic politics, a target for some, an opportunity for others. As a result, the EU, and by extension the process of European integration, is now much more visible in national politics.

The second part of the chapter focuses on Europeanization in three key member states: Britain, France and Germany. These were chosen because each in its own fashion is of critical significance to the functioning and future of the EU. The fact that Britain is outside the eurozone provides a further 'twist' to the Europeanization process. In particular, this part of the chapter explores the manner in which the EU has affected these countries' politics since the national elections in 1997 and 1998. In all three cases, a left-of-centre reforming government took power and the EU soon became a defining issue.

Increasing policy scope

From the Single European Act (SEA) of 1986 to the Nice Treaty of 2001, the EU has expanded its policy scope and, as a consequence, become an actor in many more areas of national deliberation as well as legislation. On a purely quantitative basis, the EU has come to occupy greater time and resources in the national legislative process. Qualitatively, on some of the policy issues for which it is solely or partly responsible, the EU has itself become entangled in domestic issues of a highly politicized nature.

As noted at the outset, as much as 60 per cent of domestic policy-making must be co-ordinated with Brussels. However, this conceals considerable differences among policy areas. To help understand the range of 'intensity' of the EU in national policy making, Nugent (2003) provides a spectrum of EU policy involvement, from 'extensive' to 'virtually no . . . involvement'. Focusing on the policies that range from extensive to 'responsibility shared between the EU and member states' provides a better sense of the breadth and depth of the EU's participation in national policy-making. Apart from those policies in which there is extensive EU involvement, and which happen to be the oldest – trade, agriculture and fishing – there is 'considerable' EU policy involvement in market regulation and monetary policy. The following policies are 'shared' with member states: regional, competition, industrial, foreign, environmental, equal opportunities, working conditions, consumer protection, movement across external borders, macroeconomic (especially for euro members), energy, transport, and cross-border crime (Nugent, 2003, p. 327). Although the nature of EU involvement varies from legal regulation to interstate co-operation, there are relatively few areas of national policy-making untouched by the EU.

Rather than simply listing these areas of EU involvement, it is better to consider the entire range of actors involved in policy-making at the national level in order to gain a better understanding of the EU's impact on national politics. Of course, different national styles of policy-making – for example, whether pluralist or statist (Schmidt, 1997), adds to the variation among member states. By regarding each Europeanized policy area in each member state as a case study in initiating or reacting to legislation, it is possible to get a better overall picture of the potential actors participating in EU policy-making. For example, in the area of transport policy, a wide assortment of national interest groups may be mobilized to influence a national position in interstate bargaining or in reaction to EU legislation. Consumer groups, industry groups, national parliamentary committees or sub-committees, in addition to government ministries, can all be complicit in a particular sectoral policy development. In some cases (agriculture, for example), more than one national ministry may be involved – for example, environmental, consumer or food protection, planning or land use. The main point is that because it incorporates a substantial amount of national deliberation, EU policy-making often encompasses a wide variety of actors, all of whom are potentially 'political' in the sense of placing extra burdens on national political management. The number of these actors has expanded along with the EU's policy scope.

Some policy areas have only a narrow and technical constituency, while others attract wide interest. As the EU increased its policy scope in a quantitative sense, inevitably it became entangled in highly political, and at times emotionally charged, issues. The phrase 'permissive consensus', coined by Lindberg (Lindbert and Scheingold, 1970) described a situation in which national elites' actions regarding European integration were free from public opinion constraints. The expansion of the EU into more policy areas that are highly contentious in the member states ended the permissive consensus. Instead, national politicians had to weigh the potential price paid in terms of domestic opposition to new policy developments emanating from the EU. In some cases, the issue in question was of a technical nature, and no public mobilization occurred. In other cases – for example, proposed changes in the Common Agricultural Policy (CAP) that would shift its priorities away from price supports to food quality and land management – interest group mobilization as well as protest and related social movements developed.

Whether it is agriculture or food safety, waste disposal or immigration and asylum, different constituencies and a wider public opinion have become more aware of the intrusion of the EU into previously intranational relations. According to Laffan (1999), 'the process of Europeanization disturbs domestic policy networks and territorial politics in the member states' and the 'growing visibility of the Union raises the question of public opinion and the level of support for the EU and its policies' (p. 334). Further exacerbating the image of the EU, particularly in the public's mind, is the tendency of some member states to 'blame Brussels' for the imposition of a certain policy, thereby shifting responsibility away from the national government (the implementer of the policy) on to the instigator of the policy (the EU, the Commission, or 'Brussels').

Yet this is a risky tactic both for the national governments and for the EU. Because the national government itself may have been a prime supporter of such a policy early in the process, the inclination to shift responsibility to the EU level does not necessarily lead to a perceived 'strengthening' of the national government in public opinion. Instead, it could demonstrate the growing emasculation of the nation-state, thus providing justification for Eurosceptical political opponents. As for the legitimacy of the EU, the negative connotations that are implicit in national government 'blaming' contribute to the image of a remote, bureaucratic and unaccountable entity, a development with potential drawbacks for member state–EU relations.

Economic constraints

The expanded policy scope of the EU has brought it into one of the most sensitive areas of national governance, namely that of economic management. Particularly for member states in the eurozone, the final stage of EMU has added another dimension to member state–EU relations. In the first instance, meeting the so-called convergence criteria in order to qualify for eurozone membership required measures that for some governments meant a very real constraint on public spending, and in some cases the imposition of new taxes. Although all member states supported the Maastricht Treaty, there was lively debate about it within governing and opposition political parties (Notermans, 2001). Those governments with a high inflation rate and substantial budgetary deficits required tough economic and financial medicine for qualification, and anti-EU (or anti-Maastricht) political parties seized on the economic pain to denounce the EU for usurping a critical domain of national sovereignty.

Qualification for membership in the eurozone and the launch of the euro itself did not end national conformity to EU rules and guidelines (Dyson, 2002). The Stability and Growth Pact, signed in December 1996 at Germany's behest, is a means of ensuring that eurozone member governments continue to manage their finances in such as way as to maintain low budget deficits and low inflation. In particular, governments may not exceed a deficit of more than 3 per cent of GDP without risking censure from the Commission and the Council of Finance Ministers, possibly resulting in a fine. The consequences of the pact are at least twofold for member state–EU relations. First, the Commission is charged with the surveillance of eurozone national finances and with publicly warning (if not reprimanding) governments that approach the 3 per cent limit. Public opinion and the media, as well as the governments concerned, are highly sensitive to the possibility of a reprimand or sanction, which are highly symbolic of the interdependence and constraints of national economic management in the EU. Second, the pact has a very real and explicit EU impact on governments with public finances approaching the 3 per cent limit. Those governments may either undermine the legitimacy of the pact and perhaps even EMU by refusing to rein in public spending (or raising taxes), or conform to the pact's guidelines and thereby exacerbate domestic economic turmoil. The pact, in other words, has become the most significant and symbolic instrument of supranational influence on national affairs since the revival of the integration process in the late 1980s.

EMU is not a political issue when national economic conditions are generally favourable. It is precisely when domestic economic conditions deteriorate that the 'grand bargain' of the Maastricht Treaty (including the subsequent Stability and Growth Pact) comes back to haunt national politicians. The pact forces national governments to choose between extra deficit spending in order to revive economic fortunes and risk the wrath of Brussels, or conform and risk losing at the next election. In both of these cases, the role of Brussels is made much more explicit in domestic economic policy-making and reported on widely. Moreover, the number of interested parties has expanded from economic and financial experts to a much larger cross-section of the population. Whereas the national media continue to under-report or ignore much of EU policy-making (Schlesinger and Kevin, 2000), member states' problems with the EU in the context of EMU and the Stability and Growth Pact receive wide coverage in both print and electronic media. An increasing number and assortment of domestic audiences see the achievement of EMU as having come at a high price.

There are other economic constraints on member states apart from EMU. The general economic policy orientation of the EU, born in the 1980s during the high point of neo-liberal ideological ascendancy, began to be felt by a wider audience from the mid-1990s onwards. In particular, EU competition policy, which is designed, among other things, to scrutinize state aid and monopolies, has had ramifications for those member states with large public sectors (Héritier, 2001). National conformity with competition rules has highlighted, in some countries, the very relationship between state and society. Efforts to protect certain state monopolies from privatization have drawn public-sector trade unions and political parties of the left to challenge the national government, and indirectly the EU. The sense of economic constraint imposed by the EU on national economic policy-making, although agreed to by earlier governments with regard to EMU and the SEA, has increased since the late 1990s, introducing new political dynamics between national governments and their domestic constituents.

Blurring the left/right divide

Competitive politics in EU member states are characterized by a left/right axis. Apart from the extremes of the political spectrum, the main government parties of the centre-left and centre-right are those for whom the EU has become more than a foreign policy issue. The EU's general policy orientation has contributed to the loosening of the ideological moorings of the two largest political party families, the social democrats and Christian democrats. The causes of change in these two families pre-date the relaunch of European integration in the late 1980s; nevertheless, certain features of the single market programme and EMU further stimulated their evolution. As a result, national debates concerning the future of social democracy or Christian democracy are linked explicitly to the operation of the EU itself.

Social democratic parties are present in each member state. All of them have experience of government, mainly in coalitions. Most suffered from the 'decline of social democracy' that originated in the 1970s, when changes in economic conditions, new trends in social relations, membership decline in trade unions, and challenges from the new left and the

Greens combined to undermine the membership and voter base of social democratic parties. This situation was further aggravated by the apparent ideological hegemony of neo-liberal policy prescriptions (for example, Thatcherism), and the electoral success of parties more or less advocating this programme.

The response of social democratic parties in the 1990s became intertwined with the renewed momentum of European integration. The single market programme challenged social democrats in particular because it represented a neo-liberal response to the problem of poor economic growth. By promoting the liberalization of many sectors, such as telecommunications and energy, and curbing state aids (subsidies) to industry and national companies such as airlines, competition policy hurt governments with extensive public sectors. In most cases, political parties and public-sector trade unions have mobilized in reaction, sometimes pressuring governments to challenge the European Commission directly. The emphasis on labour flexibility has also provoked heated debates within some social democratic parties and trade unions. While acknowledging national variations, most social democrats now appreciate that the EU is a critical feature in any reformed ideological landscape.

Christian democratic parties, although closer than social democratic parties to business interests, have also been influenced by the general economic orientation of the EU. Constraints caused by budgetary limits affect Christian democrats in government as much as they do social democrats. Although Christian democratic parties may have less of a relationship with trade unions, they too must respond to the trade unions' opposition to certain neo-liberal policies. More important, the underdeveloped social dimension of the EU, while a notable cause for concern among social democrats, also affects the evolution of Christian democracy. As a movement generally supportive of European integration, and especially European federalism, throughout the post-war period, Christian democracy has been uneasy with conservative ideology, especially of the neo-liberal kind. As a result, Christian democratic parties have traditionally given considerable prominence in their national programmes to preserving social welfare. That facilitated coalition building between Christian democrats and social democrats in countries such as Belgium and the Netherlands after the Second World War. Principled support for the EU's liberalization project, however, makes the chances of such national coalitions less likely. That, in turn, has fuelled debate about the future direction of Christian democracy.

For both social democrats and Christian democrats, EU-imposed constraints on national governance has blurred the differences between left and right (Mair, 1995). Debates within each party family are complemented by a wider disillusion with 'politics as usual', with voter choice on significant issues appearing attenuated at best. Moreover, a commitment to further European integration exposes both parties to charges of abandoning the national interest and sovereignty. This gives an opening to small, often anti-EU parties on the left and right, and makes the task of future referendums on EU issues – for example ratification of the draft constitutional treaty – look less secure for national governments.

Domestic agenda-setting

The EU has developed a visibility in domestic politics beyond its policy orientation or scope of policy intrusion into domestic areas. National governments now link the attainment of certain goals quite explicitly to the agenda and operation of the EU itself. This is most obvious when governments host the six-month rotating presidency of the EU. Over the course of the 1990s, the rotating presidency, with its concluding summit, has given the government-in-office an opportunity to accomplish a number of goals, ranging from influencing the development of particular policies to launching new initiatives. Especially for small member states, the presidency provides a much higher European and international profile. The end-of-presidency summit, as well as the increasingly common mid-term, issue-specific summits, provide a measure of success for government-in-office, demonstrating its prowess on the international and European stage.

Other occasions of high politics (in the EU context), such as the conduct of intergovernmental conferences, have also had a bearing on the presidency. From 1991 to 2000, three year-long conferences were held, involving six presidencies, each referred to by the summit at which the negotiations ended: Maastricht, Amsterdam and Nice. The host country invested heavily in a successful outcome, for domestic as well as EU interests. The results reflect national diplomatic skills, and the presidency gives a member state the chance to steer the negotiations in a particular direction.

The draft constitutional treaty proposed ending the six-month rota by introducing an elected president of the European Council, with a term in office lasting from two and a half to five years, an institutional innovation that would alter the domestic impact of EU membership. In addition, the Convention method itself, with its diverse membership and relative openness, may go some way towards broadening and perhaps 'democratizing' large-scale debates within the EU, thereby slightly diluting the control of national governments (Maurer, 2003).

Finally, specific national characteristics may affect a member state's relationship with the EU. For instance, latent Euroscepticism within public opinion and the political parties may be a significant issue in competitive domestic politics, and as such, can influence the timing and agenda of a national government. Thus the EU, beyond the control of a government-of-the-day, can erupt into a politicized issue in sometimes unpredictable ways. It is little wonder that in some member states ministerial responsibility for EU affairs has been transferred to the prime minister's office. This is an acknowledgement of just how politically sensitive the EU has become in domestic politics.

Three key member states

The various issues considered above do not resonate equally in all three of the following case studies. Different national characteristics, political institutions and traditions, such as the presidential system in France or the federal system in Germany, have a particular impact. Nevertheless, the EU has certainly added a new dimension to domestic politics, whatever their manifestation. Indeed, in order to understand contemporary British, French or German politics, it is imperative to appreciate that the EU is a part of domestic policy-making, not confined to some 'extra-national sphere'

Britain

Britain has been described as the 'awkward partner' in the EU (George, 1998). This pertains to its difficult relations with other member states and EU institutions, especially under prime ministers Margaret Thatcher and John Major. Although Major pledged that Britain would be 'at the centre of Europe', domestic politics prevented him from moving there (Conservative party conference, 11 October 1991). In 1997, New Labour formed a government with a commanding majority. In the years since its election (and re-election in 2001), the British government has become more of a 'team player' within the EU. Nevertheless, the EU continues to occupy a visible and controversial place in British domestic politics. The main determinants of British domestic attitudes towards the EU, and consequently the filter through which EU issues are manifested in British politics, are the nature of the political system and cultural factors. Thus party politics are the central arena in which the EU has affected Britain since the late 1990s. By contrast, a generally favourable economic climate (year on year growth with rising expenditures on public goods such as hospitals and education) meant the issues related to EU economic conformity were largely absent in Britain.

As George and Bache (2001) and others note, constitutional and institutional factors make British politics far more confrontational than those on the Continent. This is not to say that a 'left versus right' competition does not structure party politics elsewhere, but simply to point out that majoritarian government is the norm in Britain, whereas coalitions, and by implication a greater stress on consensus, are the rule in most other European countries. Cultural factors deepen the political antagonism with regards to the EU. These help to explain the prominence of Eurosceptical attitudes among politicians and commentators in addition to popular opinion and the tabloid media. In no other member state is one of the two largest parties, a historic party-of-government (rather than an anti-system party), as explicitly anti-EU as is the British Conservative Party. The conversion of the Labour Party in the late 1980s from its hostility towards the EU was hastened by domestic political considerations, namely the strident opposition of the Conservative Party under Margaret Thatcher towards some EU policy initiatives, especially social policy.

Thus party politics have been the central stage on which Britain has reacted to the EU. The decision by the government of Prime Minister Tony Blair to take a positive stance towards adopting the euro, once it was determined that conditions were finally ready with regard to the British national interest, led the Conservatives to promote themselves as the 'saviour' of the pound. William Hague, Tory party leader after John Major, elevated the 'save the pound' commitment to a central place in his 2001 general election campaign. His departure as party leader after the election defeat opened up the party to a succession battle that pitted pro-EU/euro against Eurosceptic candidates. By 2001, it appeared that what had been a vocal minority of Conservative Eurosceptics in the early 1990s had become a mainstream sentiment in the party, both in Parliament as well as on the ground (Baker *et al.*, 1999; Forster, 2002). Hague's successor as party leader, Iain Duncan Smith, had been one of the Conservatives who voted against the Maastricht Treaty under Major's government, like Duncan Smith's own successor, Michael Howard, had been associated with the Eurosceptics in John Major's cabinet. Party politics, as far as the EU was concerned, reflected a Tory scepticism, a Labour cautiousness and a Liberal Democrat enthusiasm.

The position of the Conservative Party on EU issues helped to frame political debate, and to some extent public opinion, on several issues. The Labour Chancellor of the Exchequer (finance minister), Gordon Brown, felt the need to tread carefully regarding the evaluation and timing of Britain's possible euro entry. By stating that five economic tests would have to be completed before any commitment by Britain to join the euro, the government was able to portray itself as acting in a prudent manner and in the national interest. This position deterred those for whom adoption of the euro was seen as being necessary and achievable sooner rather than later. Pro-euro organizations were unable to mobilize in the country because of the Treasury's stance, leaving the terrain of public opinion open to the Eurosceptical 'default' position. Other public policy issues that were affected by the pro- and anti-EU axis included food safety, with regard to the so-called mad-cow crisis of the mid-1990s, including EU restrictions on the export of British beef, and the foot-and-mouth crisis in 2001. In both cases the government sought to maintain the viability of British agriculture.

On the latter issue, a rethinking of the CAP by the Commission became intertwined with British debates about the future direction of its agriculture, and this too attracted partisan considerations. A seeming urban–rural divide became politically mobilized, pitting traditional ways of rural life and agriculture (and fox-hunting) against an urban, cosmopolitan and EU backed-Labour government. The Countryside Alliance, supported by the Conservative Party, mobilized supporters to march on London and kept resistance to change very much in the media during the early 2000s. The EU was portrayed as an agent of change, undermining traditional British – more specifically English – identity.

Other policies involving the EU resonated in domestic politics and were also exploited in a partisan fashion. Perhaps the most serious was the evolution of immigration and asylum policy. As part of its strategy to attract and keep hold of 'middle England' voters (white, middle-class and suburban), the Labour government sought to portray itself as 'tough on crime', breaking the monopoly of the Conservatives as the party of law and order. A series of incidents involving illegal immigrants, together with a government attempt to restructure domestic policies regarding illegal immigration and asylum, led this issue to become highly politicized as well as having an EU dimension. While the degree of EU competence in this policy area has accelerated over recent years, the intent of the government was to shape EU policy in ways congenial to domestic considerations. Essentially, the government's response to Tory accusations of losing control over the nation's borders was a more restrictive policy to keep out illegal economically-motivated migrants and a speedier process for handling refugee cases.

British partisan politics, with their constitutional and cultural foundations, also explain the government's position with regard to agenda-setting in the EU itself, for instance in the Convention on the Future of Europe. With public opinion on the euro mixed at best, any future EU constitutional change could not be seen as a risk to British sovereignty, especially as the Conservatives would link the two issues in the referendum which the government promised on euro entry. Consequently, Blair proposed essentially intergovernmental changes, the most prominent being that of a president for the European Council, a position replacing the six-month rotation for a two and a half or five-year term. British delegates to the

Convention, whether Labour or Conservative, sought to dilute or minimize any proposals that mentioned explicitly the word federal or other vestiges of power for the EU. As for promoting New Labour's domestic economic prescriptions for the rest of the EU, Blair used summits and initiatives such as the so-called Lisbon strategy to speed up liberalization of certain industries and argue for faster progress on labour flexibility (see Chapter 6).

Yet the impact of the EU on British politics since the election of New Labour in 1997 revolved mainly around the issue of adoption of the euro. Although agriculture and immigration and asylum policies generated considerable political heat, EMU remains the key issues in Britain's relations with the EU and its member states. The Conservatives realize this, and exploit the fact by portraying Labour as 'soft on Brussels', willing to sell out the nation's birthright. Mindful of public opinion, the government therefore proceeded cautiously on the timing of a referendum on euro entry and took every opportunity to suggest that it was reforming the EU in ways compatible with British political and economic interests.

Germany

German politics has witnessed the emergence of a more complex relationship with the EU. Usually portrayed as a staunch supporter of ever-deeper integration, and of a federal EU, since the election of the Social Democratic Party and Green Party coalition in 1998 Germany has begun to act more in line with its fellow member states – that is, promoting its national interest explicitly. Under Chancellor Gerhard Schröder, the German government, while not necessarily turning away from its strong pro-EU stance, has moderated its position with more public calls for the Commission to reform specific EU policies. Unlike Britain, where the rules of EMU are not explicitly binding, the sense of economic constraint imposed by EMU has been the single greatest issue affecting German politics. The re-election of the social democrats and greens in 2002, by the barest of majorities, decreased the government's latitude in economic management. Party politics among the four main political parties (the greens, social democrats, Christian democrats and free democrats) has remained more or less united around the post-war consensus on the importance of the EU for German interests, economic and political. Pressure from the Länder (states) has pushed the German government into supporting EU constitutional change in favour of the regions. Indeed, it was at Schröder's insistence that the EU committed itself at the Nice summit to holding another intergovernmental conference in 2004, which in fact began in 2003 and was prepared for by the Convention on the Future of Europe.

Germany's post-unification economy has had a difficult time. The costs of rebuilding eastern Germany, involving a 'solidarity tax' among other measures, has taken far longer than the politicians of Helmut Kohl's government contemplated. Economic woes, plus financial corruption, contributed to the election of Schröder's government in 1998. Unfortunately for Schröder, the unemployment figures, which declined during most of his first term in office, began an inexorable rise in 2001 (Silvia, 2002). How to combat that problem and rejuvenate a stagnating economy became the central issue and main political problem for Schröder and his coalition government, whose popularity after re-election in 2002 plummeted faster than that of any post-war German government. It is with regard to the challenge of restoring economic growth that the EU became a scapegoat for the government, as well as the possible solution to its problems (Smith, 2001).

The slowdown of the German economy, together with EU efforts to make member state economies more competitive through the Lisbon strategy, put enormous pressure on the coalition government. Additionally, the Stability and Growth Pact began to make itself felt by limiting the possible budget deficit. Thus EU-related economic issues were the paramount concern in Germany, a point not lost on the government as it faced re-election in September 2002. That led the government to assert itself *vis-à-vis* the Commission in order to demonstrate to the public that it was not afraid to press the EU on behalf of the national interest. Thus a string of 'debates' with the Commission, but also with the European Central Bank (ECB), between 1999 and 2004 impressed upon the German public the interdependence of the German economy with the development of the EU. At the same time the unloved euro replacement the cherished Deutschmark.

These Berlin–Brussels skirmishes revolved around three issues in particular. First, EU competition policy rules regarding state aid undermined certain government actions to support former East German industries. The German government lost some cases having to do with subsidies, and was obliged to take back the funds in question. As a result, the government had to find other means of assisting eastern German economic regeneration, which slowed to a crawl (unemployment in eastern Germany remained over twice as high as that in western Germany). In western Germany, the system of state (Land) banks was found to be in violation of EU competition rules. State governments duly threatened to withdraw support for monetary union unless the Commission backed down. In the end, the German government launched a reform of this sector, much to the delight of the commercial banks.

Second, the German government made it known that the ECB should be more proactive with regard to lowering interest rates. The first finance minister of the Schröder government, former social democratic leader Oskar Lafontaine, called publicly for the ECB to be more 'growth friendly' and less obsessed with inflation. This overt political challenge to the ECB – and, for that matter, to the EU – contributed to a showdown with Schröder, as a result of which Lafontaine quit the government, thus consolidating the Chancellor's position. Nevertheless, the affair added to the public appreciation of the extent to which Germany's economic fortunes were dependent on EU decision-making.

Finally, the slowdown in the German economy brought the government squarely into trouble with the Commission over the Stability and Growth Pact. This turn of events, more than any other, drew attention to the straitjacket that EU rules had seemingly placed on the German government. The Commission warned the German government in both 2002 and 2003 that Germany was likely to breach the budget deficit limit, forcing the government either to conform or to ignore the pact and spend according to its planned targets. Unfortunately for the government, its own projections of future economic growth were themselves revised downwards as 2003 wore on. Throughout that time the government, together with the French government, which was in a similar predicament, prevaricated by suggesting that the rules of the pact itself required reform. With unemployment rising, growth slowing to near stagnation and government revenue decreasing, Schröder was hoping not to have to conform too strictly to the pact. But his finance minister was determined to keep the German budget on the straight and narrow, much to the consternation of the left of the Social Democratic Party. This generated a great deal of attention in Germany, with the press and opposition parties keeping the episode in the public eye, especially after Commission President Romano Prodi stated publicly that the rules of the pact were 'stupid' and too 'rigid' (*Le Monde*, 18 October 2002). The Iraq war, which caused an additional blow to the economy of the eurozone, seemed to offer a pretext for a temporary budget overspend. In the end, attempts by Schröder to revive and modernize the German economy were overshadowed, and indeed sidelined, by the discipline of the Stability and Growth Pact.

Despite the acrimony between Schröder and the Commission, the Chancellor maintained German support for the integration process, and in particular for a stronger role for both the Commission and the European Parliament (EP) in the EU system. In the Convention on the Future of Europe, the German government collaborated with the French in submitting a proposal that called for the election of the Commission president by the EP, an expansion of Commission power, and a higher profile for the Council presidency. In general, however, while economic issues have dominated and sometimes strained EU–German relations, they have not altered fundamentally Germany's post-war support for European integration. Instead, the EU has intensified the need for reform of Germany's social market economic model, a tricky issue for a social democratic government.

France

Following a snap election called by conservative president Jacques Chirac in 1997, a coalition of left-of-centre parties formed a government in France, under the prime ministership of Lionel Jospin. French party politics and the impact of the EU resemble German more than British politics. That is not to say that there are no anti-EU parties in France, only that such parties are small and, in the context of the French electoral and political system, relatively marginal. Nevertheless, the reason why Chirac called parliamentary elections a year early was closely related to the EU. Specifically, the European Council was due to decide in 1999 which member states qualified for participation in the third stage of EMU. The convergence criteria for participation in the third stage had already forced governments to tighten their budgetary belts, and France was no exception. However, in 1995, while attempting to rein-in public-sector spending, the government triggered the largest public-sector strikes in a generation, forcing the government ultimately to back down. With that in mind, Chirac gambled that it was better to renew his parliamentary majority as soon as possible before the inevitable pain of austerity undermined his government's electoral chances in 1998. However, with the unexpected election of the left coalition, dubbed the plural left (*la gauche plurielle*), Chirac had to 'cohabit' with a socialist prime minister, at least until the end of the parliamentary mandate in 2002. Domestic policy therefore came under the direction of Jospin.

The Jospin government set out in a determined manner to demonstrate its 'left credientials'. The exit of the Socialist Party in the 1993 elections had had a huge impact on the party, as its massive defeat was blamed on its lack of a clear direction. With a government coalition that included the socialists, communists and greens, a demonstrably left orientation was *de rigeur*. This was notably presented in the promulgation of a 35-hour workweek and government spending on public-sector jobs for young people (Milner, 2002). However, the Jospin government could not escape some of the pressures from the EU that had undermined the previous government of conservative Prime Minister Alain Juppé. As in Germany, competition policy rules on state aid and the Stability and Growth Pact were the primary issues with which the French government had great difficulty. Until 2003, however, the government largely escaped some of the more immediate problems relating to budgetary constraints, as the French economy grew at a reasonable rate compared to that of its German neighbour.

France has a large public sector, and with it, very determined public sector unions. This public sector includes public utilities, which the French refer to as public services, including the post office, gas, electricity and railways. These are run as monopolies, being either state owned or state-regulated. Further, the constitution of the French Fifth Republic (the regime in place since 1958) guarantees access to these services for all citizens. The French 'social contract' is respected across the political spectrum, ranging from the parties of the left to the neo-Gaullists, the largest party formation on the right. Public and interest group support for this state–society relationship to remain in place was demonstrated not only during the 1995 strikes, but also on almost every occasion when the state has tried to reform the public sector. Consequently, the French government, whether of the centre-left or the centre-right, has resisted EU pressure for liberalization.

Although it is a signatory to the Rome Treaty and subsequent liberalization measures (for example, in telephony), successive French governments have called for a special status for the public services in order to deflect pressure to deregulate or privatize. For the Jospin government, relations with the public sector unions added an extra complication. Some of these unions (for example, Electricité de France workers) have close ties with the Communist Party and have slowed indirectly the French implementation of electricity liberalization. Nevertheless, the Jospin government continued with a policy of privatization, although not wanting to be accused of pursuing a right-wing agenda, the prime minister was at pains to emphasize the need to bring in more capital for modernization purposes. The discomfort in France with what is perceived to be the neo-liberal thrust of EU competition policy continues to resonate in the electorate and prompt government proposals for reform at the EU level (Cole and Drake, 2000).

Finally, like Germany, although not to the same degree, France began to slow economically in 2002. The constraints of the Stability and Growth Pact attracted much attention. The most visible difference with Germany regarding the pact was that the French government, regardless of its political persuasion, sought actively to change the pact itself. This followed a pattern, similar to French views on competition policy, to challenge publicly certain EU policies in order to promote French interests. Although not couched in such narrowly nationalistic rhetoric, French governments, whether of the left or the right, have not hesitated to confront the EU. To a large extent this represents French EU policy: broadly supportive of the integration process while insisting on certain changes and then accepting a compromise (Howarth, 2002).

Coupled with French self-identification as the political leader of the EU, these challenges proved popular among the French public. In early 2003 (by which time Chirac had been re-elected as president but this time with a conservative majority in parliament) the finance minister flatly refused to make any substantial change when the Commission began to warn that the French budget deficit would breach the limits of the pact. In a way he was tied to Chirac's promises, made during the 2002 election campaigns, to cut taxes and spend more, especially on defence and police. Freezing tax cuts or spending programmes would represent a big turn-around for Chirac and undermine his electoral chances in the future (part of the reason for losing the 1997 parliamentary election was a reversal by Chirac of election pledges made during his 1995 presidential election campaign). As in the case of Germany, the constraints on the French government's manoeuvrability resulting from EU commitments were all too apparent.

Conclusion

The EU has become part of the domestic political landscape of its member states. Adjusting to its output – directives, regulations and other types of legislation – as well as its indirect influence on national policy development has been necessary for a wide variety of domestic actors and institutions. Given that each member state has its own traditions, policy styles, and political and institutional configurations, it is impossible to generalize about the domestic impact of the EU. Nevertheless, some common points seem valid, especially in light of recent developments in the EU and further afield.

First, the final stage of EMU has had a deep and profound effect on member states. In the case of Germany and France, the Stability and Growth Pact has had a considerable and highly visible impact on national economic management. The general economic downturn in the early 2000s exacerbated the situation and highlighted, in the German and French cases, the tension between promises made at election time and binding commitments to the EU. It is not surprising, therefore, to see the French and Germans, along with some (but not all) other EU member states press for a reform of the pact. These concerns are also shared by Britain, even though it has yet to adopt the euro. The government very much needs to present EMU as a positive step for Britain, and its five tests revolve essentially around the compatibility of the eurozone and the British economy. But beyond the 'goodness of fit' argument, there is the operation of the eurozone itself. In this respect, the British have voiced support for a more flexible interpretation of the pact.

Second, for centre-left parties in government, the wider environment of the EU has been a stimulus to change, especially in their traditional programmes and identity. The rigours of EU competition policy, limits on economic management and EU-sponsored liberalization have forced social democratic parties to reassess their traditional policy packages as never before. All three of the country case studies saw reform-orientated governments take office in 1997 and 1998 and subsequently make compromises that satisfied the Commission but distressed traditional left-wing supporters.

Third, external events also affect the Europeanization process. The war in Iraq in 2003 is a striking case in point. The noticeable distance between the Commission and the French and German governments from the British and American positions justifying the military intervention led to a significant debate in Britain about the country's non-participation in the eurozone and its close relationship with the USA. As shown in Chapter 12, criticism of the British government's alignment with the Bush Administration highlighted the alternative of strengthening ties with the EU, notably through the mechanism of a beefed-up Common Foreign and Security Policy (CFSP). For France and Germany, the Iraq war demonstrated the continuing weakness of the CFSP and emphasized the need for institutional reform. Hence the call in the Convention on the Future of Europe for an EU foreign minister. Thus the fall-out from the Iraq war has stimulated a perceived need to 'use the EU' for national purposes in developing a truly European security identity and strategy, by complementing rather than replacing national goals. The Iraq war therefore demonstrated how external events could act as a catalyst for deeper European integration through the generation of a national response to wider change.

Finally, it appears that member states now acknowledge more explicitly the utility of the EU as a tool for domestic change. Thus member states have used the European level of governance to achieve certain domestic goals during EU presidencies, special summits and intergovernmental conferences. The outcome of the 2003–4 intergovernmental conference may change the process of treaty reform and alter the nature of the EU presidency, but political opportunities for national governments will undoubtedly remain. As a result, the Europeanization of national politics would appear to be a two-way street.

Chapter 4

Supporting the Union? Euroscepticism and the Politics of European Integration

PAUL TAGGART AND ALEKS SZCZERBIAK

Throughout the European Union (EU), in both new and old member states, political forces are increasingly sceptical of the 'European project'. This may not be a bad thing for advocates of European integration because it means that EU politics have become more like other politics. Yet it causes problems for a project that relied on a 'permissive consensus' on the part of European citizens and voters to give elites the leeway to construct European institutions from the top down. Given that it is a union of democratic states, it is somewhat paradoxical that Eurosceptics chastise the EU for its 'democratic deficit', although such critiques are by no means the sole source of Eurosceptical sentiments. Although Euroscepticism has not increased in scale (relative to the size of the European project), it has become far more visible in recent years and is much more consequential for the EU (the term 'Euroscepticism' departs from the literal meaning of 'scepticism' and refers to negative evaluations of European integration). As the EU becomes ever deeper, ever bigger and ever more ambitious, so opposition and scepticism become more prominent for citizens and more problematic for elites. 'Europe' has become more contested as a political issue because the EU has become a larger and more complex project.

Opposition to the European project is not new, but has become more apparent in recent years, allowing parties with Eurosceptical agendas such as the Austrian Freedom Party and the French National Front to achieve significant electoral support. Euroscepticism has emerged for a number of reasons. Successive enlargements widened the membership of the EU to include states whose populations are less supportive of integration than the populations in the original six member states. For example, Britain has long had a reputation for Euroscepticism, both in terms of public attitudes and the government's behaviour in the EU, which was especially apparent during Margaret Thatcher's period as prime minister in the 1980s. The Nordic enlargement in 1995 bought in Sweden and Finland, whose populations were highly sceptical of the EU. The most recent enlargement, incorporating eight central and eastern European states, plus Cyprus and Malta, is bringing in a large number of new members (compared to previous enlargements), with many different orientations towards the European project. As the EU grows in size, the scale of Euroscepticism within it inevitably increases.

At the same time, the process of integration has thrown up more opportunities for popular expressions of disquiet. As the EU deepened, those with a negative view of European integration had more incentive to avail themselves of those opportunities. The use of referendums to endorse or legitimate major changes (invariably extensions) to EU institutions, processes or membership highlights the possibility of mass (negative) reactions to the EU. The Maastricht Treaty of 1992 faced two such setbacks. First, the Danes rejected the treaty in a referendum in June 1992; it was only after some renegotiation later in the year that a majority of Danes endorsed the treaty in a second referendum in May 1993. Second, French voters ratified the treaty in September 1992 but the result was so close in such a key member state that it represented a victory for Euroscepticism and a close call for French Europhile elites. A similar pairing of Nordic rejection and unexpected Euroscepticism from a historically Europhile state occurred when Denmark and Sweden rejected the adoption of the euro (in September 2000 and September 2003, respectively), and Ireland rejected the Nice Treaty in June 2001. Ireland held a second referendum and the ratified treaty in October 2002. Nevertheless, these referendum results made it clear that European elites could no longer afford to rely on a permissive consensus in support of further integration.

Euroscepticism has also become more visible because of the nature of the EU. As it grows in membership, in scope and in complexity, inevitably it becomes more distant from European national populations, who then view it differently. It also becomes objectively more difficult to sustain. Member states and EU institutions are aware of the problem. For example, the debate about EU governance represents an acknowledgement that the system emerging from a relatively contained project intended to integrate a small number of states is no longer effective in an EU of twenty-five member states. The Nice Treaty was an attempt to renegotiate the governing principles of the EU in preparation for the 2004 enlargement. The Convention on the Future of the Europe was a far more explicit recognition of the need to develop the democratic credentials of the EU.

This chapter develops three key points. The first is that Euroscepticism is part and parcel of a widening and deepening European project, and therefore integral to the emergence of any new European politics. The second is that there are important differences between the way the public and the political parties see the European project, and that both perspectives are important in understanding the extent to which integration has become a contested issue in European politics. The third is that, while the EU has been roundly criticized for its democratic deficit, the EU institutions themselves provide little scope for the expression of Euroscepticism. In order to develop these points, the chapter begins by examining the types of Euroscepticism that exist. It then looks at how Euroscepticism is expressed in party systems and in public opinion. Finally, the chapter addresses the impact of the EU's democratic deficit on Euroscepticism.

Types of Euroscepticism

Criticisms of the EU come from very different quarters and are framed in very different ways. Some people and parties criticize the EU for being too socialist, while others, on the left, criticize it for being too capitalist. Parties on the extreme right, concerned about immigration, think that the principle of the free movement of people enshrined in the EU treaty is too inclusive. Some green parties regard the EU as being too exclusive because it amounts, they say, to a 'Northern' region. There is something about European integration that makes the same set of institutions and processes particularly susceptible to competing ideological interpretations.

Whatever the reasons for Euroscepticism, it is useful to differentiate between types of Eurosceptical position (Szczerbiak and Taggart, 2000; Szczerbiak and Taggart, forthcoming 2004). On the one hand, 'hard Euroscepticism' exists where there is a *principled* opposition to European integration based on the ceding or transfer of powers to supranational institution. And on the other, 'soft Euroscepticism' exists where there is *not* a principled objection to the transfer of powers to a supranational body such as the EU, but there is opposition to the EU's current or planned trajectory based on a further extension of supranationalism.

Hard Euroscepticism is relatively easy to see. It is prevalent among those who argue that their countries should not be in the EU. In the case of member states, that amounts to a withdrawal from the EU. In the case of candidate states, it obviously means ultimately not joining the EU. Hard Euroscepticism is most apparent in those political parties whose sole reason for existing is to oppose EU membership, although such parties are relatively rare. The most prominent of these are in Denmark: the June Movement and the People's Movement against the EU, which contest European Parliament (EP) elections and advocate Danish with-drawal from the EU. Neither stands in national elections, and both define themselves explicitly as movements rather than as parties (Knudsen, forthcoming 2004). In Britain, James Goldsmith set up the Referendum Party in 1995, whose sole rationale was to call for a referendum on Britain's EU membership. Although Goldsmith claimed that his goal was simply to have a referendum, it was clear that his preference, and that of his supporters, was for withdrawal from the EU. The party contested the 1997 national election but faded after Goldsmith's death. Nevertheless, the UK Independence Party, formed in 1993, still carries the baton of hard Euroscepticism in Britain (Baker *et al.*, forthcoming 2004; Forster, 2002).

Soft Euroscepticism is harder to discern. It exists among those who, while not advocating non-membership, criticize the EU in such trenchant and sustained terms that they may fairly be viewed as oppositional. Soft Euroscepticism is both much more widespread than hard Euroscepticism and much more important for the EU as it bubbles around the edges of political discourse in many European states. Simply criticizing the EU is not the same as expressing soft Euroscepticism; after all, it is difficult to find leading European politicians who have never criticized the EU. Although is would be wrong to say that someone particularly critical of one policy area is Eurosceptical, it seems fair to say that criticism of those policy areas at the 'core' of the European project amounts to soft Euroscepticism. The euro, one such core area, represents something of a touchstone for wider attitudes towards European integration. In general, sustained criticism of a number of key areas and aspects of integration amounts to a consistent position of soft Euroscepticism.

The party politics of Euroscepticism

European integration is central to contemporary European politics, but has rarely been at the heart of party politics. Because of a powerful elite consensus, major parties supported the European project almost univer-sally. Therefore integration has not emerged as a divisive issue in compet-itive party politics. Moreover, European integration has usually been a secondary issue. For example, elections to the EP have been described as 'second order elections' (Reif and Schmitt, 1980) because they have not resonated with the public as national elections have. This also applies to party politics in general, as national elections are invariably fought on 'domestic' or national issues. This does not mean that Europe is unim-portant, but rather that European issues are often subsumed into domes-tic issues, and parties prefer to compete at a national level on these issues.

The second-order status of European integration means that some parties can take positions on Europe with little cost to themselves. Parties unlikely to get into government can advocate negative positions about Europe that will have little practical implication for them. For example, the far-right Flemish Block in Belgium, whose Euroscepticism is only a small part of its agenda, often takes strong positions against the EU. However, as parties become less marginal, they tend to change their stance on Europe. Thus the German Green Party moved simultaneously from being a marginal party to a party of government, and from ambiguous support for the EU to a much more positive position (Lees, 2002). Parties likely to participate in government know that, if successful, they will have to engage actively with EU institutions. If they take highly visible, hostile positions toward the EU, parties in power have either to maintain that hostility, thereby impairing their effectiveness at the EU level, or change their stance and risk being perceived as inconsistent by the electorate. Marginal parties may find that a Eurosceptical stance reinforces their outsider status and increases their appeal to the electorate. They are able to 'use' Europe in a very different way than are parties in government.

This is evident in the behaviour of new parties in Western Europe that stress their populist roots and portray themselves as outsiders, opposed to the consensus of the major parties. Being opposed to European integration, or at least ambiguous about it, fits into this identity. Jean-Marie Le Pen, leader of the French National Front, has consistently opposed France's participation in the EU because it embodies the challenge of globalization and threatens French identity. In Austria the Freedom Party of Jörg Haider opposed Austria's accession to the EU in 1995 and has portrayed the EU consistently as a 'swamp of corruption, nepotism and waste' (Fallend, forthcoming 2004). Even in Italy, traditionally one of the most Europhile countries, the Northern League of Umberto Bossi has been opposed to, sceptical of, or ambiguous towards the EU (Quaglia, 2003).

At the opposite end of the spectrum, the same is true of green parties when they first entered party systems in Western Europe. The greens emerged as challenger parties to the dominant parties, seeing themselves as anti-establishment, and they were drawn from the new social movements. They were therefore predisposed to challenge an issue such as European integration, on which there was a powerful consensus among the parties they sought to oppose (Rüdig, 1996). Yet the greens are now in a dilemma over Europe: their ideological instincts are powerfully internationalist, but they are also at odds with the 'bureaucratic' nature of EU institutions and policies. Most green parties have reconciled themselves to European integration, emphasizing the potential benefits of environmental regulation at the EU level. But some green parties remain broadly

Eurosceptical, such as the Green Party of England and Wales, and the Green Party in Sweden (Aylott, forthcoming 2004).

Despite these examples, looking for European integration in European party politics is like looking for 'the dog that does not bark'. In other words, what is most noticeable is the frequent absence of contestation around the issue of Europe. European integration only becomes an issue of party politics when a major party, or part of a major party, takes a Eurosceptical position. This does not mean that European integration is not an issue for pro-EU parties, but that European integration only becomes an issue in party politics when Euroscepticism is present. And even when Euroscepticism *is* present, there are different degrees to which the issue is taken up and contested as part of domestic politics.

Generally, there are three patterns of competition over the European issue. In the first case, where the major parties are explicitly and consistently pro-EU, there is only limited contestation over the question of European integration. Although smaller parties at the margins of the system may have Eurosceptical positions, the EU has largely remained absent from domestic politics. In the second case, major parties (or significant sections of major parties) have either flirted with Euroscepticism or taken Eurosceptical positions, as a result of which European integration has become an issue of domestic competition. In the final case, which applies only to pre-accession countries, parties have taken Eurosceptical positions in the debate about European integration but within an overall and powerful pro-EU consensus (see Table 4.1

Systems of limited contestation

The most common type of competition over European integration is one

Table 4.1 *Party system types*

Limited contestation	*Open contestation*	*Constrained contestation*
France	UK	Poland
Germany	Greece	Hungary
Italy	Sweden	Slovakia
Belgium	Austria	Latvia
The Netherlands	Malta	Lithuania
Luxembourg	Czech Republic	Estonia
Spain	Denmark	
Portugal		
Finland		
Ireland		
Slovenia		

in which there is a strong pro-EU consensus at the heart of the party system and where, as a result, there has been relatively little discussion of the issue. In such party systems historically there has been a widespread elite consensus in support of European integration. The parties that have usually dominated government are united in their support for the European project. As those parties dominate the electoral competition, there was little space for the issue of European integration to emerge, and there has also been little incentive for these parties to push forward an issue that gives them no competitive advantage over their rivals.

This pattern of party competition applies to most of the long-standing member states, and specifically to the founding members (France, Germany, Italy, Belgium, the Netherlands and Luxembourg). The consensus is partly a function of the dominance in these countries of Christian democratic and social democratic parties, which have played a key role in both advocating European integration and pushing the project forward. Major parties, such as the Christian Democratic Union in Germany, have been crucial to European integration and have provided strong leadership, notably under Konrad Adenauer in the 1950s and Helmut Kohl in the 1980s and the 1990s. The consensus also reflects the effects of long-term involvement with European integration, which tends to 'normalize' what is, after all, quite an unusual international project for citizens in those countries.

The strong pro-European integration consensus does not mean an absence of *any* Eurosceptical parties. And it does not mean that Europe *never* plays a role. Much to the disquiet of French political elites, for example, the referendum on the Maastricht Treaty produced an extraordinarily close result. Lees (2002) shows that, although Euroscepticism exists in Germany, European integration is unlikely ever to become an issue of contest because of institutional barriers in such a consensual party system, and because of the compatibility of the federal system with the EU's political system. The Netherlands, traditionally one of the most pro-EU countries, recently saw the emergence of an avowedly Eurosceptical movement when Pim Fortuyn, a colourful anti-immigration populist politician, established a party – the List Pim Fortuyn – that broke with the pro-EU consensus of the other parties by characterizing the EU as a 'private affair' of elites.

Fortuyn had a fully developed Eurosceptical position on the basis of which he produced a nine-point plan for the reform of the EU. This included holding a conference on repatriating powers from Brussels, and undertaking a critical review of the EP which, if abolished, Fortuyn said, 'would be missed as one misses a toothache' (Harmsen, 2002). Following Fortuyn's murder just before the 2002 election, his party received a massive vote and found itself in the government. However, without

Fortuyn, the party (and the government) collapsed. Nevertheless, the party's initial success demonstrates how even a powerful pro-EU consensus, such as that in the Netherlands, is susceptible to Euroscepticism.

Ordinarily, however, countries that are traditionally pro-European display Euroscepticism only at the margins. What characterizes such states is that the major parties hold firm to a pro-European consensus, and that even if Euroscepticism emerges, party competition does not really gel around the issue of European integration. Euroscepticism is, therefore, marginal and marginalized. A pro-EU orientation prevails, resembling the permissive consensus.

Systems of open contestation

The second category of party a system is one in which there is open competition over the European issue. For this to occur, major parties have to contest the EU. Generally speaking, governing parties have not taken Eurosceptical positions, although in a few cases Euroscepticism has crept into the political mainstream (Taggart, 1998).

The UK is the most obvious case of a party system in which a major party has taken a Eurosceptical position. Britain has long had a number of single-issue anti-EU parties, most notably the UK Independence Party and the Referendum Party. But what really makes Britain a case of open contestation is that the European issue has entered domestic politics and played a part in unseating party leaders. Since the 1980s, the Conservative Party has become the most prominent mainstream party throughout the EU to take a Eurosceptical position. It has caused the party profound difficulties and triggered intense factional conflict. British politics is the only case where the fate of party leaders has hinged on the European issue. Margaret Thatcher's eventual fall was in large part a consequence of Conservative Party disputes over European integration.

Apart from the Conservative Party's difficulties over the EU, the changed nature of the British party system is truly remarkable. Today, the party of the right is avowedly Eurosceptical and the party of the centre-left is pro-European. Yet as recently as the late 1980s the position was exactly reversed, with the Labour Party advocating withdrawal from the EU and the Conservative Party, the party that took Britain into Europe, stoutly defending European integration. In the 1983 general election the Labour Party, under the leadership of Michael Foot, reached the zenith of its leftward shift and was badly defeated at the polls on a platform of radical economic protectionism and hard Euroscepticism. The party then began to move back to the centre of British politics under the leadership successively of Neil Kinnock, John Smith and Tony Blair. At the same time, Margaret Thatcher, the leader of the Conservatives and standard-bearer of the right, moved in the early 1990s from a position of supporting the Single European Act in 1986 to opposing European integration. Her successors have found the European issue profoundly difficult to manage.

Greece has had extremely high levels of both public and party support for European integration but, as with Britain, it also had a major party that switched from being Eurosceptical to supporting European integration. PASOK, the Greek socialist party, strongly opposed European integration when it was founded in 1974, but moved to a pro-EU position from the late 1980s onwards. The party's original hostility came from an anti-Western orientation and a desire to attain full Greek 'independence' (Featherstone, 1988, pp. 175–7), and it opposed Greece's application to join the EC in 1975. The subsequent pressures of being in power, however, together with the end of the Cold War, bought PASOK to an entirely different position, as a result of which it emerged as being solidly within the pro-EU consensus of European social democratic parties.

Danish politics have had a powerful impact on European integration, with the Danish public being one of the most Eurosceptical in the EU. Denmark's rejection of the Maastricht Treaty in 1992 represented the first-ever failure to ratify an EU treaty, a highly symbolic event that marked the end of the permissive consensus. It also had a substantive impact, as the treaty had to be renegotiated in order to give Denmark some specific opt-outs, to enable a second referendum to be held. In 2000, Denmark continued this trend by rejecting the euro, even in the face of almost universal support for the new currency from the parties and the media. The prime minister appeared on television with tears in his eyes when the results were known.

Nevertheless, it is remarkable that, domestically, the country's treatment of the European issue protects the largely Europhile political elite from the popular Euroscepticism that has caused the EU such problems. Denmark has long had explicitly Eurosceptical forces, notably two of Europe's very few single-issue Eurosceptical parties – the June Movement and the People's Movement Against the EU. The small 'new populist' party, the Danish People's Party, was the only party to oppose Danish euro entry in the face of the overwhelming pro-euro consensus. Putting these together means that 'Europe' is an openly contested issue in Danish politics, yet that contestation only really occurs in either elections to the EP or in referendum campaigns, and not in domestic elections (Knudsen, forthcoming 2004). By parcelling out the issue of European integration to specifically European forums, the Danish system insulates national elites from what is clearly a potentially explosive political issue.

In Malta and the Czech Republic, major political parties have championed Euroscepticism, and the issue of European integration has fed into domestic elections. In the Czech Republic, the right-wing politician

Václav Klaus has been a vocal critic of European integration, arguing that the EU is too bureaucratic and too ready to intervene in domestic economic affairs. In his positions as party leader, prime minister and (later) president, Klaus brought the issue into domestic politics, as in the 2002 elections when the nature of accession and its consequence were debated (Hanley, forthcoming 2004). In Malta, the Labour Party (one of the two major parties) opposed EU membership, which suceeded with only 53.6 per cent of the vote in the May 2003 referendum and became the main issue in the subsequent general election (Cini, 2003a, 2003b).

Party systems in which there is open contestation over European integration are relatively few. Indeed, they are the exception rather than the rule. This shows that European integration is rarely an issue of domestic competition. While domestic policy-making has become Europeanized, European politics has not been domesticated.

Systems of constrained contestation

The final category of party system is made up entirely of the post-communist new member states, where parties expressed hostility to European integration but where the European issue was of such low importance, or participation in the European project was considered to be so likely, that such hostility was marginal in importance. For many post-communist European states, the choice of whether to join the EU was seen as no choice at all. There seemed to be no alternative and, while there might have been doubts about specific aspects of European integration, the larger goal of 'returning to Europe' ultimately necessitated EU membership (Henderson, 1999).

There were prominent Eurosceptical parties in Poland, in the shape of 'Self-Defence' and the League of Polish Families. In the accession referendum these ensured that the campaign included anti-EU arguments suggesting that Poland was being offered a 'second-class membership package', or that EU accession would lead to the liberalization of abortion laws and the sanctioning of same-sex marriages (Szczerbiak, 2003, p. 6). In the end these arguments had little impact, and the country voted overwhelmingly to join the EU.

In Hungary the accession referendum in 2003 delivered a huge endorsement of membership. This reflected a long-standing sense that Hungarian accession was inevitable. But Victor Orbán, leader of the Hungarian Civic Party and prime minister in 2002, opened a debate about 'good' and 'bad' accessions, thereby introducing a sense of disquiet into the pro-European consensus. For Orbán, a 'good' accession was one in which Hungarian interests prevailed over the 'fashionable' European discourse of the day . . . and, naturally, it could only be negotiated by his government (Batory, 2002). The case of Hungary demonstrates that EU issues can sometimes become a means for political parties to compete against each other without jeopardizing an overall pro-EU consensus forged by an elite safe in the knowledge that the issue has relatively low importance for domestic electoral audiences (Batory, forthcoming 2004; Fowler, 2002).

The key question is, what becomes of these systems of constrained contestation after EU accession? Once the new member states settle into the EU, Euroscepticism generally either 'hardens' into political debate, making them systems of open contestation, or drops out of politics as a significant factor, making them systems of limited contestation. New member states are therefore likely to emulate the EU politics of the established member states.

Public opinion and European integration

A survey of Euroscepticism requires the consideration of both what positions the parties take and what the population thinks. The two are not the same and can be at odds with each other. To become important as a political force, Euroscepticism has to reflect a significant level of popular sentiment and register as an issue worth pursuing by political parties. At the popular level, support for the EU in member states since the start of the 1990s has been remarkably stable. Table 4.2 shows that, on average, 52 per cent of EU citizens see their country's membership as a good thing, while only 13 per cent see it as a bad thing. The long-term trend is one of stable levels of support and opposition to the EU.

There are some significant differences in national levels of support for integration, however. Looking across the EU's new and established member states, it appears that in some countries the public remain more sceptical of the European project than in others (see Table 4.3). Although the picture is not entirely clear, it is possible to identify the extremes and to name the states where the public is consistently either more or less supportive of European integration.

The final column of Table 4.3 contains a calculated measure of overall Euroscepticism. This is arrived at by subtracting the levels of those who think EU membership is a bad thing from those who think it is good. This means taking into account both how supported and how opposed EU membership is, and gives a better overall sense of the national public orientation than just by looking at the minorities who oppose membership.

At the top of the table there are relatively high levels of Euroscepticism combined with relatively low levels of support for European integration.

Table 4.2 *Support for European Union membership in member states,*
1994–2003

Eurobarometer (Year of fieldwork)	A good thing	A bad thing
EB 59 (2003)	54	11
EB 58 (2002)	55	10
EB 57 (2002)	53	11
EB 56 (2001)	54	12
EB 55 (2001)	48	13
EB 54 (2000)	50	14
EB 53 (2000)	49	14
EB 52 (1999)	51	13
EB 51 (1999)	49	12
EB 50 (1998)	54	12
EB 49 (1998)	51	12
EB 48 (1997)	49	14
EB 47 (1997)	46	15
EB 46 (1996)	48	17
EB 45 (1996)	48	15
EB 44 (1995)	53	15
EB 43 (1995)	56	14
EB 42 (1994)	58	12
EB 41 (1994)	56	13
Average	51.68	13.11

Sources: European Commission (1994–2003).

In relative terms, these states constitute the Eurosceptical end of the spectrum. Britain has the most Eurosceptical public opinion, followed by Sweden, Estonia, Austria, Latvia, Malta and the Czech Republic. It is difficult to say what really unites this set of member states, which includes countries large and small, new and old; and from the north, south, east and west. There is a notable similarity between this grouping and the category of party systems of open contestation, however. With the exception of Latvia and Estonia, all these countries have party systems where European integration is openly contested.

At the other end of the spectrum are member states with high levels of support for European integration and low levels of Euroscepticism. These are the most Europhile states. Luxembourg is at the top, followed by the Netherlands, Ireland, Belgium and Italy. One feature uniting these states is that all have party systems with only limited contestation on European integration issue. This grouping also includes a high percentage of founding member states. As some scholars have argued, duration of EU membership may therefore have an impact on levels of Euroscepticism (Gabel, 1998). But not all the founding states are found at that end of the spectrum.

Table 4.3   *Public opinion and European integration in EU member and candidate states, 2003*

Country	A good thing	Neither good nor bad	A bad thing	Overall national levels of support for EU membership (col. 2 minus col. 4)
UK	30	31	25	5
Sweden	41	30	27	14
Estonia	31	42	16	15
Austria	34	41	19	15
Latvia	37	40	15	22
Finland	42	37	17	25
Malta	51	24	19	32
Czech Republic	46	32	13	33
France	50	34	12	38
Denmark	63	17	16	47
Slovenia	57	33	7	50
Germany	59	26	8	51
Portugal	61	24	9	52
Greece	61	29	8	53
Slovakia	59	30	5	54
Poland	61	23	7	54
Spain	62	27	6	56
Hungary	63	23	7	56
Lithuania	65	23	9	56
Italy	64	22	6	58
Belgium	67	20	7	60
Ireland	67	16	5	62
The Netherlands	73	18	5	68
Luxembourg	85	11	4	81
Average	55.38	27.21	11.33	34.05

Notes: Candidate states in italics.
Sources: European Commission, (2003d); European Commission, 2003c.

In the middle is the largest group of states, including Germany and France, in which there are not particularly high levels of Euroscepticism or Europhilia among public opinion. With the exception of Britain, this group includes the most populous member states (France, Germany, Poland and Spain). This suggests that, in some sense, the norm of the EU is to have populations that are sceptical in the true sense of the word. A 'Europeanized' public therefore does not mean a public increasingly convinced of European integration, but rather one that is divided, yet with a generally pro-EU orientation. The difference is important. With the decline of the permissive consensus, the EU is not necessarily facing increased Euroscepticism among the European public, but rather is

Table 4.4   *Support for EU membership by demographics in candidate states, 2002*

	A good thing	A bad thing	Neither good nor bad	Don't know/No answer	Overall group levels of support for EU membership (col. 2 minus col. 3)
Gender					
Men	64	11	20	4	53
Women	58	8	23	11	50
Age					
15–24	68	8	19	5	60
25–39	64	8	22	5	56
40–54	59	12	23	6	47
55+	54	10	23	13	44
Years in education					
Less than 15	57	11	22	10	46
16–19	58	10	25	7	48
20 and above	69	7	19	5	62
Still studying	73	6	17	4	67
Main economic activity					
Self-employed	60	15	20	4	45
Managers	73	5	18	4	68
Other white collar	63	9	21	7	54
Manual workers	60	8	27	5	52
House persons	61	10	20	9	51
Unemployed	59	9	24	8	50
Retired	54	10	23	13	44

Source: European Commission, *Candidate Countries Eurobarometer*, 2 (2002).

acquiring an increasing space and potential for European integration to become a contested political issue, even if it does not always become so.

There are four demographic variations worth considering that hold across member and candidate states: gender, age, education level and employment (see Tables 4.4 and 4.5). The data show a slight gender gap: with women tending to be more Eurosceptical than men. In the candidate states in 2002, 64 per cent of men saw EU membership as a good thing, whereas for women the figure was 58 per cent. In the then member states, 58 per cent of men thought that EU membership was a good thing, but only 50 per cent of women thought so. Age also has an impact on support for EU membership, with younger people being more positive. A consistent trend is that, going up the age scale, the respondents were less likely to see the EU as a good thing. Higher levels of education generally meant higher levels of support for EU membership in both member and candidate states.

The data show that managers were the most supportive of EU member-

Table 4.5   *Support for EU membership by demographics in EU member states, 2002*

	A good thing	A bad thing	Neither good nor bad	Don't know/No answer	Overall group levels of support for EU membership (col. 2 minus col. 3)
Gender					
Men	58	12	25	5	46
Women	50	11	30	10	39
Age					
15–24	58	7	25	9	51
25–39	57	8	13	14	49
40–54	54	13	27	6	41
55+	50	14	28	8	36
Years in education					
Less than 15	43	15	31	11	28
16–19	52	11	29	7	41
20 and above	68	8	22	3	60
Still studying	63	7	22	8	56
Main economic activity					
Self-employed	61	10	25	4	51
Managers	69	7	22	3	62
Other white collar	60	9	26	5	51
Manual workers	49	12	32	7	37
House persons	43	11	34	12	32
Unemployed	49	12	29	10	37
Retired	51	15	25	9	36

Source: European Commission, *Eurobarometer*, 58 (2003).

ship in both candidate and member states. The least supportive were 'house persons' in the member states, and the unemployed in the candidate states. Looking more broadly at employment patterns and other demographic factors, it appears that those who support membership tend to be in a better position to enjoy the benefits of being in the EU. Those with higher levels of education and with more mobile employment skills are more likely to support European integration. This fits in with the thesis that European integration is supported by those in more secure positions who can benefit more easily from the advantages of integration (Gabel, 1998).

Clearly, there is both a range of different levels of support and opposition to the EU and some similarities in the structure of opinion about it. For example, the similarity in the support levels among different demographic groups in both member states and candidate countries is striking.

Yet there are significant differences in the national levels of support, notably between public opinion in the most Eurosceptical and the most Europhile countries. This shows how the EU is understood differently in various national contexts. Countries emerging from the shadow of communism and facing major readjustments inevitably have a different view of the European project than do (west) European countries such as France and Germany, with a history of successful integration in the EU. But there were also differences among post-communist candidate countries and existing member states. In many ways, the candidate countries seemed destined to disperse among the existing member states when they acceded, rather than to cluster together as a group of member states with a similar public attitude to European integration.

The European public sees the EU largely through a lens of domestic politics, as there are, as yet, no significant European or EU-wide forces. There are no European-level parties, popular newspapers, or other media. Instead, the media are nationally segmented and the party groups in the EP are a long way from being cohesive political parties. This means that the European debate is usually a domestic one. National parties, politicians and media effectively define European integration for European citizens. As domestic politics across Europe differ widely, it is important to be sensitive to different national party systems, different national debates, and sometimes very different views on European integration. That may explain the relationship between the way in which the party system deals (or does not deal) with the issue of European integration, and the nature of public opinion. The key question is whether public opinion determines the shape of party competition, or whether party competition determines public opinion.

The democratic deficit and Euroscepticism

Much is made of the 'democratic deficit' and the indirect links between European citizens and EU institutions. Some argue that undue emphasis on the democratic deficit misconstrues the nature of the EU, which is not the equivalent of a national state (Moravscik, 2000). Others point out that simply strengthening representational links will not necessarily solve the problem of legitimacy (Weiler, 1999, p. 186). Whatever the diagnosis, there can be little doubt that the notion of a 'democratic deficit' is both a cause and a weapon of Euroscepticism. In any event, the EU has taken criticism of the democratic deficit to heart.

Concern about the EU's democratic credentials brings together people with very different ideological positions. The (far) left sees the EU as insufficiently representative of the working class, as an exclusive club dominated by business interests. The populist right, by contrast, sees the

EU as a corporatist bureaucratic institution insufficiently sensitive to the common-sense wisdom of ordinary citizens. Green critics of the EU share with the populist right concern about the dominance of bureaucrats. It is unusual to find an issue that can bring together the far left, the populist right and the greens, but European integration seems to do it.

The EU is especially vulnerable to criticism about its democratic nature because it does not fit easily into a familiar national context. This can fuel Euroscepticism. European citizens who find the EU puzzling because it is such an unusual beast are likely to be sceptical or suspicious of it. Even if they have a good understanding of the EU, citizens may conclude that although the European institutions are not like national institutions, for democratic reasons they *should* be.

The unusual nature of its institutions means that the EU provides very few a venues for the expression of Euroscepticism. As Peterson (2001, p. 292) points out, there is no room in the EU political system for an 'opposition' (as understood in national terms). There are four possible occasions and places where Euroscepticism could be articulated and represented: in elections to the EP, in the EP itself, in other EU institutions, and in the process of treaty ratification. But in each of these, the effects of Euroscepticism are limited.

The purpose of direct elections to the EP was to encourage the democratic linkage of citizens to the EU. In practice, however, these elections are fought by national parties, often on domestic issues. Voters are largely driven by domestic concerns (van der Eijk *et al.*, 1996). No EU-wide parties have emerged to contest the elections, and so national parties have dominated the campaigns (Hix and Lord, 1997, pp. 88–90). Electorates have been motivated by a desire to pass judgement on governments of the day (van der Eijk *et al.*, 1996). EP elections have therefore been a collection of domestic electoral competitions that lead, almost by the way, to the creation of an EU institution. This has not meant that Eurosceptics have not been elected to the EP, but that they have been few in number and, perhaps more significantly, the election campaigns themselves have rarely been dominated by discussions of European integration.

Eurosceptics who have been elected to the EP tend to work alone and are therefore largely ineffective. Their position is complicated by the fact that they are part of an institution whose existence they fundamentally oppose. Given that they may have been elected in order to retain 'national autonomy', it is difficult for them to work with colleagues committed to supranational co-operation. The EP also presents some structural problems for Eurosceptics. Its size, pro-EU orientation and working methods all militate against them. Their small numbers mean that they either have to compromise with pro-EU parliamentarians and join groups large enough to have an impact, or remain isolated and marginal players (Benedetto, forthcoming 2004).

The Council of Ministers and the European Council, forums for the representation of national interests and institutionally at the heart of EU policy-making, are potential loci of Euroscepticism. Yet the failure of Eurosceptics generally to get into government means that the Council and European Council are usually free of them. The Commission is hardly a forum for Euroscepticism as its role is to drive European integration forward. The institutions of the EU therefore do not provide much space for Euroscepticism. Nevertheless, attempts to remedy the democratic deficit are usually focused on the very institutional arrangements that provide limited scope for expressing Euroscepticism. This supports the proposition that the most effective democratic contestation over Europe takes place at the national levels rather than at the EU level.

Referendums over EU issues are becoming an almost regular feature of the domestic politics of European integration. They have occurred over accession to the EU in candidate states and over treaty ratifications and euro membership in existing member states. In all cases, one of the major determinants of the outcome appears to be how the government of the time is perceived. The picture is by no means clear, but citizens seem to use referendums to pass judgement on domestic politicians and parties (Franklin *et al.*, 1995). The case of Ireland in 2001 is revealing. The rejection of the Nice Treaty in a country long considered to be highly supportive of European integration was caused in part by dissatisfaction with the governing parties (and their failure to sell the Nice Treaty), as well as specific concerns about Irish neutrality and abortion issues.

Eurosceptics often claim to oppose European integration because the project is insufficiently democratic, although Euroscepticism is generally *not* based on fears about the democratic deficit. Instead, Eurosceptics base their views mainly on a perception that European integration is not in their interests. This has been shown clearly in terms of public opinion in the member states, where attitudes reflect very much the perceived costs and benefits of EU membership (Gabel, 1998). It was also clear in the case of candidates such as Hungary and Poland, where the debate on EU membership was often more about the terms of accession than about the principle of European integration.

The democratic deficit, therefore, does not underlie all Euroscepticism. Even when it is prominent, it comes in very different forms and from different quarters. This suggests that other elements of European integration may well be at the 'core' of different Eurosceptical arguments. It also implies that the EU's efforts to tackle Euroscepticism by beefing up links to its citizens may not affect the issue materially.

Conclusion

Euroscepticism is not a growing phenomenon, but the EU itself is growing. The EU's larger scale, scope and size means that Euroscepticism matters now more than it did previously. Yet there is very little 'hard' Euroscepticism – the kind that advocates withdrawal or non-membership of the EU on the basis of principled opposition. Euroscepticism is mainly of the 'soft' type: not principled opposition to the idea of European integration but suspicion of the further extension of EU competences. Scepticism about European integration arises when the theoretical aspects of the project become tangible in European citizens' lives. What links Polish farmers and Swedish women as particularly Eurosceptical groups is not their opposition to Europe as an idea, but rather the threat that the EU supposedly poses to the interests of agriculture in Poland and women's welfare benefits in Sweden.

With the demise of the permissive consensus at the time of the Maastricht Treaty, the EU began to face a more precarious basis for a more ambitious project. As a result, proponents of European integration began to show greater sensitivity to the problem of Euroscepticism. Euroscepticism is now more salient than in the past, although European integration is rarely an issue of competition in domestic politics. Nevertheless, sustained criticism and open contestation over Europe is still a potential threat to the European project. The EU has recognized this and responded in part with the Convention on the Future of Europe.

Euroscepticism tends to appear at the margins of political systems. What matters more than the strength of Eurosceptical forces, however, is the degree to which the issue of European integration is contested within party systems. Despite much talk of Europeanization, and of an integrated Europe, there are still significant differences between domestic forms of politics, which have a great sway in determining whether and how Europe is contested. In fact, European integration is rarely an openly contested issue in the domestic politics of the member states, most of which have limited or constrained party systems on the EU issue. Although the permissive consensus may have passed away, most party systems still operate within its confines.

Public opinion across EU member states varies in terms of levels of support and opposition to the EU, but those levels have remained rather stable during the 1990s and beyond. There are obvious differences between Europhilic Luxembourg and the Netherlands, on the one hand, and Eurosceptical Britain and Sweden, on the other. Public opinion in the candidate countries was not that different, with variation among the candidates looking much like those within the EU. The candidates occupied positions right across the spectrum. It is also notable that the same demographic trends appear to transcend national differences. Older people, those with lower education levels and the unemployed are more likely to be Eurosceptical than the young, the well-educated and managers. But it is also apparent that levels of support and opposition are remarkably stable over time.

The 2004 enlargement brought ten new countries into the EU. Their public opinion and the contestation of the party system suggest that the EU has acquired many different types of new member states. Some may be awkward partners (Henderson, 1999) but others may be more accommodating. In short, the new member states look like the older ones in terms of the variety of opinion they bring to the European integration debate. Enlargement of the EU has not greatly changed the range of views within it on the nature of European integration, but in the enlarged EU Euroscepticism may become more pronounced.

Chapter 5

The Euro and the European Central Bank

AMY VERDUN

European integration witnessed a remarkable leap forward in the area of economic and monetary union (EMU) in the late 1990s and early 2000s. A new institution, the European Central Bank (ECB), was established and a single currency, the euro, introduced. Without doubt, these were major achievements in the history of European integration. Although the euro got off to a good start, it is still too early to judge whether, in the long term, it will live up to its promise and potential.

EMU was launched for political and economic reasons. These included the promotion of trade and economic activity more generally through the abandonment of national currencies and exchange rate uncertainty. EMU would encourage deeper integration and symbolize the success of the European project. Member states took the decisive step of giving up policy instruments used in earlier years to stimulate economic growth, such as the ability to devalue the national currency, raise interest rates, or run high budgetary deficits. Yet such instruments had generally lost their utility, as most member states had already submitted to an exchange rate regime (for the sake of price stability) in the European Monetary System (EMS). Other policy instruments, such as monetary financing of the budget (using the printing press to create money) or other policies that could lead to a significant increase in inflation had also lost their salience as other means emerged to deal with economic downturns (for example, restructuring rigid labour markets by making them more flexible as well as adopting proactive retraining policies to increase employment among young adults).

This chapter discusses developments relating to EMU since May 1998, when the European Council decided which countries fulfilled the criteria for adoption of the euro, seven months before the start of the third stage in the process of achieving a single monetary policy and a single currency (the first stage began in 1990 and the second in 1994). The first section provides a brief historical background and discusses the main issues at

85

stake. The second discusses the performance of the euro and the economy of the eurozone (the collection of countries participating in the final stage of EMU). The third section assesses the management of EMU and the role of the Stability and Growth Pact. The fourth section looks more specifically at the European Central Bank. The final section draws some conclusions about EMU based on developments in recent years.

From idea to reality

EMU was an objective of European integration for almost four decades, based on the idea that integrated macroeconomic and monetary policies would make Europe politically and economically stronger as well as more competitive globally (Dyson and Featherstone, 1999; Verdun, 2000). Though not mentioned explicitly in the Rome Treaty, the idea of monetary policy co-operation gained momentum in the late 1960s, as the Bretton Woods system of fixed exchange rates came to an end. The key questions were what kind of European monetary system would work, under what conditions, and with which participants. Some member states, notably France, Belgium and Luxembourg, subscribed to the so-called 'locomotive' theory, whereby monetary union could precede, and in turn contribute to, deeper economic and political integration, while others, notably Germany and the Netherlands, subscribed to the contenting 'coronation' theory, whereby deeper economic and political integration was a precondition for moving towards monetary union.

The Werner Report of 1970 contained the first detailed plan for EMU (Werner Report, 1970). Like the Delors Report of 1989, the Werner Report advocated a single monetary policy and, preferably, a single currency as well. Both blueprints presupposed greater market integration (indeed, the Delors Report coincided with the single market programme). Moreover, economic policy would have to be co-ordinated at the European level to ensure a proper mix between monetary and fiscal policies. The Werner Plan failed in the 1970s because of difficult international circumstances that led each member state to pursue its own policies (Tsoukalis, 1977). Inflation rose in all the member countries (but in some more than others), and exchange rates fluctuated greatly. Some member states launched a rudimentary system of fixed but adjustable exchange rates (the so-called snake), but without much success.

In response to further international currency fluctuations, member states launched the European Monetary System in 1979. Britain decided to stay out of the system's exchange rate mechanism (ERM), in which most participating member states allowed their currencies to fluctuate no more than ± 2.25 per cent from an agreed parity (some, such as Italy up to

1990, could fluctuate by ± 6 per cent). The EMS functioned more or less successfully until the exchange rate crises of the summers of 1992 and 1993. Thereafter, member states agreed to widen the bands to ±15 per cent, while aiming for a much smaller fluctuation, and named the new system 'EMS-2'. With the introduction of the euro, very few member states remained in the ERM-2.

The experience of the EMS from 1979 to the early 1990s was crucial in shaping the ideas of experts and politicians regarding EMU. The EMS owed its success in the late 1980s to the member states' willingness to keep their monetary policies in line with that of Germany, the country with the strongest currency in the system. In practice, the Deutschmark became the anchor currency, and most of Germany's partners aligned their policies with those of the German central bank, the Bundesbank. Member states that did not pursue German-type policies experienced higher inflation rates, higher interest rates, and frequent devaluations. Thus, by the late 1980s, monetary policy convergence had occurred through policy learning and practical experience. In effect, countries had already given up their sovereignty over monetary policy. Germany, the policy leader, was the notable exception (Garret, 1993). Germany would only agree to give up the Deutschmark if it was convinced that a new European regime would replicate its own institutions and policies, and benefit the country in other ways.

The Single European Act of 1986, which paved the way for completion of the single market, included a reference to EMU. Indeed, the single market programme included liberalization of capital movements, a precondition for EMU. It also intensified member states' interest in EMU, which culminated in the establishment of a committee of national central bank governors and independent experts, under Commission President Jacques Delors, to draft a plan for a single monetary policy (Delors Report, 1989). Member states negotiated the terms of EMU in the inter-governmental conference of 1991, which resulted in the Maastricht Treaty. They generally endorsed the Delors Report and agreed to launch the third stage of EMU in January 1997 if a majority of them met the treaty-specified convergence criteria. Otherwise, those member states meeting the criteria would launch the third stage in January 1999.

The convergence criteria covered inflation rates, interest rates, exchange rates, budgetary deficits and public debts. The budget and debt criteria were the best-known, and were seen as being crucial. They stipu-lated that prospective participants in the third stage of EMU would have to have a deficit no larger than 3 per cent of Gross Domestic Product (GDP) and a public debt lower than, or close to, 60 per cent of GDP. The rationale for the criteria was to ensure economic convergence among member states before launching the euro. Otherwise, member states with debts, deficits or inflation rates higher than the average would push up the inflation rate of the entire eurozone and possibly trigger higher interest rates by the ECB. If member states' fiscal policies were broadly in line with each other, the common monetary policy would benefit them equally. This represented a triumph for the German position, going back to the 1970s, on the importance of economic convergence preceding monetary union. Nevertheless, the treaty also reflected French interests. Thus the model agreed upon in Maastricht did not have too many stipulations in the area of fiscal policy or political integration that could genuinely be described as 'positive integration', a term used to indicate the creation of common supranational policies (negative integration refers to the abolition of barriers, such as rules or policies that obstruct integration).

The institutional provisions of the Maastricht Treaty reflected German preferences. There would be a politically independent central bank, which member states later agreed to locate in Frankfurt, home of the Bundesbank, and a single currency, referred to in the treaty as the European Currency Unit (ECU), would be created. The name was later changed, on the insistence of the Germans, to the euro, as the ECU was also the name for the artificial unit of account made up of a basket of participating currencies in the ERM (because that ECU had steadily depreciated *vis-à-vis* the Deutschmark, Germany did not want the new single currency tainted by association). Fiscal and budgetary policy remained the responsibility of national governments, although the treaty called for co-ordination in those areas.

Throughout the 1990s, member states worked hard to meet the convergence criteria, which turned out be more difficult than many had anticipated at the time of the Maastricht Treaty (Dyson, 2002). By the mid-1990s it was clear that the majority of member states would not be ready to launch the third stage of EMU by 1997, which meant that the deadline was postponed automatically to 1999. 'Core' EU member states, such as Belgium, France, Germany and the Netherlands, had great difficulty meeting the criteria, whereas traditionally weaker economic performers such as Ireland, Portugal and Spain, were among the first to qualify for entry. In the end, EU leaders decided at a special summit in May 1998 that almost all the member states wanting to do so could participate in the third stage the following January (Greece was the exception, but finally joined in January 2001).

Following the electorate's rejection of the Maastricht Treaty in the June 1992 referendum, Denmark asked to be given the same right to opt out from the third stage of EMU as the UK had secured in the original treaty. That concession facilitated ratification of the treaty in a second referendum, in May 1993. The Danish government wanted to adopt the euro, but lost a referendum on the issue in September 2000, when 53 per cent voted against (see Marcussen and Zølner, 2001). Since early 2003, however, polls have showed public opinion in Denmark to be warming towards the euro. Nevertheless, the government was not willing to hold a new referendum until after ratification of the constitutional treaty, meaning 2005 at the earliest. The sovereignty-conscious Swedes were as apprehensive about EMU as the generally Eurosceptical Danes, but delayed holding a referendum until September 2003. As in Denmark, public opinion in Sweden ran against the euro, and the majority voted against adopting it.

Although Britain's Conservative government had negotiated an opt-out from the euro, the new Labour government, which came to office in May 1997, wanted to build bridges with the rest of the EU and signalled its interest in adopting the euro at a later date, perhaps during the government's second term. Having won re-election in 2001, the government outlined five economic tests that would have to be met before Britain was willing to adopt the euro. These included the impact of full EMU participation on jobs, foreign investment and the City (London's international financial district), as well as an assessment of the British economy's convergance with the eurozone economy and ability to adjust to eurozone membership. Despite their seeming objectivity, the tests were highly political and difficult to apply from a purely economic perspective. When it decides that Britain has passed the tests, the government would organize a referendum on adopting the euro. Once the government decided in June 2003 that four of the five tests had not yet been passed, the promised referendum seemed somewhat remote. Nevertheless, lively debate persisted in Britain about the merits of euro membership (see, for example, http://www.eurocoins.co.uk/britaintheeuroshouldbritainjoin.html). The British Treasury provided the population and the business community with a considerable amount of information, although it was very careful not to take a formal position until the government decided whether to hold a referendum (http://www.euro.gov.uk).

Performance of the euro and the eurozone economy

The introduction of the euro in financial markets in 1999, and subsequently of banknotes and coins into general circulation in January 2002, went without a hitch. However, the value of the euro in financial markets has fluctuated considerably. Having begun at a rate of 1.17 to the US dollar, the euro rapidly depreciated against the US and other leading currencies. By July 1999 the euro was barely above parity with the dollar, and in October 2000 it reached its lowest point of 0.8252 to the dollar. The euro's declining value surprised many, given that EMU was built on a number of principles that normally lead to a strong currency, such as a focus on low inflation, no monetary financing of debts and deficits, and a high exchange rate *vis-à-vis* other currencies. With responsibility for monetary policy in the hands of an independent central bank with a mandate to safeguard price stability, many observers presumed that the euro would increase in value. Moreover, as interest rates in the eurozone were likely to stay relatively high (and notably higher than those in countries with leading currencies, such as the USA), it seemed likely that international investors would put their money into European banks. Instead, investors put their money into US stocks, which soared throughout the late 1990s as the US economy continued to grow.

Yet the depreciation of the euro did not last for ever. It continued until early 2002 after which the euro began to rise rapidly in value. By the spring of 2003, it had regained its original standing against the dollar. Thereafter, analysts puzzled over the euro's strength. Most agree that the euro owed its revival to declining American performance rather than to the economic situation in the eurozone itself, which remained weak. Although EU politicians and officials took pride in the rise of the euro, eurozone exporters were less pleased with the ensuing loss in competitiveness.

The performance of the eurozone economy is equally interesting. Advocates of economic and monetary union argued that it would be good for economic growth. They presumed that the constraints of EMU would stimulate reform of the participating countries' welfare states, labour markets and the public sector at large. Many felt that such reforms were long overdue, and that EMU would be a welcome external impetus for national governments to act. But nothing of the sort happened. Instead, continuing rigidities in the market, together with low economic growth caused by a cyclical downturn, exacerbated the eurozone's poor economic performance. Critics of EMU claimed that lack of national recourse to interest rate adjustment, exchange rate changes and greater deficit spending made the problem worse (Moss and Mitchie, 2000). Yet one of the original reasons for EMU was the growing realization that intra-EU monetary stability and greater economic activity outweighed the loss of these policy instruments.

The eurozone has a mixed record on inflation. Despite having a clear mandate to maintain price stability, the ECB has only a few instruments with which to do so. None of them is entirely adequate. The ECB can set interest rates. By raising them, the ECB discourages borrowing and encourages saving, thereby slowing down the possible upward trend of prices and wages. The ECB also controls the money supply (the amount of money in circulation). More money (or a loose monetary policy) can fuel inflation, whereas less money (or a tight monetary policy) can restrict inflation. However, the ECB does not pay too much attention to total money supply as an instrument of monetary policy.

In retrospect, it appears that the architects of the Maastricht Treaty did not give enough thought to the question of how to secure the same rate of inflation throughout the eurozone, focusing instead on rules to manage budgetary deficit. The idea was that, by having rules on debts and deficits, inflation would be constrained. No explicit sanctions were envisioned for countries experiencing high inflation. It was simply presumed that inflation differentials would even out through market mechanisms (a country with a higher inflation would lose competitiveness *vis-à-vis* other eurozone countries, causing prices to go down in that country).

The introduction of the euro notes and coins had a significant economic impact, as manufacturers and retailers used the opportunity of the changeover from national currencies to make once-off price increases. Although EU and national authorities had warned against this, business people could not resist the temptation. This was especially the case in the entertainment sectors, notably in bars and restaurants. At the same time, other sectors, notably food and energy, witnessed a jump in prices caused by factors such as exceptional weather conditions and more expensive fuel. Inevitably, people drew general conclusions from personal experiences, and blamed everything on the introduction of the euro. In Germany, for example, it became fashionable to refer to the euro as the *teuro* (playing with the word '*teuer*', meaning 'expensive').

Despite ample evidence that prices peaked in some sectors in some regions, the ECB's inflation index did not show a significant price increase on the whole over that period. ECB statistics indicate that inflation for the entire eurozone was just above 2 per cent in the early 2000s. The reason for this discrepancy is unclear. The most likely reason is that the aggregate numbers do not show price peaks that consumers notice most when doing their daily shopping and buying cups of coffee, as such small transactions are only part of the larger consumption price index that features many larger transactions, notably spending on houses, cars or consumer electronics.

The stability and growth pact

In 1995, the German finance minister suggested that some arrangements regarding fiscal policy would have to be made for the period after EMU became fully operational. The Treaty had some wording to that effect, but under pressure from a public that had turned against EMU, the German government wanted stronger language. In December 1996, the European Council agreed to adopt the so-called Stability and Growth Pact (SGP). Originally it was to have been named the 'Stability Pact' but, prompted by

France, the European Council decided to add the word 'growth', largely for symbolic reasons (Costello, 2001). In fact, EU leaders agreed to deal with growth in separate forums, outside the SGP framework. The gist of the SGP was that member states would have to keep their budget deficits below 3 per cent of GDP, and would aim to have their budgets 'close to balance or in surplus' over the medium term (Artis and Buti, 2000). This was because of a concern that, if an EMU participant borrowed much more than others, it would benefit unfairly by triggering only a slight increase in interest rates through its demand for money. If all member states borrowed excessively, the cost of money would go up significantly because of increasing interest rates, and governments would start to crowd out private investors in financial markets. Given that intra-euro-zone exchange rates no longer existed, the market would not act as an immediate discipline when exchange rates came under speculative pressure. Moreover, the Maastricht Treaty only included measures to force member states to stick to the rules on budgetary deficits and fiscal debts in the run-up to the third stage, without specifying what was to happen afterwards. Just as the convergence criteria covered the period preceding the launch of stage three, the Stability and Growth Pact imposed rules for the follow-on period (Heipertz and Verdun, 2003).

Based on principles contained in the treaty, the SGP was developed in secondary legislation (EU rules and regulations adopted under the auspices of the treaties). The Maastricht Treaty mentioned sanctions, but remained vague on when and how they were to be imposed. Finance ministers agreed that countries exceeding the 3 per cent norm should be punished. The rules on this matter, called the Excessive Deficit Procedure, set out the conditions and procedures for the Council to determine whether an excessive deficit (more than the 'reference value' of 3 per cent of GDP) existed and, if so, what action to take. Exceptions could be made if the deficit was 'exceptional' and 'temporary'; the result of an 'unusual event outside the control of the Member State'; or the result of a severe economic downturn (that is, if real GDP declined by 2 per cent or more compared to that of the previous year). In the event of a decline of between 0.75 and 2 per cent, the finance ministers could decide if the situation was exceptional. If indeed an excessive deficit existed, the country in question would be given four months to make corrections in order to bring the deficit below 3 per cent in the following year. If the member state failed to take corrective measures, the Council could impose sanctions ten months after it first reported the existence of the excessive deficit. Sanctions would initially consist of a non-interest-bearing deposit with the Commission of 0.2 per cent of GDP, plus a variable component linked to the size of the deficit. This would be converted into a fine if the excessive deficit had not been corrected after two years.

For obvious political reasons, there were intensive negotiations among member states as to whether fines should be imposed automatically or only under special circumstances. A compromise emerged whereby a country exceeding the 3 per cent ceiling on budget deficits would normally be fined unless it was going through a major economic downturn (a contraction of two or more percentage points of GDP). Nevertheless, the finance ministers had the discretion to decide if a member state was experiencing exceptional difficulties and, if so, whether to allow it temporarily to run a higher deficit.

When EU leaders agreed on the SGP, none of them thought that the finance ministers would ever have to fine a member state. The idea was to discourage member states from incurring large deficits and running the risk of being fined. In the mid-1990s, in the run-up to stage three, several member states had difficulty keeping their deficits under or at the 3 per cent ceiling. In 2002 and 2003, with the third stage already launched, some member states suffered economic setbacks and triggered the excessive deficit procedure. Ironically, they included Germany, the author of the SGP. Still struggling under the weight of reunification and enduring major economic difficulties, Germany increased its deficit and public debt. Clearly, Germany needed to undertake structural reform, but failed to act decisively because of its federal structure and the unpopularity of any reform measures.

Germany's situation focused considerable public and political attention on the SGP. In a famous outburst in October 2002, Commission President Prodi called the pact 'stupid' (*Le Monde*, 18 October 2002), but none the less justified its existence. By contrast, ECB president Wim Duisenberg and his successor Jean-Claude Trichet, the Commissioner for economic affairs, and many of the smaller member states resolutely and unequivocally supported the Pact, of which France, one of the worse offenders when it comes to budget deficits, has been extremely critical.

A number of arguments can be made for and against the SGP (Heipertz and Verdun, 2003). First, the rules are arbitrary. There is no economic law to justify the 3 per cent threshold, which member states chose at random. Economic experience and common sense nevertheless suggest that it is sensible. The important thing is that at least there is *a number*. This ensures transparency and consistency regardless of who is in power. Second, there is a problem with fining a country that may already be in recession, and therefore not have the financial wherewithal to lose more money, even if it is in breach of the SGP. Nevertheless, the original idea was to encourage countries to be in budgetary balance or, ideally, in surplus over the medium term in order to have some room for manoeuvre if a downturn occurred. Moreover, there is quite a bit of flexibility in the SGP, even for countries that hit the 3 per cent ceiling, including procedures and measures to help countries to reverse a downturn and improve their economic performance. As long as it formulates sound plans and eventually improves its performance, a country can avoid sanctions.

With as many as four countries possibly in breach of the SGP in 2003 and 2004, the issue became highly sensitive politically. EU leaders struggled with how to interpret the pact, and whether to impose sanctions. Would letting one or more countries off the hook be a bad precedent for others, which could subsequently claim an exception if they too got into difficulties? Should the SGP be revised during difficult times? Doing so under pressure from member states, especially large ones, would have a negative effect on the SGP and on the EU as a whole. Creating another set of rules would be harder if the SGP failed completely. Given that the European Council devised the SGP largely for symbolic reasons, to ensure the credibility of ECB, and to put in place a firmer arrangement than the general principle set out in the Maastricht Treaty, it was essential to keep it intact in order to signal to markets that the ECB and the member states were serious about fiscal discipline and did not condone excessive spending (Artis and Winkler, 1997). Thus, EU leaders tried to exploit the flexibility of the existing institutional framework before considering formal changes to the SGP.

The European Central Bank

The realization of EMU marked a new era in monetary policy-making in Europe. Rather than having the monetary authorities of the EU member states set their own policies, the entry into the third stage of EMU meant that the ECB set a single monetary policy for all member states in the eurozone. The Maastricht Treaty gave the ECB a clear mandate: to maintain price stability. Without compromising that objective, the treaty also mandated the ECB to support the general economic policies of the EU and to act in accordance with the principles of an open market economy. This section discusses the governing structures of the ECB, the politics behind changes in those structures, and how the ECB has pursued its mandate since becoming responsible for monetary policy in 1999.

The ECB is part of the European System of Central Banks (ESCB), which also includes the national central banks of all the member states. The national central banks operate like branches of the ECB. The term 'eurosystem' refers to the ECB and the national central banks that have adopted the euro. The ECB has three decision-making bodies: the *Executive Board* comprises the president, vice-president and four other members (all chosen from among persons of recognised standing and professional experience in monetary or banking matters); the *Governing*

Council consists of the six members of the Executive Board and the governors of the national central banks of the member states in the eurozone; and the *General Council*, which includes the Governing Council plus the governors of the national central banks of member states outside the eurozone (formally known as 'member states with a derogation' and informally known as the 'outs').

The main responsibility of the Governing Council is to formulate the monetary policy of the eurozone, which involves setting key interest rates and determining the supply of reserves in the eurosystem. It meets twice a month, but since November 2002 has taken monetary decisions in only the first of those two meetings. The Executive Board implements monetary policy thought the national central banks, and executes powers delegated to it by the Governing Council. The General Council performs whatever tasks necessitate the involvement of all EU member states. These include collecting statistical information; preparing the ECB's annual reports; establishing the necessary rules for standardizing the accounting and reporting of operations undertaken by the national central banks; determining the conditions of employment of the members of staff of the ECB; and making the necessary preparations for the irrevocable fixing of the exchange rates of the currencies of the 'outs' *vis-à-vis* the euro.

Although the Governing Council consists of representatives of the national central banks, the euro system is independent of national influence or control. Neither the ECB nor the national central banks should seek or take instructions from any external body. In turn, the EU institutions and bodies, and national authorities, should refrain from influencing the members of the decision-making bodies of the ECB and the national central banks. To help ensure their independence, European and national bank governors have reasonably long terms in office.

Impending enlargement necessitated a review of the voting procedure in the ECB decision-making bodies, which under the terms of the Nice Treaty could be changed without recourse to another intergovernmental conference. Under the terms of the Maastricht Treaty, the Governing Council operated on the principle of 'one person, one vote'. With six members of the Executive Board and twelve member states having adopted the euro, that meant eighteen votes in total. Decisions tended to be taken by consensus, generally on the basis of the Executive Board's position. A dramatic increase in the membership of the Governing Council as a result of EU enlargement, and participation in the third stage of EMU by many more countries would have weakened the relative influence of the Executive Board and could have jeopardized prospects for consensus. If the ten acceding member states and the three outs (Denmark, Britain and Sweden) joined the eurozone, there would be an additional thirteen votes in the Governing Council.

In December 2002, the ECB submitted a proposal to reform the voting rules, prepared secretly by its staff. The Governing Council was to consist of six Executive Board members and a maximum of fifteen national central bank governors. If the number of national central bank governors in the Governing Council exceeded fifteen, they would be limited to fifteen votes, although members of the Executive Board would keep their voting rights. Moreover, the rotation was designed so that the national central bank governors with a right to vote would came from member states that, taken together, represented the eurozone economy as a whole. Thus member states would be placed in either two or three categories, based on the relative size of their economies. At first there would be only two groups: large and small. When the eurozone increased to twenty-two member states there would be three categories: large, medium-sized and small. In that case, the five large member states would share four votes, and the right to cast a vote would rotate. Half of all the member states would form the second category, sharing eight votes. The last category would consist of the remaining member states, sharing three votes. The categorization of each member state would depend largely on its GDP and on the aggregate size of its monetary and financial institutions, thus ensuring that Luxembourg would be in the 'medium-sized' category. Poland, by contrast, would be in the 'small' category. These apparent anomalies generated considerable controversy throughout the EU (de la Hesa, 2003; Gros, 2003)

The European Council adopted the new rules in March 2003, following input from the Commission and the European Parliament. Whereas the Commission broadly supported the proposed change, the European Parliament opposed ending the 'one member, one vote' principle (not all national central bank governors would have a vote at all times), and complained that the new rules were unnecessarily complicated. Others expressed concern that the Governing Council would still be too large and would find it difficult to manage monetary policy efficiently, given that all of its members would be able to participate in discussions even if they did not have a right to vote. Yet those who were entitled to vote would constitute a large group; larger than the composition of any other comparable central bank in the world. Although approved by the European Council, the proposed change had to be ratified by all fifteen member states (the change deliberately preceded enlargement, thereby obviating the need for ratification in the acceding countries).

The interest rate is the ECB's main monetary policy instrument. When setting interest rates, the ECB weighs expectations about inflation in the entire eurozone, and the effect of a possible change on economic performance. The ECB bases its decision on data that is no longer national, but covers the entire eurozone. The challenge for the ECB is to anticipate change in prices in the medium term. Once it has done so, it determines which interest rate would work best for the growth of the euro area economy without risking an increase in inflation. Of course, this balancing act is a difficult one.

It is difficult to judge the performance of the ECB, which does not publish the reasons for its decisions and does not disclose the minutes of its meeting. Nevertheless, the president of the ECB makes a public statement immediately after the first of the bank's bi-monthly meetings, and reports to the European Parliament four times a year. The ECB also publishes speeches by the president and provides other information through its website. Based on these and other sources, reviews of the ECB's performance so far are mixed. Some commentators argue that the ECB is doing well, citing low inflation and the rising euro as indicators of EMU's success. Critics counter that deflation, or falling prices, could be a greater problem than inflation. A deflationary spiral of falling prices is every bit as worrying as rising inflation, and is equally undesirable. Despite stipulating price stability as the ECB's primary objective, the bank's statutes do not define the term. Initially, the ECB interpreted its mandate to mean an inflation rate of no more than 2 per cent in the medium term. In response to fears of deflation, which was more likely to happen if the inflation rate approached zero per cent, in May 2003 the ECB changed its understanding of price stability to mean an inflation rate of between 1 and 2 per cent.

In an effort to promote economic growth, the ECB focused less on price stability, perhaps at the expense of a little more inflation in the short term. Having created conditions conducive to economic growth, the ECB may still raise interest rates to dampen the boom and slow down any ensuing inflation. In fact, inflation for the whole eurozone has been above 2 per cent since the launch of the euro, so it seems that the ECB has indeed taken growth into consideration. In other words, it looks as if the ECB has been acting responsibly to set monetary policy for the whole eurozone, meeting the challenges of slow growth and the risk of deflation in some countries, and higher inflation in others. So far, the ECB has done a creditable job, given its mandate. But the bank has been in operation for only a relatively short time – too short to reach a definitive judgement about an institution of its import and stature.

Conclusion

The launch of the third stage of EMU was a major, unprecedented development in the history of European integration. Apart from its policy implications, the introduction of the euro in financial markets in January

1999, and in general circulation three years later, was one of the biggest logistical operations in peacetime. Never before had eleven countries with highly developed economies transferred sovereignty in the area of monetary policy to a new supranational institution.

There were surprisingly few problems when the euro was introduced. Automatic teller machines dispensed the new notes after midnight on 1 January 2002, and most people seemed to understand and accept the changeover. The euro's large drop in value against the US dollar initially caused some dismay and disappointment. However, major currencies fluctuate against each other all the time, and the euro gradually regained its original level. The initial depreciation damaged the euro's image, but not the eurozone economy. Because eurozone countries trade more with each other than with the rest of the world, the real effect of the exchange rate of the euro was less important than intra-EU exchange rates used to be when member states had their own currencies.

It is difficult to judge the impact of the euro on the performance of the eurozone economy as valid comparisons are impossible to make. For example, what if member states still had their own currencies and monetary policies during the period 1999–2003? How would they have reacted to the terrorist attacks of September 2001, the stock exchange crisis, or the war in Iraq in the spring of 2003? There might have been heavy speculation, in which case each country would have been affected differently. Would changes in intra-EU exchange rates have depressed trade and investment among member states? At least we know that EMU weathered the storm of major international economic shocks.

In one respect, however, EMU delivered much less than promised. It did not prompt member states to undertake serious structural reforms, which may have contributed to the eurozone's poor economic performance. The convergence criteria prompted member states to take some painful decisions in the run-up to the third stage, although these may have been detrimental to the EU's economic well-being and contributed in part to the subsequent downturn. Academic research should be able to clarify the situation at some point in the future. Member states devised the Stability and Growth Pact to succeed the convergence criteria once EMU had been implemented fully, but the results have been mixed. Some member states took the pact seriously and reduced their budget deficits; others were less responsive and allowed budget deficits to reach and even exceed the ceiling of 3 per cent of GDP. It remains to be seen what the EU will do about the SGP, and whether some member states will reject it definitively.

The ECB has managed interest rates and the money supply reasonably well, helping to keep inflation low while appreciating the danger of deflation. Initially, financial markets were unsure how to interpret ECB's actions, which were often at odds with market expectations. More recently, financial market analysts have anticipated the ECB's moves, much to the bank's credit. As for its main mandate, the ECB adjusted its definition of price stability in light of the fear of deflation, although to what effect remains to be seen.

All in all, it seems fair to conclude that the introduction of the euro has been a success. The main disappointment has been poor economic growth in the eurozone, although it is difficult to assess the euro's responsibility for that. Nor is it possible to predict what will happen when more countries adopt the euro (after enlargement), and the euro itself matures. Continuing to look to the future: will the euro ever rival the US dollar internationally? Definitely not in the short run, but it will probably increase in importance as currency traders become more familiar with it. If all goes well, by 2010 the euro should be traded quite a bit more on international financial markets. One thing, at least, is certain: more political and economic challenges lie ahead. It remains to be seen how EMU will cope with them.

Chapter 6

Completing the Single Market: The Lisbon Strategy

ANTHONY WALLACE

The idea of a single market in which goods, services, capital and people could move without restriction across national borders was the centerpiece of the Rome Treaty. The architects of deeper integration realized that the European Economic Community (EEC) had to go beyond a customs union, which dealt only with tariff and quota barriers, and eradicate the subtle non-tariff barriers to trade. Hampered by the need for unanimity in Council decision-making, the Community did not really begin to move past the customs union stage until the mid-1980s, when pressure from the European Round Table of Industrialists (ERT), keen interest in the member states, and an activist Commission president made the acceleration of economic integration a top priority.

In its 1985 White Paper on Completion of the Internal Market, the European Commission set a deadline of 31 December 1992 for implementation of the roughly 300 measures necessary to put the single market in place, many of which had been lying around for years without approval. The Single European Act of 1986, which introduced qualified majority voting for most single-market measures, facilitated their enactment in the Council. Since 1992, the Commission has pressed member states to transpose directives into national law, pushed for passage of proposals still in the pipeline, added new measures in areas such as energy and the environment, and submitted proposals to revise existing legislation that has been overtaken by events.

The single market process was an ingenious one. In telecommunications (not part of the original programme but introduced later), for example, it involved opening up the least controversial segment of the market, non–voice communications (representing only 10 per cent of the business in the late 1980s) to cross-border competition. A second phase of liberalization, involving the much larger voice communications segment, was scheduled for completion in 1994. Since then, the Commission has proposed additional measures to reflect the drastic changes in the sector brought about by recent advances in technology.

This so-called 'salami process' of gradual market opening worked because the benefits of liberalization (the introduction of competition into a sector hitherto ruled by public monopolies, leading to greater choice of supplier and lower prices) resulted in further liberalization. The process of market opening generated a seemingly unstoppable momentum. The abolition of restrictive national regulations and laws strengthened market forces. Greater competition resulted in price reductions for consumers, and concentration and consolidation (business savings and some closures) for firms. It was an exercise in deregulation at the national level and re-regulation at the supranational level.

Indicators of the success of market liberalization include the extent to which prices of goods and services fall; the scope of restructuring within sectors; and the amount of reduction in 'home market bias'. In the measurement process, the 'network sectors' – major service sectors such as transport, energy, postal services and telecommunications – are more important than others because they 'connect' every sector in the economy and affect the levels of output and employment. The financial services sector plays a similar role. Several years after the single market deadline, however, the record of completion was most deficient in these network sectors, which proved difficult to liberalize because of their political importance to the member states. Many network sectors have been, or still are, public monopolies, or are subject to restrictive national regulation. Member states have failed to implement measures or refused to grant mutual recognition to other legal regimes.

This chapter examines two important works in progress in the European Union (EU) in the early 2000s: the completion of the internal market in financial services, and the elaboration of a new social and employment policy. These are the key elements of a major initiative to modernize the EU: the so-called Lisbon strategy. This chapter reviews the Lisbon strategy for economic modernization; assesses developments in the financial services sector, and social and employment policy; and discusses the difficulties of meeting the Lisbon goals because of deep differences in socio-economic structure, culture and ideology among the member states. It concludes that, in order to meet the Lisbon objectives in these areas, the EU will have to make some important decisions about the nature of economic governance and the feasibility of maintaining Europe's distinctive social market model of capitalism.

The Lisbon strategy

Market integration slowed in the late 1990s, as the Council grappled with more challenging proposals than it had dealt with earlier in the decade. British Prime Minister Tony Blair and Spanish Prime Minister José Aznar, who prided themselves on their market-orientated, business-friendly approach, pushed for an acceleration of integration involving more co-ordination among enterprises and national governments, and less regulation by the EU. They had strong support from European business organizations, notably the European Round Table and UNICE, the European employers' federation. All were concerned about the EU's poor performance *vis-à-vis* the USA, where economic growth and job creation soared in the 1990s. Blair and Aznar called for a special summit to push economic modernization in the EU. Portuguese Prime Minister Antonio Guterres took up their call and convened a special meeting of the European Council during Portugal's presidency, in March 2000. Guterres was particularly interested in tax and financial market initiatives that would encourage entrepreneurship and generate more modern, high-skilled jobs.

EU leaders set an ambitious goal at the Lisbon summit: within ten years the EU would become 'the most competitive and dynamic knowledge-based economy in the world, capable of sustainable economic growth with more and better jobs' (Presidency Conclusions, 2000). The USA was the obvious point of reference, although there was no mention of it in the official record of the summit. In one respect, however, the EU's approach was fundamentally different from that of the USA. In addition to economic growth, the EU aimed for 'greater social cohesion', a term unheard of in the USA but beloved in the EU, especially in social democratic circles. The European Council identified a number of policy targets under the rubric of the overall Lisbon goal, and placed special emphasis on achieving a more flexible labour market and wider, deeper capital markets because of the importance of these for strong economic growth. The Lisbon targets are listed in Figure 6.1.

France and Germany are usually the prime movers behind major EU initiatives, but this time Britain, Portugal and Spain led the way. The Commission was not a key player, but quickly appreciated the political and economic importance of the Lisbon goals. French Prime Minister Lionel Jospin, a traditional socialist, signalled that France would emphasize employment and social policy measures on taking over the Council presidency from Portugal. France and Germany expressed dissatisfaction with the proposed Lisbon target of 2004 for full deregulation of the traditionally-protected gas and electricity sectors.

The Lisbon European Council outlined a new strategy for economic modernization as well as a series of policy goals. Building on practices such as benchmarking, target-setting and peer review developed at previous European summits in specific policy areas (the so-called

Figure 6.1   *The Lisbon targets*

1 Fully integrate and liberalize the telecommunications market by the end of 2001.
2 Speed up liberalization of the gas and electricity markets.
3 Establish a Europe-wide patent.
4 Liberalize the postal system.
5 Open rail transport, rationalize road tax system and air traffic control.
6 Enact the take-overs directive.
7 Make labour markets less rigid, improve pension portability, raise the employment rate and lower unemployment.
8 Develop a common tax policy for savings.
9 Move towards EU-wide harmonization of corporate taxes.
10 Take steps to shift the EU to a digital, knowledge-based economy characterized by higher education and greater use of the Internet and eCommerce.
11 Establish a European Area of Research and Innovation.
12 Complete the single market in financial services.
13 Complete the transposition of government procurement directives and reduce state subsidies that distort trade.

Source: Presidency Conclusions, 2000.

Luxembourg, Cardiff and Cologne processes), the Lisbon strategy represented a shift away from uniformity and regulation towards a more flexible 'open method of coordination' (Hodson and Maher, 2001; Sisson and Marginson, 2001). Although certain sectors, such as financial services, would remain subject to traditional Community legislation, others, such as employment and social policy, lent themselves to the new process, which involved setting specific objectives and benchmarks (and concrete measures to attain them), and putting peer pressure on laggards. Thus the European Council called for the use of 'quantitative and qualitative indicators' to set standards and benchmarks for the attainment of economic and social policy objectives, in close co-operation with the Commission, thereby assuaging concerns in the Commission that the new process would pre-empt its powers (Scharpf, 2002). Apart from its merits as a management technique, the open method of co-ordination provided a means of promoting intra-EU co-operation without further undermining sovereignty.

Business interests strongly supported the Lisbon strategy, which Blair called 'a new direction away from the social regulation of the 1980s towards enterprise, innovation, competitiveness, and employment (The Guardian, 25 March 2000, p. 8).' French President Jacques Chirac preferred to describe the outcome of the summit as a reaffirmation of the European social model. Nicole Fontaine, president of the European Parliament (EP), underlined the huge doctrinal split between the Anglo-Saxon and 'social Europe' models when, at the opening session of the summit, she warned against 'untrammelled capitalism and remorseless pursuit of profit at the expense of working men and women' (*Agence Europe*, 3 March 2000).

The Lisbon strategy includes annual follow-up summits to review progress and build political pressure for economic modernization. These are held every spring. Inevitably, they tend to be overshadowed by current events that demand the EU leaders' time and attention. For example, the imminent war in Iraq dominated the follow-up summit in March 2003. Instead of impelling economic modernization, these summits tend to disguise the slow progress to date on the Lisbon agenda. The economic climate is partly to blame for this. No sooner did the European Council proclaim the Lisbon strategy, at the height of the dot.com bubble, than the global economy began a severe downturn.

Despite its initial scepticism, the Commission became an enthusiastic participant in the Lisbon strategy, acting as a gadfly to maintain the momentum for reform. Commissioners Erki Liikanen (communications) and Frits Bolkestein (single market) were particularly effective in setting scorecards, posting deadlines and scolding laggards by name. The European Round Table and the European employers' federation also participated actively in the benchmarking process. Indeed, Europe's leading industrialists praised the Commission's contribution to market liberalization and integration in a submission to the Convention on the Future of Europe. Nevertheless, progress since Lisbon has remained spotty. France and Germany have dragged their feet on energy and transport liberalization (France finally agreed to an unsatisfactory compromise on opening its energy market at the Barcelona summit in March 2002). Member states such as Britain, the Netherlands, Spain and the Nordic countries have generally received high marks for their implementation of the Lisbon strategy, in particular for pursuing the financial services and labour market objectives. These two key areas are examined in the rest of this chapter.

A single market in financial services

Paolo Cecchini's massive study, *The Economics of 1992* (European Economy No. 35, March 1988), provided the rationale for completing the single market by enumerating the costs to Europe of not doing so. Cecchini believed that the liberalization of financial services such as banking, insurance and investment would serve as a vital catalyst for the entire economy. By bringing down barriers to cross-border trade in financial services, European businesses would save money, and consumers would pay less for a wider range of insurance, brokerage and banking services, while benefiting from competitive interest rates on loans and deposits. Firms and individuals would enjoy access to wider and deeper capital markets that would provide better investment and growth opportunities. Cecchini recorded great variability in prices for financial services across the EU, with divergences of more than 50 per cent because of differences in local customs and culture, and restrictive – often protectionist – regulations (Cecchini, 1992, p. 38).

Types of financial services

The banking sector, divided into wholesale and retail activities, covers a variety of providers, including commercial and savings banks, co-operatives, and specialized long-term lenders (mortgage and finance banks). The securities sector, wholesale and retail, consists of primary (buying for account) and secondary (buying for other parties) traders in stocks, bonds and other financial instruments, as well as portfolio managers, underwriters and investment counsellors. The insurance sector provides property and casualty insurance, and life insurance. The business is divided into 'mass risk' products (small policies purchased by individuals) and 'large risks' products (large policies for companies). It is not unusual in the EU for a large commercial bank to offer services in all sectors. In some countries, regulations forbid banks from engaging in both primary and secondary securities trade.

In addition to lowering prices by bringing competition in the provision of financial services, the single market programme aims to improve the process of intermediation, whereby institutions such as banks attract, pool and lend funds to the widest possible range of borrowers, individual and corporate. Intermediaries generally perform their functions in stock, bond and money markets, although individuals may participate directly in these markets as well.

Because of the risk of loss stemming from participation in financial markets, regulation is necessary to protect savers and investors. Prudential rules, regulations and deposit insurance programmes help to assure investors that institutions will set aside sufficient reserves to cover negative contingencies. EU-wide regulations are also necessary to ensure that practitioners meet certain standards of honesty and competence before being allowed to handle deposits and manage investment funds. In general, smaller-scale consumers need a higher level of regulatory protection.

Another critical element is the role of competition policy to govern mergers and takeovers, and reduce barriers to new market entrants. Fair rules for mergers and takeovers are an essential element of a modern capitalist system because they facilitate structural change and economic growth. Tax policies governing cross-border services, such as insurance and interest on savings accounts, are necessary, as are the convergence of accounting rules and the costs of cross-border payments.

The liberalization process

Liberalization proceeded smoothly for several years. By the mid-1990s, capital controls had been lifted, despite the fall-out from the 1992 exchange rate crisis. Providers of banking, insurance and securities gained a 'single passport', which allowed a firm incorporated in one member state to provide the full range of services through branching or cross-border sales to all member states. Investment firms gained access to foreign stock exchanges. For example, a British-headquartered bank establishing a branch in France would be subject to British banking regulations (such as capital adequacy and ownership conditions) but would have to comply with local conduct of business regulations (such as operating hours) and host country prudential rules. Directives were adopted to ensure capital adequacy and solvency of financial institutions (Pelkmans, 1997).

By 1997, financial services liberalization slowed down as concerns grew over possible job losses and damage to national champions. Continuing fragmentation of the market meant only small decreases in prices (in spite of the cross-border price transparency created by the introduction of the euro) and national barriers to the free flow of financial capital remained in place. This was true especially in retail markets. Competition and consumer choice were still restricted, with significant price differentials between markets. In banking, for example, branches in foreign countries found it hard to break into the local markets because of different national rules and business practices. Concentration (reduction in the number of banks) did take place, but most mergers and acquisitions were domestic.

In investment services, multiple stock exchanges, clearing systems and payment arrangements prevented the type of scale economies achieved in the USA. In wholesale markets, integration progressed further, in part because of the introduction of the euro, which gave participating countries a single financial market for cash. This helped to integrate segments of the bond market and spurred technological innovation to reduce processing costs. Noting the importance of the US venture capital market in creating new firms and additional jobs, the Commission drafted a Risk Capital Action Plan (1997) to increase venture capital resources in the EU. In the insurance sector, cross-border high-risk business (especially property and casualty) grew, but local unfamiliarity with foreign products limited penetration in life policies, especially for mass risks.

In order to rejuvenate the liberalization process, the Commission issued the Financial Services Action Plan (FSAP) in May 1999, which called for the implementation of approximately forty measures necessary to complete the single market in financial services and establish a common set of regulations for service providers, consumers and investors by the target date of 2005 (European Commission, 1999a). Some of these measures were difficult ones not yet tackled; others were new proposals justified by recent technological changes. The Commission's strategy was consistent with its general approach to market integration in the EU. Like the original single market programme, the FSAP included a number of measures and a deadline for enacting them. Also like the single market programme, the Commission hoped that the FSAP would generate political, popular and business support.

The European Council endorsed the FSAP in March 2000, at the Lisbon summit, making it a key component of the Lisbon strategy. France, in the Council presidency during the second half of 2000, proposed setting up a small committee of 'wise men' under Alexandre Lamfalussy, a retired Belgian banker and former head of the European Monetary Institute (the forerunner of the European Central Bank), to review the FSAP. Reporting in February 2001, the Lamfalussy Committee complained that EU decision-making was too slow, did not allow swift adjustment to a rapidly changing market environment, and produced poor-quality directives. The Committee urged faster and more efficient financial services legislation, involving greater consultation with investors, issuers, and financial intermediaries. It also recommended bringing forward the deadline for implementation of the FSAP to 2003 (European Commission, 2001d).

To ensure the prompt enactment of FSAP legislation and regulations, the Lamfalussy Committee proposed a two-track decision-making procedure. Primary legislation, in the form of directives, would contain general framework principles. To speed up the co-decision procedure, which can take up to two years to complete, the Committee recommended more consultation in the pre-proposal stage, and that the Council and the EP reach a decision after the first reading stage.

The other track involved detailed technical provisions and terms for implementation and enforcement. Here the Committee proposed establishing two new committees: the European Securities Committee (made up of senior representatives of the Commission and the member states) and the European Securities Regulators Committee (made up of national regulators). The European Securities Regulators Committee would advise the Commission on technical implementing measures; the European Securities Committee would vote within three months on Commission proposals, which the Commission could then adopt.

Member states and the Commission approved the Lamfalussy Report in 2001, but the EP objected to the new, accelerated approach, fearing that it would not be able to shape important legislation. Only when the Commission promised to keep it fully informed of the European Securities Committee's work, review the new procedure in due course and support its call for a debate on EU policy implementation in the forthcoming intergovernmental conference, did the EP approve the report, in February 2002.

The regulatory and business landscape

There are more than forty financial market regulatory structures in the EU, with different responsibilities and powers. They do not work well together, which adds greatly to the cost of doing business. Some countries, notably Germany, have separate regulators for banking, securities and insurance. State governments in Germany also have regulatory powers. France has separate regulators for the stock market and banking. Belgium, Finland and Luxembourg have merged supervision of banking and securities. In Austria, a government department oversees financial markets; while the central bank plays that role in Ireland. Three countries (Britain, Denmark and Sweden) now have a single national regulator for all markets. German states have opposed the federal government's move towards a single regulator.

The Lamfalussy Report recommended a single national regulator in each country, and even suggested that at some point there might be a single super-regulator in the EU. This provoked intensive debate. Sullivan (2002, pp. 112–13) argues that the introduction of the euro strengthens the case for a single regulator. After all, the eurozone now has a single regulator for monetary policy, the European Central Bank. If a single regulator is not possible politically, Sullivan recommends a process of mutual recognition leading to regulatory convergence in which states co-operate fully on regulatory matters without transferring their regulatory power to a central EU authority. The problem lies in getting to that level of regulatory co-operation between member states.

Lack of regulatory convergence is not the only barrier to further integration. There are also different levels of innovation among member states. Britain and Germany have highly sophisticated financial services sectors, with cutting-edge financial instruments, many of which are not permitted in other countries. There is an important difference between member states that protect their financial services' 'national champions' and those that have truly contestable markets with few barriers to foreign competition. Another dichotomy exists between Britain, Ireland and the Scandinavian countries, whose legal systems do not discourage hostile cross-border takeovers, and continental countries such as France and Germany, whose legal systems make such takeovers extremely difficult. This became dramatically apparent in 2001, when Germany successfully led the charge against a proposed directive to facilitate transnational takeovers, which had been on the drawing board for twelve years. Germany strongly objected to a provision that would have required company boards to be consulted before a firm took defensive measures (known as poison pills) against a hostile takeover. The Commission's view (and that of the European Central Bank) was that mergers and takeovers are an important mechanism for forcing weak businesses to become more efficient or leave the market.

Prospects for liberalization

Given the continuing difficulties in enacting FSAP measures, prospects for the single market in financial services do not look good. Cultural, administrative, technological and legal differences among member states inhibit agreement on common approaches that could remove remaining national barriers, provide more information to purchasers of securities, bridge the differences in levels of innovation, establish a system of single national regulators, and change the culture on hostile takeovers. A recent OECD survey of the eurozone described the situation succinctly: 'The remaining obstacles to deep integration, which are rooted in different legal, administrative accounting, tax and consumer protection systems will need to be dismantled. Ways should be explored to reduce the effects of other obstacles, such as differences in language, business culture or habit persistence' (OECD, 2002, p. 73).

A veritable thicket of European financial services trade groups, each with its own agenda, reinforces national opposition to many FSAP initiatives. A common thread runs through the groups' concerns. Thus, Angela Knight, head of Britain's Association of Private Client Investment Managers and Stockbrokers, warns that it would be better to 'take a little longer and get it right' (APCIMS, 2001). Nigel Wicks, head of a high-level London-based working group of financial companies, observes that 'We have 15 member states with financial markets at different stages of development with different values, conventions, structures, ways of doing business and cultures.' Adam Ridley, of the Investment Bankers Association, laments that 'We are trying to do things no one fully understands, seek outcomes neither clearly specified nor agreed with inadequate resources . . . at an unrealistic, dangerous pace' (*Financial Times*, 29 December 2002, p. 2).

Lamfalussy pointed to another reason why implementation of the FSAP is proving elusive. In an article in March 2002, he argued that one of the main obstacles is inadequate staffing in the Commission, the EP and the new European Securities Committee (*Financial Times*, 17 March 2002, p. 6). 'Without sufficient and able staff,' he wrote, 'it will be virtually impossible to respect legislative deadlines while maintaining adequate standards.' Lamfalussy called for more staff to be seconded from national regulatory authorities for two- or three-year periods. This is unlikely to happen, not only because national authorities are short-staffed, but also because the powerful staff unions in the Commission and the EP fiercely resist the secondment to their institutions of national officials.

Lamfalussy's concerns, as well as those expressed by national governments and industry groups, point to the formidable difficulties in completing the single market in financial services, despite the Commission's view that failure to liberalize fully would reduce the benefits to the EU of the broader single market programme and Economic and Monetary Union (EMU), and weaken prospects for economic growth and employment. Given the economic downturn, member states are less inclined to co-operate for fear that major structural reforms would threaten the viability of their financial services sectors and deepen economic woes. For countries such as France, fear of job losses trumps zeal for reform.

Don Cruickshank, Chairman of the London Stock Exchange, contends that a truly integrated financial services market is incompatible with a Europe of strong nation-states. Only with deeper integration, he believes, is such a market possible. 'The current process of national bargaining over EU laws is unlikely to produce a well functioning market in financial services . . . We need institutions that can act [in] the interests of Europe as a whole. And we need constitutional arrangements that give those institutions democratic legitimacy.' Only in a more federal Europe could a stronger Commission deal with national protectionism by pushing for greater harmonization of laws, transparency and accountability (*Financial Times*, 22 January 2003 p. 12). For that reason, the outcome of the Convention on the Future of Europe and the ensuing intergovernmental conference were of considerable importance for the future of the EU's financial services sector.

Social and employment policy

Europe has a long tradition of concern about working conditions and social welfare. Continental Europeans, in particular, exert formidable political pressure nationally and in the EU to preserve 'social Europe' and avoid moving towards 'heartless American capitalism'. Britain is an outlier in that respect. Even under the Labour government, it drew the line at certain social welfare practices that it saw as interfering with the market process.

The then Commission President, Jacques Delors, a French socialist, thought it necessary to add a 'social dimension' to the single market programme, which originally did not include any social policy measures. Delors was concerned about the impact of market liberalization on workers and regions forced to adjust to the reduction of barriers and deregulation. In 1989, with strong French support, the Commission issued a Social Charter listing workers' fundamental rights. These included freedom of movement, improvement of working conditions, social protection, freedom of association, collective bargaining, information and consultation, health and safety in the workplace, and equal treatment for men and women. Britain did not adopt the charter. Nor did it sign on to a protocol attached to the Maastricht Treaty that allowed qualified majority voting on most worker rights proposals listed in the social charter. Only when Labour came to power in 1997 did Britain sign up to the protocol.

Despite the adoption of the social protocol, the Council shied away from enacting many social policy measures (for example, legislation requiring worker participation in management), even under qualified majority voting. This reflected a major policy shift, with Delors emphasizing the need for more employment rather than traditional social policy measures. Thus, at the Copenhagen summit in June 1993, Delors warned about the negative effects of increasing unemployment on the EU's attempts to compete with the USA and Japan. The Commission followed up with a White Paper stressing job creation, labour mobility, equal opportunities, and the integration of social and economic policies, and calling for a 50 per cent cut in unemployment and the creation of 15 million new jobs by the year 2000. (European Commission, 1993). At Sweden's insistence, the Amsterdam Treaty of 1997 included a chapter that made employment a matter of major concern for both the EU and its member states.

The European Council held a 'Jobs Summit' in Luxembourg in November 1997 and established a non-binding peer review process (the European Employment Strategy) with a view to promoting full employment, increasing labour force participation, creating better jobs, providing life-long learning, and encouraging social dialogue. Launched in 1998, the process involves the following steps: (i) the Council drafts a set of Employment Guidelines, based on employability, adaptability, entrepreneurship and equal opportunities; (ii) governments translate the Employment Guidelines into National Action Plans; and (iii) the Commission and the Council review the National Action Plans and present the results in a Joint Employment Report (this helps member states to monitor labour markets and share best practices).

The Lisbon employment initiative

At the Lisbon summit, EU leaders credited the European Employment Strategy with helping to reduce unemployment. They urged the Council to strengthen the guidelines by providing more concrete targets and drawing on other initiatives, such as the Broad Economic Policy Guidelines developed by the finance ministers as part of EMU. The European Council then set the targets for more and better jobs, greater social cohesion, and better preparation for participation in a dynamic, knowledge-based economy.

Specifically, the European Council suggested raising the overall employment rate from 61 per cent to 70 per cent by 2010 (the benchmark for this target, not specified in the Lisbon conclusions, was the USA, which maintains an overall labour force participation rate of about 74 per cent). The European Council also called for an increase in the number of women in employment, from 51 per cent to 60 per cent, and older workers (aged 55–64) from 35 per cent to 50 per cent. Achieving these targets would require the creation of 20 million new jobs, including 11–12 million for women and 5 million for older workers.

There was some improvement in unemployment and employment figures between 1995 and 2001. Overall, unemployment fell from 11.3 per cent to 8 per cent. Employment rose from 58 per cent to 63 per cent for the 15–64 age group, and the numbers for women and older workers have also improved. Nevertheless, the record varied considerably across the member states, with Germany and Italy performing poorly and the Nordic countries performing well.

The Lisbon strategy has encouraged member states to deal more effectively with the groups that contribute most to the EU's low levels of employment: those who do not work but are looking for jobs; those who are of working age and healthy but not looking for work; those who have disabilities but could be helped to find meaningful work; and third-country nationals living in Europe who are not covered by many employment regulations and may feel discouraged from looking for work. It has also helped to improve the European Employment Strategy (through better use of targets, impact evaluations and structural funds to meet the strategy's pillars). Finally, the Lisbon strategy has sharpened the dichotomy between those in Europe who seek real structural reform, labour mobility and flexibility to meet the job targets, and those who believe that old-fashioned 'social Europe', with stronger worker rights and welfare programmes, should not be sacrificed to meet the Lisbon goals.

Poor labour market flexibility

Labour market structures differ widely among member states. The better functioning ones are highly correlated with economic growth. Adair Turner, a management consultant and former head of the Confederation of British Industry (CBI), developed a useful typology to analyse the problems that the EU faces in this area, devise possible remedies, and set benchmarks for success. He identified six dimensions of labour market flexibility (Turner, 2001, pp. 89–91):

1 Functional flexibility: the ability of workers to shift between jobs and functions in a particular workplace.
2 Skills flexibility: whether workers have widely applicable skills and/or the ability to change or update them.
3 Working time flexibility: the range of work schedules available, such as part-time, temporary and flexible hours, that differ from the standard full-time job.
4 Numerical flexibility: the ability of an employer to hire and fire without unreasonable restrictions.
5 Real wage flexibility: wages set by market forces rather than largely by collective bargaining or social policies.
6 Geographical flexibility: the willingness and ability of a worker to travel from home to work (perhaps across a border), and to move to pursue a job opportunity.

A number of factors militate against labour market flexibility in the EU, although the situation differs from country to country. Strong unions play a major role in setting wages, which are subject to collective bargaining according to a number of formulas (by plant, industry or sector). Broad, rigid wage deals make it difficult for firms, sectors and nations to adjust to changing economic conditions. Yet the parties at the table vary from country to country. Germany and the Netherlands use a corporatist approach in which the 'social partners' (business, labour, and the government) seek to achieve consensus. At the other end of the scale, in Britain, organized labour is weak and wage negotiations fragmented.

In general, Europe also has a noted 'downward stickiness' in wages, unlike the USA, where negotiated wage cuts during an economic downturn are increasingly common. Statutory minimum wages, where they exist in Europe, also tend to be higher than in the USA. Employers are therefore discouraged from hiring low-skilled workers because wages are often higher than the value of the marginal product of labour. Similarly, restrictions on hiring and firing are greater in Europe than in the USA. In France and the Netherlands, the government must approve large layoffs and there is a presumption that no profit-making enterprise should be allowed to fire workers. Firms faced with heavy restrictions on hiring and firing often invest in machines instead of workers, or hire temporary help. High payroll taxes (a total of more than 50 per cent of the wage bill in France and Germany) also discourage hiring and encourage the substitution of machines for labour.

European countries have more rules governing working time, from the EU-wide limit of 48 hours a week to restrictions on night work, hours for minors, part-time work and temporary contracts. Generous social benefits such as unemployment compensation encourage employees to 'game the system' and discourage an active job search. Finally, differences in language and cultural practices limit cross-border working and relocation for employment to other countries.

Yet Nickell (1997) cautions against making generalizations. For example, generous unemployment benefits do not always encourage unemployment if they have strict criteria and are time-limited. There is not a high correlation between unemployment on the one hand, and high employment taxes and high minimum wages on the other. Nor, as a general rule, do restrictions on firing increase unemployment. Strong unions, if offset by coordination with employers in wage bargaining, need not discourage hiring.

Commission initiatives

The Commission has moved away from the idea of a strong, centralized social policy. Instead, member states now take the lead in setting policies that meet the general guidelines set by the Commission and Council. Nevertheless the Commission continues to play a key role and launch various initiatives. Following the review of the Lisbon process at the Stockholm summit in March 2001, for example, the Commission set out to encourage more open and accessible labour markets by 2005. At the Commission's behest, a High Level Task Force on Skills and Mobility produced an Action Plan to accelerate progress on meeting the Lisbon targets, by creating 'opportunities for citizens to move around the EU for educational or professional purposes and make it easier to take advantage of the benefits of integration by improving skills levels and removing barriers to mobility'. The Plan seeks to remedy skills mismatches that are increasingly costly in the EU's knowledge-based service sector economy, and ensure both 'employability and adaptability of workers throughout their working life, thereby enhancing . . . mobility' (European Commission, 2002a).

The Action Plan complements other Commission initiatives, notably 'Making a European Area of Lifelong Learning a Reality' (European

Commission, 2001a); 'A Mobility Strategy for the European Research Area' (European Commission, 2001b); and a communication on the impact of the eEconomy on European enterprises (European Commission, 2001c). The Commission is particularly concerned about education levels in the EU, which correlate with employment growth. Thus, the Commission wants to boost the share of 25–64-year-olds who have completed secondary education from the current level of 60 per cent, and reduce the secondary level dropout rate (18.5 per cent). The quality of education is increasingly important, as jobs in the newer sectors require a higher level of literacy and numeracy. The Commission also wants to provide specialized training for those in the workforce, notably for workers with low-to-medium levels of educational accomplishment (only 6 per cent of workers in this category received on-the-job training in 2000). Other priorities in this area include special training programmes for women, low-skilled workers, the unemployed and older workers who could benefit from on-the-job training.

The Commission's concern stems partly from demographics: as birth rates across Europe continue to decline, the average age of the workforce is increasing. It is extremely important to retain older participants in the workforce by upgrading skills and discouraging early retirement. The Commission is placing special emphasis on extending retirement eligibility dates, on active ageing and lifelong learning initiatives, and on helping to equip the disabled, the long-term unemployed and third-country nationals for jobs in the new economy. These groups are needed in the labour pool to compensate for the falling numbers of young workers.

As well as taking initiatives and launching programmes to address labour market flexibility, however, the Commission continues to propose legislation in the areas of health and safety, and worker rights. For example, the Commission proposed a directive requiring small and medium-sized firms (with 50 or more employees) to 'inform and consult' workers about company plans. Britain opposed an earlier proposal covering companies with 1,000 or more employees and operations in more than one EU country, but agreed to the directive when the Labour government signed on to the social protocol. Britain also opposed the new proposal, which the European employers' federation deemed to be a burden on business that would limit labour market flexibility. Realizing that it would probably be outvoted, Britain finally accepted a face-saving transition.

A separate directive would appear to work against Commission efforts to increase employment. It required firms to give temporary workers the same pay and conditions as full-time traditional employees. For each temporary worker hired, the firm would have to locate a comparable full-time person on the staff and demonstrate that the part-timer would earn an equal wage. In industries such as travel, construction and financial services, temporary workers would enjoy the same perks (such as reduced-fare air tickets or preferential insurance rates) as full-time employees.

The temporary workers directive seemed unlikely to increase market flexibility. By making it harder to hire labour from temp agencies, the Commission went against the stated Lisbon goals of addressing the needs of service firms that want to use part-time workers for uneven work-loads. According to the OECD, half of the new jobs created in Europe are temporary. European unions, long critical of temporary work as being 'not real jobs', undoubtedly influenced the tabling of this directive. Employers' associations throughout the EU attacked the directive. The EP added more than ninety amendments to it in the first reading, and the Commission accepted thirty-one of them. The revised proposal is not considered to be any better, but it may be adopted because Britain and Ireland, its fiercest opponents, cannot defeat it under qualified majority voting.

Different national approaches

For historical, cultural and political reasons, national approaches to the challenge of unemployment differ considerably. France and the Netherlands are interesting examples. Having endured unemployment levels approaching 13 per cent during the mid-1990s, France adopted several measures to deal with the problem. In 2000, Prime Minister Jospin announced a major initiative to place thousands of young work-ers in government jobs. He also reduced the working week from 39 to 35 hours (with no reduction in pay). Employers strongly opposed the measure, which many economists scoffed at because it treats work as requiring a fixed 'lump' of labour. Nevertheless, it appears that some jobs have been created, because employers were able to freeze wages and negotiate time off on a fixed schedule over a one-year period. This appealed to workers and gave companies the flexibility they sought in scheduling work, enabling them to hire more workers. Indeed, at the time of writing unemployment in France has moved down to about 8.5 per cent, near the EU average. The 35-hour week and the youth employ-ment scheme have been expensive, however, increasing budgetary pres-sure at a time when France hovered around the 3 per cent deficit limit prescribed in the Stability and Growth Pact.

The Netherlands, which also suffered from high unemployment in the 1980s, took several steps that eventually reduced unemployment to about 2 per cent. The Netherlands has a corporatist approach to wage negotiations: business, government and labour sit together and negotiate a mutually agreeable solution. In return for limiting wage demands, labour won early retirement benefits, although this went against later efforts to get older workers to stay in work for a longer period. The government tightened eligibility for unemployment benefits and cut the lowest rate of income taxes, giving workers more take-home pay. It also cut public spending and employment taxes. The Dutch employment figures are somewhat distorted by the large number of people on disability benefits, but the reduction is still impressive.

Will the EU meet the Lisbon goals?

Those in the EU who call for more and better jobs by increasing labour market flexibility may be on a collision course with the doctrine of a 'social Europe'. The measures needed to increase employment by matching specific categories of labour supply and demand are not accepted by all member states. Employers face constraints in hiring the labour they need; key skills are lacking; and generous welfare programmes tilt the work/leisure trade-off. High effective minimum wages (including high employment taxes), expensive sector-wide wage negotiations, restrictions on firing, and increasingly strong activities of workers' councils all militate against the Lisbon goals.

Governments face strong union pressure for regular rises and political forces advocating greater social protection, making it difficult to constrain wage increases and reduce the social safety net. Because it is difficult politically for them to cut expenditure, governments have difficulty reducing the employment tax 'wedge' that discourages employers from hiring. They also face fiscal constraints in increasing education and retraining programmes designed to improve occupational mobility, information and technology skills, and lifelong learning initiatives. Workers are reluctant to move across borders or even within their own countries to seek employment, because of cultural and language factors, or for tax, pension and social security reasons.

Turner believes that the EU faces a choice. It can move towards the Anglo-Saxon model, accepting growing income inequality (the working poor) with higher levels of employment and economic growth. Alternatively, it can continue to offer high minimum wages, generous benefits and extensive worker rights measures, thereby maintaining a lower level of inequality at the expense of high unemployment, lower growth and increasing welfare outlays (Turner, 2001, p. 191). The two models seem basically incompatible. For example, France's adherence to the social market model may well prevent the EU from going as far as it could with structural reforms.

The Lisbon strategy has challenged the EU to accelerate market liberalization and labour market reform if it wishes to realize the full potential of economic integration. Yet it is difficult for the EU, whose member states remain jealous of their prerogatives and sensitive to domestic political pressures, to embrace the many changes called for at the Lisbon summit. Despite its impressive rhetoric, the EU may simply be incapable of meeting the high goal it set for itself in 2000.

Chapter 7

The Common Agricultural Policy and Cohesion

DESMOND DINAN AND MARIOS CAMHIS[*]

The budget of the European Union (EU) is unlike that of any other international organization, let alone a sovereign state (Laffan, 1997). On the disbursement side of the ledger, the EU expends about € 100 billion annually. That is a lot of money for an international organization, but not a lot by the standards of a developed country. The most unusual aspect of the EU's expenditure is that almost half of it goes to the Common Agricultural Policy (CAP), and one-third to social and economic cohesion (see Figure 7.1). In the case of agriculture, the EU spends about € 50 billion annually to subsidize farmers for a variety of reasons, such as keeping them on the land, ensuring food security and improving food safety, and protecting the countryside. In the case of cohesion, the EU spends about € 35 billion annually through the so-called 'structural funds' to help close the socio-economic gap between rich and poor regions (including entire countries) in the EU.

The size and configuration of the EU budget is increasingly anomalous. For an entity that is constitutionalizing itself as a quasi-federation, with a single market, a single monetary policy and a high degree of involvement in almost every area of public policy, the EU spends its money in unusual ways. Yet there is no fiscal federalism in the EU. Member states retain responsibility for fiscal policy (within certain constraints, notably the Stability and Growth Pact), and spending on 'big-ticket' items such as social welfare and defence is the responsibility of national governments. Agriculture became an item of major EU expenditure for domestic political reasons (mainly in France) and because of French diplomatic power in the early years of European integration. The CAP has changed a lot since then, but remains deeply entrenched politically at the national and EU levels of government. Cohesion policy developed later in the history of the

---

[*]The views expressed by Marios Camhis, an official of the European Commission, are his own and do not necessarily reflect the Commission's position.

119

Figure 7.1 *EU budget expenditures, 2001*

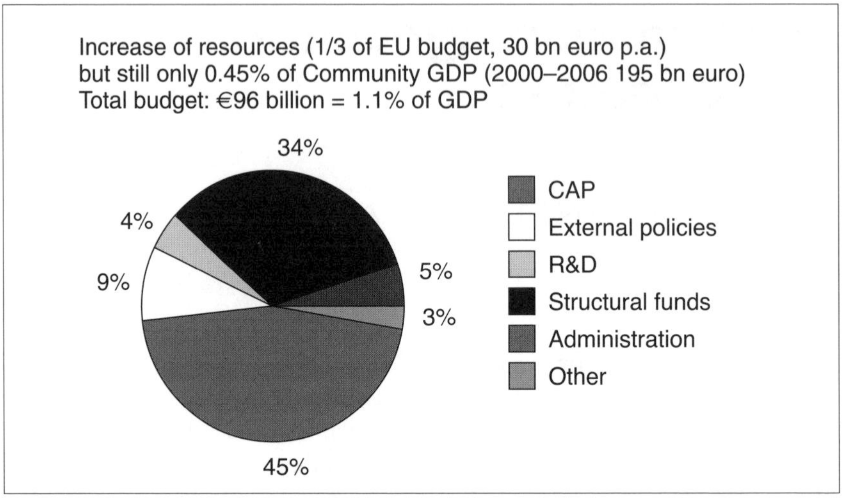

Increase of resources (1/3 of EU budget, 30 bn euro p.a.)
but still only 0.45% of Community GDP (2000–2006 195 bn euro)
Total budget: €96 billion = 1.1% of GDP

34%

4%

9%

5%

3%

45%

- CAP
- External policies
- R&D
- Structural funds
- Administration
- Other

Source: European website http://www.european.eu.int/comm/budget/index_en.htm

EU, largely as a result of concerns that completion of the single market in the late 1980s and early 1990s would exacerbate the plight of the poorer regions and countries, including new entrants Portugal and Spain. Astute political manoeuvring by the poor member states and the Commission, with the support of some of the rich member states, resulted in a radical reform of the structural funds, including a huge increase in the budget for cohesion policy.

The recipients of CAP and cohesion largesse – farmers, regional development authorities, programmes to retrain unemployed workers and help disadvantaged groups – have a vested interest in perpetuating both policies. National governments, which benefit politically and economically from the redistribution of EU funds, spearhead local and regional efforts to keep the money flowing from Brussels. Nevertheless, the EU is under pressure to curb spending on agriculture and cohesion, or at least to ensure that the money is better spent. In the case of agriculture, that means assisting small rather than big farmers; reducing the trade-distorting effects of price supports and other subsidies; and promoting 'multi-functionality' (emphasizing rural development, environmental protection and animal welfare). In the case of cohesion, it means spending less on administration and channelling the money to the truly deserving regions and groups. In both cases, enlargement is a main driver of reform. The new Central and Eastern European member states have relatively large agricultural sectors and relatively poor regions (arguably, they constitute a vast disadvantaged region). The EU cannot afford to increase its budget to support Central and Eastern European farmers and regions to the extent that it supports Western European farmers and regions. Hence the difficulty in 2002 of negotiating the agriculture and cohesion 'chapters' of the accession agreements, and in 2004–6 of negotiating the size and shape of the next financial perspective (2007–13).

The Common Agricultural Policy

The CAP seems ripe for root-and-branch reform. Assailed inside the EU by consumers, environmentalists and advocates of greater assistance to farmers in the developing world, and outside the EU by almost the entire international community, the CAP's days would appear to be numbered. Looking at the CAP from a purely economic perspective, a group of experts appointed by Commission President Romano Prodi concluded in July 2003 that the CAP should indeed be wound down, with responsibility for farm subsidies returned to the member states, an option known as renationalization (Sapir *et al.*, 2003).

Yet the irate reaction to the so-called Sapir Report throughout the EU demonstrates a fierce attachment to the CAP. Politicians, officials and farmers defended the CAP in predictable ways: as the oldest and most emblematic of the EU's policies, the CAP is sacrosanct; it guarantees an abundance of food in a continent historically subject to occasional shortages and famine; the CAP is not just about economics, but assures the livelihood of Europe's farmers, the guardians of the countryside and of a distinctive culture and lifestyle.

Defenders of the CAP admit that the policy is far from flawless, and point out that it is already undergoing major reform. Indeed, in an effort to curb the kind of food surpluses that gave the CAP such a bad name in the 1980s, and to make it more compatible with the international trading regime, the EU began, with the so-called MacSharry reform of the early 1990s, to shift subsidies away from production and towards direct payments to farmers. In response to pressure later in the 1990s and in the early 2000s from consumers concerned about food safety and environmentalists concerned about the ecological consequences of the CAP, farmers and politicians tried to recast the CAP as food-safety-conscious and environmentally friendly.

The incompatibility of the CAP with freer and fairer world trade is an ongoing reason for reform. Just as pressure to complete the Uruguay Round of the General Agreement on Tariffs and Trade tipped the balance in favour of the MacSharry reform, so too did pressure to complete the Doha Round of the World Trade Organization (WTO) more than a decade later impel the EU to accelerate the reform process. Moreover, because the Doha Round is linked specifically to global development, the EU was under added pressure to change the CAP so that farmers in the developing world would not be disadvantaged by it.

In the meantime, the accession of the Central and Eastern European member states with their large, under-developed agricultural sectors increased pressure for CAP reform. Advocates of far-reaching change confidently predicted that the financial impact of enlargement would force the EU to overhaul, or even scrap, the CAP. Instead, the EU made enlargement conform to the CAP rather than the CAP conform to enlargement. The CAP triumphed yet again because of the politics behind it. Indeed, the CAP is best understood not in economic but in political terms.

The politics of the CAP

In an article published in 1996, Keeler explained 'the puzzle of continued European Community support for a CAP that seems on the surface to be increasingly untenable' (Keeler, 1996, p. 127). Despite some significant political changes since then, notably the formation of a social democratic–green coalition government in Germany, increasing concern about food safety, and the growing clout of the European Parliament (EP), Keeler's analysis remains compelling. The politics of the CAP still favour the status quo – gradual reform but maintenance of the policy's underlying characteristics – rather than radical change.

The CAP enjoys residual support because of its supposed role in the establishment of the European Community (EC) and its status as the EC's first common policy, forged in the formative decade of the 1960s. One of the most enduring myths of EU history is that France and Germany struck a bargain at the time: France agreed reluctantly to establish a common market in industrial goods (a cherished German objective) in return for European subsidization of France's large agricultural sector. But the situation was more complicated than that: France wanted an industrial common market (about which Germany was equivocal) in any case, but domestic opinion was strongly divided on the issue. French negotiators rallied sceptical farmers around the idea of a putative CAP in order to swing support behind the proposed EC. The German government acquiesced in it, as long as the level of EC agricultural subsidies would approximate the high level of domestic German subsidies (Dinan, 2004).

Rather than dwell on the contentiousness of its CAP-driven positions in the 1960s, which contributed to a major constitutional crisis in 1965–6 and Britain's exclusion from the EC until 1973, France cultivated the myth that the CAP was the bedrock of its post-war rapprochement with

Germany, a fundamental element in the historic European project. This may seem irrelevant several decades later, yet it resonates at the highest level of EU decision-making. Generally fearful of the impact of enlargement and determined to resist pressure for additional agricultural trade liberalization, France increasingly cites the CAP as the touchstone of its commitment to European integration and the perpetuation of the Franco-German axis. French President Jacques Chirac, a Gaullist and a former agriculture minister, is especially adept at playing the CAP card. German Chancellor Gerhard Schröder may have strained relations with Chirac and be uninterested in agriculture, but he is willing to preserve the CAP for the sake of (relatively) harmonious relations with France. By the same token, Britain's historically different approach to the CAP is one of a number of factors making it unlikely that the Franco-German axis will ever broaden to include Britain, or be replaced by contending Franco-British or German-British axes.

The more practical, day-to-day politics of the CAP underpin support for it at the highest reaches of the French and German governments, and make it difficult for other national governments to bring about radical change. Agriculture may be a shrinking sector, but agri-business is a going concern. The farm lobby, including not only farmers but also business people with agricultural interests, is as politically powerful as ever. Keeler ascribed the success of the farm lobby in thwarting far-reaching CAP reform to 'its asymmetrical interest, extraordinary organization, and remarkably biased enfranchisement' (Keeler, 1996, p. 128). Not much has changed since the early 1990s. The farm lobby would feel the financial pain (substantially lower incomes) of meaningful CAP reform much more acutely than would consumers appreciate the gain (marginally lower food prices). The farm lobby is extremely well organized at both national and European levels. Nationally, farm lobbies are tied closely into bureaucratic and decision-making structures. They are particularly close to leading political parties, notably the Gaullists in France and the Christian democrats in Germany (especially in Bavaria). Most national political systems over-represent rural constituencies, and farmers and their friends constitute a strong voting block.

The farm lobby is less influential, although influential none the less, at the European level. The Committee of Agricultural Organizations in Europe (COPA) is one of the oldest and largest lobbying groups in Brussels. Nevertheless, farmers are not as influential in the Commission as they are in national bureaucracies. Despite its image as a staunch supporter of the CAP, the Commission favours a much less costly and trade-distorting agricultural policy. Historically, the French government sought to colonize the Commission's agriculture directorate-general (DG) with sympathetic French officials. National governments still influence the appointment of senior Commission officials, but are generally less blatant about doing so. Moreover, the French government lost its lock on DG agriculture during the Commission reforms of the early 2000s. Even when the French were most successful in influencing DG agriculture, however, the Commission continued to advocate CAP reform.

The power of the farm lobby at the European level is concentrated not in the Commission but in the Council. Considering that the Council consists of government ministers, and that the Agriculture Council consists of agriculture ministers with close ties to national farm lobbies, this is not surprising. Moreover, a special committee of national agriculture experts, again tied closely to national farm lobbies, serves the Agriculture Council. Given that, at the European level, the Commission proposes but the Council disposes, the farm lobby's tight grip on the Council's decision-making machinery militates against a radical overhaul of the CAP. Given also that a minister's and a government's domestic position often depends on maintaining the farm lobby's support, members of the Agriculture Council, and EU leaders in the European Council, are not averse to using (or threatening to use) the national veto to block unpalatable proposals to reform or revise the CAP.

The politics of the CAP are not immutable, however. The increasing clout of the environmental movement and the increasing emphasis on environmental policy in the EU, reflected in successive treaty changes, is potentially detrimental to the CAP. Gerhard Schröder took the unusual step of appointing as minister for agriculture a member of the Green party in his coalition government, thereby breaking one of the 'unwritten rules' of German politics, whereby the minister of agriculture 'has to come from the farmers' lobby' (Sturm, 1994, p. 82). Not only that, but Schröder included consumer affairs in the new minister's portfolio. As food safety is of keen concern to the consumer lobby, which considers the CAP culpable for recent food scares, this seemed to represent a blow to the farm lobby.

Yet the German minister's apparent timidity on the environmental and consumer fronts, compared with her record of agricultural accomplishments, indicates the pervasive power of the farm lobby and the political realities of agricultural decision-making in the EU. Sensitive to shifting political winds, the farm lobby now portrays itself as a champion of environmental protection and food safety, while the EU lists these as key policy objectives for the CAP. Agriculture ministers and the farm lobby are busy recasting the CAP, to blunt criticism from consumers and environmentalists. Although fundamentally unfriendly to the environment and unlikely to make European food any safer, the CAP is now described as being essential for 'rural development', 'multifunctionality' and preserving the 'European model of agriculture', phrases intended to evoke

warm and fuzzy feelings of social responsibility and political indispens-
ability.

A number of food safety scares in the 1980s and 1990s, in particular
the outbreak of so-called 'mad cow disease' in Britain, had important
institutional implications for the CAP. Critical of the Commission's
handling of the crisis, the EP flexed its muscles and launched a committee
of inquiry. The committee's report castigated the Commission and
demanded a greater role for the EP in policy-making on consumer protection. At a time of major treaty reform in the run-up to enlargement, the EP
also began to push for a voice in CAP decision-making, hitherto the exclusive preserve of the Commission and the Council (Roederer-Rynning,
2003a).

The Commission responded by moving responsibility for veterinary
and plant health issues from the agriculture to the consumer affairs DG,
thereby further limiting DG agriculture's usefulness to the farm lobby.
The extension of the co-decision procedure to consumer and public health
issues gave the EP an indirect role in agricultural policy-making, much to
the chagrin of the farm lobby, which has a far weaker hold over the EP
than over national parliaments. Emboldened by this development, and
thirsting for additional power, the EP pressed during the constitutional
convention in 2002–2003 for an extension of co-decision to the CAP. It
was difficult for national governments to refute the logic of EP's position,
but politically expedient for them to try to keep the EP out of CAP decision-making.

Enlargement brought many more farmers into the EU, thereby
strengthening implicitly the power of the farm lobby. Yet farmers in
Central and Eastern Europe, while not uninfluential politically, lack the
domestic clout of their Western European counterparts. Because they will
receive fewer subsidies than Western European farmers, they may also be
less enamoured of the CAP in its present form. While they are unlikely to
become a major force for change, Central and Eastern European farmers
may not be stout defenders of the status quo either. The impact of enlargement on the politics of the CAP is therefore less clear-cut than the EU farm
lobby would like it to be.

From Agenda 2000 to the mid-term review

Regardless of the political implications of enlargement, the anticipated
budgetary impact of the accession of ten Central and Eastern European
countries with large, and largely poor, agricultural sectors was a major
impetus for reform in the late 1990s and early 2000s. Enlargement
entailed a 50 per cent increase in agricultural land and a doubling of the
farm labour force in the EU. Given the political realities of the CAP,

however, it is not surprising that neither *Agenda 2000* nor the subsequent mid-term review (half-way between 2000 and the negotiation of a new financial perspective in 2006) resulted in a radical reduction of agricultural expenditure. Yet there was no question either of simply increasing the EU budget to subsidize Central and Eastern European farmers at the same level as their Western European counterparts. Apart from the catastrophic effect of such a massive infusion of money into economies without the capacity to absorb it, existing member states wanted, if possible, to cut the EU budget. 'Net contributors' – member states that, by a strict financial calculation, were paying more into the EU budget than they got out of it – were at the forefront of the cost-cutting campaign. Still reeling from the costs of unification, Germany led the charge. A change of government in late 1997, when the largely unknown Schröder replaced Helmut Kohl, a long-time advocate of deeper integration and a strong believer in the Franco-German axis, suggested that major change might finally be imminent.

France, under the relatively new presidency of Jacques Chirac, was aghast as the prospect of a large-scale cutback in CAP spending. Chirac strongly resisted German calls for a partial renationalization of the CAP, and would countenance only small reductions in direct payments to farmers. Negotiations on *Agenda 2000*, based on a Commission proposal of July 1997, culminated in a bruising encounter at a special summit in Berlin in March 1999, when Chirac prevailed over the inexperienced Schröder, who may have been more accommodating because Germany was then in the Council presidency. Predictably, EU leaders declared the summit, which agreed to some cuts in guaranteed prices and in direct payments, a success. A related decision to limit the EU budget to 1.27 per cent of EU GNP satisfied the net contributors. Enlargement, the ostensible reason for *Agenda 2000*, hardly intruded on the agreement. By that time, the expected date of enlargement was slipping later into the decade, and it still looked as if only five of the Central and Eastern European candidates would join in the first round. As Ferrer and Emerson (2000) showed in their detailed study of *Agenda 2000*, the original aims of the reforms 'were practically forgotten'.

Agenda 2000 mandated a budgetary review in 2003. This time the existing member states could hardly ignore enlargement, the negotiations for which were due to end by December 2002. Before presenting proposals for the mid-term review, the Commission submitted separate proposals in January 2002 specifically on agriculture expenditures after enlargement. These called for the phasing in of direct payments to farmers in Central and Eastern Europe during the current and succeeding financial perspective, ending in 2013. The net contributors, led by a now more experienced Schröder, again responded with a demand for radical

CAP reform, including the phasing out of direct payments throughout the enlarged EU and the renationalization of agricultural subsidies. Defending the status quo, France led a group of countries, including Greece, Ireland, Portugal and Spain, which benefited greatly from the existing CAP. Britain, traditionally in the forefront of CAP reform, was in a difficult position, as both sides took aim at its budget rebate, negotiated by Prime Minister Margaret Thatcher in 1984 and considered sacrosanct by subsequent British governments, regardless of their political stripe.

The Commission's proposals for the mid-term review, submitted in July 2002, sought to strike a balance between the contending French and German positions. On the one hand, the Commission upheld the French position that direct payments are an integral part of the EU's *acquis* and could not be phased out entirely; yet on the other hand it sided with Germany by proposing cuts in direct payments of 20 per cent (see Roederer-Rynning, 2003b, pp. 145–6). In keeping with the direction of CAP reform in recent years, the Commission's proposals linked direct payments to environmental, forestation and animal welfare measures (so-called 'cross-compliance'), thereby advancing the broader objectives of EU agricultural policy.

The budgetary negotiations reverted to their usual pattern of Franco-German deal-making when Chirac and Schröder reached agreement just before an EU summit in October 2002 to keep annual expenditure on agriculture in the forthcoming financial perspective (2007–13) at the 2006 level of approximately €45 billion, with a 1 per cent increase for inflation. Much to the consternation of the reform-minded member states, Chirac and Schröder pushed this agreement through at the summit itself. Once again Schröder chose Franco-German harmony over discord, perhaps fearing that, without a guarantee of continued agricultural largesse, France would delay a final agreement on enlargement. The emerging Franco-German consensus on the deepening crisis in Iraq may also have inclined Schröder towards a compromise with Chirac. Whatever its provenance, the agreement on overall CAP funding postponed difficult decisions about the size and allocation of agricultural subsidies until 2006, when the new financial perspective would have to be agreed upon and the existing pie divided among many more member states.

EU leaders also agreed at the October 2002 summit to phase in direct payments for the new member states, beginning at 25 per cent in 2004 and ending at 40 per cent in 2007, when the new financial perspective would begin. Far from accepting a fait accompli, the candidate countries pressed for larger allocations in the run-up to the Copenhagen summit in December 2002, where a final decision on enlargement was due to be made. As anticipated, agriculture therefore became the most contentious, longest-lasting issue in the accession negotiations. The summit ended successfully when the Danish presidency managed to find some more money for farmers in the new member states, thus paving the way for enlargement to take place in May 2004. But the entire affair left a bitter aftertaste in the mouths of the representatives of most member states: the candidate countries resented the second class citizenship implicit in the CAP agreement, and existing member states chafed at what looked like another example of Franco-German high-handedness.

The outcome of the separate, but related, mid-term review was equally unedifying. The European Council's agreement on the size of CAP spending for the period until 2013 robbed the Commission's reform proposals of much of their meaning. Although hailed by the protagonists as a major breakthrough in the history of CAP reform, the ensuing agreement was a patchwork of compromises and concessions to recalcitrant member states such as France and Spain. The agreement further decoupled subsidies from production, reinforced cross-compliance, tipped the balance towards a more equitable distribution of payment from big to small farmers, and introduced price cuts in some hitherto unreformed agricultural sectors (although the sugar sector once again emerged unscathed). Essentially, the 2003 reform was a continuation of the MacSharry reform of 1992. It changed the modalities, but not the munificence, of EU agricultural subsidies.

The Doha Round

Like the MacSharry reform, the 2003 reform was driven in large part by the EU's need to curb the trade-distorting impact of the CAP in order to facilitate completion of a multilateral round of trade negotiations, this time the Doha Development Round. Even more so than in the early 1990s, a decade later the EU's trading partners targeted the CAP as an obstacle to the success of a decisive effort to liberalize global trade and investment. In the late 1990s, the EU fiercely resisted holding separate talks on agriculture in the WTO, preferring to bundle agricultural and other issues in order to link and leverage to the full any concessions on its part. The agricultural talks became a key part of the Doha Development Agenda – the basis of the new round of WTO negotiations launched in Doha, Qatar, in November 2001 (see Chapter 11).

Developing countries long damaged by the pernicious impact of EU agricultural export subsidies, the Cairns group of agricultural free traders and the USA all took aim at the CAP. The USA lost the moral high ground after giving massively increased subsidies to its own farmers under the 2002 Farm Bill, although Washington claimed that the CAP was still much more trade-distorting than its American counterpart. Regardless of its impact on world trade, however, the US Farm Bill was a propaganda coup for the EU, whose politicians and officials seized on it to deflect criticism from the CAP. EU farmers were impressed by the generosity of the American measure. Reuters (2003) quoted Gerd Sonnleitner, president of COPA, the EU-level farm lobby, complaining at a protest against CAP reform in Strasbourg, in June 2003, that 'We [EU farmers] need support like the US gave its farmers'.

Far from letting the EU off the hook, enactment of the 2002 Farm Bill merely put the USA in the dock alongside the EU in the Doha Round. Yet the EU was under more pressure than the USA, not only because EU tariffs and export subsidies obviously distorted global agricultural trade, but also because the EU was more sensitive than the US to the needs of the developing world. Having made North–South global development a cornerstone of its foreign policy (see Chapter 15), the EU had to do something, or at least be seen to be doing something, about the impact on developing countries of the CAP. External and self-imposed pressure on the EU to reform the CAP intensified further after the WTO missed a deadline of March 2003, because of US and EU intransigence, to agree a framework for the negotiations to reduce farm subsidies.

Growing WTO-related pressure for CAP reform gave the EU a strong incentive to introduce changes under the auspices of the mid-term review. Chirac, who announced in October 2002 that CAP reform was off the agenda until 2006 (*European Report*, 2002, p. 480), may have relented in order to try to avoid a collapse of the Doha Round, paving the way for the agriculture ministers to reach agreement in June 2003 on the Commission's proposals. Inevitably, the EU claimed that the outcome of the mid-term review would facilitate a breakthrough in the WTO negotiations on agriculture, and in the Doha Development Round as a whole. Indeed, more direct payments to farmers reduced the scope for overproduction, import levies and export subsidies, thereby lessening the trade-distorting impact of the CAP. Nevertheless, the EU's trading partners remained sceptical, preferring to see concrete proposals for agricultural trade liberalization in the WTO negotiations.

The EU touted its CAP reform at a WTO 'mini-ministerial' in Montreal in July 2003. The following month, the USA and the EU, hitherto highly critical of the impact of each other's agricultural policies on prospects for a Doha Round agreement, came together and presented a 'joint approach' to agricultural issues in the WTO, dealing with the 'three pillars' of domestic support, market access and export competition. The US–EU initiative in the WTO was analogous to a Franco-German initiative in the EU: when the two key players lead, the others have little choice but to follow. Nevertheless, the US–EU initiative was insufficient to ensure the success of the Cancun ministerial in September 2003, the Doha Round's own mid-term review (although a host of other factors accounted for the meeting's collapse).

With the WTO in danger of missing the deadline of January 2005 for completion of the Doha Round, thanks in part to dissatisfaction among the Cairns Group and the developing countries with the Europeans' and the Americans' offers of agricultural trade liberalization, the EU is under additional pressure to reform the CAP. Such pressure will intensify in 2006, when the EU must conclude a new financial perspective. The European Council already agreed on the size of the CAP budget for the period 2007–13, but not on the allocation of agricultural expenditure among a considerably enlarged EU, including new member states that deserve more support than most of the old ones. Despite the pressures of enlargement and multilateral trade negotiations, however, the history of the CAP suggests that a core group of member states will continue to ensure that farmers receive generous subsidies, albeit for multi-functionality rather than overproduction. Although its modalities may change over time, the CAP will probably endure for ever, a symbol and instrument of EU altruism for a favoured socio-economic sector.

Economic and social cohesion

A commitment to economic and social cohesion – to reducing disparities between the levels of development of the various regions and the backwardness of the least favoured regions or islands, including rural areas – is anchored firmly in the EU treaties. Cohesion has benefited the EU in a number of ways. For one thing, it has a redistribution function in favour of the less well-off member states and regions, with a significant macroeconomic impact, and has promoted genuine convergence. For another, cohesion has, directly or indirectly, helped member states and regions to improve their administrative structures, adopt strategic programming on the basis of guaranteed funding, develop partnerships, and evolve a culture of evaluation.

Cohesion facilitates the implementation of other EU objectives, such as sustainable development, the e-Europe initiative, and, of course, the single market. Financial transfers to the poor member states also help the rich ones directly as well as indirectly. For example, recipients of cohesion funding spend a significant amount of their financial assistance on goods and services in other member states, ranging from 42 per cent of what Greece receives, to 15 per cent of what Spain receives. Cohesion policy provides the only EU instruments that can help regions to restructure in the event of a crisis, thereby helping member states to maintain the budgetary discipline imposed by the Growth and Stability Pact, as well as helping to consolidate the euro.

Perhaps most important of all, cohesion policy helps to keep alive a certain model of Europe: a system of economic organization based on market forces that nevertheless includes a commitment to the values of solidarity and equal access to services of general benefit. Because it has an impact on almost every European region, cohesion has become a point of contact with the EU for ordinary citizens. Together with a number of other policies that have a territorial impact – environment, transport and competition – social and economic cohesion can be envisioned as a large-scale planning operation on an unprecedented scale. It helps a divided and fragmented European territory, with diverse cultures and administrative systems, to operate as a unified and interconnected whole. Better infrastructure networks, easier access to the European marketplace for remote regions, and closer cross-border co-operation have strengthened economic and political integration in the EU.

Early years

The development of cohesion policy is intimately linked to the history of the EU itself. The preamble of the Rome Treaty mentioned the need 'to ensure [the] harmonious development [of the member states] by reducing the differences existing between the various regions and the backwardness of the less favoured regions'. The treaty itself envisaged instruments for social and agricultural policy – the European Social Fund (ESF) and the European Agricultural Guidance and Guarantee Fund (EAGGF) – but none to tackle regional disparities.

The prevailing idea was that market forces would, by themselves, help to remove disparities and inequalities between the regions of the EC. Only Italy, with its impoverished Messogiorno, supported the creation of a special fund to help the less favoured regions, but the other five member states were unconvinced. Lacking political clout, Italy succeeded only in getting the others to agree to establish the European Investment Bank (EIB), whose primary task was to provide loans to national governments and regions for development projects.

During the 1960s it became increasingly obvious that relying on free market forces was not enough to reduce regional disparities. In the early 1970s, the EC's first enlargement changed the character of the EC: Ireland, at the time, was a very poor and underdeveloped country; Denmark bore the burden of Greenland; and Britain included Northern Ireland and a number of other regions suffering from structural problems of industrial decline. The economic crisis of the mid-1970s exacerbated these regional problems.

Before the economic recession and on the eve of enlargement, EC leaders called in December 1972 for a Community Regional Policy, and asked the Commission to submit proposals for a European Regional Development Fund (ERDF). Negotiations on the ERDF were bogged down when the recession hit, and became bound up in Britain's demand for more favourable EC membership terms. Because it got relatively little from the CAP, Britain wanted to get the lion's share of the ERDF. Agreement by EC leaders in December 1974 on the size and disbursement of the ERDF facilitated the renegotiation of Britain's membership terms and the successful outcome of the British referendum on whether to stay in the EC.

The ERDF Regulation of 1975 set out the terms of EC regional policy. Thus the EC provided co-financing for regional projects selected by the national governments within their quota of the fund's resources. The EC only supported new projects, which member states would otherwise not have undertaken (this is the principle of 'additionality'). The EC confined its assistance to purely economic projects in underdeveloped regions; nobody thought at the time that the EC should assist black spots of under-development within otherwise prosperous cities or regions.

The Single European Act and Maastricht

Regional policy remained largely unchanged until the early 1980s when EC leaders agreed, as part of a broader effort to revive European integration, to revise the ERDF. By the time the Council adopted a new regulation in 1984, on the basis of a Commission proposal, the situation in Europe was changing rapidly. European integration quickly gathered momentum with the conclusion of the Single European Act (SEA). Apart from facilitating the single market programme and heralding various other initiatives, the SEA included a commitment on the part of the member states to promote 'social and economic cohesion'.

Implementation of the SEA and the accession of Spain and Portugal triggered new ideas for regional development that still predominate at the time of writing. Together with the new ERDF regulation, which came into effect in 1985, the EC launched the Integrated Mediterranean Programmes (IMPs) to counteract the impact of Spanish and Portuguese accession on Greece, which joined in 1981, and on poor Italian and French Mediterranean regions. By introducing the idea of an integrated approach to development, programming and partnership between the Commission, national governments, and regional and local authorities, the IMPs became an important testing ground for what was later applied throughout the EU.

In December 1988, after long and difficult negotiations based on Commission proposals, the Council adopted a multi-annual programme of EC expenditure (the so-called Delors package), including a new set of regulations and a doubling in size of the structural funds (the regional development fund, social fund, and guidance section of the agricultural fund) by 1993 (the various development funds are outlined in Figure 7.2). In so doing, the Council transformed regional policy from a supporting role for national regional policies to a fully-fledged European policy. As with all political processes, the purity of the original ideas was not completely retained, but the new approach nevertheless represented a breakthrough.

It included five clear territorial and thematic objectives on the basis of EC-wide (not national) criteria. 'Objective 1' covered regions having less than 75 per cent of average EU GDP – in effect, Greece, Portugal, a large part of Spain, Ireland, the Italian Messogiorno, and, later, the former East Germany. Other objectives included regions with a high level of unemployment and dependence on industrial sectors in crisis, and assistance for long-term and youth unemployed. The new approach concentrated resources in the most problematic regions, in order to maximize their impact; mandated multi-annual programming and new procedures of decision making; and established a partnership between the Commission, member states and relevant regional and local authorities. The Delors reforms also included new 'Community Initiatives' – Community-wide actions to promote economic, social and territorial integration, such as

Figure 7.2   *The Regional Development Funds*

ERDF	European Regional Development Fund	Finances infrastructure, job-creating investments, local development projects and aid for small firms.
ESF	European Social Fund	Promotes the return of the unemployed and disadvantaged groups to the workforce, mainly by financing training measures and systems of recruitment aid.
EAGGF	European Agricultural Guidance and Guarantee Fund	The 'Guidance' Section of the EAGGF finances rural development measures and aid for farmers, mainly in regions lagging in development The 'Guarantee' Section also supports rural development under the Common Agricultural Policy in all other areas of the Union.
FIFG	Financial Instrument for Fisheries Guidance	Helps to adapt and modernize the fishing industry.
PHARE	Poland, Hungary: Actions for Economic Reconstruction	€1.6bn p.a. to assist applicant countries of CEE in their preparation for joining the EU financing institution building; investment and measures similar to those supported in member-states through the structural funds.
ISPA	Instrument for Structural policies for Pre-Accession	€1 bn p.a. for environment and transport projects to familiarize applicant countries with the policies and procedures of the Cohesion Fund.
SAPARD	Special Accession Programme for Agriculture and Regional Development	€0.5 bn p.a. to help applicant countries deal with the problems of structural adjustment in rural areas, and in the implementation of CAP.

'cross-border co-operation' in which the Commission acts as a catalyst for two or more member states to launch development projects in border regions.

Some have argued that the radical change in regional policy amounted to a handout to the less prosperous member states so they would refrain from creating obstacles to market integration. Others hold that it was an essential ingredient in the success of the single market programme and revitalization of European integration. To bolster their case, they point to the failure of market integration in other parts of the world where important inequalities persist between countries and regions.

The reform of the structural funds coincided with a paradigm shift in regional development theory. From the mid-1980s onwards, new concepts of an effective regional development emerged (Bachtler and Yuill, 2001). Development was attributed increasingly to a region's ability to innovate, facilitate learning and encourage networking between enterprises. At the same time, technological changes altered the way in which companies organized their activities. The acceleration of globalization resulted in the freer movements of labour and capital, the internationalization of economic activity, greater foreign investment, and more acquisitions and mergers. Development came to be seen as a multi-dimensional process requiring integrated strategies, in which all factors – economic, social and environmental – were taken into account. Under the circumstances, a decentralized approach seemed to be more effective than centralized decision-making. These new perspectives influenced and were incorporated into EC policies and programmes.

The Maastricht Treaty of 1992 emphasized the importance of cohesion policy alongside Economic and Monetary Union (EMU) and the single market. Accordingly, member states committed themselves to establishing a special solidarity fund, the Cohesion Fund, to assist those with less than 95 per cent of the EU's GNP to meet the convergence criteria for EMU. This would provide assistance to Greece, Portugal, Ireland and Spain to finance major projects in the fields of the environment and transport. Moreover, Maastricht established a new programme, the Trans European Networks, to facilitate the spatial integration of the unified economic space established by the single market. In a repeat of the post-SEA procedure, the Commission and the member states thrashed out another Delors package (Delors II) in December 1992 to provide the resources necessary to meet the Maastricht commitments.

Enlargement

Negotiation and implementation of the Maastricht Treaty took place against a background of profound change in Central and Eastern Europe. With the collapse first of the Soviet Empire, and then of the Soviet Union itself, the newly-independent Central and Eastern European countries announced their intention to join the EU. Both the EU and the aspiring member states knew that the road to enlargement would be long and difficult. First the European neutrals – Austria, Finland and Sweden – negotiated EU accession. Because of their affluence, their membership had little impact on regional policy, although a new objective (Objective 6) was added to the list of regional goals, to tackle problems of remote, sparsely populated areas.

The likely impact of Central and Eastern European enlargement on regional policy began to dawn on EU politicians and officials only in the late 1990s, when the accession negotiations began and the extent to which enlargement would dramatically change the face of the EU finally became apparent. Disparities and diversities would intensify greatly, and competitiveness and internal cohesion diminish. The gap in per capita GDP between the 10 per cent of the population living in the most prosperous regions and the 10 per cent living in the least prosperous ones would more than double. When all ten Central and Eastern European countries joined, 116 million people (25 per cent of the EU's total population) would live in regions with a per capita GDP below 75 per cent of the EU average, compared with 68 million (18 per cent of the population) in the EU of fifteen member states. In future, the EU would have three types of member state with regard to economic development: those slightly above the average per capita GDP (such as Germany, Ireland and Finland); those slightly below the average (such as Spain, Portugal, and Slovakia); and those far below the average (such as the Czech Republic, Poland and Romania) (European Commission, 2003a).

There would also be a less advantageous employment situation, with the rate of employment declining and the rate of unemployment, and especially of long-term youth unemployment, increasing. Three million new jobs would be needed to bring the average level of employment in the new member states up to that of the rest of the EU (in the event, 3 million net jobs were created in the year 2000 in the EU, while 600,000 jobs were lost in candidate countries). Related issues include the sectoral distribution of employment, the role of agriculture, productivity in industry and employment creation in services (European Commission, 2003a).

The lack of adequate infrastructure in Central and Eastern Europe was another huge drawback. Massive infrastructural investment would be needed in all new member states. Of 30,000 km of roads in Hungary, for example, only half were asphalted and a paltry 448 km were motorways. The agglomeration of Budapest still had 1,000 km of unmetalled roads at the time of enlargement. The Czech Republic, a transit country, had 500 km of motorway. It took five hours to cover the 360 km between Prague and Bratislava, in Slovakia. Poland had less than 400 km of motorways, and only 1 per cent of its 360,000 km of roads reached EU standards. Similarly, only 1,500 km of Polish railway tracks (out of a total network of 29,000 km) met EU standards. The EU estimated that it would take twenty years for most of the Central and Eastern European countries to catch up with the EU 15 average.

On the positive side, the candidate countries had a higher rate of economic growth than the existing member states (3.2 per cent versus 2.4 per cent for the period 1995–9), and a higher level of education, particularly at the intermediate level. By contrast, poor educational levels remained a problem in certain regions in Portugal, Spain, Italy and Greece (European Commission, 2003a).

Agenda 2000 gave the EU an opportunity to tackle the implications of enlargement for regional policy. EU leaders decided at the Berlin summit in March 1999 to spend over €30 billion per year on the structural funds between 2000 and 2006 (€213 billion over seven years), and to develop special programmes to help the candidate countries. The Instrument for Structural Policies for Pre-accession (ISPA) and the Special Accession Programme for Agriculture and Rural Development (SAPARD) would therefore complement the PHARE programme to promote the economic and social development of the Central and Eastern European countries. EU leaders also agreed a number of changes with regard to the operation of the structural funds and adjustments to the operation of the cohesion fund, to which they allocated an annual budget of €2.5 billion (€18 billion over seven years).

The new wave of regulations covering the period 2000–2006 attempted to rationalize the functioning of the funds and improve their management, but the main philosophy behind the 1989 reform remained intact (European Commission, 1999b). One of the most noteworthy changes was to reduce the number of objectives from six to three. As a result, some regions would receive less assistance or no longer receive any assistance (following a phasing-out period) because they had achieved the relevant development objectives either by raising their level of GDP over the threshold (75 per cent of the EU per capita average) or reducing unemployment. Ireland is a classic example of a country that graduated out of large-scale EU assistance.

Objective 1 (territorial) – helping poor regions (those with less than 75 per cent of EU average GDP) – remained practically unchanged. The new Objective 2 (territorial) brought under one umbrella all non-Objective 1 industrial, rural, urban and fisheries-dependent regions facing structural difficulties and increased levels of unemployment. The new Objective 3 (thematic) covered the development of human resources aiming at modernizing systems of training and promoting employment. For the period 2000–2006, about 22 per cent of the EU's population came within the purview of Objective 1, and received about 70 per cent of total available funding; about 18 per cent of the EU's population came within the purview of Objective 2, and received about 11.5 per cent of total available funding; and Objective 3 received about 12 per cent of total funding. Thanks to greater funding, the European territory at the time of writing is a huge construction site: more than 500 programmes comprising about 100,000 projects are being implemented. Forty per cent of the EU's population – living in Objectives 1 and 2 areas – benefit from these projects, and regional transfers have grown since 1989 from €143 to €217 per capita.

Agenda 2000 included a number of managerial reforms intended to take advantage of improvements in the administrative capacities and structures of the less developed regions, and necessitated a large increase in the number of cohesion programmes, which was not accompanied by a proportional increase in the staff required to monitor them. Hence the move towards a more decentralized approach, giving more responsibility to the member states and to the regional authorities concerned. Under the new system, the member states have established a Managing Authority, in which the Commission has an advisory role, to assume general responsibility for implementing, monitoring and evaluating programmes.

In return for less intervention in the planning and implementation stages, the Commission gained more financial control. In keeping with a general trend in the EU, financial management of cohesion policy has become much stricter. Whereas the member states are responsible for ensuring the effectiveness of the supervisory systems and correcting irregularities, the Commission may reduce or suspend payments if irregularities persist. Moreover, if a programme is not implemented on time, the resources allocated to it may be removed and transferred to other programmes. In addition, the EU has set aside a performance reserve to reward successful programmes. The rates of co-financing depend on a number of factors, including key EU objectives such as environmental protection and the promotion of equality between men and women (European Commission, 1999b).

In the run-up to enlargement, the future of regional policy rose to the top of the EU's internal agenda. Although priorities shifted to the prospective new member states, the EU also had to maintain support for the less developed regions of the existing member states. The inclusion of a large number of regions with a very low GDP has caused a 13 per cent fall in EU average per capita GDP. As a result, numerous regions in the EU 15, with a population of over 20 million, now find themselves above the new 75 per cent ceiling for Objective 1 assistance on the basis of a statistical change rather than real convergence. The EU is looking for a reasonable solution, involving a transition period and a gradual phasing out of support for the affected regions.

A number of other questions remain unanswered. Will there be adequate funding for cohesion during the 2007–13 financial perspective? What should the level of assistance be? It is doubtful that the current level of 0.45 per cent of EU GDP for cohesion policy will be sufficient for the scale of economic and social disparities in the enlarged EU. Will all the regions of the enlarged EU be treated in the same way? Because of the limited capacity of the new member states to absorb large financial infusions, the EU is imposing a strict limit of 4 per cent of national GDP for structural and cohesion transfers.

Joint management between the Commission and the member states will become even more complex. Although there will be more programmes, the number of Commission officials will remain constant, or increase at lower rates. The new member states, which have little experience of the management of the structural funds, may not be able to cope with the more decentralized approach to cohesion now favoured by the EU, counter-balanced by stricter financial control. They will have to increase their administrative capacities and endure closer monitoring by the Commission. Thus enlargement will aggravate the tension between a more decentralized delivery system, on the one hand, and more effective financial control by the Commission, on the other.

Given the vast differences in needs, types of assistance and available resources, the EU might have to adopt a differentiated approach to cohesion in the enlarged EU by applying the principle of proportionality. The Commission needs to become less involved in small programmes while providing more technical assistance to the new member states. Although the current system is based on uniform rules that apply to all member states, in fact, different practices, linked to different political and administrative situations, apply. De facto differentiation has become the norm under the cover of uniform rules (European Commission, 2003b).

Any modifications to the management system will have to conform to the treaty provision that gives responsibility to the Commission for the implementation of the budget. Further decentralization would need to be accompanied by a clearer definition of responsibilities, giving the necessary assurances on the use of scarce EU resources. In this context, a contractual approach between the Commission and national authorities (and/or regional authorities), to identify the results to be achieved with EU funding, may be appropriate. Thus the Commission could monitor progress on the basis of a series of indicators and allocate resources in relation to specific objectives.

The third Cohesion Report, presented by the Commission in February

2004, contained concrete proposals for the future of cohesion policy (the first report, in 1996, formed the basis for *Agenda 2000*; the second report appeared in 2001). The Third Report urges the EU to focus on convergence efforts by the least developed member states and regions; improve competitiveness and employment in the more developed areas of the EU; and assist cross-border co-operation. It is a key element of the Commission's planning for the financial perspective for the period 2007–13. During the inevitably contentious negotiations culminating in 2006 on the size and shape of the EU budget for the following seven years, the CAP and cohesion, on which the EU spends most of its money, will once again be at the forefront of EU affairs.

Chapter 8

Environmental Policy: At a Crossroads?

ANDREA LENSCHOW

'Environment policy is one of the EU's success stories – thanks to EU legislation we have seen big improvements in cleaning up the air and our rivers, for example. But we still face major problems and in some cases the environment is actually getting worse'. This statement by Margot Wallström, commissioner for the environment, at the unveiling of 'Environment 2010: Our Future, Our Choice', reflects a real puzzle in EU environmental policy-making (European Commission, 2001f). On the one hand, the EU has arguably the most progressive environmental policy in the world, one that continues to grow in depth and breadth. But on the other hand, the state of the European environment is a cause of growing concern. Economic activity continues to deplete natural resources and pollute the atmosphere despite the enactment of far-reaching environmental policy measures.

This chapter focuses on recent efforts to ensure that EU policy-making succeeds in improving the environment, and investigates the relative standing of environmental policy *vis-à-vis* other areas in daily EU policy-making. The progressive anchoring of an environmental agenda in the EU, beginning with the Single European Act (SEA) of 1986, suggests that the environment is a political priority. Since the early 1990s, member states enshrined the principles of sustainable development and respect for the environment in the EU treaties. By integrating environmental protection requirements into the definition and implementation of other policies and activities (a process called environmental policy integration, or EPI), the EU put environmental consciousness at its core (Jordan, 1998). As a result, environmental policy is approaching a crossroads. It may become simply another policy area in the EU's *acquis*, or the next 'big idea' in European integration, influencing the nature of all internal policies as well as the EU's mission in external relations.

Moving to centre stage

Environmental policy did not develop in the EU as a coherent area with agreed-upon objectives and clearly defined boundaries. Environmentally-minded officials in the Commission initially used their exclusive right of initiative to develop 'green' policies in certain niches of the single market programme – for example, by establishing environmental product standards to facilitate the free movement of goods. Alternatively, they pushed environmental policy under the aegis of industrial policy – for example, in the chemicals sector. The Commission also responded to a number of environmental disasters in the 1970s to build support for transnational initiatives. Until the SEA, which inserted environmental policy objectives into the Rome Treaty and provided a legal basis for future policy-making in this field, environmental policy measures needed to be 'hooked' to established European Community policy objectives and gain support inside the fragmented bureaucracy of the Commission as well as among relevant national policy-makers.

Even after implementation of the SEA, environmental policy evolution via issue linkage continued (Weale *et al.*, 2000). As decision-making procedures varied across policy areas, allowing for qualified majority voting (QMV) on single market measures but requiring unanimity on environmental policy, policy-makers pursued the linkage strategy in order to push an environmental agenda through the easier decision-making route (via market-building measures). Hence many industry- and trade-related environmental standards where agreed (or amended) in the post-SEA period, leading to a rapid expansion of the environmental *acquis*. Subsequent treaty revisions, decided in Maastricht (1991) and Amsterdam (1997), changed decision-making procedures towards co-decision with the European Parliament and QMV in the Council on most environmental proposals. As a result, the pattern of linking pragmatically environmental policy objectives to legal and procedural niches in the treaties became less common – a sign of the political consolidation of the environmental policy field.

For a long time, protection of the environment and economic development/growth appeared to be competing objectives. Given the market-bias of the European project, this placed environmental policy at a disadvantage. Therefore, the endorsement by leading policy makers in the member states and the Commission of the 'ecological modernization' and 'sustainable development' paradigms, with their central claims of compatibility of environmental and economic (and social) objectives, was a critical juncture for the environmental agenda inside the Union. The sustainable development paradigm in particular, and the associated environmental policy integration principle calling for the 'greening' of all sectoral policies, became the main vehicle for environmental policy expansion after implementation of the Amsterdam Treaty in 1999. Accordingly, the EU devoted more time to environmental impact assessments, to procedures granting participatory and information rights to affected citizens, and to developing policy instruments to raise awareness of and develop incentives for environment-friendly behaviour.

Thus, while the framing of environmental concerns in terms of the economic mission of the EU shaped the evolution of this policy field, changes in the EU's institutional and normative framework triggered a dynamic that placed environmental policy-makers on a more equal footing with their economic policy counterparts – at least in theory. As a result, environmental objectives can no longer easily be ignored in EU policy-making. Nevertheless the treaty revision agreed in Nice in December 2000 failed to round off previous reforms, and raised doubts about the central role of environmental policy in the future profile of the EU. Qualified majority voting was not extended to the few remaining areas – most importantly (environmental) tax issues – and the threshold for reaching a qualified majority was generally raised, making it easier to block the enactment of progressive environmental policy, a factor that is particularly significant in the enlarging EU (Jordan and Fairbrass, 2002). Yet the double majority rule (60 per cent of the population and simple majority of the member states) proposed by the European Convention in its draft constitutional treaty, could bring about a major change in environmental decision making, as it would lower the threshold for a qualified majority, giving any coalition in favour of environmental policy greater weight.

The international environmental discourse

The correlation between institutional opportunism and environmental policy expansion is important, but does not tell the whole story of the increasing salience of environmental policy in the EU. Institutional openings are themselves closely linked to the emerging international environmental discourse. Transnational environmental problems helped to mobilize public opinion, intensify scientific research activities and instil greater responsiveness in the EU's political leadership. The establishment of international environmental institutions and regimes, typically following the lead of individual countries or groups of countries like the EU, fuelled the demand for a co-ordinated European approach in relevant issue areas. High standards of living in north-western Europe contributed to calls for, and a political willingness to embrace, a widening of the environmental policy agenda.

Thus, in the early 1970s, the United Nations Stockholm Conference on the Human Environment coincided with the first steps towards institutionalizing environmental policy in the European Commission and the Parliament, and in the formulation of multi-annual Environmental Action Programmes (EAPs). These set out the main objectives and strategies for EU environmental policy and provide the framework inside which the Commission initiates and shapes relevant proposals. Although not politically binding, EAPs guide the policy-making process.

In 1987, the influential Brundtland Report of the World Commission on the Environment and Development played a crucial role in 'Europeanizing' sustainable development, in the form of a leading principle in the EU treaties and a guidepost in programming documents. Similarly, the EU's fifth and sixth EAPs resonated closely with the international discourse following the UN Rio conference in 1992, focusing not only on pressing problems such as climate change, but also on more participatory and responsive state–society relations in environmental governance (Lenschow, 1999).

Parallels between international and EU levels are not limited to general environmental themes and principles, but also concern concrete environmental issues. Considering the often local character of nature protection and its relative independence of market mechanisms, the passage of a considerable amount of EU legislation on the protection of wildlife and biodiversity may seem surprising. Yet a closer look reveals that many of these regulations can be traced to international treaties that triggered a co-ordinated European approach. Equally, EU air pollution policy reflects international discourse: apart from market motivations (for example, in the case of car emissions), the salience of trans-boundary air pollution since the early 1970s – specifically international concerns about acid rain, the depletion of the ozone layer, and increasingly also climate change – have kept the control of various air pollutants high on the agenda of environmental policy-makers in the EU.

The EU's trans-boundary air pollution policy suggests a change in Europe's foreign environmental policy-making. Notwithstanding sometimes difficult internal negotiations, the EU has become a policy *shaper* rather than a *taker* in international environmental affairs, generating rather than simply responding to policy imperatives. While its foreign policy may be fragile in the areas of security and defence, the EU has gained much confidence and credibility in pushing for global environmental responsibility.

Member state interests

The interplay of policy shapers and takers also affects the internal dynamics of EU environmental policy-making. This holds true for the prioritizing of policy issues and the choice of regulatory approach and depth. Nevertheless, it is not easy to identify permanent policy takers (or laggards) and shapers (or leaders). While the Southern member states are reputed to lag behind, implementation records suggest other weak spots in the EU. With respect to policy shaping, there are variations over time. For example, Britain has shrugged off it image as the 'dirty man of Europe' and is actively shaping the EU's environmental agenda (Jordan, 2002b). Many countries tend to pursue (and shape) special issues and approaches, while neglecting others. The patchwork nature of EU environmental policy results in part from this disorderly pattern of individual member states pushing their particular environmental interests in the EU arena (Héritier *et al.*, 1996). All countries, regardless of the level of regulation, like to prevent high adaptation efforts and costs related to the imposition of new regulatory philosophies and structures. Hence, they attempt to embed their approaches in the EU environmental *acquis* by means of 'regulatory competition' (Héritier *et al.*, 1996).

Whereas in earlier years Germany seemed particularly successful in shaping the agenda – for example, by dealing with industrial air pollution, and in imposing its legalistic regulatory style, since the 1990s Britain has moved to the forefront. As well as proactive behaviour in the Council, Britain has played personnel politics within the Commission, placing experienced officials in key positions in the environment directorate-general (department). Smaller member states, such as the Netherlands and Sweden, have also adopted regulatory competition strategies, engaged in proactive policy shaping, and had a notable impact on the environment *acquis*. The Dutch planning system and target group approach were reflected in the 5th Environmental Action Programme adopted in 1993, and in institutional innovations in the Commission such as the installation of a range of participatory or consultative mechanisms. Sweden began to leave its mark soon after joining the EU in 1995, especially when it used its Council presidency to push the EPI principle in the formulation of all sectoral policies.

This is not to deny that conflicts of interest between member states or between environmental policy-makers and their counterparts in other sectors prevent the direct adoption of policy initiatives into decisions, or decisions into action. Lowest common denominator decisions and outright blockage often occur. For example, the British government continues to block a European carbon tax; the (largely German) chemical industry has mobilized to water down a (Swedish and Commission-inspired) chemical policy proposal; and the powerful position of agricultural policy-makers in all EU institutions and the member states has thwarted attempts to 'green' the common agricultural policy. Nevertheless, wide-ranging and in many cases high-standard environmental policy attests to the sometimes progressive dynamics of agenda setting via the initiative of member states and the Commission, resulting in the success story to which Commissioner Wallström referred.

Commission activism

The Commission has been instrumental in identifying policy niches to push the environmental agenda as well as exploiting current issues and concerns, raised in international or national circles, to launch environmental initiatives. Its history of situating environmental policy firmly in the *acquis*, thanks to ambitious and often creative entrepreneurship, is especially noteworthy.

The institutionalization of environmental policy within the Commission began in the 1970s. A working group for the environment and an administrative group within the directorate-general for technology, industry and science, were founded in 1971. In 1973, the administrative group was upgraded to the Environment and Consumer Protection Service, reporting to the vice-president of the Commission. A decade later, it became a fully-fledged directorate-general. The number of officials in the Commission working on environmental policy grew from six to over 400 officials in what is now 'DG Environment'. This initially tiny staff succeeded time and again in pushing the boundaries of its formal competence and exploiting opportunities to insert environmental objectives into the *acquis*.

In recent years, the Commission has given new or renewed priority to two environmental issues: the broad category of 'environment and health' and, more specifically, chemical policy. Under the umbrella of 'health concerns', the Commission framed a range of media- or production-specific environmental policies, dealing with air and water pollution, nuclear safety and GMOs (Genetically Modified Organisms). The so-called precautionary principle is central to the Commission's approach. Thus, in its 'new chemical strategy', the Commission placed increased responsibility – 'the burden of proof' – on industry, and aims to improve risk management actions. In so doing, the Commission developed a common framework for the 'scattered' chemical policy legislation in the *acquis* (European Commission, 2001g).

Yet the Commission's environmental entrepreneurship has come under growing pressure from a variety of critics, ranging from European federalists to Eurosceptics, and from advocates as well as enemies of environmental policy. All are concerned about the ineffectiveness and inefficiency of EU environmental policy. The Commission has responded by reorientating from task expansion to consolidation, and shifting from policy- to governance-entrepreneurship. In particular, the Commission has pushed for more co-ordination between policy sectors in order to avoid conflict, and has promoted a co-operative climate between European, national and sub-national levels of governance, and between public and private actors. The Commission – specifically DG Environment – is becoming more of a mediator and engaging with a multitude of stakeholders in an effort to raise mutual understanding and inspire concerted action.

New phase in environmental policy-making

In the mid-1990s, EU environmental policy making entered a distinct new phase. Years of EU environmental activism had not improved the state of the environment significantly (European Environment Agency, 1999). Critics questioned the effectiveness of the policy itself and, even more important, the apparent lack of co-ordination between environmental and other EU policy areas, such as transport, energy, agriculture and the single market. Smarting from an economic downturn in many member states, critics attacked the cost of environmental regulation, and condemned the EU's tendency towards *ad hoc* and 'wild' regulatory expansion. Without doubt, EU environmental policy suffered from an implementation deficit exceeding that of other policy areas such as the single market, industry and consumer affairs (Commission, 2002a). In short, the overall legitimacy of the policy was questioned both by sceptics of EU regulatory expansion and by those (still) perceiving environmental policy as a burden on the economy.

EU policy-makers responded to this challenge in three general ways: by rationalizing and streamlining the environmental *acquis*; by improving the policy-making process and system of governance; and by further emphasizing the EPI principle.

Streamlining the environmental acquis

Patterns of wild growth, a consequence of the opportunistic policy-making style of the 1970s and 1980s, come at the cost of piecemeal regulation and co-ordination failures. Beginning with the 5th EAP in 1993, the Commission began to identify priorities clearly and develop a more structured and integrated approach to environmental policy-making. The 5th EAP was modelled on the Dutch National Environmental Policy Programme, characterized by a holistic approach to policy planning and an emphasis on stakeholder involvement. The 6th EAP (2002) continued this approach, and lists the following four priorities: climate change; nature and biodiversity; natural resources and waste; and health and quality of life (a new priority of the Commission).

At the level of law making, the EU began to *consolidate* previous regulatory output – for example, by placing formerly disconnected directives in a common framework. The passage of the Water Framework Directive in 2000 exemplified this. It rationalized the EU's water legislation by replacing seven of the 'first wave' directives (surface water and two related directives on measurement methods, sampling frequencies and exchanges of information on fresh water quality, fish water, shellfish water and groundwater directives; and the directive on the discharge of dangerous substances). By requiring all member states to co-operate in river basin management, the EU brought the hitherto neglected cross-boundary and cross-media effects of water pollution into focus.

The EU also adopted a more *integrated* perspective on environmental impacts, seeking to prevent the harmful effects from one medium (such as soil) from passing into another (such as water). The environmental impact assessment (EIA) directive, revised in 1997, and the integrated pollution prevention and control directive, adopted in 1996, facilitate pollution control (and industrial permitting) beyond the initial medium (soil, air, water) affected by discharge. Plans for a strategic impact assessment that would extend an integrated and long-term impact perspective from individual projects to policy programmes, continue to float through Commission corridors. These measures point towards a more systematic, cohesive and effective approach to environmental policy making. But they also require high co-ordination capacities (and structures) on the part of national public administrations, and therefore risk implementation problems.

Good governance

Historically, EU environmental policy was characterized by a variety of regulatory philosophies, styles and instruments. In general, however, traditional EU regulatory policy in the environmental field is based on the top-down imposition of uniform standards. In light of the problem-solving difficulties already mentioned, the EU is considering new regulatory procedures and forms. These place a higher priority on responsiveness to local conditions. Flexibility (not uniformity), participation (not top-down command) and learning (not sanctioning) are some keywords signifying this new philosophy that has made inroads in EU environmental policy-making. In the policy formulation phase, the Commission has begun to involve more systematically those who bear the burden of implementation. The desire for more participatory procedures and context awareness is also evident in the choice of regulatory instruments, although traditional instruments still continue to dominate (see Holzinger *et al.*, 2002 for a quantitative study of the choice of policy instruments in EU environmental policy-making).

Indeed, in analysing the extent of the development of new regulatory forms, or the 'transformation of environmental governance' (Lenschow, 1999), it is important to distinguish between EU rhetoric, procedural reforms and policy. EU communications, ranging from the EAPs to the White Paper on Governance (European Commission, 2001h), give an impression of fundamental change, away from authoritative, hierarchical and substantive regulation to more procedural, participatory, discretionary, and hence context-orientated steering. Recent environmental policy-making shows that this is indeed the case. The Commission is interested increasingly in stakeholder involvement in order not only to tap expertise but also to pass on responsibility. While some high-level dialogue groups established in the first half of the 1990s as sounding boards for EU environmental policy were later disbanded, an implementation network (IMPEL) of Commission officials and representatives of relevant national (or local) authorities has become an important forum for considering the feasibility of EU proposals early in the game, as well as for improving the capacity and willingness of local implementers through the exchange of experiences.

The so-called auto-oil experiment has taken stakeholder involvement even further and, for some in the Commission, points the way ahead (Wurzel, 2002). This experiment can also be seen as evidence of a greater effort to optimize the relationship between costs and benefits in EU rule making. Through a 'trialogue' with the automobile and oil industries, the Commission hoped to identify cost-effective ways to meet air quality standards by way of burden sharing between the two main industries responsible for car emissions. 'Auto-Oil I' led to the proposal of directives on fuel quality and vehicle emissions. Yet the initiative did not escape criticism. Placing the exercise outside regular democratic control and limiting the stakeholders to the main industrial parties may have improved the chance of arriving at a solution, but at the expense of democratic legitimacy and potentially with the risk of industrial bias. 'Auto-Oil II', launched in the spring of 1997, had much wider stakeholder involvement, including members of the European Parliament. Once again the aim was to propose cost-effective solutions for achieving the air quality targets defined in previously adopted or proposed EU legislation. A range of technical as well as non-technical and fiscal solutions for reducing emissions were identified (European Commission, 2000c). Despite these elements of better governance, the ultimate outcome depends on bargaining in the Council, which may dilute a sensible proposal. Council resistance to proposed legislation on fiscal instruments for environmental policy proves the point.

In general, there is a large gap between rhetoric and reality in EU environmental policy-making. Few so-called new policy instruments, characterized

Figure 8.1 *Choice of regulatory instruments in EU environmental policy-making (the periods correspond to EAPs)*

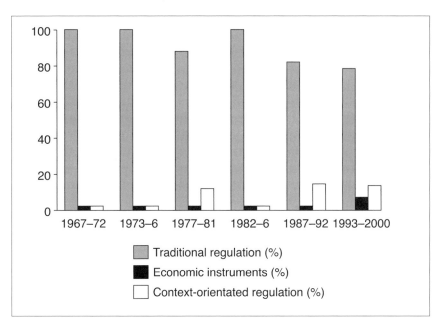

Note: Based on Holzinger *et al.*, 2002, p. 16.

by procedural law rather than standard-setting, and discretionary rather than authoritative measures, have been adopted (Héritier, 2002; Holzinger *et al.*, 2002; see also Figure 8.1). Most of these less authoritative, and hence softer, regulatory tools are applied in the 'shadow of the hierarchy', with the prospect of 'command and control' looming in case the discretionary regime fails to produce the desired results. Alternatively, they are applied together with traditional authoritative measures, indicating that steering through participatory, incentive-led or learning processes is supplementing, but not replacing, traditional legal obligation.

In fact, enforcement statistics indicate that the Commission continues to rely on the force of the law. Ironically, here there has been a true change of approach. As Figure 8.2 shows, infringement proceedings (legal action) in relation to the environmental *acquis* exceed proceedings in all other areas, including the single market, and have increased steadily in recent years. About 10 per cent of all infringement cases end up before the Court of Justice. Environment cases at the Court amounted to approximately 25 per cent of all cases in the years 1998–2000, and a remarkable 36.6 per cent in 2001 (European Commission, 1999c, 2000d, 2001i, 2002f).

Figure 8.2   *Cases under examination for which the infringement procedure has been opened*

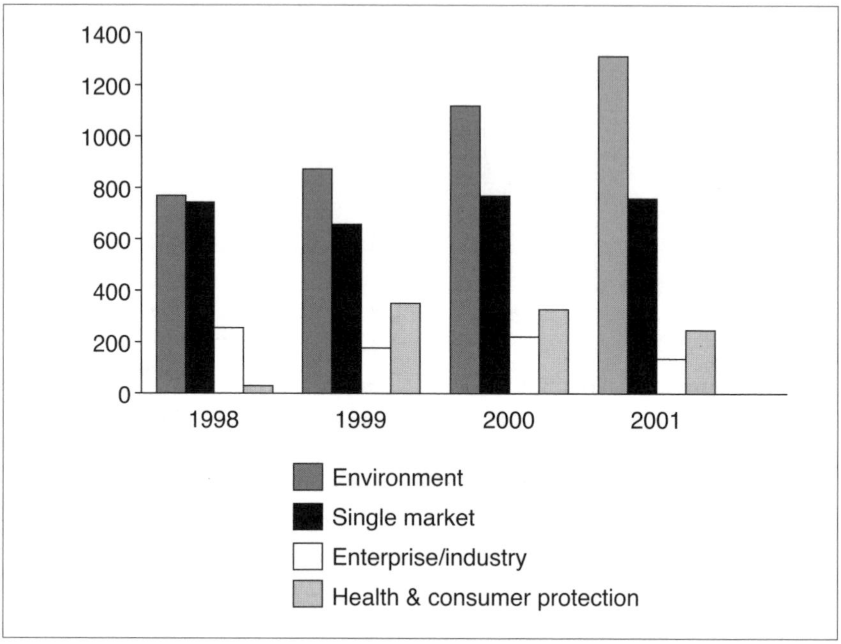

Source: Commission, 1999c, 2000d, 2001i, 2002c.

Within the environment category, waste and nature protection cases clearly lead in the infringement statistics (European Commission, 2002f). Looking at the overall state of affairs in environmental governance and policy-making, wider consultation, stakeholder involvement and responsiveness in the policy formulation phase go hand in hand with greater toughness in the enforcement phase.

Anchoring environmental policy: the EPI principle

Traditionally, the EU has treated the protection of the environment as the sole responsibility of environmental policy-makers in the Commission's DG Environment and in national environment ministries. This began to change following the adoption of the sustainable development paradigm in the late 1980s, with its emphasis on the interdependency of the ecological and the economic spheres. In operational terms, the Environmental Policy Integration principle follows from the sustainable development paradigm as each economic activity should be evaluated in terms of its environmental impact, not only for the environment's sake but also for

Figure 8.3   *Cases under examination in years 1998–2001*

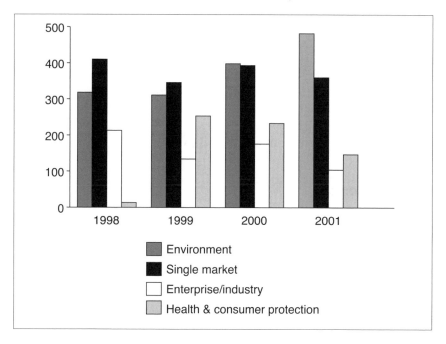

Source: Commission, 1999c, 2000d, 2001i, 2002c.

the sake of longer-term economic and social development. To the extent that EPI will be applied to all EU activities, running a common thread through the arguing and bargaining that characterize EU policy-making, environmental protection has the potential to become the next big idea of the EU, dressing the internal market in green clothes.

However, the impact of the EPI principle on EU policy-making has been slow and continues to be uneven (Lenschow, 2002). Like the related, long-standing and frequently violated 'polluter-pays' principle, the EPI principle, with its long-term and holistic perspective as a guide to production and consumption activities, suffers from the short-term costs of minimizing environmental damage. The Cardiff Summit in June 1998 represented something of a breakthrough for the EPI principle, when EU leaders pushed for its implementation. As a result, most sectoral Councils have had to review their integration performance and develop an EPI strategy. In the meantime, the Commission and the European Environment Agency began work on developing integration indicators while member states started to exchange 'best practice' models.

This combination of 'carrots' (informational tools and open dialogue) and 'sticks' (pressure from a committed leadership) is crucial for embedding

EPI firmly in EU policy-making. Such pressure, successfully applied, would go beyond merely consolidating the environmental *acquis* and mark a real move towards greening the EU. The EU is not yet at that point, however. The commitment of the EU's political leadership to EPI remains volatile, especially during difficult economic times. Ultimately, the 'pure' economic mission of the EU may trump its environmental mission. While presenting opportunities for skilful agenda-setting, the rotating Council presidency has been problematic in terms of continuity. Therefore, the strategy of opportunistic 'niche' politics is far from obsolete for policy-makers dedicated to environmental objectives.

Enlargement

In 1997, the Commission noted that 'none of the candidate countries can be expected to comply fully with the [environment] *acquis* in the near future, given their present environmental problems and the need for massive investment' (European Commission, 1997, p. 67, quoted in von Homeyer *et al.*, 2000, p. 347). Five years later, negotiations between the EU and ten candidate countries came to an end after all policy chapters, including Chapter 22 on the adoption of the environment *acquis*, were closed. Despite this outcome, enlargement will pose an enormous challenge for environmental policy both in the new member states and the EU as a whole.

While looking to the future, it is tempting to make comparisons with previous rounds of enlargement, in particular with the Southern enlargement of the 1980s when Greece, Portugal and Spain joined. These countries were known to have deficient legal and administrative structures for environmental protection, and to place a lower priority on environmental concerns than most EU member states. Notwithstanding continuing references to the 'Mediterranean syndrome' in the literature on environmental policy, the new Southern member states greatly improved their performance (La Spina and Sciortino, 1993). Their membership in the EU prevented neither the massive quantitative expansion nor qualitative advancement of the environmental *acquis*. In that case, why be concerned about Eastern enlargement?

The current challenge is different in a number of respects:

- The environment *acquis* before 1986, when Portugal and Spain joined, was relatively small (the single market programme and implementation of the SEA in the late 1980s marked the turning point for European environmental policy). Moreover, the early environment *acquis* corresponded to the economic structure of the Northern industrialized member states and their environmental problems; specific Southern problems, such as desertification and soil erosion were not (yet) on the EU's agenda. The new Mediterranean member states, therefore, did not face an insurmountable challenge as far as the *acquis* was concerned. By contrast, not only is the present *acquis* far more comprehensive, but also the economic structure of most accession countries corresponds to that of the original member states, with densely populated areas and heavy industrialized regions. The ensuing air and water pollution, as well as waste management problems, are highly regulated in the EU, requiring substantial investments in most of the new Central and Eastern European member states.

- In the late 1980s, the other member states realized that the socio-economic characteristics of the new Mediterranean member states could hamper the implementation of environmental legislation and bring EU environmental policy-making to a halt. As a result, they adopted several special programmes (ENVIREG, MEDSPA, LIFE and the Cohesion Fund) to facilitate Southern 'greening'. The cost of doing the same for the countries in Central and Eastern Europe would be prohibitive. The Commission's proposals for *Agenda 2000*, the EU's financial perspective for the period 2000–2006, assumed that only 4 per cent of the investment needs of the new member states in the environmental field could be covered.

- Many of the candidate countries already had national environmental policies with relatively tough standards. These, however, were not implemented effectively or enforced by the competent authorities (Baker and Jehlička, 1998). To the extent that this was because of administrative rather than financial capacities, the EU's enlargement strategy, paying at least some attention to the reform of administrative structures, helped to improve their implementation record in the medium term. Nevertheless, the institutional challenge remains huge and the EU tends to emphasize the legal transposition of directives and adoption of the *acquis* rather than far-reaching administrative reform. Assistance through the PHARE, ISPA and 'Twinning' programmes, which aim at capacity building and the diffusion of 'best practice', is limited financially. Moreover, capacity building in these programmes focuses almost exclusively on implementation capacity, and not on building environmental awareness and expertise independently of specific EU legislation (Jehlička, 2002).

- Economic and Monetary Union (EMU), and the associated Maastricht criteria, pose severe constraints on the investment capacity of the new member states. While these countries are not full participants in EMU, they all hope to join eventually, with the result that local and regional authorities and industry can hardly afford badly needed investments in environmental infrastructure. The initial post-1989, pro-active approach in many of the accession countries has come to an end, with the environmental *acquis* being perceived as a 'structural imperative' and burden of accession (Slocock, 1996). The practical implementation of EU law is highly questionable under these circumstances.

For these reasons, the new member states are likely to encounter considerable problems with EU environmental law. These problems are rooted especially in the financial misery and deficient administrative capacities of the Central and Eastern European countries. The cultural predispositions associated – rightly or wrongly – with the Mediterranean syndrome are of only secondary importance. The following Commission statement, weighing compliance cost against long-term and wide spread benefits, turns a blind eye to the real budgetary constraints, distributive issues, and political rationales of decision-makers in the accession countries:

> Ensuring compliance with the environment *acquis* requires an estimated investment of around € 80 to € 120 billion for the ten Central and Eastern European countries alone. However, a study financed by the European Commission shows that implementing the EU environmental directives – and the higher environmental protection they entail – in the candidate countries, will bring significant benefits for public health and reduce costly damage for forests, buildings, fields and fisheries. The estimated total value of the benefits of EU directives for the candidate countries will range from € 134 to € 681 billion. (European Commission 2002d, p. 61)

Notwithstanding the scepticism surrounding the practical relevance of the Commission's study, the adoption and implementation (however deficient) of the environment *acquis* will have a positive effect on the environment in Eastern and Central Europe, given the level of environmental degradation that exists there. In the meantime, the EU agreed transitional measures with respect to some directives requiring substantial adaptation of infrastructure in the new member states, mainly relating to waste management (European Commission 2002d, pp. 62–4).

What about the consequences of enlargement for future environmental policy-making in the EU? Assuming that the Central and Eastern European countries can be considered environmental laggards, accession is likely to put 'downward pressure on environmental policy' (Baker, 2000, p. 164, quoted in Jehlička, 2002, p. 3), or at least prevent the passage of tough measures. A related scenario points to the possible renationalization of EU environmental legislation as the Commission puts renewed emphasis on flexible regulation in order to avoid the overall demise of environmental policy (von Homeyer *et al.*, 2000). Jehlička (2002), in contrast, rejects the assumption that a 'race to the bottom' is the sole interest of the new member states, which may take a more proactive role in shaping the Community's environmental *acquis*. The evidence so far suggests that the preferred environmental policy of the Czech Republic, Hungary, Poland and Slovakia 'corresponds with the current trend in the EU towards flexibility, economic instruments, public participation and environmental integration' (Jehlička, 2002). The extent to which the new member states will be able to assume or share leadership of the environmental agenda remains to be seen. Either way, the form and content of environmental policy-making depend on their input.

International co-operation and conflict

While enlargement may put an end to deepening the environmental *acquis*, in its external relations the EU continues to push an environmental agenda and takes some pride in its 'alternative' foreign policy identity. Besides assuming leading roles in international environmental conventions (notably on climate change and bio-diversity), the EU argues that environmental concerns must be taken seriously and integrated into the activities of all international organizations. In effect, the EU is pushing the EPI principle on a global scale. This is particularly evident in the areas of trade policy, climate change and co-operation with neighbouring states.

Trade policy

Compared to traditional foreign and security policy, in international trade relations the EU is a strong actor, capable of speaking with a loud and clear voice. Together with the significant expansion and deepening of the EU's environmental *acquis*, this has led the EU to push for the greening of international trade relations.

The traditional cleavage within the World Trade Organization (WTO) on this issue has been between the USA and Europe on the one hand, and the developing countries on the other, with the latter in particular fearing 'green' trade restrictions on raw materials. Principally in favour of restricting non-tariff trade barriers, the USA and the EU shared an interest also in protecting national health, safety and environmental regulations from challenges through the WTO. Since the mid-1990s, when the Republican Party took control in Congress, the relationship between the EU and the USA has become edgy, with the EU identifying trade and the environment as an area that ought to be covered in the next trade round. Most important, the EU wanted assurances that trade restrictions contained in multilateral environmental agreements (such as the Montreal Protocol on Biodiversity) would be protected from challenges through the WTO, whereas the USA felt that WTO rules and dispute settlement procedures were already adequate. The EU also wanted WTO rules modified to protect the precautionary principle as defined in the Maastricht and Amsterdam treaties. The USA, by contrast, followed a more science-based approach to risk management and opposed such innovation. These contending approaches were at the core of the long-running beef hormone case (in which the EU banned the importation of hormone treated beef from the USA). They threatened also to become an issue regarding the trading of genetically modified organisms. Other disputes involve process and production methods, ecolabels and subsidies, with the USA being fearful that any rule change will either make future trade liberalization more difficult, or legitimate eco-protectionism (Vogel, 2002).

Climate change

Ratification and implementation of the Kyoto Protocol (1997) to cut greenhouse gas emissions by 8 per cent over 1990 levels by 2008–12 is a key priority in the 6th EAP (European Commission 2001k). In the longer term, the EU hopes to go far beyond that goal. Although it is uncertain whether the EU will succeed in reaching its own benchmarks, 'Kyoto' has become a pervasive reference point in the environmental, energy and transport policies of the Union. This reflects a general acceptance of global solutions and the authority of international conventions as legitimate constraints on national or EU action, something that distinguishes the EU from the USA, which 'appears to accept binding commitments and obligations by the international community . . . only when this brings economic advantage' (Krämer, 2002, p. 15).

Nevertheless, it is important to note that the EU has had some difficulty in developing a joint position in the initial negotiations. The problem is partly one of competence. With respect to global environmental issues, the EU generally has 'shared competence' to act, typically following a 'mixed' procedure, with the Commission making use of its right of initiative in proposing a negotiating position and often taking the lead in negotiations (acting under a mandate agreed in the Council), while the EU – strictly speaking the European Community – as a whole and the member states individually sign and ratify the international agreement, frequently after complex internal negotiations. In the climate change case, the EU argued for binding reductions for industrial countries in a fixed period, whereas the USA favoured a more flexible approach, allowing for 'banking', 'borrowing' and 'trading' of emissions, the inclusion of emission sinks in the calculation of long-term obligations, and a stronger focus on the contributions of the developing world to the climate change regime. The EU's insistence on internal burden sharing contributed to a more flexible approach, with binding reduction targets (Obertür and Ott, 2000). During the post-Kyoto conferences in Buenos Aires, Bonn, The Hague, Marrakesh and New Delhi, the EU attempted to tighten up the Protocol and close some flexibility gaps, allowing industrialized countries to avoid reducing greenhouse gas emissions. In light of the increasingly critical, and ultimately negative, position of the Bush Administration towards the Protocol, the EU attempted to rally a sufficient number of countries (responsible for at least 55 per cent of all greenhouse gas emissions) for the Protocol to come into force without watering down the initial agreement too much. Although Japan signed, Russia held out for more concessions.

In response to US efforts to undermine the Kyoto Protocol, therefore, the EU moved into a leadership and front-runner position on global climate change. The multilateral negotiations were based initially on co-ordinated member state engagement, with the Commission establishing itself only gradually as the EU representative (Sbragia, 1998). Faced with internal conflicts and growing doubts about its own ability to meet the Kyoto targets, however, the EU seems unlikely to lead an international 'flock of stubborn sheep' on such a contentious question.

Relations with neighbouring countries

The enlarged EU is surrounded by countries with problematic environmental records. In view of the risks of trans-boundary pollution, the EU is active in forming environmental partnerships with Mediterranean countries as well as with countries in the Western Balkans and former Soviet Union. These partnerships build upon the 'Environment for Europe Process', launched by the United Nations Economic Commission for Europe in 1991. This and subsequent initiatives led to the conclusion of several pan-European Environmental Agreements, including the Aarhus Convention on Access to Information, Public Participation in Decision-Making, and Access to Justice in Environmental Matters, and the establishment of a number of Regional Environmental Centres (in Budapest, Moscow, Kiev, Chişenău, Tbilisi and Almaty) to strengthen environmental awareness in civil society.

The Commission has a strategy of embedding environmental co-operation in bilateral partnerships between the EU and neighbouring countries, while adopting a regionally differentiated approach. The

Commission wants to help partner countries to implement international agreements, improve environmental laws and institution building, and launch sub-regional initiatives. Funding comes in part from EU programmes such as TACIS (technical assistance and investment co-operation in the newly independent states), CARDS (community assistance for reconstruction, democratization and stabilization in South-East Europe), LIFE (financial instrument for the environment in the EU), and Synergy (energy co-operation). The European Investment Bank also contributes to the environmental dimension of the Euro-Mediterranean Partnership and to environmental projects in the St Petersburg and Kaliningrad regions.

Besides its immediate environmental objectives, this strategy is part of a coalition-building exercise aimed at strengthening EU leadership on international environmental issues by building a critical mass of environmentally aware and increasingly capable countries willing to support the EU's positions. In that regard, the EU has been moderately successful.

Conclusion

While undoubtedly idiosyncratic in its development and composition, EU environmental policy is extraordinarily comprehensive (McCormick, 1999, p. 200). The formulation of multi-annual environmental action plans, initially little more than 'shopping lists', helped to establish a programmatic framework affecting policy making in the EU in general. Expansion, deepening and consolidation of EU environmental policy can be traced to pragmatic and adaptive policy-makers in the Commission and the environment ministries of the member states, who exploited a range of opportunities. Over the years, environmental policy principles have become institutionalized, both in specific ways and more generally. The interplay of a wide range of actors with diverse interests has led to policy expansion rather than contraction, because of a continuous institutionalization – if not constitutionalization – of environmental policy in the *acquis* communautaire and in the treaties, thereby preventing a rolling back even at times of little enthusiasm for new initiatives.

As a result, EU environmental policy is approaching a crossroads. It could become just another policy area or the next big idea in the EU's development. Either way, a period of contraction after fifteen years of occasionally rapid expansion seems unlikely. Despite current challenges, including vocal internal criticism of a policy that seems too interventionist, costly and poorly implemented, EU environmental policy has reached a high level of institutionalization and general acceptance. The progressive development of EU environmental policy is unlikely to stop after enlargement, although questions of governance will continually arise, while the problem of financing will be seen more frequently. Lack of resources may ultimately be the reason why environmental policy may not replace market integration as the next big idea in the EU. The record of implementing the EPI principle during a period of economic downturn bears out this point. Nevertheless, the consolidation of the EPI principle in the treaty will keep environmental policy at the forefront of the European project for a long time to come.

Chapter 9

Immigration and Asylum: A High Politics Agenda

VIRGINIE GUIRAUDON

In October 1999, at a special European summit on Justice and Home Affairs (JHA) in Tampere, Finland, EU leaders committed themselves to developing a comprehensive immigration and asylum policy, and decided to 'place and maintain this objective at the very top of the political agenda' (European Council, 1999). A key element in bringing about the 'area of freedom, security and justice' called for in the Amsterdam Treaty of 1997, immigration and asylum policy became a high priority for the EU, along the lines of the single market programme and Economic and Monetary Union. A year later, the European Commission issued a road map on the subject and called for a balanced approach in meeting different objectives: on the one hand, securing rights for long-term foreign residents and asylum-seekers, and assessing the need for new foreign labour in Europe; on the other, fighting illegal immigration and trafficking by reinforcing 'partnerships with the countries of origin' (European Commission, 2000b). Less than a year passed before the terrorist attacks in the USA of September 2001 pushed the EU's agenda in a new direction. At their December 2001 summit in Laeken, EU leaders linked the fight against terrorism with illegal immigration and sought to reinforce border controls by enacting a stricter visa policy. In June 2002, following a wave of electoral successes by anti-immigrant populist parties across Europe, the Spanish presidency decided to dedicate most of the Seville summit, to 'intensifying the fight against illegal migration'.

Immigration and asylum have therefore become 'high politics' in the EU: a prerogative traditionally at the core of the nation-state is now at the top of the agenda of European integration (see Figure 9.1). This is especially remarkable because there was no formal intergovernmental co-operation on the subject before the 1985 Schengen Agreement, and no EU competence for immigration policy before 1992. Yet immigration and asylum are now highly salient issues that occupy an ever-larger place in the activities of EU institutions. The Commission produces a flurry of

Figure 9.1   *Key immigration and asylum priorities set by the European Council*

Tampere objectives:
1   Partnership with countries of origin.
2   A Common European Asylum System.
3   Fair treatment of third-country nationals.
4   Management of migration flows.

Laeken priorities for 'A true common asylum and immigration policy'
1   Integration of the policy on migratory flows into the EU's foreign policy. In particular, European readmission agreements must be concluded with the countries concerned.
2   Development of a European system for exchanging information on asylum, migration and countries of origin.
3   Establishment of common standards on procedures for asylum, reception and family reunification, including accelerated procedures where justified.
4   Establishment of specific programmes to combat discrimination and racism.

Seville conclusions
1   Measures to combat illegal immigration.
2   Gradual introduction of co-ordinated, integrated management of external borders.
3   Integration of immigration policy into the EU's relations with third countries.
4   Speeding up of current legislative work on for a common policy on asylum and immigration.

Sources: European Council, 1999b, 2001, 2002.

legislative proposals, and the Council of Ministers holds innumerable meetings on JHA (about four per presidency). Moreover, immigration and asylum policy has become an integral part of the EU's external relations, and was prominent in the accession negotiations with the Central and Eastern European countries, which the existing member states viewed as 'buffer states' that had to agree to adopt the EU *acquis* in full.

This chapter examines developments in immigration and asylum policy since the Amsterdam Treaty came into effect in May 1999, and the impact of this policy area on other issues and policies, including enlargement and external relations. The chapter explores why member states gave the EU competence for an area considered to be emblematic of national sovereignty and highly sensitive politically, and outlines the decision-making rules in the post-Amsterdam period. It also looks at the way in which immigration and asylum policy aims to prevent unwanted immigrants from reaching EU territory.

The salience of immigration and asylum policy

Europe is now an immigration continent. Each year, about a million and a half legal immigrants arrive in the EU, proportionally twice as many as arrive in the USA (OECD, 2003). There were about thirteen million non-EU nationals residing legally in the EU before enlargement, making up about 4 per cent of the total population (only 2.8 per cent of the world population are international migrants). Illegal immigration into the EU can only be estimated, and figures vary greatly. For example, the International Organization for Migration estimated the upper limit of unauthorized migrants in Europe to be 3 million in 1998, and believes that anywhere between 120,000 and 500,000 foreigners enter Europe illegally every year (IOM, 2000). Beyond these aggregate numbers and estimates, national situations differ significantly. As Table 9.1 shows, some Northern member states have a long tradition of immigration with significant foreign-born populations, while Southern member states have only recently taken in migrants, many of whom transit through their territory. The numbers admitted vary: flows into Germany have been higher than into France or Britain, although Britain topped the list in 2002. Large numbers of asylum-seekers, relative to the total population, arrive in smaller countries such as the Netherlands and Denmark.

Countries such as the USA or Canada *solicit* immigration and sometimes actively recruit highly-skilled workers from abroad. Every year, the USA gives large numbers of residence permits to highly-skilled workers and to family members of US residents: the US Immigration and Nationality Act sets an annual *minimum* of 226,000 family-sponsored immigrants and 140,000 employment-based preference immigrants. By contrast, policies in Europe seek to *stem* immigration flows. Countries that had welcomed post-colonial migrants and actively sought foreign 'guest-workers' after the Second World War stopped recruiting migrant workers in 1973 at the time of the first oil crisis. Immigration continued, but most of the foreigners who came were unsolicited. New legal entrants have either been family members of foreign residents and nationals, or persons fleeing zones of conflict and escaping persecution, such as the Asian 'boat people' of the 1970s and those fleeing the Balkans or Afghanistan in the 1990s.

Given the lack of business pressures for more migrant workers and the rise of ethnocentric rhetoric and sentiment in Europe, national policies since the later 1970s have sought to reduce the number of foreigners reaching the territories of member states. Yet, based on constitutional principles such as equality before the law and fundamental rights, landmark high court rulings in the late 1970s were more favourable to immigrants than were administrative decisions and immigration laws. Thus governments could no longer prevent family reunification; foreigners enjoyed a more secure residence status; and certain categories of foreigners gained protection from expulsion. The end of the 1970s also saw the

Table 9.1 Foreign populations and asylum applications in EU countries

Rank	Percentage of foreigners as part of total population (averages 1990–9)		Asylum applications per 1000 inhabitants		Total asylum applications per GNP (US$ billion)		Total asylum applications lodged in 1997 (Amsterdam treaty)		Total asylum applications lodged in 2002 (Seville summit)		Kosovar refugees accepted per 100000 inhabitants	
1	Luxembourg	35.6	Sweden	27.71	Sweden	1049.32	Germany	104,350	UK	110,700	Austria	628
2	Austria	9.1	Germany	22.90	Germany	897.18	UK	41,500	Germany	71,127	Denmark	530
3	Germany	8.9	Denmark	21.14	Netherlands	811.97	France	21,420	France	50,798	Sweden	421
4	Belgium	8.7	Netherlands	20.34	Belgium	721.60	Netherlands	34,440	Austria	37,074	Ireland	275
5	France	5.6	Belgium	17.62	Denmark	653.95	Belgium	11,790	Sweden	33,016	Netherlands	257
6	Sweden	5.6	Austria	16.03	Austria	632.73	Sweden	9,660	Netherlands	18,667	Luxembourg	233
7	Denmark	4.8	Luxembourg	13.26	Luxembourg	316.67	Austria	6,720	Belgium	18,805	Finland	191
8	Netherlands	4.2	UK	6.29	UK	257.85	Denmark	5,090	Ireland	11,634	Germany	179
9	UK	3.8	France	5.02	Ireland	232.28	Spain	4,980	Italy	7,281	Portugal	127
10	Ireland	3	Ireland	4.89	France	207.30	Greece	4,380	Spain	6,179	Belgium	119
11	Greece	2.6	Finland	3.53	Greece	196.88	Ireland	3,880	Denmark	5,947	France	107
12	Italy	2.1	Greece	2.34	Finland	143.86	Italy	1,860	Greece	5,664	Italy	102
13	Finland	2	Spain	2.12	Spain	141.15	Finland	970	Finland	3,443	UK	72
14	Spain	1.8	Italy	1.57	Italy	76.46	Luxemburg	430	Luxemburg	1,043	Spain	36
15	Portugal	1.8	Portugal	0.56	Portugal	51.76	Portugal	300	Portugal	245	Greece	0

Sources: UNHCR (www.unhcr.org), OECD (2003) and Thielemann (2003).

first major clashes between ministries of social affairs, responsible for integrating migrants and regularizing their status, and ministries of justice and home affairs, responsible for immigration control.

By the early 1980s, justice and home affairs ministries had an incentive to seek new policy venues at the European level to circumvent domestic legal constraints and conflicting policy goals (Guiraudon, 2000). This explains the emergence of intergovernmental forums such as the Trevi Group of JHA ministers, which met regularly after 1975 to exchange information and co-ordinate positions. Migration control agencies benefited from shifting policy-making away from the national level by excluding a number of actors who were more successful at the national level where the bargaining process involved almost every ministry and many civil society groups. By contrast, JHA ministries do not broker compromises at the European level with dissenting ministries. Civil society actors do not have the resources to monitor the secretive activities of JHA ministries and mobilize against them at the European level. National parliaments have largely been bypassed and only presented with international agreements to ratify without modifications, as was the case with the 1990 Schengen implementation agreement on border controls and the 1990 Dublin Convention on asylum.

Schengen, named after the town in Luxembourg where the original agreement was signed between France, Germany and the Benelux countries in 1985, provided the first opportunity for JHA officials to set the agenda for intergovernmental co-operation. The aim was to create a 'laboratory' in which a few countries would establish an area without internal border controls while taking 'compensating measures' in the form of reinforced external controls. Illegal immigration was one undesirable activity that needed to be countered; organized crime, drugs and arms trafficking were some of the others. The Single European Act (SEA) of 1986 included a commitment to the free movement of *persons* as part of the single market programme. The first elaboration of a common immigration policy was thus bound up with the lifting of internal border checks on persons within the EC, a side-effect of the free flow of goods.

Refugee flows from Central and Eastern Europe into Western Europe rose after the fall of the Berlin Wall in 1989, especially with the disintegration of Yugoslavia. A major influx of asylum-seekers into Germany in 1992–93 provided new grounds for co-operation, as did emotional public debates in many member states about imminent 'tidal waves' of 'bogus refugees'. Military, intelligence and police officials added international migration to their list of trans-national dangers, such as Islamic fundamentalism and global mafias menacing post-Cold War Europe (Huysmans, 2000).

In a development compatible with intergovernmentalist accounts of

EU integration, member states facing such challenges sought to upgrade their common interests through policy co-ordination, specifically by including immigration and asylum in the 'Third Pillar' of the 1992 Maastricht Treaty, covering co-operation in JHA. Germany, coping with the overwhelming majority of asylum seekers (over 400,000 requests in 1992), appeared to have enough influence to convince the other member states to increase co-operation. Germany wanted a 'burden-sharing' system to distribute asylum-seekers throughout the EU. The other member states demurred. Instead, in a manner reminiscent of 'every man for himself', member states adopted various measures in intergovernmental forums to reduce their numbers of asylum seekers and move them on to other countries. For example, they concluded the Dublin Convention outside the Community framework to establish rules on the state responsible for examining asylum cases and the transfers of asylum seekers back to the member state in which they had entered the territory of the EU. Most of the policy innovations before the Amsterdam Treaty took place outside the Third Pillar framework, notably within the Schengen framework, which continued to attract new members.

The Amsterdam Treaty framework

The Amsterdam Treaty framework integrated immigration and asylum into the 'Community' pillar (the First Pillar) of the EU. Table 9.3 compares the pre- and post-Amsterdam situations. Yet intergovernmentalism continued to predominate, leaving only a limited role for supranational institutions. During the negotiation of the Amsterdam Treaty, everyone agreed that the convoluted intergovernmental framework contained in the Third Pillar needed revision if progress was to be made in the co-ordination of migration control policies. Before Amsterdam, member states had agreed on only one joint position and five legally binding joint actions on fairly marginal issues, such as airport transit and cross-border school trips. After much debate, national governments agreed to move the provisions on immigration and asylum out of the Third Pillar and into the First Pillar. Nevertheless, the Amsterdam agreement was far from simple or clear-cut.

First, the scope of policy competence delegated to the EU in this area was much wider than external border policing measures. It included the development of a common asylum policy and the harmonization of rules of entry and residence for non-EU citizens. Foreign ministry officials, shunted aside during the Schengen negotiations but at the heart of the Amsterdam negotiations, took their revenge. Keen to rein in transgovernmental processes dominated by law-and-order civil servants who

Table 9.2   *Pre- and post-Amsterdam institutional framework for
immigration and asylum*

	Post-Maastricht	Post-Amsterdam transition period (1999–2004)	Post-Amsterdam after 2004
Treaty basis	Title vi, article K	Title iv, arts 61–64 TEC	Depends on 2004 ICG
Types of legal instruments	Conventions, joint actions, declarations	First pillar instruments (directives, regulations, decisions)	No change planned
European Parliament	Limited role (visa policy mainly)	Consultation role	Co-decision after unanimous Council vote
European Court of Justice	No jurisdiction	Referral for last instance national courts	No change planned
Voting rules in the Council	Unanimity	Unanimity	Qualified majority voting after unanimous Council vote
European Commission	Shared right of initiative	Shared right of initiative	Exclusive right of initiative

had seemingly run amok, the foreign ministry officials decided to incorporate the Schengen agreement, and all subsequent measures adopted for its implementation, into the EU treaties. The Schengen *acquis*, 3,000 pages long, was published and given legal standing. Nevertheless, the treaty came into force before member states had agreed on how to incorporate the Schengen *acquis* into it, despite many expert meetings on the subject.

The Amsterdam Treaty marked an important step in the 'communitization' of immigration and asylum policy, which implies both a greater role for EU institutions in decision-making and the use of traditional EC legal instruments, such as directives and regulations. The treaty provided for the Commission to acquire an exclusive right of initiative after a five-year transition period, until which time it would share the right of initiative with the member states. Given that ministers had to approve Commission initiatives unanimously, in effect the Commission had a limited margin of manoeuvre.

During the treaty negotiations, several member states were reluctant to involve supranational institutions other than the Commission, especially those with control and review functions. The European Parliament (EP), whose opinions and reports have always defended the interests of non-EU nationals, won only a consultative role. The introduction of co-decision, whereby the EP could ultimately veto legislation, required a unanimous

Council decision. The European Court of Justice may issue rulings on the interpretation of justice and home affairs measures, but its role is circumscribed, at the insistence of the French. This followed earlier Court jurisprudence affirming that certain categories of third-country nationals – families of EU nationals, employees of EU firms contracted in another member state, and nationals of countries that had signed association agreements with the EC – could move freely within the EU.

The Court has no jurisdiction over national border-crossing measures aimed at safeguarding internal security. Therefore the Court cannot review the overwhelming majority of administrative measures either barring access to a member state or requiring the expulsion of foreigners, as they are justified by the need to 'maintain public order' and 'safeguard internal security'. More important, the application of preliminary rulings (requests to the European Court for a legal interpretation) in areas covered by JHA is restricted to the highest national courts (instead of national courts at any level). This limits the number of cases brought before the European Court and hinders the dynamics of 'integration through law' in this domain. JHA officials seeking to escape judicial constraints at the national level do not want to be faced with similar legal scrutiny at the EU level.

Accountability and democratic oversight are weak in the EU, especially with regard to immigration and asylum policy. There is a proliferation of committees of national experts, whose meetings and minutes are not made public. The most important is the Strategic Committee on Immigration, Frontiers and Asylum (SCIFA), consisting of high-level JHA officials. Euro-parliamentarians and the few non-governmental organizations that serve as 'watchdogs', such as Statewatch or the European Council for Refugees and Exiles (ECRE), denounce the lack of access to documents. European-level policy-making is much harder for 'organized publics' – relevant elected officials and civil society actors – to supervise than national immigration policy reform or local administrative decisions.

Decision-making rules in the Council undermine the 'communitization' of immigration and asylum policy. In the negotiations leading to the Amsterdam Treaty, Germany insisted successfully on unanimous voting in the Council on immigration and asylum policy, because the German state governments had lobbied against the transfer of decision-making capacity to Brussels in this area, thereby ensuring a 'lowest common denominator' approach to immigration and asylum decision-making. Negotiations on the harmonization of national legislation that need to take into account the evolving and varied interests of member states are drawn-out processes in which proposals are watered down, resulting in fairly vague and flexible final texts. One case in point, a proposed directive on family reunification, has sat on the table since 1999, despite several Commission attempts to move it along. The text finally adopted by the Council in September 2003 sets very harsh conditions for family reunification, uses a restrictive definition of the family, and in many ways goes against the fundamental right to live a normal family life.

Directives adopted quickly tend to be those that turn pre-existing Schengen rules into EU legislation. As most member states are Schengen states that adapted their legislation to comply with the agreement, no additional national transposition is necessary. Thus a 2001 regulation on the list of countries whose nationals require a visa to enter the EU states that 'it follows on the Schengen *acquis*'. Other Schengen follow-up measures include a 2001 directive on sanctions against carriers that transport foreigners without proper documentation; and a 2002 directive on unauthorized entry, transit and residence. Indeed, most of the binding EU legislation adopted since 1999 simply involves updating Schengen.

Unanimity also means that measures involving coordination, informal co-operation or technical instruments such as databases, have far outpaced directives requiring new national laws. Informal co-operation includes, for example, information exchange among consulates on 'bona fide' and 'migration risk' visa applicants. In November 2002, the Council urged the creation of a network of 'liaison officers', posted at consulates and airports, to share operational information on immigrant flows and false documents. The oldest relevant database is the Schengen Information System (SIS), revamped as SIS II to accommodate enlargement. Under the rubric of the Third Pillar (co-operation on JHA), it includes information on persons and stolen goods, as well as information provided by all participating countries on millions of 'inadmissible aliens' who should be denied entry into the EU. EURODAC, another database, stores the fingerprints of all asylum-seekers in the EU since 2003. Officials consult EURODAC to ensure that an asylum seeker has not applied for asylum in another member state. In the event of an existing request, the rules of the Dublin Convention determine which member state should process the request, in order to prevent 'asylum shopping'. In June 2003, the European Council approved the establishment of a database of visa applicants. Finally, the Commission has stated that the proposed EU global satellite navigation system (GALILEO) will be used to track people crossing the EU's external borders.

Despite these examples of technical co-operation, the decision-making rules laid out in the treaty make the harmonization of legislation difficult to achieve, and the use of legal instruments such as directives less likely. The difficulty of reaching an agreement to harmonize the rights of third-country nationals and on other aspects of asylum policy is so striking that alternative methods have been suggested in the Commission and the

Council. One is to apply to immigration and asylum the 'open method of co-ordination', whereby member states set common goals and targets rather than reaching agreement on binding EU norms (European Commission, 2001j). An alternative approach, known as 'enhanced co-operation', allows some member states to go further than others in certain policy areas.

In effect, the Amsterdam provisions on immigration and asylum policy consecrate the idea of a *Europe à la carte*. Not all member states subscribe to the policy: Britain and Ireland, for example, have negotiated a selective 'opt-in'. In practice, they ask participating member states permission to co-operate on immigration and asylum policy on a case-by-case basis. Denmark, albeit a member of Schengen, is not bound by the Amsterdam provisions and co-operates only on visa policy. That has caused a legal nightmare, as each new decision necessitates the signing of a separate Denmark–EU treaty. Norway and Iceland are not EU members, but signed an agreement in 1999 allowing them to participate in the application and development of the Schengen/EU regime in order to maintain the Nordic Passport Union (covering all Scandinavian states). The new member states have had to comply with existing EU rules. Thus immigration and asylum policy epitomizes a multi-speed Europe that extends beyond the EU's borders.

It is worth noting that the EU is not the only international entity to develop common policies on immigration and asylum, thereby undermining the idea that co-operation in this area was simply a spillover from the creation of the single market. Among the most important comparable processes are the Intergovernmental Consultations on Asylum, Refugees and Migration Policies; the Vienna Club (Germany, Austria, Switzerland, France and Italy); and the Budapest process (involving both Western and Eastern European countries). The Council of Europe and the United Nations (UN) are also actively involved in immigration policy co-operation.

The Nice Treaty did not alter the Amsterdam framework. Nor did the draft Constitutional treaty presented to the European Council in June 2003 by the Convention on the Future of Europe suggest that any changes were imminent, although the co-decision procedure and qualified majority voting may be extended to all policy domains, including this one. The draft constitutional treaty acknowledges the key role of the European Council in this area and the prerogatives of a standing committee co-ordinating 'operational co-operation between the competent authorities of the member states'. National governments will therefore remain the most important policy actors for some time to come (European Convention, 2003, p. 35).

From Tampere to Seville

At the Tampere summit in October 1999, EU leaders agreed to develop balanced common policies in the area of immigration and asylum. Although committed to fighting illegal migration, they recognized the need to give 'fair treatment to third-country nationals', fight racial and ethnic discrimination, respect international obligations relating to asylum, and even consider labour market needs for foreign workers. By the Seville summit of June 2002, however, 'balance' was no longer an objective. Instead the summit focused solely on fighting illegal migration. The change was a result of important developments in the intervening period, including the terrorist attacks on the USA in September 2001, and the electoral success of xenophobic populist parties in Europe. As a result, immigration and asylum became a high priority for member state governments, which entrusted the Commission with launching a large number of initiatives in this area.

EU leaders set an ambitious agenda at the Tampere summit in an effort to realize the putative 'area of freedom, security and justice'. The summit was intended to send a political signal that EU leaders wanted to address the daily preoccupations of European citizens, such as crime-fighting. The summit was the culmination of various Council meetings so that EU leaders could announce sixty concrete policy initiatives, some with specific deadlines. The emphasis was clearly on 'freedom' and the rights of European residents, including a possible charter of fundamental rights. The summit affirmed that a common immigration and asylum policy was necessary to lift internal borders and achieve full freedom of movement. To ensure that concrete decisions would follow, EU leaders requested the Commission to keep a 'scoreboard' of proposals and track the negotiating process every semester: a sort of 'to-do list' to monitor progress in this area.

At the time, the EU's economic prospects were relatively good. That augured well for a rebalancing of immigration policy goals. In its 'Communication on a Common Immigration Policy,' the Commission underlined that a goal of 'zero immigration' could not be achieved and was not necessarily desirable given labour shortages in certain sectors and a demographic decline in Europe because of low fertility rates (European Commission, 2000b). The External Trade Commissioner suggested that Europe could benefit from lifting immigration controls on the personnel of service companies as part of the global negotiations known as GATS (General Agreement on Trade in Services). Individual member states were already recruiting highly-skilled workers, with Germany proposing 20,000 'green cards' for Indian computer programmers. Yet they did not propose this as EU policy; after all, the point was to recruit the best for themselves rather than share with other member states. Still, the early post-Amsterdam period heralded a less repressive and restrictive policy, which non-governmental organizations (NGOs) applauded.

The reorientation of immigration policy turned out to be short-lived. The attacks of September 11 and a coincidental economic slowdown brought with them a security-orientated view of migration control. Official statements emanating from the Council and the Commission linked terrorism with immigration and asylum. At an extraordinary meeting of JHA ministers convened immediately after the attacks, Germany claimed that the fight against terrorism required the creation of an EU visa identification system, including a common database with biometric data on all visa applicants wanting to travel to the EU. EU leaders made the proposal a priority at their Laeken summit in December, and the Council approved them in February 2002, thereby illustrating the acceleration of decision-making in this area. At the October 2001 meeting of the Strategic Committee on Immigration, Frontiers and Asylum, the USA signalled a complete overhaul of its immigration system and requested detailed personal data on people flying to its territory (Council of the European Union 2001). US pressure on the EU in the area of immigration persisted, with direct consequences for EU citizens. For example, the Commission prepared legislation in the autumn of 2003 so that EU passports would meet new US document security standards (alternatively, EU citizens travelling to the USA would have to pay US$100 to obtain a visa).

For the EU, as well as for the USA, September 11 was a turning point. The Commission came under pressure to act more speedily on immigration and asylum issues. For example, the Council asked the Commission to examine the relationship between safeguarding internal security and complying with international human rights obligations, including the Geneva Convention on refugees. The Commission responded with a working document that raised concern among civil liberties groups and refugee organizations because it seemed to imply that all asylum-seekers were terrorists in disguise. António Vitorino, the Commissioner with responsibility for JHA, had to clarify and retract part of the report. After September 11, member states asked the Commission to exercise its power of initiative more frequently, putting the new, understaffed directorate-general (department) for JHA under considerable pressure, and resulting in some hastily drafted and controversial proposals.

Political developments in a number of member states that experienced electoral breakthroughs by extremist or 'populist' parties standing on anti-immigration platforms contributed to the toughening of immigration and asylum policy. Between 2000 and 2002, such parties joined the ruling coalition government in a third of the member states (Austria, the Netherlands, Denmark, Italy and Portugal). In May 2002, the candidate for the extreme-right-wing National Front party came second, with over 17 per cent of the votes, in the first round of the French presidential elections. Xenophobic parties also made headway in local and regional elections, notably in Flanders (Belgium) and Hamburg (Germany). At the same time, the Spanish Presidency in the first half of 2002 decided to make 'the fight against illegal migration' the focus of the Seville summit, after Prime Minister José Aznar and Tony Blair, his British counterpart, issued a joint statement on the subject. Since becoming prime minister, Aznar, from the right-wing *Partido Popular*, had enacted tough immigration laws, whereas Blair faced a campaign in the widely-read tabloid and regional press against the increasing numbers of asylum-seekers arriving in the south of England via the Eurotunnel. Blair and Aznar justified their focus on illegal immigration as a reaction to the French and Dutch elections.

The EU leaders' willingness to make immigration a top priority was noteworthy, as this was a policy area previously left to bureaucrats. The shift reflected not only the indirect impact of populist parties on the policy agenda but also the state of national electoral competition, where issues such as crime and immigration gained salience over older right/left cleavages regarding the economy. By lifting that particular 'hot potato' out of the national debate, EU leaders implicitly shifted the blame on to the EU for the partial failure of control policies at the national level. Despite lofty rhetoric and calls for action, the Seville summit produced nothing of substance on the harmonization of immigration policy. Indeed, by raising the stakes for a common policy that would take years to achieve and possibly strengthening the appeal of the populist parties that abhor both foreigners and European integration, the EU leaders were playing a dangerous game.

Under increasing pressure in the area of JHA both before and after the Seville summit, the Commission began to acquire more resources to develop proposals. Following the Maastricht Treaty, the Commission had only a taskforce on JHA, with a dozen bureaucrats. The directorate-general for JHA, set up in 1999 with about 180 civil servants, grew quickly to 300 staffers. Commissioner Vitorino, a Portuguese with an excellent reputation, had technical knowledge, political acumen and good communication skills. As Uçarer (2002) noted, the Commission was constitutionally, and institutionally, empowered in the area of JHA after Amsterdam. It soon established its legitimacy as a broker of compromise among member states. Yet problems of understaffing and lack of in-house expertise persisted.

Over time, member states made less use of their right of initiative, preferring instead to call upon the Commission to develop the ideas that they put forward. Member states control the agenda, but delegate policy elaboration to the Commission, as in the case of the post-September 11 demand by Germany for a new visa identification system. The Commission staff first dismissed the suggestion as an exaggerated response to the terrorist attacks. Yet Germany was so adamant about seeing it through that the Commission stressed in a green paper (discussion document) on return policy for illegal residents that the future database of scanned visa and passport pictures would play 'an essential role' in the expulsion of foreigners, as if it had been a Commission priority all along (European Commission, 2002).

As well as accommodating member state positions, Commission proposals also have to show the 'value added' of a common approach. In doing so, the Commission benefits from the experience of former members of the internal market directorate-general. Documents on immigration and asylum stress economies of scale and the advantages to be derived from 'best practices'. For example, the green paper on return stresses that multinational charter flights to take illegal residents back to their country of origin should be encouraged because they are efficient and cost saving. Human rights NGOs disagree with this approach, which is typical of the way in which the Commission argues for 'more Europe' in a number of areas. Ultimately, the Commission has had to bow to member states' demands for more restrictions on immigration and asylum policies, and package them in familiar Community language. Instead of inter-institutional competition, the Council and the Commission collaborate in producing an increasing number of proposals, all of which try to restrict immigration, and many of which are of poor legal quality.

Enlargement: a buffer zone?

As the EU enlarges, its external borders shift, and the Central and Eastern European countries have now become the 'final frontier'. Yet tensions between the new and old member states have grown, with the old member states, distrusting the new ones, wanting to impose their own border control standards and, conversely, the new member states feeling that they are being asked to do too much, in too little time, with inadequate resources.

As soon as the Berlin Wall fell in 1989, a number of East–West forums were set up, at Germany's behest, to ensure that the Central and Eastern European countries would adopt the same laws, use the same policy toolbox, and develop the same infrastructure as the Western European countries. These multilateral intergovernmental processes, with varied memberships such as the Budapest process or the Berlin Group, viewed the Central and Eastern European countries as possible 'buffer states' for immigration and asylum flows, creating a new 'wall around the West' (Andreas and Snyder, 2000). A number of bilateral readmission agreements were signed with the Central and Eastern European countries, such as the 1993 accord between Germany and Poland, which stipulated that Poland would re-admit migrants who had illegally crossed the Polish–German border.

EU institutions became more assertive once the accession negotiations began. The Commission was responsible for managing the PHARE funds intended to help the Central and Eastern European countries adapt to the *acquis communautaire*, as well as monitoring and reporting on the progress of candidate countries in meeting the requirements of membership. The question of external border controls and immigration moved higher up the agenda as the accession negotiations proceeded. Ten per cent of PHARE funding (about €131 million in 2000) was allocated to JHA, half of it for border security (mainly enhancing operational capacities on Poland's eastern border) (House of Lords, 2000, p. 4). Candidate countries began to adopt laws resembling those of the member states, but had major implementation problems. It took only a day to pass a law on asylum, but much longer to set up receiving and processing centres. Similarly, a blanket commitment to controlling borders could not hide the fact that border guards were very poorly paid and therefore subject to corruption, and that they did not possess the infrastructure to control crossings according to EU norms.

As the importance of border control grew in the enlargement process, tension, mistrust and frustrations between the EU and the Central and Eastern European countries intensified. The candidate countries were quick to point out that the existing member states were not in full compliance with the Schengen agreement (Italy and Greece had taken years to meet Schengen standards). Nevertheless, the EU demanded that the Central and Eastern European countries focus strictly on control at the risk of endangering their own interests. The Council insisted that border reinforcement was necessary because of the perceived link between immigration and international organized crime. For example, concern about the increasing activities of Russian mafias led the Council in 1998 to question the feasibility of visa-free travel between Russia and the Central and Eastern European countries (*European Report*, 1998). Yet the candidate countries, knowing that 'security' could not be enhanced without regional stability, wanted to have good relations with their eastern neighbours. Hence the reluctance of the Central and Eastern European countries to impose EU-mandated visa restrictions.

The case of Poland and Ukraine is revealing. Each year, two and a half million Ukrainian migrant workers and small traders cross the border into Poland. About 35 per cent of small enterprises in Poland depend on commerce with Ukraine, and border trade gives Poland an annual net surplus of US$1.5 billion. Polish officials wanted to impose visas only at the very last minute, and even threatened to establish an 'ultraliberal visa regime'. According to the Polish government, economic ties cannot be separated from strategic interests, as the stability of Ukraine could counter-balance Russian hegemony. The Polish government also feared that strict visa policies could hinder the activities of Ukraine's democratic opposition, which operates mainly out of Poland.

The question of the Hungarian Diaspora is similar to the Polish–Ukrainian case. Hungary, a country with 10 million inhabitants, is very concerned about the three million 'ethnic Hungarians' living abroad, mainly in Romania and Ukraine. Hungarian trade and investment are linked closely to the Diaspora, and migration to Hungary provides a livelihood for many ethnic Hungarian families in neighbouring countries. Consequently, the Hungarian government feared that complying with the EU visa regime would run counter to its commitment to ensure the well-being of Hungarians abroad.

The German–Austrian demand for a transition period of five to seven years after accession, before the citizens of all new member states (apart from Cyprus and Malta) could enjoy the full rights of free movement, was a major bone of contention between the EU and the Central and Eastern European countries. Unless they were self-employed, citizens of the new member states would not be able to work in the existing member states, and would therefore not be treated equally as EU citizens. Some member states, notably Germany, also reserved the right to limit the freedom of services inscribed in the treaty in certain economic sectors, such as construction (a move intended to limit the activities of firms from the new member states that employ their own nationals when fulfilling contracts abroad).

Candidate countries therefore had an obligation to comply with the Schengen *acquis* regarding immigration controls, which is not matched by their citizens' right to move to the older member states. Free movement of persons, reaffirmed as an important goal in the SEA and considered in the Maastricht Treaty as the cornerstone of a developing 'European citizenship', has none the less been fortified by the jurisprudence of the European Court of Justice. The idea that citizens of the new member states would not enjoy it immediately is another example of a differentiated or 'multi-speed' EU, in which not all member states and citizens are treated equally.

Demographers disagree on the scale of migration from the Central and Eastern European countries to the other member states. Estimates range from 200,000 to 1,000,000 annually. Yet demographers admit that their early predictions for the 1990s were wrong, as many fewer people than expected moved west (Christiansen, 2002). East–west migration to date has focused on the two member states that are closest to the Central and Eastern European countries, both geographically and culturally: Germany (with about 500,000 migrants) and Austria (about 100,000). Three-quarters of all Central and Eastern European workers in the EU, mainly coming from Poland, are employed in these two countries. Most Central and Eastern European migrants who settle in Western Europe are fairly young and highly-skilled, although they are concentrated in a few sectors, such as construction and agriculture, and generally work below their skill levels.

Fear that the accession of poorer countries would lead to massive immigration flows is not new. Greek, Spanish and Portuguese accession prompted similar claims, and led to short transition periods before the EC extended free movement to them. In fact, many migrants from Southern Europe returned to their countries of origin, which had become democratic and prosperous. These countries now attract migrants from elsewhere. The same could happen in Central and Eastern Europe.

Limiting access to the EU

EU measures in the area of immigration and asylum have focused on what scholars refer to as 'remote control', with the aim of preventing undesirable migrants from reaching the EU, where they could have legal protection and begin the asylum process. This strategy, which operates *before* the border, also allows for less control at the point of entry itself, thus facilitating the movement of inhabitants of the 'first world' – tourists and businessmen. The goal is to allay public anxieties over immigration while short-circuiting legal constraints and facilitating a desirable level of immigration.

Beyond the border, measures have taken various forms: visa regimes; an obligation for transport companies to check passports and visas; and co-operation with countries from which migrants come or through which they transit. In the event that undesirable foreigners reach the border, member states have set up extraterritorial waiting zones in airports. The EU has updated various Schengen decisions on visas. A regulation of March 2001 stipulated that a uniform and secure visa for visits of less than three months must be obtained by nationals of 135 countries (those of forty-six other countries are exempt). In effect, three-quarters of non-EU countries are on a 'blacklist', including most developing countries (oil-producing countries, some Asian tigers, and some Latin American countries are exceptions). After Spain experienced a significant increase in Ecuadorian immigrants, the EU moved Ecuador to the blacklist in

March 2003, As Ecuador's president wryly remarked, 'when the Spanish came to America, nobody asked them for a visa' (Statewatch, 2003). The EU's official criteria for the blacklist cover, among other things, the record of illegal immigration, public policy and security, foreign policy considerations, and regional coherence and reciprocity. It reality, each member state lobbies for countries from which it fears an influx of migrants to be added to the blacklist. The list is therefore much longer than was the case when member states were solely in charge of their visa policy. Applying for a Schengen visa is no mere formality: it requires a large number of documents to convince sceptical immigration officers that applicants are likely to return home after the visit.

A 2001 directive on carrier sanctions forces air, sea and coach companies to operate pre-boarding checks at the point of departure to verify the validity and authenticity of travel documents and ensure that non-EU citizens are in possession of the required visa. The main European airlines prevent around 5,000 people from boarding each year, something that contravenes international legal obligations under the UN Geneva Convention. Both the visa and carrier sanctions have led to a growing business in false documents, and to illegal entry over less-controlled land routes. That in turn generates more EU proposals to fight illegal immigration and smuggling.

As many legal migrants are asylum-seekers, European intergovernmental co-operation since the 1990s has sought to prevent foreigners from accessing asylum procedures. The two cornerstones of current EU policy were developed and legitimated through other European forums. First, foreigners who come from a 'safe third country' of transit or origin, a place where human rights and democracy were deemed to be adequate to send people back, were denied access to the asylum process. Second, based on the London Resolutions adopted by JHA ministers in November 1992, member states have invoked the notion of 'manifestly unfounded' requests, according to which they will not examine certain applications for asylum, including those coming from 'safe countries'.

But member states still continued to receive significant numbers of asylum-seekers. For example, Kurds flocked to Britain because of family ties and presumed economic opportunity. That led the British government to make a bold proposal: to 'externalize' asylum procedures by sending asylum-seekers to the hinterland of Europe, where living conditions are by no means as good as in Britain. At an informal meeting of JHA ministers in March 2003, in the presence of experts and officials of the UN High Commissioner for Refugees (UNHCR), Britain suggested that the UNHCR should process demands for refugee status in camps where people have fled conflict or famines. Applicants who did not go to these 'safe havens' but instead reached the EU would be immediately sent to camps just outside the EU's borders, in countries such as Albania and Ukraine that are not liberal democracies, where their applications would be examined. Despite breaching the fundamental principle of *non-refoulement* in the Geneva Convention on refugees, and being incompatible with the Dublin Convention, in which member states recognized their responsibility to examine asylum requests, most states welcomed the proposal. In doing so, they risked conveying an image of 'Fortress Europe' surrounded by refugee camps intended to keep the 'huddled masses' outside the EU. At a meeting of the Council in June 2003, only Sweden and Germany criticized the idea of 'camps' surrounding the EU, something that evokes dark historical memories in post-Nazi Europe.

Since Tampere, member states appreciate that, in order to prevent immigration into the EU, they have to create 'partnerships with countries of origin' and address what are called the 'push-factors' of immigration (such as lack of economic opportunity), as opposed to the 'pull-factors' (prosperity and family ties in the EU). In 1998, a High Level Working Group drew up action plans for Afghanistan, Iraq, Morocco, Somalia, Sri Lanka and Albania, the main source countries for asylum seekers and illegal immigrants into the EU. The group's remit was explicitly 'trans-pillar', meaning that it drew on a range of policies, such as trade and development assistance (in the First Pillar) and foreign and security policy (in the Second Pillar) to try to convince countries to prevent their nationals from leaving illegally for the EU. The group's conclusions were sobering. At that time there were no diplomatic ties with the Taliban government in Afghanistan, or agreements with Saddam Hussein's government in Iraq, thereby making 'co-operation' with such regimes illusory. Instead, EU efforts focused on countries like Morocco, through Commission programmes such as *Med-migrations* that aimed to encourage development projects involving North Africans on both sides of the Mediterranean. In June 2003, the Commission announced €250 millions in aid over the following five years for countries that signed readmission agreements with the EU.

Over time, the EU has integrated immigration issues into bilateral and multilateral agreements with developing countries in order to standardize and institutionalize instruments such as readmission agreements for illegal nationals. For example, JHA ministers insisted that the Cotonou agreement of 2000, between the EU and seventy-one African, Caribbean and Pacific countries include a standard clause whereby those countries commit themselves to taking back their nationals deported from an EU member state. At the Seville summit, the Spanish Presidency made a drastic proposal: countries not co-operating with member state authorities to readmit their nationals would face financial sanctions (cuts in aid or trade). Although some member states found that kind of blackmail counter-productive, the summit conclusions mention the possibility of retaliatory measures against noncooperating countries. In this area, as in others, the kinder, gentler approach of Tampere has evaporated. The new trend is for JHA ministers to try to use trade and other commercial exchanges as bargaining chips with third countries, rather than trying to build trust.

Another proposal to prevent unwanted foreigners arriving in the EU, also discussed in Seville, was to create a 'European corps of border guards'. Pilot programmes involving border guards from up to six member states have already been run in various parts of the EU. In February 2003, the EU launched 'Operation Ulysses'. With a budget of €1 million, 116 officers and seven vessels from five member states patrolled the area off the Canary Islands to detect and dissuade boats containing migrants from landing illegally in Spain. No boats were found, leading the EU to herald the operation as a model of deterrence.

Conclusion

Immigration and asylum policy has become a top EU priority, one largely cast in security terms since the end of the Cold War, and in particular since 11 September 2001. Supported by EU leaders under pressure to act for domestic political reasons, border and police experts and JHA officials dominate the policy process, largely free of domestic constraints. Nevertheless, other EU actors are increasingly involved as well. As immigration became a 'high politics' issue, increasing numbers of national ministries and Commission directorates-general began to play a part. Yet the cumbersome character of supranational decision-making and the unanimity rule in the Council slows down the harmonization of policy in favour of soft norms and informal and technical co-operation. Consequently, the impact of EU decision-making on national policies cannot simply be measured in terms of the transposition of EU laws. EU policies influence the way in which immigration and asylum are perceived and discussed in the member states, and legitimize a restrictive approach to migrant and refugee flows. Increasingly, EU initiatives seek to externalize or 'contract out' anti-immigration actions to buffer zone countries in Eastern Europe, and to the consulates, airports and local authorities of countries from which large numbers of migrants originate.

It is difficult to assess the direct impact of EU policy on immigration. A number of studies (Böcker and Havinga, 1997; Thielemann, 2003) show that immigration policy plays a marginal part in deterring people from migrating to a particular EU member state. Cultural and family ties, and good economic prospects, ultimately determine immigrants' actions, regardless of the strictness of the laws in place. Even with a common policy, EU member states will continue to receive varying numbers and types of migrants. The EU also needs to address the perverse effects of raising a wall around itself, such as the rise of a 'migration business' involving the smuggling of immigrants and the forging of documents. In any event, the profound reshaping of Europe's external borders as a result of enlargement is bound to keep the issue of immigration high on the EU's agenda.

Chapter 10

Police and Judicial Co-operation

JOHN D. OCCHIPINTI

Following the terrorist attacks on the United States on 11 September 2001, Justice and Home Affairs (JHA) rose to the top of the EU's policy-making agenda. Having developed slowly and in relative obscurity compared to other policy areas, JHA became a focal point in the EU for the ten-month period beginning with September 11 and ending with the Seville European Council in June 2002. During that time, JHA supplanted in political attention even the impending introduction of the euro, and the accession negotiations with the candidate countries. Rather than precipitating new forms of co-operation in the EU, however, the terrible events of September 11 served to accelerate the development of several long-planned JHA-related measures, in particular regarding police and judicial co-operation in criminal matters.

Even as the impact of September 11 began to fade, progress in this area continued under pressure from mounting public alarm over illegal immigration and the success of far-right political parties in several member states. Moreover, the EU's new ability to contribute to crime-fighting received further impetus from the anticipated internal security challenges of enlargement. As a result, concerns about terrorism, illegal immigration and impending enlargement pushed the EU towards the construction of a new legal and institutional infrastructure of crime-fighting.

With the establishment of new European-level law enforcement bodies and enhanced roles for the Commission and, to a lesser extent, the European Parliament, this development entails a shift towards a more supranational approach for dealing with transnational organized crime. Accordingly, the EU has begun to harmonize some aspects of substantive and procedural criminal law. Combined with newly implemented common training programmes and forums for the exchange of 'best practices', the approximation of criminal law demonstrates the gradual Europeanization of the fight against cross-border crime. Although national law enforcement agencies retain primary power and responsibility in the area of crime fighting, the incipient supranationalism and Europeanization of internal security is a remarkable development, especially considering that the so-called

181

Third Pillar (co-operation on Justice and Home Affairs) did not exist before November 1993, when the EU came into existence.

While heightened concerns over terrorism, illegal immigration and enlargement help to explain the recent acceleration of police and judicial co-operation in criminal matters, the ability of transnational organized criminal organizations to exploit the limits of national law enforcement agencies in a rapidly integrating Europe is the fundamental driving force behind the concerted EU action. By the early 1990s, it was clear that transnational organized crime was spreading geographically and worsening both qualitatively and quantitatively (Europol, 2003). As mafia groups emerged in Eastern Europe, unprecedented co-operation began among different ethnic crime organizations, with various links established among groups based in Romania, Russia, Turkey, China and Albania. As a result, foreign criminal organizations and emerging multi-ethnic criminal networks challenged the dominance of indigenous organized crime groups in the EU (Europol, 2003).

For example, the trafficking of illicit drugs had long been a major challenge for EU member states. Following the end of the Cold War, the establishment of new transit routes in Eastern Europe and the Balkans exacerbated the flow of drugs from Latin America, Central Asia, the Middle East and China. Social upheaval in the former Soviet bloc contributed to an increase in the illegal trafficking of human beings into the EU, frequently resulting in their exploitation or even death. More recently, in the run up to the launch of the single currency in January 2002, there were fears of widespread counterfeiting of the euro, although this did not happen.

Free movement for organized crime groups across much of the EU, a consequence of the gradual implementation of the Schengen free travel area after 1995, fuelled the perception that one member state's problems with terrorism, drug trafficking and illegal immigration would eventually affect the internal security of others. As police and judicial authorities remained restricted by territorial jurisdictions and national penal codes, organized criminal groups enjoyed unprecedented freedom to operate transnationally. The prospect of extending the Schengen regime to the Central and Eastern Europe soon-to-be member states heightened the existing member states' determination to prevent organized crime groups from using the young democracies as source- or transit-states for criminal endeavours elsewhere in the EU. National law enforcement authorities resolved to co-ordinate their work more effectively, which in turn strengthened the political will to create a new legal and institutional infrastructure of crime fighting. The EU's emerging legal and institutional infrastructure of crime fighting can therefore partly be explained as functional spillover from EU policies on the free movement of people (Occhipinti, 2003).

This chapter first examines the historical context of these developments, from the creation of the Trevi group to the coming into force of the Nice Treaty. The next section analyzes the impact of September 11 on police and judicial co-operation, not only within the EU but also between the EU and the USA. Subsequent sections detail the EU's emerging institutional and legal infrastructure relating to fighting crime, and the impact of enlargement on internal security matters. The chapter concludes with a look at some of the challenges facing the EU as it seeks to implement goals embodied in the draft constitutional treaty and ensure internal security in a rapidly uniting Europe.

From Trevi to Nice

The need for police and judicial co-operation in Europe to fight transnational crime can be traced as far back to international efforts to combat the anarchist movement at the beginning of the twentieth century. The problem of terrorism in Europe arose more recently in the 1970s, involving groups with roots in the Middle East, as well as homegrown organizations such at the Irish Republican Army, the Baader-Meinhof Gang (in Germany), and the Red Brigades (in Italy). The effort to create a common legal and institutional infrastructure of crime fighting in Europe accelerated with the creation of the so-called Trevi Group of interior and justice ministers, which began to meet regularly from 1976. Coming in the wake of the hostage-taking and murders at the Munich Olympic Games in 1972, and in response to terrorist threats with sources both within and outside Europe, as well as the problem of drug trafficking, the European Community member states created this largely intergovernmental forum for collaboration outside of the formal treaty structure. Although lacking a permanent secretariat, the Trevi Group provided law enforcement authorities in the EC with a limited but useful way to communicate and exchange information on various transnational crimes, as well as to share best practices to combat them. Much as European Political Co-operation (EPC), also founded in the 1970s, served as a forerunner for the goals and mechanisms of the EU's Second Pillar on Common Foreign and Security Policy, the Trevi Group laid the normative and institutional foundation for co-operation on JHA, embodied in the Maastricht Treaty.

The evolving Third Pillar

Functional spillover stemming from moves towards the goal of free movement among the EC's member states, enshrined in the Schengen Agreement of 1985 and the Single European Act (SEA) of 1986, provided a major impetus for the creation of the Third Pillar. These initiatives facil-itated the free movement not only of goods, labour, capital and services, but also of organized crime, creating shared challenges at the common external border and necessitating common policies on JHA. By the time negotiations on the Maastricht Treaty got under way, the end of the Cold War had begun to affect the EC's internal security agenda, including rising expectations that some of the newly free states of the former Soviet bloc would want to join the emerging EU. Moreover, by mid-1991 the burgeoning conflict in Yugoslavia led to a refugee crisis in several member states, making clear the need for common policies on border manage-ment. Combined with the federalist aspirations of some member states, notably Germany, these developments helped to shape the Third Pillar, including calls for a European Police Office, or Europol (Occhipinti, 2003).

Although the Trevi Group was founded with terrorism in mind, the political will for greater co-operation on JHA after the Cold War came mainly in response to other types of transnational organized crimes, particularly drug trafficking and illegal immigration. Yet progress on implementing the new Third Pillar initially was slow. At the same time, organized crime groups based in Eastern Europe became increasingly active, and popular perceptions of a crime problem in the EU increased as the full impact of the refugee crisis stemming from the Balkans became apparent. This led to calls for a reform of the Third Pillar, which became bound up in the negotiations that resulted in the Amsterdam Treaty of 1997, with its provisions for an 'area of freedom, security and justice' in the EU.

The new treaty also brought the Schengen *acquis* into the framework of the EU (by means of a protocol) and called for the transfer of all free-movement-related matters from the Third Pillar to the First Pillar (cover-ing traditional European Community affairs) by mid-2004. That meant extending the so-called Community method to policy-making on visas, immigration and asylum by giving the Commission the sole right of legislative initiative; using qualified majority voting in the Council; elimi-nating a member state's right to veto; and extending the European Parliament's power of co-decision. Having moved these areas into the First Pillar, member states described what was left in the Third Pillar as 'Provisions for Police and Judicial Co-operation in Criminal Matters'. Even here, however, the Parliament won the right to be consulted by the JHA Council, and, more importantly, the Commission won the power to initiate legislation, albeit a right shared with the member states. All-in-all, the Amsterdam Treaty represented a major shift towards supranational-ism on internal security issues.

A new Commission, under President Romano Prodi, took office soon after the Amsterdam Treaty came into force in May 1999. Plans were already in the works for a special meeting of the European Council devoted to JHA, in order to jump-start progress on internal security matters. The initial slow development of the Third Pillar was exemplified by the delay in ratifying and implementing the Europol Convention of 1995 and its protocols, which kept the new European Police Office from becoming fully functional until July 1999, and even then with a somewhat limited operational and crime-fighting mandate. Similarly, little had been achieved with regard to common policies on visas, immigration and asylum. As the EU moved closer towards Central and Eastern European enlargement, pressure increased to expedite co-operation on JHA before the addition of these new member states, with their relatively weaker criminal justice institutions, complicated EU decision-making, and policy formulation.

The impact of Tampere

The special European Council on JHA took place in Tampere, Finland in October 1999, and was notable for both the means and ends that it prescribed. The conclusions of the summit laid down ten general 'milestones' for progress toward the establishment of the area of freedom, security and justice, subdivided into sixty-two specific points of action. Many of these had already been proposed in previous EU action plans, but others were new, including proposals for the harmonization of criminal law in some areas, and the creation of new bodies aimed at helping police authorities in the member states to combat crime (Monar, 2000). Overall, the Tampere European Council set in motion a number of different avenues of progress on JHA, including some that forged a variety of links and common standards for crime fighting below the level of the national governments.

One new institution proposed at Tampere was a European judicial unit, or 'Eurojust', a liaison network of national criminal prosecutors, designed to facilitate judicial co-operation. Another body was the Police Chiefs' Task Force, intended to bring together high-level police officials in the EU for periodic meetings to compare strategies and exchange information on tactics. The Tampere summit also called for the creation of the European Police College (or 'CEPOL', according its French acronym), a network that links police academies in member and candidate states, and promotes training programmes for high-level police officials. Along with Europol, the new bodies proposed in Tampere would form an institutional infrastructure of crime-fighting in the EU, much of which is in place at the time of writing.

In addition, the Tampere milestones emphasized that the area of freedom, security and justice should be built on the principle of 'mutual recognition' in criminal matters, replacing the standard of 'double-criminality', which demands that member states define and sanction crimes in the same way. Just as the common market was built on a mutual recognition of standards regarding health and safety that could otherwise have impeded the free flow of goods, services and labour, the area of freedom, security and justice would be built on the mutual recognition of criminal codes and judgments, helping to fight crime by facilitating co-operation and denying criminals save havens. In this regard, for example, the Tampere European Council proposed the virtual elimination of traditional criminal extradition and its replacement with an arrest and surrender warrant that would be mutually recognized throughout the EU.

In practice, however, mutual recognition on criminal matters would have to be supplemented by some approximation of penal codes among the member states. For this, the new mechanism of the framework decision would be used, just as the legal instrument of the directive was used to harmonize commercial law in the creation of the single market. Together with the principle of mutual recognition, the approximation of criminal law gradually created a common legal infrastructure for crime-fighting in the EU. Together with the newly created JHA institutions, the approximation of criminal law is also helping to bring the proposed area of freedom, security and justice into being.

As already mentioned, the Tampere European Council was noteworthy not only for *what* it proposed, but also for *how* it suggested that the EU implements those objectives. The summit endorsed the creation of a so-called JHA scoreboard, suggested by the British, which brought together the goals of the Tampere milestones with those expressed in various EU action plans already endorsed by the European Council, but still unattained. EU leaders charged the Commission with creating the scoreboard, which eventually took the form of a chart detailing about fifty distinct objectives (divided into eight areas), the specific actions needed to achieve them, the actors responsible (Council, Commission, member states and so on), the timetable, and the current 'state of play' regarding progress on each item (for example, transposition of framework decisions into national law).

In addition, the Tampere European Council gave the Commission responsibility for monitoring progress, updating the state of play, and adding to the scoreboard any new goals set out by the Council. The JHA scoreboard was intended to foster steady progress towards completing the area of freedom, security and justice, just as the 1992 deadline had helped to complete the single market programme. The Commission prepared the first version of the JHA scoreboard during Portugal's Council presidency in the first half of 2000 and amended it every two years thereafter to include new objectives and changes to the state of play. The initial update came during the French presidency and included several new goals contained in the EU's 'Action Plan on the Prevention and Control of Organized Crime', which the JHA Council had approved in March 2000.

Beyond the genesis of new objectives and the scoreboard, the Tampere European Council was also significant for the renewed political will that it gave, at the highest level of the EU, for progress on JHA. Yet mere agreement on ambitious goals by the heads of state and government did not automatically, or even easily, translate into the implementation of actual policies. Working according to the timetable of the JHA scoreboard, progress on building the new institutions and legal framework on internal security was nevertheless more rapid than before the Tampere summit. The new role of the Commission in JHA accounted for some of this progress, bolstered by the installation of a new and able Commissioner for JHA, António Vitorino of Portugal, and the creation of a directorate-general (department) for his portfolio (Uçarer, 2001). Despite the impact of Tampere and the positive role of the Commission under Vitorino, the evolution of JHA remained dogged by disagreements among the member states and complete lack of progress in some areas, such as immigration and asylum policy.

Towards the Nice Treaty

Apart from institutional and personal factors, functional spillover stemming from several developments in the EU after the Tampere European Council contributed to greater progress on crime-fighting (Occhipinti, 2003). For example, the impending introduction of the euro prompted member states to give Europol a prominent role in combating counterfeiting and to pass a framework decision harmonizing penalties for this. Similarly, preparations for the creation of a European Rapid Reaction Force, which accelerated after the Helsinki summit of December 1999, contributed to co-operation on JHA in the form of plans for civilian policing units to carry out some of the so-called Petersberg tasks relating to peace-keeping and nation-building. Meanwhile, the single market's provisions on the free movement of capital accelerated the need to fight money laundering and financial crime, leading to increased attention to these issues during the French presidency of 2000. Finally, in March 2001, the Schengen area was expanded to include all the Nordic states, entailing freedom to travel among fifteen countries (including Iceland and Norway, but not Britain and Ireland), increasing the potential for transnational crime as well as the need for greater international police co-operation. More than ever before, enduring issues of border control and immigration, mounting attention to enlargement, and the growth of transnational organized crime with sources both inside and outside of the EU, intensified pressure to co-operate on JHA.

Although there was no federal impetus to create strongly supranational crime-fighting institutions, adherence to the principle of subsidiarity (states' rights) was not a barrier to addressing a wide range of internal security issues at the EU level. Member states recognized that 'enhanced co-operation' among some of them on various JHA matters might be desirable if the entire EU membership did not want to proceed together. This manifested itself in the Nice Treaty, which removed the so-called 'emergency brake' regarding closer co-operation, meaning that individual member states would no longer have the right to veto enhanced co-operation on JHA should such a matter be referred to the European Council.

Other than this, and a few minor innovations regarding asylum policy and family law, the Nice Treaty did little to change the nature of JHA. One exception was that it mentioned explicitly Eurojust and specified its relationship to Europol. However, by the time the treaty came into force in February 2003, this provision had largely been superseded by the actual development of crime-fighting institutions through the JHA Council, which had created Eurojust and was working on new protocols for the Europol Convention aimed at strengthening the operational capabilities of the fledgling European Police Office. In addition, by the time the treaty took effect, the ongoing Convention on the Future of Europe was well on its way to proposing dramatic changes to the EU's approach to protecting its internal security.

Finally, co-operation on JHA following the Tampere summit coincided with growing concerns about a 'democratic deficit' in this area of EU policy-making. Virtually every new treaty provision, convention, protocol or specific legislative item before the JHA Council met with calls to pay attention to personal freedom and privacy, data protection, due process, human rights or democratic oversight. Not surprisingly, the European Parliament, which continues to demand a more powerful role on JHA, has been at the forefront of such agitation. The EU's reaction to the terrorist attacks on the USA in September 2001 brought to light the inherent tension between strengthening police and judicial co-operation in criminal matters and protecting basic democratic values and civil liberties.

The impact of September 11

The deadly attacks on the World Trade Center and the Pentagon brought JHA policy to the forefront of the EU and created a new political will among the member states to make progress towards establishing the area of freedom, security and justice. The attacks of September 11 dramatically altered the policy agenda of the Belgian presidency, prompting it to call extraordinary sessions of the JHA Council and European Council, and resulting in an ambitious 'Anti-terrorist Road Map', designed to insure the rapid implementation of a variety of measures to fight terrorism. Yet apart from freezing the assets of the groups and individuals suspected of being involved in the attacks, EU actions to fight terrorism after September 11 had either already been in the legislative pipeline or were on the JHA scoreboard, having been prescribed in the Tampere milestones or in related action plans, conventions and so on. In other words, rather than inspiring a whole new range of endeavours, September 11 caused the acceleration of existing initiatives in the field of JHA. Even so, the speed at which the EU approved JHA legislation in the aftermath of September 11 was remarkable compared to the normal pace of activity in the Third Pillar, even when compared to the somewhat increased rate of progress after the Tampere summit (Occhipinti, 2003).

In its initial response to the attacks, the JHA Council called for the creation of an anti-terrorism task force within Europol, and for national police and intelligence authorities to share any relevant information with this new body. Amid reports that some of the terrorists involved had been based in Europe before moving to the USA, Europol's director, Jürgen Storbeck, complained publicly that his analysts could be much more helpful in fighting crime if national authorities would only be more forthcoming with information. By December 2001, he was able to report to the JHA Council that member states' willingness to provide Europol with intelligence on terrorism had already improved.

Beyond strengthening Europol's role, the highlight of the EU's anti-terrorism efforts was its rapid approval of two items proposed by the Commission just days after the attacks on the USA. One was a framework decision establishing a European arrest warrant that eliminates normal extradition among EU members, which could often last two years or longer. This measure specified a list of thirty-two crimes, including terrorism, for which extradition could be as fast as ten days, and take no longer than three months in the case of appeals. The second measure was a framework decision that provided a common definition of terrorism and specified minimum criminal sentences for various terrorist offences. This was necessary because only six member states had criminal legislation specifically directed against terrorism, and the terminology and penalties described in these varied wildly.

Although the EU was eager to show its commitment to the fight against terrorism, approval of these measures, though extremely rapid, was controversial. Regarding the harmonization of anti-terrorism legislation, for example, member states were careful to define terrorism in a way that would not criminalize legitimate public protests. In the end, specific types of terrorist acts were identified, which

> given their nature or context, may seriously damage a country or an international organization where committed with the aim of: seriously intimidating a population, or unduly compelling a Government or international organization to perform or abstain from performing any act, or seriously destabilizing or destroying the fundamental political, constitutional, economic or social structures of a country or an international organization. (Council of the European Union, 2002a, Article 1)

However, to assuage fears that this could be used to prevent anti-globalization demonstrations, which had begun to disrupt EU summits, the preamble of the legislation makes it clear that

> nothing in this framework decision may be interpreted as being intended to reduce or restrict fundamental rights or freedoms such as the right to strike, freedom of assembly, of association or of expression, including the right of everyone to form and to join trade unions with others for the protection of his or her interests and the related right to demonstrate.

There was even more controversy concerning the proposed 'Euro-warrant', which had long been held up by constitutional issues in several member states, and the possibility that Ireland might ask a country to extradite someone who was suspected of carrying out an abortion. However, with appeal procedures and other safeguards built into it, and abortion left off the positive list of crimes, such concerns were sufficiently mitigated. Nevertheless, Ireland initially blocked the passage of the warrant, arguing that it entailed criminal offences, such as 'extortion' and 'swindling', for which there were no common definitions. Hoping that the Euro-warrant would cover a list of just six serious transnational crimes, excluding 'corruption' and 'fraud', Italy resisted much longer. Although Italy claimed its opposition to the Euro-warrant stemmed from concerns over civil liberties and its own constitutional situation, there was speculation that Prime Minister Silvio Berlusconi feared being extradited to other EU member states for alleged tax-related wrongdoing. In any case, Italy blocked agreement on the arrest warrant at the JHA Council in December 2001, leading to unusually harsh and public criticism from several other member states, including threats to exercise the option of 'closer co-operation' and proceed without Italy on the matter. Within a week, however, Belgian

Prime Minister Guy Verhofstadt had had a personal meeting with Berlusconi in Rome and obtained approval for the Euro-warrant and its list of thirty-two crimes. This suggests that the Italian leader's opposition lay partly in his desire to assert Italy's importance in the EU.

Near the end of the Belgian presidency, the Council supplemented the framework decision on terrorism and the common arrest warrant by passing two 'common positions' regarding the fight against terrorism, as well as related measures to implement them. One of the common positions specified various initiatives to outlaw the funding of terrorism and prevent terrorist acts from occurring, while the other defined terrorism in line with the definition contained in the newly approved framework decision and established a list of specific terrorists groups and individuals whose assets were to be frozen (Uçarer, 2002). The list, updated several times, named terrorists from all over the world, but the lack of a proper legal basis in the EU's treaties prevented the freezing of assets of persons or groups based in the member states, such as those connected to Basque separatist group ETA (meaning 'Euskadi Ta Askatasuna' – 'Basque Homeland and Freedom').

The Belgian presidency concluded with the Laeken summit, which will be remembered as much for its historic decisions to proceed with enlargement and the Convention on the Future of Europe as for the petty bickering among leaders about where to locate various new EU bodies, particularly the new Food Safety Authority. The dispute delayed a decision regarding the permanent homes for Eurojust and CEPOL, which were provisionally located in The Hague and Copenhagen-Brøndby. As for JHA more broadly, the Laeken summit was significant for its long-planned assessment of the EU's progress towards the goals set at the Tampere summit.

Belgium could therefore be proud of its leadership on police and judicial co-operation regarding criminal matters, including measures approved to tighten security at international summits; the decision to expand Europol's remit to a wider variety of transnational crimes; the signing of a protocol reducing banking secrecy under the Convention on Mutual Assistance in Criminal Matters of 2000; a directive in the fight against money laundering, the final decision setting up Eurojust; the agreement between the USA and Europol; the framework decision on terrorism, and the Euro-warrant. In addition, the Police Chiefs' Task Force had already shown its usefulness, especially after September 11, when it helped to plan and oversee a meeting of anti-terrorism officials from the member states. CEPOL was up and running (and available to police officers of the candidates' countries), and the permanent Eurojust unit was ready to begin operations in 2002. In addition, framework decisions and other measures were formally adopted, or at least agreed upon, regarding counterfeiting of the euro, trafficking in human beings, and financial crime. Thereafter, the fight against terrorism remained prominent in the EU, whether directed at al-Q'aeda or, to a lesser degree, ETA.

US–EU relations

Along with giving the EU an impetus to proceed rapidly on various internal JHA matters, the terrorist attacks of September 11 also helped quicken the pace of new collaboration between the USA and the EU on internal security. This entailed an agreement with the USA on Europol, as well as a separate accord covering judicial co-operation. Although these arrangements had been in the works long before September 11, the terrorist attacks propelled them to the top of the transatlantic agenda much sooner than originally planned.

The USA and the EU signed a co-operation agreement on Europol in December 2001, which allowed the exchange of technical information regarding terrorist threats, crime patterns and smuggling routes, and about lists of criminal assets to be frozen. However, Europol's rules covering data protection prevented the sharing of specific personal information, thereby excluding the exchange of names, addresses, photographs and criminal records. Subsequently, the USA and the EU began to negotiate a supplemental agreement to allow such information to be shared, entailing assurances from the USA that it would protect adequately data supplied by Europol despite lacking a single authority responsible for this. Meanwhile, the EU and USA also began talks on a mutual judicial co-operation agreement, with formal negotiations starting in May 2002 and lasting nearly a year because of the complex issues at hand, as well as the EU's posturing on extradition where the death penalty might be applied, a point that the USA was prepared to concede from the outset.

In September 2002, Europol opened a liaison office in Washington, and progress continued on negotiations with the USA on two fronts. The supplemental agreement allowing the sharing of personal data between Europol and American law enforcement authorities was finally concluded in December of that year, after the EU was given guarantees about data protection and assurances that its officials would not be liable for civil damages awarded by US courts regarding data supplied by Europol. The outstanding differences regarding US–EU judicial co-operation in criminal matters were also resolved over the next few months, despite rising tensions over the war with Iraq, allowing the accord to be signed in June 2003, including an extradition agreement that bars the imposition of the death penalty on suspects handed over to American authorities. Overall, in its collaboration with the USA on fighting transnational organized crime, the EU demonstrated a new emphasis on the external dimensions of its internal security. This was also evident in its dealings with the candidate countries, and in its relations with developing countries on immigration and asylum policy.

The new infrastructure of crime fighting

Although the Third Pillar has been in existence since 1993, most of the progress in the EU on police co-operation and judicial co-operation in criminal matters came in the aftermath of September 11 and the run up to enlargement. This has brought about a new institutional infrastructure of crime fighting at the EU level. Certainly, the institutions listed below were established by the member states and remain under the intergovernmental control of their various management boards. However, given their pan-European approach to law enforcement and, in some cases, daily operations independent of oversight by the member states, these new bodies represent a subtle but noteworthy shift in the direction of a more supranational approach to fighting transnational organized crime in the EU.

- *Europol* is based in The Hague, and although quite small compared to the American FBI, has a sizeable budget of €55.5 million and 424 personnel (in 2003), including its own staff and seconded European Liaison Officers (ELOs) from member states. It aims to help national authorities fight a long list of transnational crimes, including all the offences mentioned in the Europol Convention and its Annex (since 2002), which entails nearly all the crimes covered by the Euro-warrant. To this end, Europol's network of ELOs facilitates international information exchanges and co-ordinates multinational operations, entailing simultaneous operations in several member states. Europol is charged with building and maintaining a database of information supplied by the member states, and using this data to analyse crimes, conduct specific investigations at the request of national law enforcement authorities, and request that the latter launch such investigations. Amid fears of widespread counterfeiting, Europol was made responsible for preventing counterfeiting of the newly introduced euro, through information-sharing and co-operation with law enforcement agencies in the member states, EU entities (such as the European Central Bank) and international bodies (for example, Interpol). Not only did this crisis fail to materialize, but euro counterfeiting into 2003 was estimated to be much less than in the cases of the currencies that it replaced. Of course, it is difficult to determine whether this was a result of Europol's efforts, the high-tech security measures built into the new notes, or other factors. Because of unease in several member states about surrendering sovereignty and a perceived lack of accountability, Europol still does not have any executive policing powers, notably the authority to make arrests, use coercive measures, and so on. Nevertheless, Europol's operational powers have been strengthened in various other ways as well. For example, it received € 3.1 million in extra funds in 2002 alone for the fight against terrorism, and was authorized to request member states to initiate investigations of particular transnational crimes. On a related note, the JHA Council decided in 2002 to provide the legal framework for the creation and operation of multinational joint investigation teams and empowered Europol officers to participate in them, short of exercising any executive policing power (pending ratification of a protocol specifying guidelines for doing so).

- *Eurojust* is also located in The Hague, and began operating officially in 2002. It oversees a liaison network of national criminal prosecutors to help facilitate and co-ordinate criminal investigations by encouraging better contacts among investigators, helping to simplify the execution of 'letters of rogatory' (that is, international court to court requests for assistance or information), and advising Europol on its operations. Eurojust operates in conjunction with the European Judicial Network (EJN), a decentralized network of legal contact points in the EU that was created in 1998. Eurojust plays a key role in the execution of the Euro-warrant, and may one day provide a home for a projected European Public Prosecutor's Office.

- *The Police Chiefs' Task Force* is an international forum to help high-level national police officials share best practices and information on current trends in cross-border crime, and contribute to the planning of joint operations. Launched during the Portuguese presidency in 2000, it meets every six months, outlining various common priority areas, such as community policing and drug trafficking.

- *The Common Unit for External Border Practitioners* was created late in the Danish presidency of 2002 under a mandate from the Seville European Council. Its main role is to oversee a larger liaison network of national immigration officers to help promote greater co-operation in border management, and co-ordinate joint operations and pilot projects. Along with the development of a common training curriculum for immigration personnel, such an agency could become the forerunner of a common border patrol for the EU.

- *The European Police College* (CEPOL) seeks to build a common police culture among law-enforcement agencies in the EU and candidate states. Yet CEPOL is only a 'virtual' training academy, with its secretariat based temporarily in Denmark. CEPOL helps to fund and co-ordinate programmes for senior officials, operated in and by the police academies of the member states. As with the other JHA bodies and programmes, CEPOL welcomed the participation of the candidate states, but its capacity and effectiveness will be greatly tested by enlargement.

Co-operation in the area of crime fighting in the EU is supported by a number of shared databases, some of them containing similar information, implying an eventual consolidation and streamlining if various technological barriers and concerns over data protection can be resolved. For example, the Europol Information System (EIS) consists of a common pool of criminal information supplied by the member states, as well as a number of 'analysis work files' generated by its own staff on particular crimes or investigations. There is also the Schengen Information System (SIS), which gives police officials in participating states access to criminal data. In 2003, the EU implemented the Customs Information System (CIS), which allows national authorities to share data to help prevent smuggling, and the Eurodac system, for storing asylum seekers' fingerprints in an effort to combat both 'asylum shopping' and illegitimate claims. By 2004 the EU was working on a similar biometric database called the Visa Information System, intended to prevent 'Visa Shopping'.

The EU offers a number of co-financing programmes to assist horizontal co-operation among law-enforcement authorities. These include the new *Agis* programme, named after a king of ancient Sparta who promoted traditional law and discipline. *Agis* combined and replaced a number of more limited initiatives (for example, *Grotius*, *Oisin*, *Stop*, *Hippocrate* and *Falcone*) to promote collaboration, personnel exchanges, training in the area of organized crime, crime prevention, customs, judicial/prosecutorial co-operation, the trafficking of human beings and so on. The new *Argo* programme, named after the mythical ship of Jason and the Argonauts, replaced the defunct *Odysseus* programme to co-finance co-operative projects for the administration of asylum, immigration and border control.

Just as the EU's *institutional* infrastructure of crime fighting must adapt to enlargement, so too must its burgeoning *legal* infrastructure continue to enhance internal security. Once transposed into national law, the European Arrest Warrant will simplify, replace and consequently expedite extradition among the member states for its list of thirty-two crimes. In addition, the principle of mutual recognition has been supplemented by a growing number of framework decisions that must be transposed into national criminal law. Pending the lifting of parliamentary scrutiny reservations in some cases, the JHA Council has approved common definitions and sanctions for the transnational crimes of counterfeiting of the euro, money laundering, terrorism, the trafficking of human beings, child sexual exploitation, fraud and counterfeiting of non-cash payments, corruption in the private sector, serious environmental crime, cyber-crime, and drug trafficking, with provisions for Dutch tolerance for the personal use of soft drugs. The harmonization of criminal law is envisioned for several other forms of trans-national crime as well.

Overall, the approximation of criminal law and asylum practices illustrates the Europeanization of internal security in the EU, which is at least partly attributable to the perceived impact of enlargement (Occhipinti, 2004). Europeanization is evident not only in the process of gradual legal harmonization, but also in the sharing of best practices and strategies for law enforcement stemming from the work of the newly created bodies that form the institutional infrastructure, and in the projects sponsored by the *Agis* and *Argo* programmes and their predecessors. The instruction- and strategy-sharing projects co-financed by these programmes will further contribute to the Europeanization of crime-fighting in the EU, as will the development of the common training curriculum for border patrol personnel and the various seminars administered and funded by CEPOL.

The impact of enlargement

The images of September 11 were still fresh when the Laeken European Council affirmed the possibility of a 'big bang' enlargement of the EU in 2004. By implication, the new member states would have to contribute to the fight against terrorism. Thanks to September 11 and the impending enlargement, JHA remained at the top of the EU's agenda when Spain took over the Council presidency in January 2002 (Occhipinti, 2003). Within a short time, the EU's attention shifted from terrorism to illegal immigration, as a result of the unveiling of a Commission action plan on the subject, followed by a series of immigration-related crises and political events in the run-up to the Seville summit in June 2002. Concerns about weak border security in the EU, raised in the context of the immigration debate, contributed to the perceived need to co-operate more effectively on crime fighting. Moreover, after the terrorist attacks on the USA, border management was viewed in terms of the overall fight against terrorism and the difficulty of maintaining internal security in an enlarged EU, which, after Laeken, seemed increasingly likely in the near term.

By the time of the Danish presidency later in the year, the EU's attention in the area of JHA had clearly shifted toward the goals, declared at the Seville summit of June 2002, regarding border management and asylum, and of finalizing the accession negotiations with the candidate countries.

Nevertheless, progress on police and judicial co-operation continued, albeit under the radar of many EU observers. In general, the quickened pace of co-operation on police and judicial co-operation in the EU since September 11 presented the candidate countries with a moving target as they struggled to conclude the terms of their membership (Occhipinti, 2004).

During this time, for example, the JHA Council was also able to make progress in the area of substantive criminal law, reaching agreements on framework decisions covering the sexual exploitation of children, corruption in the private sector and cyber-crime. By the end of 2003, the JHA Council was considering proposals covering the illegal trafficking of human organs, a European Evidence Warrant and legislation to prevent criminal double jeopardy in the EU. The long-delayed passage of a Framework Decision on Racism and Xenophobia continued to be blocked by Italy.

In the meantime, work continued on changing and enhancing the role of Europol, with an eye towards facilitating crime fighting in an enlarged EU. Near the end of the Danish presidency, ministers agreed a protocol to the Europol Convention specifying the nature of Europol's participation in the newly authorized international joint investigation teams. This was followed by progress on a second, broader protocol, which clarified Europol's mandate and ability to manage and exchange data, its direct links to national policy authorities, and scrutiny of it by the European Parliament.

The candidate countries watched these developments closely, as they completed negotiations with the EU and prepared to meet the commitments embodied in the accession treaties. These included the provisions contained in Chapter 24 of the negotiations (on JHA), which had been among the final items opened for accession talks. Hungary was the first of the aspiring member states to close the JHA chapter, in November 2001, followed by Cyprus, Slovenia and the Czech Republic a month later. The remaining candidates, with the exceptions of Bulgaria and Romania, were able to close negotiations on JHA during the Spanish presidency, with Poland being the last to do so, in July 2002.

Since 1998, the EU had reorientated the PHARE programme to encompass JHA and help prepare the candidate countries to meet the internal security commitments that would eventually be embodied in the accession treaties. In general, these activities were part and parcel of the applicants' accession partnerships with the EU, which identified the need to reinforce external border management, build new criminal justice institutions, and strengthen the administrative capacity for a whole range of JHA entities, such as sufficient and properly trained personnel for police, courts and so on. The candidates also had to reform their asylum procedures, fight organized crime, and eventually adopt and effectively implement the Schengen *acquis*.

Under the PHARE programme, the EU funded a number of horizontal programmes and 'twinning' projects (that is, personnel exchanges), entailing direct collaboration between the member states and candidate countries, as well the transfer to the candidates of technical and administrative know-how to help to improve the performance of their new criminal justice institutions. In addition, the candidate states participated with the member states in a number of so-called 'structured dialogue' sessions on JHA, resulting, for example, in an important pre-accession pact on organized crime in 1998. This spelt out a number of common objectives and priorities, including the need for the candidates to forge formal ties with Europol before their accession. Following satisfactory reports on data protection, Europol welcomed liaison officers from the candidate countries, starting with Estonia, Hungary, Poland and Slovenia in October 2001, and followed by the other aspiring new member states in the run-up enlargement.

Conclusion

Since 1999, the EU has made remarkable progress on police and judicial co-operation in criminal matters, particularly in response to the terrorist attacks of September 2001, the mounting pressure of enlargement, and the expansion of the Schengen free travel area. Although responsibility for maintaining internal security remains primarily in the hands of the member states' law enforcement agencies, the EU's emerging institutional and legal infrastructure of crime-fighting facilitates greater co-operation among these bodies. Indeed, this multi-layered approach to strengthening internal security distinguishes the area of police and judicial co-operation among EU policy areas.

Despite recent progress, the EU must meet several challenges if internal security is to be strengthened in the aftermath of enlargement. In particular, the EU needs to ensure that the newly created international criminal justice institutions, notably Europol and Eurojust, function as intended in an EU of twenty-five or more member states. To that end, these entities must be properly funded to meet the increased crime-fighting needs of the enlarged EU, and must be able to perform the tasks of strategic planning, information sharing, analysis, and co-ordination of national authorities, among a larger and more diverse group of member states. Similarly, CEPOL and the training initiatives co-financed by the *Agis* and *Argo* programmes must have the resources to foster the sharing of best practices and the development of a common culture of crime-fighting in an enlarged EU. At the same time, new and old member states alike must continue to transpose the increasing number of framework decisions into nation law in a timely fashion and be sure that their law enforcement authorities fully execute these in practice. Ultimately, for police and judicial co-operation to succeed, the evolving legal and institutional infrastructure of the Third Pillar must demonstrate that it can contribute effectively to the fight against transnational organized crime in the larger EU, especially after the eventual expansion of the Schengen free zone to include the new member states.

While strengthening new crime-fighting institutions and further harmonizing criminal law, however, the EU must be careful not to overlook enduring concerns about the perceived democratic shortcomings of co-operation in this area. It was precisely this dual challenge – fighting crime effectively while reducing the democratic deficit of the Third Pillar – that the Convention on the Future of Europe of 2002–2003 attempted to address when it laid the foundation for another round of treaty reform. Giving national parliaments an earlier and more meaningful role in the formation and oversight of police and judicial co-operation in criminal matters would be a significant step forward, although bolder plans would bring most of the Third Pillar under the 'Community method', standard operating procedure in the EU under the draft constitutional treaty. By instituting qualified majority voting in the Council and co-decision between the Council and the European Parliament in most areas of police and judicial co-operation (excluding operational co-operation involving executive police powers), as well as giving a new and influential role to the European Court of Justice, the constitutional treaty aims to insure that neither internal security, nor concerns for democracy, will be neglected in the enlarged EU.

Of course, doing so will only continue to shift the EU's approach to police and judicial co-operation in the direction of supranationalism. Similarly, the further harmonization of criminal law and the 'communitization' of much of the Third Pillar will also promote the ongoing Europeanization of the fight against transnational organized crime. Indeed, as long as the enlarged EU tries to reconcile the principle of free movement with competing concerns for internal security and the democratic deficit, the trend towards supranationalism and Europeanization in police and judicial co-operation is bound to continue.

Chapter 11

The EU and World Trade: Doha and Beyond

ALASDAIR R. YOUNG

The European Union (EU) is a leading participant in world trade and foreign investment, and the world's most successful economic integration project. It is also a crucial actor in shaping multilateral rules. The EU is therefore unique in being both an international organization for co-operation among its members and an international actor seeking to co-operate with non-members. This chapter focuses on how the EU's unusual character as an international organization affects its participation in multilateral trade negotiations.

The EU has had both intentional and unintentional impacts on the world trading system. Its intentional impacts have been political, albeit with economic consequences, stemming from its participation in multilateral negotiations and decisions to protect domestic firms from foreign competition. This participation is usually based on a common position that must be agreed among all its member states, which often have very different interests. Its unintentional impacts, on the other hand, have been economic; the external consequences of internal policies, also agreed through a complex process of compromise among its member states. Other countries, particularly the USA because of the size of its economy, have significant intentional and unintentional impacts on the world economy, but the EU's situation is different, because it is an international organization.

The beginning of the twenty-first century is a particularly appropriate time to examine how the EU interacts with the rest of the world in trade matters. First, the EU's member states have only recently agreed to increase the EU's authority with regard to some aspects of foreign economic policy. Second, the EU has embarked on its single biggest enlargement to date, with the accession of the Central and Eastern European states, plus Cyprus and Malta. This has increased significantly the number and diversity of interests that must be accommodated within the EU's common policies. Third, the nature of trade politics in the EU and elsewhere is changing as increasing numbers of diverse interest groups engage with trade policy. Fourth, the EU is engaged with more than 130 other countries in an extensive and ambitious round of multi-lateral trade negotiations within the World Trade Organization (WTO) – the so-called 'Doha Development Round', incorporating the Doha Development Agenda.

Concentrating on these four developments, this chapter explores the interaction between the EU's character as an international organization and its role as an international trade actor. It begins by establishing the EU's significance in world economic activity. It then discusses the development and character of EU trade policy-making before turning to its experience with the WTO, and particularly the current round of negotiations. It concludes with an evaluation of the EU's role as an international trade actor.

The EU in the global economy

The EU is an extremely important economic actor in the global economy. It is the second-largest economy in the world, only slightly smaller than the USA. In 2001, the EU accounted for over 18 per cent of world exports

Figure 11.1   *Destinations of EU merchandise exports, 2001*

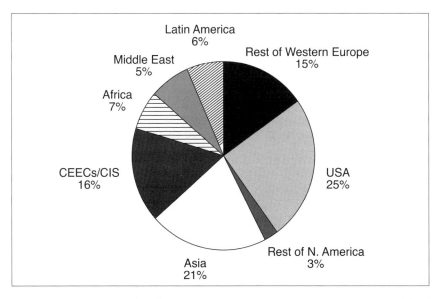

Notes: CEECs = Central and Eastern European countries; CIS = Commonwealth of Independent States; excludes intra-EU trade.
Source: WTO, 2002b.

Figure 11.2   *Origins of EU merchandise imports, 2001*

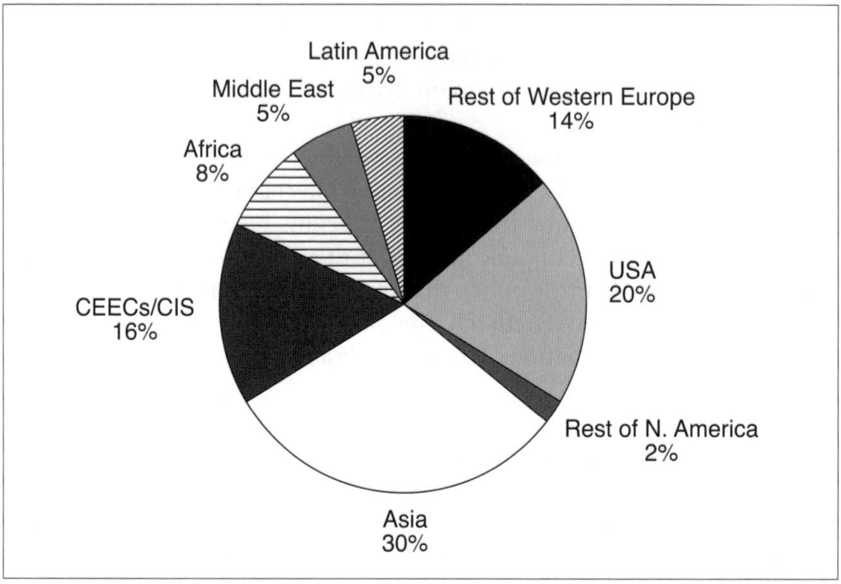

Latin America
5%
Middle East
5%
Rest of Western Europe
14%
Africa
8%
USA
20%
CEECs/CIS
16%
Rest of N. America
2%
Asia
30%

Note: Excludes intra-EU trade.
Source: WTO, 2002b.

and imports (excluding trade among its members), making it the world's largest merchandise exporter and second-largest importer behind only the USA (WTO, 2002b). In 2000, the EU accounted for 24 per cent of each of global imports and exports of commercial services – primarily transport, telecommunications and tourism (Eurostat, 2001). Figures 11.1 and 11.2 depict the EU's main trading partners.

EU trade policy: protectionist, liberal or misunderstood?

How easy it is for foreign products to enter the EU depends on a combination of policies that are either intended to affect imports or affect imports as a side-effect of other objectives. The most common intentional policy affecting imports are tariffs – a tax on imports. As a consequence of multiple rounds of multilateral negotiations, the EU's average most-favoured-nation tariff is only 4.2 per cent, and 20 per cent of tariff lines enter free of duty (WTO, 2002a). Further, the vast majority of the EU's trading partners enjoy some kind of preferential access to the EU market (see Chapter 15), although the value of such preferential access has diminished (Winters, 2001).

The EU's 'nominal' liberalism, however, is tempered by a number of very important exceptions, the most prominent of which concerns agriculture (Winters, 2001, p. 25). The common agricultural policy (CAP) functions through a system of price supports, and requires that imports of agricultural products be subject to levies to prevent them undercutting EU prices. EU agricultural tariffs on average exceed 16 per cent, and there are significantly higher tariffs on products such as wheat, sugar and dairy products (Winters, 2001).

There are also particularly high tariffs – 'tariff peaks' – on some manufactured goods, particularly footwear, leather, textiles and clothing. These reflect the tendency of the EU's member states to translate each government's protection of particular sectors into a common policy, rather than to challenge the policies of another government (Winters, 2001). Further, there are a number of trade defence instruments that can be imposed on specific foreign producers following complaints by domestic producers of 'unfair' competition. The EU is an extensive user of such measures and has been making increasing use of them (Allen and Smith, 2001). As a consequence of anti-dumping duties, fertilizers, VCRs, integrated circuits, photocopiers and clothing have estimated total rates of protection exceeding 30 per cent (Winters, 2001).

As tariffs have (generally) fallen and quantitative restrictions have been eliminated, regulatory barriers to trade have become more prominent (World Bank, 2000). As a product sold in a country must comply with that country's rules, any rule affecting the character of a product may impede imports from another country where a different rule applies. The EU's regulations and standards now represent significant barriers to market access (WTO, 2002a).

Studies of the external impact of the single market find that the adoption of common rules has, overall, benefited non-EU firms (WTO, 1995). This is largely because, rather than having to comply with different national rules in order to sell a product throughout the EU, now a firm has to comply with only one common rule. In some cases, however, the single market programme has resulted in very strict common rules being adopted, thereby increasing regulatory barriers to imports. These 'regulatory peaks' cluster where the regulatory differences among the member states are most pronounced. Substantial differences among member state rules are particularly common where there are uncertainties about the risks involved. Where the member states' rules diverge the dynamics of European market integration tend to push for approximation at the level of the most stringent national rule (Vogel, 1995; Young and Wallace, 2000). Examples of this process include the EU's ban on hormone-treated beef and strict limits on aflatoxins in ground nuts. Again, the need to agree common internal rules among its members affects the EU's external economic relations.

As with other large economies, the EU's importance as a market for goods and services, whether supplied through trade or investment, means that its policies affect producers in other countries, whether intentionally or not. The importance of EU firms as providers of goods and services, whether through trade or investment, means that the EU takes an interest in the policies of other countries. The EU's economic importance thus gives it an interest in the functioning of the global economy and the ability to affect it.

The development of EU trade policy

In order to understand how recent and imminent changes in the EU's institutions, membership and internal trade politics affect its engagement in the Doha Development Round, it is necessary to review how the EU's trade policy has developed. Because the EU is an international organization, the allocation of authority (competence, in EU parlance) for trade policy between the member governments and the EU is a crucial issue that has long been a source of tension. The result has been an uneven and sporadic process of political and institutional adaptation.

Who's in charge? The allocation of competence

The EU is the world's most highly institutionalized international organization. The most fundamental impact of its institutional framework on foreign economic policy is in determining whether authority for particular issues resides with the EU, the member states or both. In other words, the EU's institutions determine whether the member governments must participate in international negotiations through the EU, or if they can choose to participate unilaterally.

Where exclusive external competence resides with the EU, the member states cannot pursue unilateral policies. In such circumstances, there are clear procedures, and decision rules facilitate collective participation in international negotiations. Where competence resides with the member states, national governments can choose whether or not to co-operate in order to increase their influence in a negotiation.

Disputes about the allocation of competence between the EU, represented by the European Commission, and its member governments have been a persistent feature of EU foreign economic policy since the signing of the Rome Treaty in 1957, which established the common commercial policy (CCP), the keystone of the EU's trade policy. From the outset, there have been two cross-cutting tensions in EU trade policy: liberal versus protectionist; a strong Commission role versus a strong member state role.

The compromise that squared these tensions in the Rome Treaty left open the question of precisely where the boundary between EU and member-state authority lay. This came to matter more and more as the international trade agenda expanded to include issues such as services, intellectual property rights and foreign direct investment (FDI). Differences among the member governments, however, meant that they were unable to agree (unanimously) to expand the EU's authority for these 'new' trade issues until the Nice Treaty of February 2001.

Creative tension and adaptation

In the absence of formal treaty change, the EU's member states and the Commission agreed repeatedly to co-operate beyond what is strictly required by the legal allocation of competence. Disagreements over the allocation of competence, however, frequently arose after the internal co-operation had succeeded and the external agreement had been concluded.

The European Court of Justice (ECJ), in passing judgment on the compatibility of the resulting arrangements with the treaty's provisions, shifted authority progressively for a wide range of trade issues from the member states to the EU (Weiler, 1991). This shift occurred along two dimensions. First, the ECJ broadened of the scope of the CCP itself. Second, and more profoundly, the ECJ established parallelism between the internal development of the EU and its exclusive external competence. The 'doctrine of implied powers' holds that where the EU has adopted common rules that would be affected adversely by an agreement between a member state and a third country, exclusive external competence in that area transfers to the EU. The EU's dual character as an international organization and international actor are, therefore, explicitly linked. As the EU's network of internal rules expanded, particularly in the wake of the single market programme (see Chapter 6), so too did the scope of its external economic policy authority.

The Nice Treaty: negotiated reform

The Nice Treaty therefore marks a sharp and significant departure from the sporadic and gradual process of adaptation that had come before it. By extending the scope of the CCP to encompass trade in services, with a few notable exceptions, as well as all trade-related aspects of intellectual property rights, the treaty improved the fit between the EU's procedures and the breadth of the international trade agenda.

The Commission and the Belgian, Dutch, Italian, Finnish, Luxembourg and Swedish governments had become increasingly concerned that, in the absence of a mechanism to manage internal differences in areas where competence was shared, the EU would not be able to participate effectively in WTO negotiations (Meunier and Nicolaïdis, 2001). The Commission has long been a proponent of extending exclusive competence to the 'new' trade issues, because it would make the EU a more effective negotiator and enhance the Commission's role in trade policy. The smaller member states too have been consistent advocates of a wider and stronger EU (and Commission) role in trade policy, particularly as a way of increasing their influence in international negotiations. The more liberal of the smaller member states – Finland, the Netherlands and Sweden – also saw the extension of EU competence, and with it qualified majority voting, as a way of weakening the influence of the more protectionist member states.

Britain, Denmark and Germany also generally favoured giving the EU greater authority, but had some reservations, particularly with respect to retaining control of transport services, ensuring that external commitments would not drive internal policies, and retaining scope for unilateral action (Meunier and Nicolaïdis, 2001). Spurred by concerns about the increasing penetration of trade policy into domestic policies, such as health care and culture – in particular, retaining the ability to protect its film industry from Hollywood – France vigorously opposed extending EU competence comprehensively (Holmes and Rollo, 2001; Meunier and Nicolaïdis, 2001). Alongside Greece, Portugal and Spain, France particularly sought to retain authority over education, social services and health policy, as well as audio-visual services.

Finland advanced the artful compromise on which the final agreement was based (European Commission, 2000a). It used the principle that the EU's external competence should 'parallel' the EU's internal decision-making authority to address a number of concerns. As a consequence, the Treaty extended the CCP to encompass trade in most services as well as all trade-related aspects of intellectual property rights, while respecting the main concerns of the reluctant member governments. The principle of 'parallellism' addressed the British and German governments' general concerns about external agreements not driving internal policy. It also (conveniently) excluded education, health care and social policy from exclusive EU competence, because the EU does not have exclusive authority for them internally, thus assuaging French, Greek, Portuguese and Spanish worries. The agreement also excluded transport services – a concern for Denmark, Germany and Greece – from the CCP, on the grounds that they were already governed by the EU's common transport policy. While these policy areas were excluded explicitly from the CCP, FDI in non-service sectors and non-trade-related intellectual property rights were excluded by not being included.

An important part of the Nice compromise, particularly for Britain, was that member states retain the ability to act unilaterally with respect to trade in services and trade-related intellectual property rights, so long as such actions do not contravene the EU's rules. This was a marked departure from the CCP's treatment of trade in goods, which prohibits member states from acting unilaterally.

Changing trade politics

Institutional reform is not the only recent change in EU trade policy. The politics of trade have also changed. Trade is no longer simply the purview of trade ministers, firms and, to a lesser extent, trade unions. As the multilateral trade agenda has expanded to tackle politically sensitive regulatory barriers, as the implications of free trade for the environment have become more apparent, and as trade has become linked to issues such as human rights, so too has trade policy become politicized (Hocking and Smith, 1997). This was illustrated most vividly at the WTO Ministerial meeting in Seattle in December 1999, where 30,000 demonstrators from trade unions, environmental groups and groups concerned about development caused chaos on the streets. As a consequence of the broadening trade agenda, many more, and more diverse types of, interest groups are seeking to influence trade policy.

In response, the Commission has stepped up and formalized its consultations with civic interest groups. In 1998, it established a Civil Society Dialogue and an informal Contact Group to help disseminate information. These outreach activities engage diverse interests: trade unions, environmentalists, consumers and business (see Table 11.1). The frequent meetings of the Dialogue, which closely parallel developments in the negotiations, certainly increase transparency in both directions – letting interest groups know what is going on and keeping the Commission in touch with what the groups think about developments.

The politicization of trade is not a phenomenon unique to the EU. It is occurring throughout the developed world, and increasingly in developing countries. The EU, however, has emerged as the primary champion of two issues of particularly concern to public interest groups: labour standards and environmental protection. The theory is that countries should be able to use trade sanctions to encourage other countries to improve their labour and environmental standards. These ideas resonate with many business groups as they provide an appealing way of justifying protectionism. Such social pressures exist in a number of developed countries. The Clinton Administration in the USA, for example, championed labour standards at Seattle but the Bush Administration has dropped the issue (Panagariya, 2002). Now the EU is their most aggressive proponent. This stance, along with the CAP, has put the EU at odds with developing countries in the current Doha Round.

Table 11.1   *Members of the Commission's Trade Contact Group*

Constituency	Member
Social partners	Economic and Social Committee
Employers	Union of Industrial and Employers' Confederations of Europe (UNICE)
Trade unions	European Trade Union Confederation (ETUC)
Agricultural producers	Committee of Agricultural Organizations – General Committee for Agricultural Co-operation (COPA–COGECA)
Service industries	European Services Forum
Commerce	Foreign Trade Association
NGOs: Environment	Worldwide Fund for Nature (WWF)
NGOs: Animal welfare	Eurogroup for Animal Welfare
NGOs: Health issues	European Public Health Alliance
NGOs: Social issues	Platform for European Social NGOs
NGOs: Consumers	European Bureau of Consumers' Unions
NGOs: Development	International Co-operation for Development and Solidarity (CIDSE)
Eurochambres	Eurochambres
Commerce	Eurocommerce

Note: Order and description of 'constituency' as provided by the Commission.
Source: http://trade-info.cec.eu.int/civil_soc/contact.php.

Enlargement: increased size and political complications

Enlargement has increased the size and importance of the EU's market, and considerably complicated the politics of trade policy-making. That said, enlargement is unlikely to make any radical alterations to the character of the EU's trade policy. Because the new member states, though numerous, are relatively small economically, they will not increase the EU's market size dramatically. In 2001 they accounted collectively for only 3.6 per cent of world merchandise exports and 2.6 per cent of imports (European Commission, 2002b). They did, however, account for 9.8 per cent of EU exports and 12 per cent of EU imports. Enlargement therefore further reduced the EU's dependence on external trade.

The new members, however, are unlikely to tip the existing balance dramatically towards either greater protectionism or greater liberalism. The most likely impact of significance is that enlargement will bolster those opposing reform of the CAP (Johnson with Rollo, 2001). Poland, by far the largest and most politically weighty of the new member states, in particular, is likely to defend the CAP vigorously from outside pressure for reform, whatever its problems with the policy internally (too little rather than too much support). In other areas, the new member states are experiencing adjustment costs from opening their markets fully to EU competition, and are unlikely to want to create additional pressures by pushing for external liberalization (Winters, 2001). Further, in a few sectors – iron, steel, chemicals and non-ferrous metals – joining the EU has required the new members to lower their tariffs on non-EU products as well. As a consequence, there may be an increase in anti-dumping cases involving these sectors (Johnson with Rollo, 2001).

Trade policy-making: institutions and power

These three developments – the extension of EU competence, changing trade politics and enlargement – are affecting how the EU makes trade policy even though the procedures and practices for conducting the EU's trade policy have changed little since the launch of the European Community. On matters falling within the CCP, the Commission represents the EU. It proposes a negotiating directive to the Council of Ministers. Although the treaty states that only a qualified majority is needed to adopt a negotiating directive, in practice the Council proceeds on the basis of consensus.

The Commission alone conducts the negotiations, but consults regularly with the 133 Committee (named after the relevant treaty article), composed of member states' trade officials. Frequent and close consultations between the Commission and the 133 Committee mean that the member states are well aware of the status of negotiations, and the Commission is clear on what the member states will accept. It is only in the final, hectic, closing stages of a negotiation that consultations loosen and the Commission has a freer hand.

The Council must ratify all agreements reached under the CCP. Although only a qualified majority is required, again in practice the member governments prefer to proceed on the basis of consensus. Before the Maastricht Treaty (1992), the European Parliament had no role in ratifying international trade agreements other than through association or accession agreements. The Maastricht Treaty required Parliament to give its assent (a simple majority in favour) to international agreements that establish specific institutional frameworks for co-operation, have significant budgetary implications or affect internal rules that have to be agreed under the co-decision procedure.

Each member state must also ratify the agreement if aspects of it fall outside the EU's exclusive competence. This means that each government has an effective veto over the agreement. Even though the Council tends to operate on the basis of consensus even within the CCP, there can be a big difference between a consensus reached in the 'shadow of the vote' and one reached where each party has a veto. The need for unanimity therefore has significant implications for the substance of the EU's external policy, as a veto strengthens the hand of the most reluctant (that is, most protectionist) member state (Woolcock, 2000). The ethos of consensus, particularly when strengthened by the threat of a veto, encourages package deals in which each member state gets collective protection for its favoured sector (Winters, 2001). This tends to make the EU's positions both more protectionist and more difficult to change. Nevertheless, an advantage of the need for unanimity is that it strengthens the EU's hand in a negotiation (Meunier, 1998). The need to keep all member governments on-side makes granting concessions difficult. Consequently, any concessions by the EU command a high price from its negotiating partners.

While having to maintain unanimous support for a negotiating position might have benefits where the EU is on the defensive, the need for unanimity may undermine the EU's capacity to play a proactive role in multilateral negotiations (Meunier, 1998). That is not, however, necessarily the case. Where the member governments have previously agreed an internal regime that is more ambitious than that under negotiation at the multilateral level (usually the case with respect to services), the obstacle of unanimity is neutralized (Young, 2002). Thus there is a link between the adoption of common internal rules and the member states' ability to play a leading role in negotiations involving issues of mixed competence.

None the less, as the multilateral trade agenda expanded in the 1980s and 1990s, increasing numbers of issues fell outside the scope of the CCP. This was the problem the Nice Treaty was intended to fix. To the extent that mixed competence increases the leverage of the most reluctant member government on any issue, however, it is a problem that the treaty did not fully solve. Because a number of particularly sensitive service sectors were identified explicitly as being of mixed competence, and FDI in non-service sectors was not incorporated in the revised CCP, the member governments will still have to ratify individually any agreement that addresses such issues. This implies that aspects of the negotiations falling within the CCP can still be held hostage by protectionist member governments.

Enlargement has not made any formal changes to the EU's trade policy-making procedures, Arguably, however, the increase in the number of members and diversity of their interests benefits the Commission (Johnson with Rollo, 2001). When the Council cannot agree, the Commission has a freer hand, and when there are many actors the one that proposes a compromise is in a stronger position.

Having established how the EU's character as an international organization affects its performance as an international trade actor, it is time to examine how it has engaged with the multilateral trading system.

The EU's experience with the WTO

Before turning to the round of multilateral trade negotiations current at the time of writing – the Doha Development Round – it is necessary to establish the point of departure, from the EU's perspective. This means examining how the WTO has functioned to date, with particular reference to how the it has met the EU's expectations.

The EU and the Uruguay Round

It is best to begin with a brief look at the origins of the WTO in the Uruguay Round of trade negotiations (1986–93), and the EU's objectives in the talks. An examination of the Uruguay Round also reveals some patterns of EU behaviour that are recurring in the current round of negotiations.

The CAP was the main problem for the EU in the Uruguay Round (Woolcock and Hodges, 1996). The issue divided the member states, making agreement on a common position difficult. When a common position *was* eventually agreed, after and on the basis of internal reforms, it was inflexible and reflected the preferences of the more protectionist member states, particularly France and Ireland. This in turn created problems with the EU's negotiating partners, particularly the USA and the Cairns Group of seventeen agricultural exporting countries, including Australia, Argentina and Indonesia, which co-operate to press for the liberalization of trade in agricultural products.

In an attempt to provide benefits that would help to compensate the more protectionist member states for anticipated concessions on agriculture, the EU sought to broaden the negotiating agenda to seek concessions in services, intellectual property rights and market access (Woolcock and Hodges, 1996). Ultimately though, the deal on agriculture did not go nearly as far as the USA or the Cairns Group wanted. And even the limited deal was only possible after the EU promised internal compensation to farmers if the implementation of the Uruguay Round agreement constrained subsidies more than had been agreed in the internal reform (Devuyst, 1995).

Textiles was another awkward subject for the EU. Both Italy and Portugal resisted the phasing out of the Multifibre Agreement (Devuyst, 1995). Portugal objected to the position taken by the Commission in the negotiations and threatened at the final hour to block the conclusion of the Uruguay Round. It dropped its opposition only after the other member states agreed to provide financial assistance to modernize the Portuguese textile industry. Thus, on the two thorny issues of agriculture and textiles, the EU had to agree internal compensation in order to accept external liberalization.

In other areas, however, the EU's dual character as an international organization and an international actor posed less of a problem. Its experience of internal liberalization was at times even a boon. In particular, the EU was able to make innovative proposals for liberalizing services, an area in which the single market was well advanced (Woolcock and Hodges, 1996; Young, 2002). Progress on internal integration, while helpful, was not a prerequisite for EU leadership in the round. Where member states' interests were congruent, as on intellectual property rights, the EU was able to make comprehensive proposals even though internal rules were largely lacking (Woolcock and Hodges, 1996).

The EU was also a successful champion of strengthening the multilateral system. Although the USA had originally advocated a shift to a more rule-based, less diplomatic system, its support began to wane as concerns about the implications for the autonomy of US policy increased. The EU, along with Canada and a number of newly industrialized countries, picked up the baton and pushed successfully for a binding dispute-settlement system, arguably the most significant development of the round (Woolcock and Hodges, 1996).

What was new with the WTO?

As the preceding discussion suggests, the Uruguay Round covered a great deal of ground. In particular, in addition to continuing the process of lowering tariffs and removing quantitative restrictions, the Uruguay Round broadened the scope of multilateral rules substantially, and made them more binding. The Uruguay Round brought agriculture and textiles under multilateral disciplines for the first time. It also addressed trade in services (the General Agreement on Trade in Services (GATS)), intellectual property rights (the Agreement on Trade-related Intellectual Property Rights (TRIPs)), and foreign direct investment (the Agreement on Trade-related Investment Measures (TRIMs)).

A significant difference between the Uruguay Round and those that preceded it was that, with a very few exceptions, it was a single undertaking. This meant that developing countries could not opt out of individual agreements or decisions taken, although there were special treatment clauses in many parts of the agreement. As a consequence, developing country governments engaged more actively than previously in the negotiations

(Martin and Winters, 1996). That developing countries are bound by new multilateral disciplines is an important part of the context of the current round.

Developed and developing country governments tended to line up against each other on the new issues of the Uruguay Round agenda, although developed–developing country alliances were not uncommon. The developing countries, with the USA and the Cairns Group, sought the liberalization of agriculture, with the EU and Japan as the principal resisters. Developing countries also pushed for the liberalisation of trade in textiles. The USA, eventually with the support of the EU, advocated the liberalization of trade in services and foreign investment, and guarantees regarding the protection of intellectual property rights (Woolcock and Hodges, 1996).

Because of resistance from developing countries, particularly Brazil and India, both GATS and TRIMs represented only limited liberalization. The GATS essentially resulted in governments binding existing levels of liberalization, rather than accepting additional obligations (Hoekman, 1996). The TRIMs agreement, arguably, did not go much beyond codifying existing disciplines on local content and export requirements (Trebilcock and Howse, 1995). The TRIPs agreement, however, was much more radical in that essentially it established minimum requirements for the national protection of intellectual property rights (World Bank, 2000).

The establishment of a binding dispute settlement system heightened the significance of these new disciplines. Disagreements between contracting parties about the application of the rules are heard by an independent tribunal (panel) with the possibility of appeal. Whereas previously either participant could block the adoption of a panel's report, now the decision of the panel or Appellate Body is adopted unless all the contracting parties vote against it. If the respondent fails to comply adequately with an adverse ruling, the complainant may be authorized to impose sanctions or claim compensation. As of the end of June 2003 there had been 294 complaints, the vast majority of them being resolved without WTO adjudication; sanctions were authorized in only seven cases and applied in only three.

The Uruguay Round therefore made dramatic changes to the multilateral trading system within which the EU operates. It extended the scope of multilateral rules to new issues, broadened their coverage to developing countries, and made them more binding through a robust dispute-settlement system.

The EU and the WTO's rules

Thus far the EU has fared reasonably well under the new trading system.

That should not come as too much of a surprise, as the EU was able to fend off significant concessions on agriculture and was an advocate of binding dispute settlement, the GATS, TRIPs and TRIMs. The EU has used the WTO's rules and dispute settlement system actively to open other countries' markets. It is second only to the USA as the most active user of the dispute settlement system, accounting for 21 per cent of all complaints during 1995–2002. During that period, the EU filed complaints against eleven countries, although more than 40 per cent of the EU's complaints were against the USA (see Table 11.2).

The EU has scored a number of important successes, particularly with regard to US extraterritorial legislation, which punishes foreign firms for their activities outside the USA, and contingent trade protection, such as anti-dumping or countervailing duties, which seek to off-set 'unfair' competition by particular foreign firms. The EU also challenged successfully the

Table 11.2 *EU participation in WTO trade disputes, 1995–2002*

	As complaintant	As respondent		
		EU	Member state	Total
USA	25	12	16	53
India	6	4		10
Brazil	3	6		9
Canada	3	6		9
Argentina	5	2		7
Japan	6			6
Chile	3	1		4
South Korea	4			4
Mexico	1	2		3
Honduras		2		2
Panama		2		2
Peru		2		2
Thailand		2		2
Indonesia	1			1
Pakistan	1			1
Australia		1		1
Ecuador		1		1
New Zealand		1		1
Uruguay		1		1
Total	58	38*	16	112*

Note: *Some complaints filed by more than one contracting party.

Source: Compiled from the WTO's dispute-settlement database accessible at: http://www.wto.org/english/tratop_e/dispu–e/disput–e.htm

US Foreign Sales Corporation legislation, which gives tax relief to exporters. Having challenged changes that the United States adopted to that legislation, the EU has received WTO authorization to impose US$4 billion in sanctions, by far the largest complaint in value terms. Yet the EU has been reluctant to impose those sanctions, although it had published its list of targeted products in the hope that this would increase pressure on the US Congress to bring the law into compliance.

The EU, however, has not had it all its own way. As Table 11.2 shows, the EU has been the respondent in almost as many cases as it has been a complainant. Fifteen countries have filed complaints against the EU, but the USA accounts for over half of them. Significantly, a third of all complaints against the EU have targeted the measures of individual member states. The EU is unique in this respect, as the rules of the subunits of other federal systems are generally not bound by WTO rules. Being an international organization again affects how the EU engages with the world trading system.

The EU and the Doha Development Agenda

The rocky road to Doha

The current round of multilateral trade negotiations has its roots firmly in the Uruguay Round. In exchange for accepting less liberalization of trade in agriculture and services in the Uruguay Round than it would have liked, the USA insisted that these issues be revisited in negotiations scheduled to start in 2000. Agriculture and services therefore constituted the 'built-in agenda' of the current round. In addition, developing countries wanted to redress some of the perceived imbalance in the Uruguay Round Agreement. This perception rests both on expected benefits from developed country liberalization of key developing country exports of textiles and agricultural products not being realized, and on the heavier-than-anticipated burden on developing countries of some of the 'new' commitments, such as the protection of intellectual property rights (Panagariya, 2002).

The EU, given its internal problems with accepting the liberalisation of agricultural imports, has long been an advocate of a 'comprehensive' round that would include a wide range of issues in addition to agriculture and services, and so permit gains in some areas to offset anticipated concessions in agriculture (Allen and Smith, 2001). The EU was thus a crucial champion of the Doha Development Round.

Although most of the EU's wider agenda – investment, competition policy, trade facilitation and transparency in public procurement – reflects business interests, one component (labour standards) reflects the concerns of European civil society. These issues, often referred to as the 'Singapore issues' because they were first discussed at the WTO Ministerial meeting in Singapore in 1996, are opposed by many developing countries, which perceive them as benefiting primarily the developed countries and being demanding to negotiate. The Singapore issues were on the agenda of the Ministerial in Seattle in 1999, which was intended to launch a new round of multilateral trade negotiations (Hoekman and Kostecki, 2001). The developing countries' opposition to their inclusion on the agenda, and resentment at being excluded from the 'green room' negotiations within the negotiations – combined with inadequate preparation and poor organization, scuppered the launch of a 'millennium' round (Hoekman and Kostecki, 2001).

Subsequent attempts to entice the developing countries back to the negotiating table led to the focus on development issues in the current round. In particular, there has been the need to address developing country concerns about the 'implementation' of the Uruguay Round commitments (Hoekman and Kostecki, 2001). These include:

- ensuring that the developed countries deliver on their commitments to developing countries, particularly with regard to liberalizing trade in agricultural products, textiles and clothing, and curbing the use of contingent protection;
- responding to the problems developing countries are encountering in implementing the agreements before transition periods expired (particularly with regard to TRIMs); and
- addressing whether some of the substantive disciplines of some of the WTO agreements (notably TRIPs) were compatible with national development priorities.

The Doha Development Agenda

The WTO Ministerial meeting in Doha, Qatar, in November 2001 launched a new trade round successfully around what was dubbed the Doha Development Agenda. The US-government's determination, shared by the EU and others, to demonstrate that the terrorist attacks of 11 September 2001, two months earlier, would not undermine the resolve to liberalize world trade, contributed to a general willingness to compromise (Panagariya, 2001). In addition, the Bush Administration, less beholden to domestic trade unions than its Democratic predecessor, was not interested in pushing for WTO rules on labour standards, which were anathema to developing countries. More than ever before, developing countries participated actively and co-ordinated their positions in meetings. The EU came with the most ambitious agenda and, given the need for all member states to agree, was slow to compromise on it (Allen and Smith, 2002; Thompson, 2001).

Consequently, whereas the Uruguay Round began with the USA and the developing countries on opposing sides, with the EU in the middle, in Doha the EU was in opposition to the developing countries on a number of key issues, despite its public protestations about concern for development. Not only did the EU, particularly France, resist the inclusion in the agenda of the objective of phasing out agricultural export subsidies, but it was alone in advocating a comprehensive agenda that would have included the 'Singapore issues' that many developing countries, India in particular, dislike so much (Panagariya, 2002; Thompson, 2001).

At the last minute a form of words was found that satisfied the EU, and, after a delay, clarifications of the text enabled India also to accept the agenda. On agricultural export subsidies, the Ministerial Declaration (WTO, 2001, p. 3) stated that the agenda did not 'prejudge the outcome of the negotiations' and clarified that the aim was the 'reductions [sic] of, with a view to phasing out' export subsidies. The decision to start negotiations on the Singapore issues – investment, competition policy, trade facilitation and transparency in government procurement – was postponed to the Cancún Ministerial in September 2003. India sought, and received, explicit clarification that the decision to start negotiations on the 'Singapore issues' could be blocked by any contracting party (Thompson, 2001). The EU was not able to get core labour standards included on the agenda, with the Ministerial just reconfirming its earlier call for co-operation between the WTO and the International Labour Organization (European Commission, 2001e).

The EU did score some successes. In exchange for accepting the deferment of the start of negotiations on investment and competition policy, the EU secured a commitment that the negotiations will seek to clarify the relationship between the WTO and multilateral environmental agreements (Thompson, 2001). The EU also got formal recognition that 'nontrade' aspects of agriculture would be taken into account in the negotiations. This refers to the concept of the 'multifunctionality' of agriculture, which captures the role of agriculture in rural development and environmental protection, as well as the associated issues of food safety and animal welfare (European Commission, 2001e). This provides scope for the continued subsidization of agriculture, but disconnected from production, and therefore less trade-distorting. Further, the Ministerial, facing the threat of a veto by the African, Caribbean and Pacific (ACP) countries (*Financial Times*, 14 November 2001), granted a waiver for their preferential trading relationship with the EU (see Chapter 15). On other issues, such as the trade in services and market access for industrial products, the EU's preferences were in line with those of the bulk of the members, and it got what it wanted on the agenda.

The EU was not consistently in opposition to the developing countries. For example, again reflecting pressure from civil society, it played an important part in securing an agreement in principle that the TRIPs agreement should be interpreted and implemented in such a way as to permit WTO members to manufacture or import any drugs necessary to deal with public health crises, such as the HIV/AIDS pandemic in southern Africa (Panagariya, 2002; Thompson, 2001).

The crunch in Cancún

Even before the Ministerial meeting in Cancún in September 2003 ended without agreement, the round had lost momentum. Initially, the USA and EU were at the core of the problem. The USA was guilty of sins of commission – namely, imposing safeguard measures on steel imports and substantially increasing its agricultural subsidies, while the EU was guilty of sins of omission – for example, having trouble agreeing negotiating positions in agriculture and services, and struggling with agricultural reforms, which stemmed from the need to reach agreement among the member states.

Agriculture was an early sticking point. The USA, the Cairns Group and a number of other developing countries said that unless the EU reduced import barriers and slashed subsidies aggressively, there could be no deal (*Financial Times*, 23 January 2003). Although not alone in resisting agricultural liberalization – Japan, Norway, South Korea and Switzerland also do so – the EU received the brunt of the criticism, as it was the last of the major trade powers to table firm agricultural proposals. This was because France and Ireland had blocked the negotiating position until references to the elimination of export subsidies for specific products were removed (*BRIDGES Trade BioRes*, 7 February 2003). In June 2003, however, the EU agreed reforms to the CAP (see Chapter 7). This cleared the way for a joint EU–US proposal on agriculture, which was announced in August 2003 during the run-up to Cancún.

Although not sufficient to please everybody, this proposal, combined with an agreement at the end of August on the details of squaring TRIPs with developing countries' access to essential medicines, contributed to a degree of renewed optimism going into the Ministerial (The *Economist*, 16 August 2003). But that optimism was misplaced. Agriculture, however, was not (at least on the face of it) the biggest problem. The Group of 21 (G 21) – a new alliance of developing countries, including Brazil, China and India – was critical of the EU–USA proposal, demanding more extensive changes from developed countries while offering less. Another group of developing countries, mainly from Africa, were very concerned that agricultural liberalization would erode the value of their preferential trading relationships with developed countries (see Chapter 15) and expose their small farmers to intense competition (The *Economist*, 20 September 2003). These differences, however, seemed manageable, and the Mexican foreign minister, who was chairing the talks, decided to concentrate first on the more seemingly intractable Singapore issues (*BRIDGES Daily Update on the Fifth Ministerial Conference*, Issue 6, 15 September 2003).

The EU had been the principal raiser of Singapore issues, but at the start of the Ministerial ninety governments had stated their opposition to starting negotiations on them. It was only on the last day of the talks that the Commission dropped its insistence on talks on investment and competition policy. The Africans, however, deeply dissatisfied with the draft text on agriculture, refused to negotiate on any of the Singapore issues (The *Economist*, 20 September 2003). On the other side of the coin, Japan and South Korea, both of which had been resisting the liberalizing of their agricultural markets, insisted that all four Singapore issues be included in the Round (*BRIDGES Trade BioRes*, 19 September 2003). Thus, while the EU eventually showed flexibility, the two issues in the round to which it had been central– agriculture and the Singapore issues – were linked in a destructive way by others.

In the light of these differences, the chair decided to end the negotiations on the afternoon of 14 September. This surprised a number of participants, who had anticipated an all-night push to reach an agreement. All the members did agree on was that they would carry on with the negotiations below ministerial level.

Setbacks such as those at Cancún have been overcome before. During the Uruguay Round, for example, the Brussels Ministerial (in 1990) also collapsed, but the negotiators pressed on, and eventually reached a far ranging agreement, albeit five years later than planned. Nevertheless, the negotiating landscape has since been profoundly changed by the emergence of combative developing-country alliances. Moreover, as was the case during the Uruguay Round, governments are likely to turn to bilateral and regional trade liberalization, thus further dissipating negotiating energy. Almost certainly, however, the deadline of December 2004 for completing the round will be missed.

Conclusion

The EU's character as an international organization means that the interests of its member states must be aggregated in trade policy. In particular, where member state competences are involved, the hand of the government most opposed to change is strengthened. As the Nice Treaty left some of the items on the agenda of the Doha Round in the hands of the member states, those governments most resistant to liberalization have significant power. Moreover, the traditional protectionist influences within the EU have been bolstered by the engagement of a wider array of civil society in trade politics and the associated demand to promote labour and environmental standards abroad. Enlargement further complicates EU trade policy-making as there are more interests that need to be accommodated. Consequently, the treaty reform agreed in Nice does not appear to have been sufficient to offset the negative impacts on decision-making effectiveness of changed trade politics and increased EU membership. It is thus even harder for the EU to agree compromises during the Doha Round than it was during the Uruguay Round.

In addition, the EU's common agricultural policy and single-market programme, although formally internal policies, arguably have a greater impact on the EU's trading partners than does its formal trade policy. The EU's character as an international organization exacerbates the difficulties of CAP reform and tends to make the single market rules more trade restrictive, thereby leaving its mark on the world. Ultimately how the EU manages the twin internal challenges of CAP reform and enlargement will be a crucial element in determining the success of the current multilateral trade round.

Chapter 12

The Foreign and Security Policies of the European Union

ANAND MENON

The last few years has been a period of extremes for the EU in the foreign and security policy spheres. On the one hand, the development of the European Security and Defence Policy (ESDP) following the December 1998 Franco-British summit at St. Malo; the high profile initiatives embarked on by both External Relations Commissioner Chris Patten and Common Foreign and Security Policy High Representative Javier Solana; and the increasing salience of security issues following the terrorist attacks in the United States on 11 September 2001 have focused considerable scholarly and public attention on this policy sector.

On the other hand, it would be all too easy (and understandable) to lapse into fatalism, not to say profound cynicism, about the EU's foreign and security policies. After all, the EU played no role in either the crisis leading up to, or the subsequent prosecution of, the war against Iraq. Indeed, in so far as the EU figured on the international politics radar screen at all, it did so largely via periodic appearances to air divisions among its member states.

Although events such as those in Iraq necessarily dominate the headlines and the international agenda, there is far more to contemporary international affairs than sporadic military crises. Out of the limelight, and often in areas of little interest to either the European public or many of their political leaders, the EU has in fact become a highly active, and in some respects highly influential, actor on the international stage. High-profile crises, in other words, have overshadowed low-profile achievements.

It is worth adding a rider to what follows at this point. In so far as the EU's role in international politics is concerned, events move fast. The combination of the war in Iraq, the Convention on the Future of Europe, and the ensuing intergovernmental conference mean that the EU's external policies are a rapidly moving target. What follows, therefore, is an attempt both to analyse current events and to put them in a broader context. The chapter is divided into four parts. The first section provides the background to recent developments, placing foreign and security policy in its historical context. The second section looks at the reality of EU foreign, security and defence policy in the early twenty-first century, and the third and fourth sections assess future prospects in the light of the war in Iraq in 2003 and the negotiation of a constitutional treaty for the EU.

Background

From its inception, European integration has been concerned with issues of foreign and defence policy. Indeed, its first institutional embodiment was the 1948 Brussels Treaty of Economic, Social and Cultural Collaboration and Collective Self-Defence. Similarly, France and Germany would not have created the European Coal and Steel Community had it not been for a desire on their part to eliminate the possibility of future conflict between them.

However, following the failure of the French National Assembly to ratify the European Defence Community in 1954, foreign and security affairs were effectively removed from the agenda of European integration. While EC member states took steps to co-ordinate their foreign policies from the 1970s in the framework of European Political Co-operation (Nuttall, 2000), it was not until the Single European Act of 1986 that the EC itself formally acquired a purview over this policy sector.

The Treaty on European Union, signed in Maastricht in February 1992, built significantly upon those foundations and provided the legal basis for the development of a common foreign and security policy (CFSP). Maastricht incorporated European political co-operation into the legal structures of the EU, and empowered the EU to implement a common foreign and security policy, including the framing of a common defence policy, which might in time lead to a common defence. On defence matters, the EU received the right to request the Western European Union (WEU) to 'elaborate and implement decisions and actions of the Union which have defence implications'.

Member states agreed in the Maastricht Treaty to review the CFSP in a later intergovernmental conference, held in 1996. The ensuing Amsterdam Treaty reformed the CFSP in several significant ways. First, it empowered the European Council to provide a general framework and strategic direction for foreign policy activity across the EU's three pillars via the definition of common strategies, by means of consensus. Once a common strategy was agreed, the Council could implement it through joint actions and common positions adopted by a qualified majority. A safeguard clause enabled member states to block majority voting for important reasons of national policy. In such cases, once the member state in question stated its reasons, the Council could decide by a qualified majority to refer the matter to the European Council for a unanimous decision. As early as December 1998, the Council recommended three common strategies to the European Council – on Russia, Ukraine and the Mediterranean.

Second, the treaty provided for the creation of a High Representative for the Common Foreign and Security Policy, responsible for assisting the Council in CFSP-related matters by contributing to the formulation, preparation and implementation of decisions. At the request of the presidency, the High Representative engages in political dialogue with third countries on behalf of the Council, and endeavours to improve the visibility and consistency of the CFSP. Meeting in Cologne in June 1999, the European Council appointed Javier Solana, then NATO Secretary-General, as the first incumbent.

To offer administrative and institutional support to the High Representative, a policy planning and early warning unit was set up in the General Secretariat of the Council under the authority of the High Representative. The unit was charged with monitoring and analysing developments in areas relevant to the CFSP; assessing the EU's interests in relation to the CFSP; providing timely evaluations of events, potential political crises and situations that might have significant repercussions for the CFSP; and producing policy option papers for the Council.

Finally, the Amsterdam Treaty made modest amendments to the provisions concerning defence policy. A semantic shift in wording enabled the European Council to 'avail itself' of the WEU rather than simply 'request it' to carry out missions, as stipulated in the Maastricht Treaty. In October 1999, the High Representative became Secretary-General of the WEU in order to preside over another major change in the Amsterdam Treaty: the incorporation of the WEU into the EU. The new treaty also incorporated into the EU the so-called Petersberg tasks, namely 'humanitarian and rescue tasks, peacekeeping tasks and tasks of combat forces in crisis management, including peacemaking'.

No sooner had the ink dried on the new treaty than startling developments occurred in an area where progress had been minimal at the Amsterdam summit itself. At Amsterdam, as at the Maastricht summit in December 1991, Britain stymied progress in the sphere of defence. The new British prime minister, Tony Blair, arrived in Amsterdam – his first EU summit – armed with the arguments of his predecessors against involving the EU in defence issues. As he reported to the House of Commons after the summit: 'Getting Europe's voice heard more clearly in the world will not be achieved through merging the European Union and the Western

European Union or developing an unrealistic common defence policy. We therefore resisted unacceptable proposals from others' (House of Commons, Hansard, 18 June 1997, Col. 314).

Yet within months of the summit, the British position began to shift. A myriad of possible explanations for this change have been put forward, ranging from increasing dissatisfaction with the USA following experience in the Balkans; to a desperate desire for Europe to do more in order to convince the USA of the continued vitality of NATO in the light of increasingly clear concern in Washington about the military utility of the Alliance; or to Blair's desire to assert 'leadership' in Europe (Howorth, 2000; Whitman, 1999).

Whatever the root cause, the shifting British position led to dramatic results. On 4 December 1998, Tony Blair and French President Jacques Chirac signed the St. Malo Declaration advocating the development of an 'autonomous' political and military capacity for the EU. At the Cologne summit the following June, EU leaders created the institutional framework necessary to take political decisions concerning defence matters, and at the Helsinki summit in December 1999 they established the so-called Headline Goals, setting force targets for the EU's military capabilities (for a full discussion, see Howorth, 2002; pp. 37–41). Foremost amongst these was the decision to create, by December 2003, an EU Rapid Reaction Force capable of undertaking the full range of Petersberg tasks and be self-sustaining militarily with the necessary command, control and intelligence capabilities, logistics, other combat support services and, as appropriate, air and naval elements.

The changes brought about at successive European Council meetings were codified at the Nice summit of December 2000. Few changes of any significance were made to the provisions for foreign policy. In terms of defence, however, the Nice Treaty removed virtually all references to the WEU, thereby underlining the fact that the EU itself was now empowered to take and implement defence decisions. Moreover, a report by the French presidency submitted to the summit formalized the existence of the interim ESDP institutions (the Political and Security Committee, the Military Committee and the Military Staff) which, by then, were in operation. These became permanent institutions in January, April and June 2001, respectively. A year later, EU leaders proclaimed the ESDP operational, in the Laeken Declaration.

The reality of foreign, security and defence policy

EU foreign and security policy has therefore undergone a process of rapid institutional change. Yet the Union did not enjoy the luxury of perfecting gradually the institutional architecture intended to prepare the ground for common external policies. Being overtaken by events was not a new experience for EU leaders attempting to forge a collective capacity in foreign and security affairs. Discussions about foreign and security policy during the pre-Maastricht intergovernmental conference were overshadowed by the outbreak of the Gulf War, while the implementation of the Maastricht provisions and negotiation of the Amsterdam reforms were dominated by the deteriorating situation in the Balkans. Similarly, less than a year after the Nice summit, the terrorist attacks of 11 September 2001 rocked the world and, in particularly, the USA. Such was the impact of these events that international politics came to be dominated by their aftermath: Washington's 'war on terrorism'. Consequently, and somewhat unfortunately as far as the EU was concerned, it was in the context of the post-September 11 world, and of America's activist policies, that the EU's emerging foreign and security policies came to be judged.

The inability of the EU to make any kind of military contribution to the post-September 11 American military campaign contributed to a growing sense that, once again, expectations in the area of EU foreign and security policies had clearly exceeded capabilities, although it is debatable whether Washington would have wanted such a military contribution even if the EU could have provided it. In the event, profound and highly public disputes between EU member states over the conflict with Iraq led many to proclaim that the EU's foreign and security policies were effectively moribund. Thus Alexander Stubb, an adviser to the European Commission, wrote in the *Financial Times* that 'in the past few weeks we have been subjected to an unprecedented European foreign policy cacophony. The Union had a unique chance to show that Europe can speak with one voice in international crises. The failure was as fantastic as the opportunity, and it seems that everyone is to blame' (13 March 2003).

In even more striking tones, Anatol Lieven declared in the same newspaper that it 'may be time to admit that there will never in fact be a common European foreign and security policy' (*Financial Times*, 3 February 2003). It is certainly understandable why they and others reached those conclusions. Yet a more balanced assessment suggests that such judgements may have been too hasty.

ESDP

If any area exemplified informed frustration about the chasm between stated intentions and outcomes, it was defence policy. Following the St. Malo Declaration, the conference circuit was overflowing with those confidently predicting that, because of the political momentum behind closer defence co-operation, the EU was about to take a qualitative step forward and equip itself with a meaningful defence policy (Howorth, 2002).

Yet for all the fanfare accompanying the development of the ESDP, the EU made no military contribution to either of the major military actions undertaken by the Americans as part of the war against terrorism. Indeed, following the apparent triumphs of St. Malo, Helsinki and Nice, it become increasingly difficult to discern when, if ever, the EU would be able to act militarily at all. Therefore, when the Belgian foreign minister announced to the press at the time of the Laeken summit in December 2001 that the EU was going to send a 'multinational force' to Afghanistan, he was reminded publicly, almost immediately, by both the British minister for Europe and the German foreign minister, that it would not be an EU but an international force backed by the UN (*Europe*, 15 and 16 December; *Guardian*, 15 December). Throughout 2002, despite much public speculation about the possibility of the EU replacing the NATO peacekeeping force in Macedonia, nothing if fact happened.

At least three factors explain this apparent lack of progress. First, the EU was, of course, not the only institution interested in stamping its imprimatur on European security affairs. While the EU was striving to establish incipient structures to handle defence policy, NATO was in the process of adapting its own structures to handle the new security threats of the post-September 11 world. Most striking in this regard was the decision taken at the NATO Prague summit of November 2002 to create a rapid response force. The stark differences with the EU's planned force could hardly have been more striking: the NATO undertaking was predicated on the reorganization of existing capabilities for high intensity war fighting (Interview with Lord Robertson, NATO Secretary General, *European Voice*, 21 November 2002). In terms of actual military capabilities, while the EU rapid reaction force of 50,000–60,000 troops was to be available at 60 days' notice and capable of remaining in the field for one year, the NATO equivalent was up to 21,000 troops, to be deployable within 5–30 days. As a senior source in the Council of Ministers remarked, the EU's undertaking was 'not necessarily rapid, not necessarily reactive and not necessarily a force' (*European Voice*, 21–27 March 2002).

Second, the EU was hamstrung by a simmering row involving Turkey and Greece, which stymied negotiations with NATO for almost two years about EU access to NATO assets. The heart of the problem was that, given its limited military capacities, the EU relied for most conceivable military operations on guaranteed access to NATO experts and planning facilities – the so-called Berlin Plus formula that had been agreed in June 1996. However, Turkey initially blocked the signing of implementation agreements between the EU and NATO because, in its opinion, the EU's new defence policy decision-making arrangements discriminated against non-EU NATO European countries (*International Herald Tribune*, 26 January 2001). At the end of 2001, a deal was finally struck whereby the EU guaranteed that its rapid reaction force would not intervene near Turkey's geopolitical sphere of influence. In return, Turkey gave up its demand for a right to a say in the operational decisions guiding the force (*Le Monde*, 15 December 2001). Following this, the Greek government complained that too much had been conceded to the Turks, and promptly blocked the signing of the agreement. It was not until mid-December 2002, at the EU summit in Copenhagen, that a solution was finally arrived at.

Third, the slow progress in setting up an operational defence policy was because of the misgivings of certain EU member states concerning the viability and value of the project. From the start, EU member states had vastly different opinions about the idea of ESDP (Menon, 2001). Crucially, the Britain, the single most important country in terms of the effectiveness of any EU defence initiative, was far from totally committed to the undertaking, and certainly uncommitted to ambitious French objectives for it. Britain's preference for working with the Americans was never in doubt. Indeed, it was illustrated clearly by British participation with the US in bombing raids on Iraq a mere two weeks after the St. Malo Declaration. From the first, Britain openly viewed the EU defence initiative as a means to an end rather than as an end in itself; as a tactic to improve military capabilities rather than a political project intended to strengthen the EU. As Britain's defence minister stated in Washington in January 2000: 'Helsinki is all about enhancing military capability. It is not about political niceties . . . If hanging a "European" tag on it is what it takes to make it happen, then so be it.' Moreover, at British insistence, the EU stressed its relatively limited defence ambitions and the continued primacy of NATO over security affairs. Accordingly, the Helsinki Declaration stated unambiguously that 'The European Council underlines its determination to develop an autonomous capacity to take decisions and, where NATO as a whole is not engaged, to launch and conduct EU-led military operations in response to international crises. This process will avoid unnecessary duplication and does not imply the creation of a European army' (European Council, 1999c).

The events of September 11 and America's activist foreign policy thereafter forced Britain to make a more explicit choice between the EU and the USA – something that British policy makers could possibly have foreseen at the time of St. Malo. While the choice has been neither as clear-cut nor as definitive as those who portray Blair as simply a 'poodle' of President George W. Bush imply, it is clear that the divisions in the EU over Iraq, divisions that centred on a confrontation between the two leading proponents of ESDP, will severely impair progress in that particular field for some time to come (Menon and Lipken, 2003).

Nevertheless, it is not yet time to sound the death knell for the ESDP. For one thing, given the events of September 11, it is simply unfair to judge the EU's nascent military capabilities against the backdrop of American military might revealed so massively and effectively in the war against terrorism. The lack of an EU military response to September 11 should be seen in context. First, the EU is not Europe. Whereas the EU found itself unable to act, several European states made important contributions, both to the operations in Afghanistan and to the conflict in Iraq. The picture that Charles Grant (2002) painted of 'US forces hunting for terrorists in caves, and Europeans keeping the peace on the streets of Kabul' is misleading in that several European countries made major contributions to the war by fighting in Afghanistan. It was often British Special Forces that did the searching in caves, with the French military contribution also being highly significant (Shapiro, 2002). Nor should the importance and difficulty of peacekeeping, whether in Kabul or elsewhere, be underestimated.

Moreover, for all its failings, ESDP has finally become operational. The deployment of peace-keeping troops to Macedonia (operation Concordia), launched in April 2003, was a good illustration of both the shortcomings and the strengths of ESDP. For six months, approximately 400 troops from all fifteen EU member states participated in the Berlin Plus mission under the operational command of German Admiral Rainer Feist, Deputy Supreme Allied Commander Europe, with the objective of overseeing the agreement reached in 2001 between the Macedonian government and Albanian rebels. (Altogether, twenty-seven countries were involved in the mission, their soldiers wearing national uniforms with insignia bearing the letters 'EUfor' and badges with the European colours – blue with gold stars – on the right shoulder). France, which sent the bulk of the troops, assumed most of the responsibility on the ground.

The lessons of Macedonia were threefold. First, discussions over its inception illustrated the divisions among member states concerning the scope of ESDP. The EU was originally supposed to take over the NATO mission in October 2002. However, the simmering dispute with Turkey about ESDP meant that the requisite agreements with NATO could not be signed. Several member states, including France and Belgium, argued that, because the operation was relatively small (the NATO force numbered only some 800 troops) the EU mission should go ahead even in the absence of any EU–NATO accords. Britain, Spain and Germany blocked that proposal. Not only were they concerned about the implications for the transatlantic alliance of such a move, but their military commanders pointed out that, while the proposed mission itself was small, there was still the possibility of escalation, in which case the EU would need support from NATO. According to the senior EU official in charge of the operation, 'We should never exclude even the worst case scenario. If there would be a requirement to extract the force, then that would be done under NATO command and control with the assistance of NATO-led forces' (BBC News online, 28 March 2003).

The second lesson therefore was that, by designating the Macedonia mission a Berlin Plus operation, member states recognized that, even in undertaking small-scale missions, the EU faced the possibility of escalation and would need to be able to turn, in the last resort, to NATO for back-up and assistance. As NATO Secretary General Lord Robertson pointed out, it 'marks an important milestone in the development of the EU–NATO strategic partnership. The full set of agreements for ready access by the EU to the collective assets and capabilities of NATO for EU-led operations is the key for the European Union to take over NATO's mission in Macedonia' (*EUobserver.com*, 19 March 2003).

Third, Macedonia was symptomatic of an emerging functional division of labour between the Europeans and Americans. Operation Concordia was in keeping with a broader pattern whereby the Europeans compensated for American troop withdrawals from the Balkans. There was a real possibility that this trend would be taken further as and when the EU took over NATO operations in Bosnia. Further afield, European forces made up the bulk of the International Stabilization and Assistance Force patrolling the streets of Kabul. Thus, at the lower end of the military spectrum, the EU, or European states acting through other forums, were increasingly complementing and reinforcing American military might.

ESDP also includes non-military tasks. Away from the public gaze, which focused very much on the military dimension, the EU has also created a civilian ESDP. The Nordic countries, in particular, drawing on their strong traditions in the area of conflict prevention and supported by Germany's social democratic–green coalition, insisted that civilian crisis-management capabilities be developed alongside the military aspects of ESDP. At a series of summits in 1999 and 2000, EU leaders therefore developed a civilian ESDP. In keeping with the approach adopted for military forces, the European Council emphasized four non-military areas of ESDP: policing; the administration of justice; civilian administration; and civil protection. In June 2002, the EU established the Committee for the Civilian Aspects of Crisis Management, reporting to the Political and Security Committee. The Danish presidency declared five months later that specific objectives for the four civilian headline goals had been met. Shortly after that, in January 2003, the EU embarked on its first civilian ESDP mission: the deployment of a police training force to Bosnia.

Certainly, one should not exaggerate the significance of the EU's first police mission. It was a rather unchallenging debut for the civilian ESDP in that it followed in the footsteps of a United Nations' mission that had been on the ground since 1995, and the EU had twelve months' warning before taking over. However, the importance of civilian ESDP is that its existence gives the EU a full gamut of foreign and security options on which to draw. It also marks an acceptance of the fact that military power is not the only aspect of external policy with a role to play in contemporary external relations, a notion stressed by Scandinavian officials in the EU (Interviews, Brussels, January 2003).

CFSP

If civilian ESDP serves to show that military force is not everything in international affairs, other aspects of the EU's foreign and security policies reinforce that message. The term 'soft power' is an ambiguous one, used in some cases pejoratively, in others to refer to non-military forms of power, and still others as power to attract, rather than coerce, others. Whatever the definition, the fact is that the EU's foreign and security policies have considerable resources at their disposal. Indeed, one of the problems with over-hasty judgements about the EU's international performance in recent years is that debates about the EU's foreign policy role have been subsumed beneath public and political discussion about the state of the military aspects of ESDP.

On a non-military level, the EU's response to the attacks of September 11 was both more rapid and more united than most would have predicted. As early as 14 September, the EU issued a joint declaration on the situation at the level of the heads of state and government. More practically, the day after the attacks, the Commission tabled proposals for a European Arrest Warrant, and the EU moved quickly to upgrade its co-operation with the USA in the area of Justice and Home Affairs (Den Boer and Monar, 2002).

EU diplomatic activity also had a more direct impact on events following September 11. The EU had already been building links gradually with the Iranian regime. This process of constructive engagement culminated on 10 September 2001 in a meeting between External Relations Commissioner, Chris Patten, and the Iranian foreign minister, at which the EU announced its intention to negotiate a trade and co-operation agreement. Following the events of September 11, the EU played a crucial role in bringing Iran within the ambit of the global coalition against terrorism and, through High Representative Solana, in liaising with Iran on the future of Afghanistan (Allen and Smith, 2002).

The EU was also active in helping to bring about a successful resolution to the Afghan conflict itself. Two respected observers commented that the

'UN-backed agreement on political transition in Afghanistan signed in Bonn on 5 December [2001] would not have been possible in its final form without EU efforts in the CFSP context' (Den Boer and Monar, 2002). Moreover, not only was it predominantly European troops that made up the bulk of the stabilization force in Kabul, but the EU, following the end of hostilities, remained engaged economically in Afghanistan, providing €280 million in 2002, and in March 2003 pledging a further €400 million package of reconstruction for the country.

The real test of the EU's ability to wield political influence through the exercise of soft power, however, has been the Middle East. In terms of direct political influence, the EU has clearly been dwarfed by the USA. That being said, the EU has become an irreplaceable source of aid in the region, particularly for the Palestinian Authorities. From 1993 to the end of 2001, the EU committed about €1 billion in grants and loans to the region (Soetendorp, 2002). Together with the contributions of individual member states, the EU contributes about 50 per cent of the total aid to the Palestinian Authority (Everts, 2003). As Ginsberg has noted, 'the Palestinians have come to depend as much on the EU for an economic life-line and diplomatic support as the Israelis have come to depend on the United States for diplomatic support, military co-operation and economic aid' (Ginsberg, 2001).

From such economic beneficence stemmed a degree of political influence. In 1999, the EU was instrumental in persuading Palestinian President Yasser Arafat to step back from his threat to declare Palestinian statehood unilaterally (Soetendorp, 2002). The following year, Solana was present at the summit meeting in Sharm el-Sheikh, where Arafat, the Israeli prime minister, the US president, the UN Secretary–General, and the leaders of Jordan and Egypt tried to find a way to end the violence between Israel and the Palestinians. Solana became one of the five members of the Sharm el-Sheikh Fact Finding Committee (the so-called Mitchell Committee). In April 2002, Solana and the EU Special Representative brokered the agreement on the release of the Palestinians holed up in the Church of the Nativity in Bethlehem.

Certainly it would be foolish to exaggerate the EU's influence in this volatile region. While it has become a recognized partner of the USA (as shown by the establishment, at a meeting in Washington in May 2002, of a quartet on the Middle East, composed of the USA, EU, Russia and the UN), the EU could do little but watch as Israeli troops brutally destroyed the infrastructure it had funded. In April 2001, Israel refused to allow a high-level EU diplomatic mission, which included Solana, to visit President Arafat in his besieged headquarters. It is hard to argue with a cynical British foreign ministry official who observed that it will be clear if and when the USA ever becomes serious about promoting peace in the

Middle East: at that moment, Washington will cease working through the quad, as it does when it is keen to share out the blame for failure, and act alone (Interview, London March 2003).

Soft security therefore has its limits as a means of exerting global influence. Yet it remains the case that, often behind the scenes, and certainly with little, if any, political or public recognition, the EU has been both active and surprisingly effective in the foreign and security policy spheres. Clearly, it is extremely difficult to measure the effectiveness of such policies in terms of their impact on security, and particularly on Western security. Yet, as Javier Solana commented recently:

> as far as contemporary security is concerned, there is no standard 'unit of account'. How much additional security does an aircraft carrier bring? Is it more or less than spending the equivalent amount of money on peacekeeping or the reconstruction of failed states? Security today is a multi-dimensional concept. Bringing peace, stability and order is an effective way of 'draining the swamp'. Nation building is not for wimps, as we have found out in Afghanistan and as we will be reminded in Iraq. And Europe's security contribution and her ambitions are relevant and useful. (Solana, 2003)

The impact of Iraq

The Iraq conflict not only dominated headlines during the spring and early summer of 2003, but also had a profound effect on the EU's aspirations to become an influential global actor. In the first place, the crisis heightened fears, already prevalent in many parts of Western Europe, concerning the dangers of American unilateralism. Such fears have hardly been lessened by the rhetoric of the neo-conservative right in Washington, which criticized European weakness and painted the EU as a powerless actor in the face of American might (Kagan, 2003).

Moreover, sections of the American right not only encouraged the US administration to adopt a unilateralist approach to international affairs, but also propounded a policy of divide and rule towards the Europeans themselves. Certain right-wing commentators in the USA have propounded 'cherry picking' explicitly as an approach destined to maximize American influence while minimizing the constraints upon it. A striking feature of US policies towards Europe has been the willingness of the administration to promote divisions among Europeans on issues ranging from the International Criminal Court, where the administration placed heavy pressure on European states to sign bilateral agreements exempting US personnel from the jurisdiction of the court, to Iraq. At the annual Wehrkunde meeting in the spring of 2003, Secretary of Defence, Donald Rumsfeld, made a point of insisting that there were more differences among Europeans on Iraq than between the USA and Europe (*Financial Times*, 10 February 2003).

Not that outside intervention was necessary in order to foster divisions over Iraq among EU member states. Public differences between the major European players were marked and increasingly vitriolic in the build-up to war. Perhaps most significantly, the Iraq crisis drove a wedge between France and Britain. Immediately before the war, relations between London and Paris degenerated to an alarming degree. Each side clearly had a different agenda concerning transatlantic relations at a time when they appeared to be converging over the necessity to create an EU defence capability. It will take time to appreciate the full implications of the high degree of personal resentment generated by the crisis. What is clear is that the public falling out between the EU's two most powerful states militarily will almost certainly stymie developments in the sphere of ESDP, if only because it has reopened old divisions about whether ESDP has a 'Europeanist' or an 'Atlanticist' vocation (for a fuller discussion of this, see Menon and Lipken, 2003).

Constitutional reform

The Convention on the Future of Europe in 2002–2003, and the ensuing intergovernmental conference of 2003–2004, introduced another source of uncertainty concerning EU foreign and security policy, about which the debate in both forums focused on the twin issues of coherence and leadership. Multiple actors are involved in the formulation and implementation of the EU's foreign and security policies, including four Commissioners, several Council formations (above and beyond the General Affairs and External Relations Council), the Council presidency, and the High Representative. Perhaps inevitably, therefore, the Union is plagued with problems when it comes to ensuring the coherence of its actions in the international system. In an internal memo of June 2000, External Relations Commissioner Patten complained of an 'unresolved tension' between the intergovernmental and community methods in external relations, and that the creation of the High Representative's office had complicated EU foreign policy (*Financial Times*, 6 July 2000).

Indeed, certain aspects of external policies are characterized by multiple overlapping institutional jurisdictions. Thus, although they come under the formal authority of the High Representative, the EU's special representatives in international trouble-spots are financed from the Community budget. While civilian ESDP belongs in the Second Pillar (the

Common Foreign and Security Policy), the Commission paid for some 80 per cent of initial training for the civilian ESDP experts. Moreover, in the wake of the development of a civilian ESDP, the EU operated two different civil protection schemes concurrently, one under the Council and the other under the Commission.

Perhaps predictably, the Convention on the Future of Europe was dominated by the need for big ideas to rejuvenate the EU's international role. Consequently, it focused on the need for clear and effective leadership as a way of resolving the issue of coherence and making the EU a more effective presence on the international stage.

The perceived need to reform the rotating Presidency of the Council was a particular concern. According to Tony Blair, 'The [six-monthly rotation system] has reached its limits. It creates for Europe a weakness of continuity in leadership: a fatal handicap in the development of an effective Common Foreign and Security Policy. What's worse, each Presidency sees itself as setting its own distinctive agenda for the Union' (Blair, 2002). There is indeed reason to believe that successive presidencies have projected their own preferences on to the EU foreign policy agenda. From the Northern dimension favoured by the Finns, to the emphasis on Mediterranean characteristics by French and Spanish presidencies, this is hardly a new trend. Hence the desire to overcome the perceived deficiencies of the rotating presidency, while at the same time avoiding 'duplication' between the Council of Ministers, responsible for decisions concerning foreign and security policies, and the Commission, charged with other aspects of foreign policy, including crisis management (*European Voice*, 11 July 2002).

The problems with proposals in the draft constitution – to create a European foreign minster based simultaneously in the Council and the Commission, as well as a permanent European Council chair with some responsibility for representing the EU in the outside world – are manifold. Two in particular stand out. First, providing the European Council with a permanent chair, and the Council of Ministers with an input into the Commission via the new foreign minister, is bound to exacerbate tensions between the large and small member states. The small member states generally perceive moves towards greater intergovernmentalism not only as a direct attack on the Commission, which they see as their defender, but also as an attempt on the part of the big member states to create a directorate for foreign and security affairs. Tensions between the big and small member states came to the surface at a meeting of the European Council in October 2001, when Blair, Chirac and German Chancellor Gerhard Schröder held informal talks on Afghanistan an hour before the summit started, infuriating both the presidency and the Commission. More strikingly, they broke out openly on the occasion of a Downing Street dinner the following month when, initially uninvited, the prime ministers of Belgium (in the Council presidency), Italy, Spain and the Netherlands, as well as the High Representative, Solana, forced their way to the table (*The Economist*, 10 November 2001). Fostering such fears on the part of the small member states hardly helps in the quest for foreign policy consensus or effectiveness.

Second, it was obviously tempting politically for the Convention to come up with high profile institutional initiatives. However, doing so ran the risk of both undervaluing what had already been achieved and introducing gimmicks that played well domestically in the short term, but had few, or even negative, practical effects in Brussels. Certainly, the EU's institutional system is far from perfect. Yet much has been accomplished, as argued above, in the realms of foreign and security policy. And much of what has been accomplished – the judicious use of aid and trade, the use of soft security tools and so on – has been managed relatively effectively by the Commission. Moreover, alongside the Commission, the High Representative has, slowly but surely, begun to assume a higher profile and play a more important role. In June 2002, *Newsweek* claimed that 'quietly and almost unnoticed, Javier Solana has done the unthinkable. He has created a common European foreign policy'. This is doubtless overstated. Yet the fact remains that the jury is still out on the performance of the institutions created at Amsterdam and Nice for the conduct of EU foreign and security policy. Rushing to reform them before they became properly embedded, on the basis of judgements concerning their performance in a post-September 11 crisis that only one country in the world proved able to confront, smacked of the worst kind of shortsighted short-termism.

Conclusion

In only a decade the EU moved from being a new kid on the block in terms of foreign and security policy to being a high profile and surprisingly effective international actor. Certainly, the EU failed to match the ambitions of some of its most enthusiastic proponents. Certainly, too, the European public know next to nothing about what the EU really does in the international realm. For that reason, despite their potential and effectiveness to date, EU actions in this sphere were widely derided as failures as soon as the attacks of September 11 shook the world to its core. Yet even in the crises that succeeded the terrorist attacks in New York City and Washington, European states, and in certain instances the EU itself, responded rapidly and effectively.

The Convention on the Future of Europe and subsequent intergovernmental conference set out to make significant institutional changes to the

EU's foreign and security policy systems. In undertaking these reforms, Convention members and national government representatives were doubtless motivated by the laudable objective of enabling the EU to do more on the international stage. The danger, however, was that they would simply propose reforms for their own sake and, in the process, undermine a system that, to the surprise of many, has continued to function respectably in an ever more complex and ever more dangerous world.

Chapter 13

The European Union, the United States and Asia-Pacific: A New Trilateralism?

MICHAEL SMITH

In the external relations and policies of the European Union (EU), the links between the EU and the USA (on the one hand) and the EU and the Asia-Pacific countries (on the other) occupy a central place. At various times, analysts and policy-makers have discerned in these links a 'triangle of forces' around which much of the activity in the global economy and the global security system appear to revolve. During the late 1970s, the US administration spent much of its time developing strategies of 'trilateralism', both at the level of government policy and at the level of private networks among business and other communities. During the late 1980s and early 1990s, there was again a wave of interest in the competition between the European Community, the US and Asia-Pacific, based on the assumption that both the European and the Asian sides were becoming capable of competition with the USA (see, for example, Thurow, 1992).

During the 1990s, however, the expectation of increasing symmetry between the three 'poles' of international political and economic interaction was severely challenged. The USA seemed to emerge from the Cold War as the sole superpower, with no realistic rivals in the political and security spheres, and with a renewed economic vitality, which seemed to undermine the view of Europe and Asia as potential superpower rivals. In the meantime, German unification, halting progress towards eastern enlargement, and the management of conflict within Europe itself preoccupied the EU, while the states of East Asia found themselves confronted by a variety of political and economic setbacks, most notably the Asian financial crises of 1998 and after.

This chapter centres on the implications of these developments for the EU and its external policy-making. Among the significant partners and targets for EU external policies, the USA is the longest-standing and arguably the most important in all areas of policy-making. The challenge for the EU is how to manage a mature but deep and broad relationship,

237

which is heavily politicized and securitized, and engages almost every area of the EU's economic activities. Dealing with Asia is very different. It involves handling a dynamic emerging region characterized by great diversity and often political and economic fluidity. A study of recent developments in these relationships thus holds the promise of opening up central questions about the EU's role in the global arena and its capacity to form a cohesive and adaptable global strategy.

The chapter has two major sections. The first centres on the challenges posed for the EU by its relationships with the USA and the Asian countries, with the aim of identifying the key variables in the relationships, and EU attempts to handle them. The second emphasizes the development of EU policy during the past few years, with the aim of showing how the EU has met the central challenges and dealt with some of the key issues and policy dilemmas that have occurred. The conclusion explores the possible emergence of a 'new trilateralism' in EU relations with these two crucial partners and rivals.

Challenges for the EU

The first key challenge in dealing with the USA and with Asia-Pacific is that of handling relationships that exist at many levels and in almost all areas of EU activity. Table 13.1 shows the 'vital statistics' of these relationships, especially in economic terms. A number of key features are apparent. First, relations with the USA and Asia-Pacific constitute a very large part of the EU's international economic activity: trade with the USA remains the EU's single most important relationship, and constitutes a huge amount of bilateral exchange, much of it in areas where the EU competes directly with US producers. It also extends for beyond trade in goods to include the world's most important relationship in services trade (such as financial services, information services and so on).

Not only that, but the EU–US relationship is very extensive in terms of mutual investment: the EU is the single largest source of direct investment in the United States, and the United States is the single most important source of direct investment in the EU. The challenge that emerges from this intense interdependence is that of managing the inevitable disputes and conflicts that emerge while continuing to collaborate in order to gain maximum mutual benefit for the partners (Guay, 1999; McGuire and Smith, 2004, chs 1–2).

Economic exchange with the Asia-Pacific region is also a vital part of the EU's external relations, but it is very different from that with the USA. First, the intensification of economic relations with Asia-Pacific is more recent than that with the USA, and the pace of intensification has accelerated since

Table 13.1   The EU, the US and Asia-Pacific

Partner	Population (m 2002)	GDP per capita (euro 2002)	Trade in goods (bn euro 2002)		Trade in services (bn euro 2001)		FDI flows (bn euro 2001)	
			EU exp.	EU imp.	EU exp.	EU imp.	EU out	EU in
USA	288	38,609	238.7	174.2	116.8	120.8	107.9	82.1
ASEM	1,999	3,364	132	232	33	28	16.3	10.9
ASEAN	539	1,217	39	61	9.1	10.8	4.2	6.8
China	1,285	1,027	34.0	81.3	3.4	3.9	1.7	0.2
Japan	127	33,420	42.2	67.8	17.6	11.0	10.2	3.9

Source: http://european.eu.int/comm/trade/, June 2003.
Note: ASEM members: Brunei, Cambodia, Indonesia, Laos, Malaysia, Philippines, Singapore, Thailand, Vietnam, China, Japan, South Korea.
ASEAN members: Brunei, Cambodia, Indonesia, Laos, Malaysia, Myanmar, Philippines, Singapore, Thailand, Vietnam.

the 1980s. Second, the diversity of the economic relationship is much greater, reflecting the diversity of the Asia-Pacific partners: at one end of the spectrum the EU–Japan relationship is centred on trade in industrial goods and on investment; at the other end, the EU is engaged with other countries primarily in trade in raw materials and other commodities. A number of these partners fall into the 'less developed' category, and others fall into the 'rapidly developing' category, thus posing very different challenges for management and policy-making in the EU. Perhaps the most striking recent development is the rapid rise of China as a key economic partner for the EU, but also the fact that the EU trades at a loss with China, in the form of a large and continuing trade deficit (Dent, 1999).

The economic challenges of dealing with the USA and Asia-Pacific are very different, but are almost equally important for the EU. That has not always been true of the political challenges, however. From the start of European integration, the USA has been a constant and dominant political influence within the process. US support for the 'European project' began with the onset of the Cold War in the late 1940s, continued through the vicissitudes of European integration during the 1970s and 1980s, and was renewed with the collapse of the Soviet bloc and the Soviet Union itself in the early 1990s. At times, it appeared that the USA was not only an external political partner or patron for the European project but also almost part of the process itself. That led to friction and misunderstandings over the years, but whatever the tensions and conflicts, the political importance of the USA to European integration cannot be denied. Political changes in both the USA and Europe are therefore closely linked, with events on one side of the Atlantic often having a great impact on the other, not least because large numbers of Europeans and Americans have got 'under the skin' of their partners through the processes of investment and exchange outlined above (Peterson, 1996; Pollack and Shaffer, 2001).

Political connections with Asia-Pacific form a very different type of challenge for the EU and its member states. As can be seen from Table 13.1, Asia-Pacific (based on the definition adopted in this chapter) consists of ten very diverse countries, with very different histories and connections with the EU. Several of the countries have at various times been colonies of EU member states (for example, Indonesia is a former colony of the Netherlands, Vietnam of France, Malaysia of Britain); others have been dependent upon them economically and politically; and still others have been adversaries and even enemies in wartime or during the Cold War. Legacies of post-colonial conflicts, such as that in East Timor, persisted into the 1990s and beyond. Some became mixed up with issues such as Islamic fundamentalism, with direct and indirect implications for the EU (Smith, 1998a; Wiessala, 2002).

The political systems of many of these countries have also followed very different trajectories from those of the EU or the USA. This is not simply a question of institutional differences: there are also differences of values and political ideas that can have a strong cultural impact on political dealings (Wiessala, 2002). It is thus not surprising that, given the geopolitical difference between the EU and the Asia-Pacific region, there is a kind of political 'distance' between EU policy-makers and their Asia-Pacific counterparts that does not exist to the same degree with the USA (yet there is plenty of scope for misunderstanding and differences of opinion with Washington). In addition, whereas the EU's dealings with the USA can take for granted the Americans' capacity to act cohesively (whether Europeans like the results or not), the capacity of Asia-Pacific countries to develop such cohesiveness is in question. Diversity and distance greatly affect the possibility of a coherent EU–Asia-Pacific 'leg' to the EU–USA–Asia triangle.

Finally, the relationship between the EU and the USA has from the outset been very heavily securitized, in the sense that it has been linked with the patterns of military and political collaboration and competition growing out of the Cold War and its aftermath. One way of looking at the EU is to see it as part of the 'Cold War system' in the period before 1990, alongside the North Atlantic Treaty Organization (NATO). Not only did NATO carry part of the security burden for the EC's member states, but there was also a constant tension between what the Europeans wanted to do about security in the EC context and what they were able to do or allowed to do in the broader NATO context (Smith, 1984).

The tension has persisted in the post-Cold War period, although the context has changed. The enlargements of EU and NATO have been parallel processes, each with a different pace and rhythm. At the same time, the increased incidence of armed conflict within Europe itself has led to mutual entanglement of a much less 'tidy' kind between the EU and the USA; leading in turn to difficulties concerning the political management of security for the EU itself. There has also been a perpetual tension between the intimate entanglement of the EU and the USA in the defence of Europe, and the more fluid and politically sensitive issues arising from what used to be called 'out of area operations' – those falling outside the remit of NATO and involving broader issues of global security (Gompert and Larrabee, 1998).

Whereas the security relationship between the EU and the USA, whatever its ups and downs, has been intimate and compelling, that has not always been true of the EU's security interests in Asia-Pacific. The political 'distance' between the EU and Asia-Pacific is paralleled by a security 'distance' in which the Asia-Pacific countries are seen as a far-away and relatively insignificant concern for EU security policy-making (Maull *et al.*, 1998, ch. 4). Certain EU member states, because of their colonial history, are concerned directly about developments in certain Asia-Pacific countries, while others are relatively uninterested. There is nevertheless a general concern with stability and security in the Asia-Pacific region, often connected with the need for stable security arrangements as a prerequisite for the growth of trade and investment. As in other areas of EU relations with Asia-Pacific, the contrast with EU–US relations is one of depth, breadth and diversity.

A number of key aspects of the challenges posed for the EU by the USA and Asia-Pacific emerge from this broad picture. These can be summarized as follows:

- *The challenge of range and diversity.* Relationships between the EU and these two regions are shaped by historical variety, by different political processes and ideas, and by diversity of security concerns. The issue for the EU is how to manage the different demands and opportunities offered by this diversity and range, while the issue for the EU's partners and rivals is that of shaping a coherent set of expectations and policies towards 'Europe'.

- *The challenge of change.* Most obviously, relations between the EU, the USA and Asia-Pacific have been shaped by the end of the Cold War. This had a different impact in different areas, and was also accompanied by economic change and by domestic political change in both the USA and the Asia-Pacific region. Here, the issue for the EU is how to monitor and respond to these changes.

- *The challenge of resources and leverage.* As the result of diversity and change, the EU has been faced with questions about how it can respond to the demands and opportunities offered by relations with the USA and Asia-Pacific. This intersects with the internal development of the EU, and particularly the development of its 'foreign economic policy' and its foreign and security policies. What resources and strategies can the EU muster to pursue these relationships?

- *The challenge of institutions.* The EU has a strong preference in its external policy-making for negotiation and for institution building. Relations with the USA and Asia-Pacific raise important questions about how the EU can pursue negotiation and institution building on the one hand with the sole superpower and on the other hand with a diverse and dynamic collection of countries. How has the EU been able to pursue these processes, and with what success? Have the EU's partners and rivals entered fully into the building of institutions within the triangle?

- *The challenge of symmetry and asymmetry.* The EU is presented in its relations with the USA and the Asia-Pacific with two overarching sets of relationships, but within each of which is a range of different balances (economic, political, security) that have to be managed. Moreover, the engagement and commitment of EU member states in certain areas are likely to vary, giving added importance to the internal balance of views and interests. So there is an enormous burden on the EU in attempting to strike a balance between these pervasive and persistent asymmetries.

Recent developments

This section explores recent developments in economic, political and security relations. It aims to provide evidence from the past few years, as well as to show how the three areas of activity relate to the key features of the relationships, as already outlined. A key source for evidence in this and the following section is Allen and Smith (annual since 1993).

Economic relations

As has already been noted, the economic relationships between the EU and the USA and the EU–Asia-Pacific have seen important changes during the 1990s and beyond. The end of the Cold War was not just a political event; it had important economic repercussions as well. How has the EU responded, and what do its responses say about the nature of EU external policy-making?

In the case of EU–US relations, a number of key areas of economic tensions and dispute, and of attempts to underpin economic co-operation, can be discerned (Guay, 1999). The first, and historically the most persistent, concerns trade. During the late 1990s and early 2000s, EU–US trade – and trade disputes – continued to grow, but there have been some significant changes relating to how the tensions have been handled. Some trade disputes have had a very traditional flavour: for example, EU–US tensions over a range of agricultural trade issues have persisted since the 1960s.

The period since the later 1990s has seen a continuation of this trend, but also the addition of new factors. For example, a number of agricultural trade disputes are now really about food production and food safety. The US imposition of sanctions on the EU because of the EU's ban on the use of growth hormones in beef (on health and safety grounds) is one such case; others include the dispute about the EU's effective embargo on the introduction of genetically modified organisms into food production within the EU. The US imposition of tariffs on steel imports in 2002 triggered another apparently traditional trade dispute, against which not only the EU but also a range of other steel producing countries reacted very strongly. In the steel dispute, and other cases, the EU and the USA were both able to make use of the World Trade Organization (WTO), established in 1995, as a new and more powerful court of appeal on trade issues.

Some key trade issues with the USA were much less 'traditional'. For example, a dispute over so-called 'open skies' agreements between the USA and a range of European countries that aroused the opposition of the European Commission, which wanted to establish its competence in the area of air transport, began to be a significant point of contention during the later 1990s. Similarly, there has been a series of disputes surrounding EU and US regulatory policies, many of which appeared to have been entirely 'domestic' in origin but which affected firms on both sides of the Atlantic. For example, US legislation demanding changes in firms' accounting practices (the so-called Sarbanes–Oxley Bill) had important implications for accounting practices by European firms with US operations, and caused a sharp transatlantic dispute in 2002–2003. At the same time, the EU achieved a major victory in the WTO by getting the US tax treatment of multinational companies via so-called foreign sales corporations declared illegal, which entitled the EU to impose US$4 billion of sanctions on the USA. Not surprisingly, Brussels hesitated to deploy such a 'doomsday weapon' against Washington.

Although trade disputes form some of the most obvious examples of the EU–US 'adversarial partnership', other areas of economic activity have also been important. The investment relationship between the EU and the USA has continued to grow, to the extent that it is often difficult to say what is a 'European' or an 'American' company or product, which makes some of the trade disputes outlined above very difficult to handle. A host of firms on both sides of the Atlantic have a foot in both camps and an interest in avoiding the escalation of disputes or the breakdown of relationships. Many of them are actively involved in the Transatlantic Business Dialogue (TABD), established during the mid-1990s. Equally, there has been an intensification of technological competition between the EU and the USA, but this is often very difficult to see as a simple bilateral set of disputes. There has been a continuing dispute between the Americans and the Europeans over the trade in large civil aircraft (essentially between Boeing and Airbus), but in many cases the growth of transnational production processes means that Boeing and Airbus aircraft are 'international', with large proportions of their components coming from either the EU or the USA.

Finally, in this area of 'competitive cooperation' (Smith, 1998b), two great events in contemporary European integration have affected EU–US economic relations. First, the introduction of the euro brought about a situation in which there are now, in effect, two 'world currencies': the dollar remains predominant, but after a shaky start the euro has become in many respects a real alternative. This has caused some EU–US tensions, notably over the management of international currencies and membership of international financial institutions. More important, perhaps, it represents the early stages of a potentially major shift in international monetary power. At the same time, the process of EU enlargement has generated EU–US economic friction; for example, over the potential diversion of trade from central and eastern European markets or over the treatment of US investment in the new member states. Each previous enlargement necessitated adjustment of trade and other relationships with the USA. The enlargement taking place in 2004 is no exception.

The intensity of transatlantic economic relations means that there is a strong incentive for policy-makers to develop mechanisms to manage them. At the bilateral level, the key mechanism is the New Transatlantic Agenda of 1995, which encompasses areas of political as well as economic partnership. The Transatlantic Economic Partnership of 1999 developed this further in some areas of economic activity. A number of early-warning and other mechanisms for handling specific conflicts have also been put in place.

Apart from their bilateral dealings, the EU and the USA play a central role in managing the world economy. This has been especially evident in recent years, as the WTO began to have a major impact on international trade. The EU and the USA are key players in the handling of trade disputes under the WTO and in the generation of momentum behind world trade negotiations. In contrast, disagreement between them can imperil the future of the world trading system and severely damage third parties. The EU and the USA therefore played a major part in launching the so-called Doha Development Round of international trade negotiations in 2001, but a wide range of disputes between them, especially over agricultural subsidies, imperilled prospects for the success of the negotiations (see Chapter 11).

EU–US economic relations are broad, intense and difficult to manage, yet highly institutionalized – qualities that have become even more apparent in recent years. What can be said in comparison about EU–Asia Pacific economic relations? A key feature, especially apparent recently, has been their unevenness (Dent, 1999; Wiessala, 2002). The EU and its member states have widely differing relationships with the Asia-Pacific countries, covering both trade and investment. One of the most important of them is with China, the most rapidly growing of all the EU's trade relationships. Inevitably, there has been a series of disputes about the terms on which trade is carried out and the ways in which it might be managed. China has been a major target of EU anti-dumping cases, and a range of European industries and member states have demanded defensive measures.

Nevertheless, the threat from 'Chinese' products is tempered by the fact that they are made under licence on behalf of EU companies. The major thrust of EU efforts in relation to China has been towards the creation of institutional and other frameworks for the handling of trade and investment, at bilateral, interregional and multilateral levels.

By comparison with the EU's 'China problem', which has intensified in recent years, the EU's 'Japan problem' has retreated into the background (Gilson, 2000). Whereas in the early 1990s there was a kind of paranoia in some EU circles about the methods used by the Japanese to gain access to the European market, this issue became manageable and less significant. This is because the EU established a continuing dialogue with Tokyo, encompassing a number of areas of industrial and technological co-operation as well as co-operation on a number of more political issues. EU concern about Japan has also retreated into the background because of two developments: first, the increasing tendency of Japanese producers (for example, in the motor industry) to invest in the EU and produce there; and second, the stagnation of the Japanese economy in general, which has made it a less dynamic (though still formidable) competitor for the EU. Some of the same assessment can be applied to the EU's relations with South Korea, although there are still several important areas of dispute with Seoul, such as that over subsidies for the shipbuilding industry.

Other Asia-Pacific trade and economic partnerships are clearly less significant in quantitative terms than those with China, Japan and Korea, but they have been a continuing focus of EU attention in recent years, partly for political reasons. For example, the imposition of trade and other sanctions on some South-East Asian countries, and the development of economic partnerships with others, has been a continuing theme. As a result, the EU's economic presence in South-East Asia has become more salient and more heavily institutionalized in recent years. This has been alongside an active EU strategy for the development of interregional economic partnership.

Central to this effort has been a series of bilateral agreements (for example, with China), as well as an EU effort to relate to the Asia-Pacific countries as a group. A long-standing agreement between the EU and the members of the Association of South-East Asian Nations (ASEAN) formed the core of a wider initiative in the mid- and late 1990s to establish an institutional framework for EU–Asia-Pacific relations through the Asia–Europe Meeting (ASEM). The first such meeting took place in 1996 in Bangkok, and subsequent meetings have taken place every two years, alternating between European and Asian locations. Although these meetings have been criticized as lacking in substance, they have been accompanied by the development of a large infrastructure for EU–Asia-Pacific relations (see Figure 13.1), which at least potentially constitutes the basis

Figure 13.1   *Institutional arrangements between the EU, the USA and Asia-Pacific (selected)*

Partner	Arrangements	Notes
USA	1990 Transatlantic Delaration 1990> Networks of co-operation in areas such as anti-trust, biotechnology, etc. 1990> EC(EU)–US summits (biannual, later annual) 1995 New Transatlantic Agenda and Action Plan 1995> Public–private dialogues (Business, Legislative, Labour, Environment) 1999 Transatlantic Economic Partnership	Bilateral EU–US institutions supplemented by sectoral dialogues, public–private partnerships, specialized agreements – for example, on 'earlywarning' for trade disputes, mutual recognition. Importance of World Trade Organization (WTO) as a framework for disputes and co-operation. Significance of NATO and security co-operation involving EU member states.
Asia-Pacific	1980 EC–ASEAN Agreement (links to ASEAN Regional Forum (from 1994) and other bodies) 1991 EU–Japan Declaration (industrial dialogues, etc.) 1996 ASEM (biennial) Bilateral Partnership and Co-operation Agreements (e.g. with China, including specialized dialogues)	Diversity of interregional and bilateral arrangements, relatively 'light' institutionalization in many areas, indirect relationships with security issues, persistence of EU member states' 'special relationships' with historic partners/ex-colonies. Importance of WTO as a channel for the handling disputes and generation of rules.

for a continuing and deepening partnership. Yet this partnership is by no means as robust as that between the EU and the USA, especially as the impact of Asian financial instability and other difficulties in the late 1990s slowed down the process of institutionalization and co-operation.

Political relations

Although the foundations of both EU–US and EU–Asia-Pacific relations have primarily been economic, there has been a consistent and continuing trend towards the politicization of the relationships. In other words, it has been impossible to insulate the economic relations from the broader impact of political change. Three political issues, in particular, have affected the EU's role in the world, and therefore its dealings with the USA and the Asian-Pacific countries: the exercise of leadership, the impact of change, and the impact of values in areas such as human rights and global development.

In relation to the USA, the EU has experienced a continuing and intensifying set of tensions over political leadership. The evolution of the EU's Common Foreign and Security Policy (CFSP) during the mid-1990s, accompanied since the late 1990s by the emergence of the European Security and Defence Policy (ESDP), has generated a good deal of friction over leadership in the Western alliance. For example, over whether the EU or European members of NATO should have a more substantial role in determining strategy (Sloan, 2003). Moreover, the changing of the political guard in the USA, with the installation of the Bush Administration in 2001, was a further source of friction. During the early part of the new century, Europeans have increasingly protested US unilateralism and the Bush Administration's determination to use its new-found dominance in the world arena. For their part, Americans have complained about the Europeans' inability or unwillingness to confront thorny political problems.

Three examples illustrate these trends. First, there have been continual tensions between the USA and many EU member states over the treatment of 'rogue regimes', especially after the USA proclaimed the 'axis of evil' (Iraq, Iran and North Korea). At the same time, the EU has confronted the USA on the subject of global environmental change, most clearly in the transatlantic conflict over the ratification and implementation of the Kyoto Convention on global climate change, but also in a series of issues linking environmental and development policies. Finally, the EU and the USA have been at odds over questions of international order and justice, not only over human rights but also over institutional issues such as the introduction of the International Criminal Court (ICC). In each of these areas, the USA's assumption of a unilateral right to leadership (or to independent action) came up against the EU's preference for negotiation and dialogue as a means of resolving international disputes.

As a result, the EU and the USA have experienced continual problems recently over the handling of political change and the application of political ideas and values. Some people have argued that, unlike the economic sphere, the realm of political ideas and institutions has seen a fundamental divergence between the EU and the USA since the late 1990s. On one side of the Atlantic, there is the assumption of leadership and the unilateral right to apply American power, while on the other, there is the reliance on institution building, negotiation and dialogue. One position reflects Europe's essential weakness; the other America's overwhelming strength in key areas of international power (Kagan, 2003; Kaldor, 2003).

For the EU, the impact of Washington's approach has at times been disabling and divisive. Whereas the British are generally pro-American, the French and Germans are generally more sceptical or cautious of the implications of US leadership. As noted by Anand Menon in Chapter 12, US unilateralism has had a negative effect on the development of the CFSP and the ESDP, and has thrown into doubt the ability of the EU itself to exercise 'hard power' rather than simply diplomatic co-ordination. There is also a basic difference between the American approach to human rights, which sees them as an instrument of foreign policy, and the European approach, which is based on the universality of conceptions of justice. Similar differences pertain to global development policy.

If the problem with the USA in recent years has been that of handling a dominant power, the problem with Asia-Pacific has been that of engaging with a fluid and rapidly changing region (Wiessala, 2002). Although the issue of leadership is certainly important within the Asia-Pacific region, and EU policies are shaped at least partly by the implicit triangular competition with the USA, the political context is far less settled. As noted above, in the early 1990s the EU was preoccupied with the economic challenges posed by Japan, and to a certain extent Korea; and these in turn were part of a broader challenge from the so-called 'Asian tiger' economies of South-Eeast and East Asia.

Yet this economic challenge was embedded in a wider sense of political difference: the 'Asian model' of modernization and development embodied values and political practices significantly different from the assumed liberal democracy of the EU and the USA (Smith, 1998a; Wiessala, 2002). So the challenge of political difference was felt broadly in the EU, primarily but not exclusively in the sphere of economic competition. This challenge was all the more substantial because development policy is a key source of 'soft power' for the EU, and a source of tension with the USA. Issues such as human rights became, during the 1990s, part of the EU's agenda for dealing with East and South-East Asian regimes. Although this was not a major problem in the case of Japan, or even South Korea, the politics of South-East Asia posed a series of dilemmas for the EU and its member states. To a large degree, these centred on Myanmar (formerly Burma), where the EU imposed an economic boycott. This caused two problems. First, a number of European companies saw opportunities for investment in Myanmar and ways to circumvent the sanctions. Second, the predominant feeling among South-East Asian regimes was that Myanmar should be treated as a regional problem and not seen as an acid test for the modernization of the region as a whole at the global level.

A number of other problems of political order and disorder were also characteristic of the late 1990s and early 2000s. The EU inevitably was engaged – because of former links and economic and political interests in stability – in the conflicts that occurred in Indonesia, Cambodia and elsewhere. For example, the conflicts that led to the independence of East Timor engaged the interest of the EU in general, but specifically of Portugal, the ex-colonial power, and of others with links to Indonesia, such as the Dutch. But much of the EU's leverage in such cases was indirect and often exercised through the concerns of specific member states. The EU clearly preferred multilateral solutions via the United Nations (UN), whereas the USA appeared to prefer bilateral pressure and the (albeit distant) threat of force or coercion. Political fluidity and tensions also fed into EU–Asia-Pacific relations at a more general level, shaping the capacity of the Asia-Pacific countries to enter into a collective partnership with the EU.

The key emerging political issues in EU–Asia-Pacific relations during recent years, though, have been linked to China. As previously noted, the emergence of China as an economic great power, and efforts to draw it into the multilateral system through the WTO and other institutions, was a central preoccupation of the EU in the late 1990s. This was also linked with a range of often agonising political problems, especially relating to human rights. The late 1980s had seen major tensions in this area, which came to a head with the events in Beijing's Tienanmen Square and the subsequent repression of reforming and democratic movements. Throughout the 1990s and into the 2000s, the EU has sought a practical balance between its commercial interests in the fast-emerging Chinese market and its broader system of values, which sees the Chinese state as a cause of political concern. The EU's concern mirrors that of the USA, which has maintained pressure on China in respect of human rights, but which also has a key set of commercial interests (not to mention broader interests in regional security) to defend. The EU maintains a strong and growing political relationship with China, linked to commercial relations in the EU–China Partnership and Co-operation Agreement, but these tensions remain at the centre of its Asia-Pacific policies.

The political dimension of the EU's relationships with the USA and Asia Pacific thus demonstrates not only the difference between the two sets of strategic partners, but also some of the ways in which the two sets of relationships intersect. For the EU, the problem of balancing commercial interests and political values, of engaging in a triangular game of 'competitive co-operation' with the USA in the Asia-Pacific region, and of coping with the changing nature and priorities of 'the only superpower', are major political challenges for the twenty-first century.

Security relations

Much of the foregoing review implies that global security is one of the most dynamic and difficult challenges facing the EU in the twenty-first century. This broad concern is often linked to issues much closer to home, through the politics and economics of the 'new Europe'. This section focuses on the changing nature of these challenges and how they have affected the EU's relations with the USA and Asia-Pacific.

Security considerations have had a long-standing and central role in EU–US relations. Simply put, the EU–US relationship has always been heavily securitized. This has had profound implications both for the development of European integration and for the handling of change in the wider Europe (Peterson, 1996; Smith and Woolcock, 1993). During the 1990s and early 2000s, several new and profoundly important elements have been added to this mix. The USA has emerged as the incontestable military leader in the international arena, with global engagements and with an unmatched (perhaps unmatchable) technological and logistical advantage over its potential challengers. But at the same time, America's global engagement has contributed to a heightened sense of vulnerability arising from the potential global risks to which the world's sole superpower might be exposed.

The result has been a volatile mixture of supremacy and perceived risk from which Europe has not been immune. The development of a more explicit and institutionalized foreign and security policy, and especially of the ESDP, inevitably brought the EU into collision with the development of US policies (including those conducted within the NATO context). Surrounding both the EU and the USA was a global security complex in which the traditional instruments of military might were not always the key to success: new areas of economic security, environmental security and what has been called 'societal security' have created new challenges and the potential for effective security measures through non-military means (McGuire and Smith, 2004; Sloan, 2003).

The most direct security encounters between the EU and the USA during the late 1990s occurred over the Balkans. Here was a region, bordering the EU and touching on the vital interests of a number of member states, in political and ethnic turmoil. The Balkan wars exposed the limits of the EU's security role, with the Dayton agreement of 1995 symbolizing what the EU could not do, and what the USA could through the mobilization of military force. In 1999, the Kosovo crisis again exposed the limits of EU security and crisis management capabilities, with NATO being the key instrument for the co-ordination of military action.

But Kosovo also prompted a number of European initiatives for a more decisive security role. First, it produced the Stability Pact for South-Eastern Europe, which linked bilateral Stability and Association Agreements for Balkan states with the promise of eventual EU membership (and membership has always had a potent security dimension). Second, the EU's role in post-conflict reconstruction, already apparent in Bosnia, was underlined; to this was added the possibility of EU management of stabilization efforts involving a military presence, as the ESDP produced more tangible commitments of military forces by member states. Indeed, the perceived failure in Kosovo was a key stimulus to the further development of the ESDP, starting with the St. Malo declaration in 1998 and building rapidly as the conflict unfolded.

By the year 2000, when conflict erupted in the Former Yugoslav Republic of Macedonia, the EU was arguably in a stronger position than ever to make its presence felt: the Macedonian government was in the process of negotiating its Stability and Association Agreement, and the EU could use its newly developed security instruments to offer a stabilization force. As a result, by 2003 the EU was leading the stabilization effort there. For some, this heralded a new division of labour in European security, accompanied as it was by the enlargement of the EU and of NATO towards Central and Eastern Europe.

Such a division of labour was far more difficult to find in the broader development of global security. Here, the defining episode was the terrorist attacks in New York and Washington on 11 September 2001. These underlined sharply the tension in US policies between supremacy and vulnerability, and led directly to the proclamation of the 'war on terror,' including a conventional conflict in Afghanistan, which emphasized the USA's potential for global power projection, and in which a number of EU member states (notably Britain) participated. The limits of the EU in the military sphere were again exposed; so were the divisions among member states over appropriate diplomatic and other responses. As such, the conflict was a major challenge for the CFSP and the emerging ESDP (see Chapter 12).

Yet in some respects war played to the EU's strengths. It linked closely to the new issues of economic security and produced a major effort in the sharing of intelligence, in police and judicial co-ordination, and in other areas under the rubric of Justice and Home Affairs (see Chapter 10). One effect was to intensify the interactions between the EU and US authorities. Another was to highlight new roles for the EU in the evolving security area, in sharp contrast to the initially marginal role of NATO, which the USA pointedly ignored when presented with the opportunity for collective action under Article 5 of the North Atlantic Treaty.

Whereas the war on terror and the search for Al-Qaida in Afghanistan and elsewhere presented new opportunities for the EU in its relations with the USA, the same could not be said for the ensuing conflict in Iraq. Throughout the 1990s, the aftermath of the 1991 Gulf War saw the USA and Britain engaged in ongoing military activity while multilateral sanctions through the UN were imposed on Saddam Hussein's regime. The EU and its other leading member states pursued a more equivocal policy, stressing the need for multilateral action as well as in some cases pursuing commercial activities relating to the oil industry. This was linked to the broader EU stance on other conflicts in the Middle East, notably between Israel and the Palestinians, which tended to stress 'constructive engagement' rather than confrontation. The EU also adopted a policy of 'critical dialogue' with Iran, which contrasted significantly with America's portrayal of Iran as possibly the 'next Iraq'.

As a result, the Bush Administration's determination to tackle Saddam

Hussein was a recipe for splits and tensions within the EU. Britain immediately and consistently aligned itself with the USA, albeit stressing the need for action within a multilateral framework and the need for a link to the Israel–Palestine dispute. But as time went on, the French and the Germans in particular become confirmed opponents of what appeared to be an increasingly unilateral US policy. In late 2002, this tension centred on the UN Security Council and the need for an authorizing resolution to justify the use of force; by the spring of 2003, however, it was clear that the USA and Britain were prepared to go ahead regardless. This led to a major split in the EU and to the marginalization of collective European efforts as the Americans and British organized for and undertook an attack on Iraq. Despite a strong effort to re-establish a collective EU position after the war, with the EU closely involved in discussions about humanitarian assistance, it was not clear that the rebuilding of confidence would be easy or rapid. The implications for the broader development of the EU's security and defence roles were unclear yet bound to be far-reaching, involving potential further clashes about Iran and the Palestinian–Israeli conflict.

One of the implications of the globalization of risk and security referred to above was that the EU's relations with Asia-Pacific would also become securitized, even if only by reference to the impact of US policies and actions. The impact of the war on terror was felt in South-West Asia or the South Asian sub-continent (where it intersected with the conflict between India and Pakistan, two nuclear powers) as well as permeating. In a number of areas where the EU or its member states had significant historical or commercial interests, there was the threat of disorder, of 'regime change' and of broader impacts on the trading environment. Thus, in Indonesia, which was a focus of conflict (for example, over East Timor) during the late 1990s, and which then felt the force of Muslim fundamentalism (for example, through the Bali bombing of 2002 and the rebellion in Aceh province), the EU had important historical connections through the Dutch and a range of significant economic interests.

In other areas of South-East Asia, there was a less specific but none the less important EU interest in regional stability. This found expression both through EU contacts with ASEAN (particularly in the context of the ASEAN Regional Forum) and in the ASEM process. There was also an EU engagement in the affairs of the Korean peninsula, where the nuclear threat from North Korea constituted a continuing element in both commercial and political dealing. The EU was engaged in efforts to contain and neutralize the North Korean threat via the Korean Peninsula Energy Development Organization (KEDO), but the limits of the EU's role were again exposed when the North Koreans denounced this arrangement and threatened to reactivate their nuclear weapons programme.

It is clear from this account that the EU has at best had only an indirect role in the conflicts that have emerged in Asia-Pacific, given its political and strategic distance from the region. But that indirect role can none the less be important, providing a diplomatic voice for European interests and a contribution to regional stability (Wiessala, 2002). Can it (or should it) be developed to give the EU a more concrete involvement in 'hard security' in the Asia-Pacific theatre? The posing of such a question points back again to the ways in which the EU's security policies have developed, both in the area of 'soft security' and in the deployment of limited 'hard security' measures. But it also points to the key contrast between the roles of the USA and the EU in the post-Cold War global security system.

Conclusion

This chapter identified a number of key challenges concerning the EU's links with the USA and Asia-Pacific. EU–US and EU–Asia-Pacific relations involve challenges of *range and diversity*. These are expressed in very different ways in each relationship, but are crucial to the evolution of EU policies and institutions. Has the EU been able to handle this diversity and to reconcile member state's interests with the demands of collective action? Has it been more effective in doing this in areas of economic or political activity than in areas of security policy?

This is accompanied by the challenges of *change* and of *resources and leverage*. Does the evidence assembled here show that the EU has developed and mobilized resources appropriate to the challenges posed by change (economic, political, security) in these two arenas, or does it show that there is a long way to go before the EU can fully meet the challenges of either, or both? This in turn is reflected in the challenge of *institutions*: both within the EU itself and around these two relationships there has been a persistent problem of institutional capacity and development, which has not been resolved. Do the current institutional arrangements enable key issues to be handled effectively? Where they do not, what would be necessary in order to resolve this issue, or should the EU even try to resolve it?

This leads finally to the challenge of *symmetry and asymmetry*: the evidence shows clearly that the EU has to handle multiple imbalances in these two relationships and that these multiple imbalances often intersect (for example, in dealing with issues of human rights, or the war against terror, or the building of global economic institutions). Has the EU succeeded in managing these multiple imbalances? If not, what would be needed to act as the foundation for more effective management?

Given the EU's uncertain political situation, such questions will inevitably remain unresolved, at least for the foreseeable future. The relationship with the USA has always been at the centre of the integration project; as the EU's most significant other, the USA will continue to be a constant but constantly changing point of reference. The relationship with Asia-Pacific poses key questions about the EU's ability to link commercial interests with political and security problems, and to adapt to a dynamic and diverse region. Recent EU activities demonstrate clearly the challenges and the constraints on the EU's responses, but they also demonstrate the distance that the EU travelled during the late 1990s and early 2000s. The EU finds itself positioned between East and West in the new trilateralism of the early twenty-first century, but in an increasingly complicated and interconnected world, in which its growing presence and leverage create as many problems as they solve.

Policy Towards the Extended Frontier: The Balkans and the Newly Independent States

JOHN VAN OUDENAREN

The enlargement to include Central and Eastern Europe in 2004 brought the European Union into direct and extended contact with two potentially unstable regions: the Western Balkans (Albania, Bosnia and Herzegovina, Croatia, the Former Yugoslav Republic of Macedonia (FYROM), and the federation of Serbia and Montenegro) and the newly independent states (NIS) of the former Soviet Union. Both regions present danger and opportunity for EU external policy. Both are also capable of generating spillover effects that include terrorism, cross-border organized crime, narcotics trafficking, direct migration, transit migration from other regions, transmission of HIV/AIDS and other infectious diseases, environmental degradation, and the proliferation of conventional and nuclear, chemical and biological weapons.

Failure to address these problems would have direct implications for the security and prosperity of the EU, in particular for the new member states of Central and Eastern Europe. Instability in the Balkans and the NIS also could damage the credibility of the EU's Common Foreign and Security Policy (CFSP), which has set the creation of a stable and prosperous 'wider Europe' as one of its key priorities. Conversely, by addressing the problems of these regions successfully, the EU can develop new markets and trading partners for itself, as well as prove the effectiveness of its CFSP in a way that will lay down the foundation for a stronger role in the international system beyond Europe.

While the Balkans and the NIS present similar challenges to the EU, and call for similar policy responses in many areas, there are also crucial differences between the two regions, in particular with regard to long-term membership prospects. Eventual expansion to the Western Balkans has been implicit in the logic of EU enlargement since the Copenhagen summit of June 1993, when the EU elaborated its accession criteria. With Greece already a member, and Bulgaria, Romania and Slovenia accepted as candidates in the mid-1990s, this subregion in effect became an enclave surrounded by current and future member states, which for practical and political reasons would be invited to join the EU at some point. The problem for EU policy has been to relate the long-term logic of eventual EU accession to the short- and medium-term challenge of dealing with a region characterized by war, ethnic hatred and cross-border crime. The NIS, in contrast, have not been accepted by the EU as candidates for membership – a situation that some of these countries (notably Ukraine) resent, but is not likely to change in the foreseeable future. The challenge for EU policy with regard to these countries has therefore been to develop forms of co-operation that fall short of membership but that none the less are 'privileged' in some sense, and that address the economic and political challenges and opportunities that these countries present to the EU.

This chapter examines EU policy towards these crucial regions, focusing on the implications for enlargement. It examines first the Western Balkans, and then the NIS. The latter are, in turn, broken into three subgroups: Russia, a country that is historically European but is probably too large and diverse to be considered for EU membership; Moldova, Ukraine and Belarus, smaller countries that border an enlarged EU that could at some point be considered for membership; and the countries of central Asia and the Caucasus, which traditionally are culturally and geographically closer to Asia and the Middle East, and generally are not regarded as potential candidates for EU membership. A concluding section evaluates the effectiveness of EU policy towards these regions, and its possible implications for an enlarged EU.

The Balkans

European Union policy in the Balkans in recent years has made a slow but as yet incomplete recovery from the disasters of the early 1990s, when it declared prematurely that it could handle the developing crisis in its own backyard, only to fall into intra-European squabbling and a severe transatlantic political crisis as the region descended into a series of wars that the EU was powerless to stop. With the civil wars that followed the break-up of the former Yugoslavia finally over, the EU has begun the task of integrating these countries into a wider Europe in preparation for eventual accession. This, in turn, requires that problems of crime and corruption are dealt with, and the weakness of civil society and domestic institutions are overcome.

A turning point in EU policy towards the region was the November 1995 Dayton General Agreement on Peace for Bosnia and Herzegovina which, even as it highlighted American military and political predominance in the

1990s, established the groundwork for the EU to bring into play its strengths in aid, trade and integration with the rest of Europe. In the Dayton negotiations, the European members of the Contact Group insisted that the civilian administrator for Bosnia be a European, thus counterbalancing US command of the NATO-led Implementation Force (IFOR). The post of High Representative established by Dayton has since been filled by a succession of prominent Europeans, beginning with former Swedish Prime Minister Carl Bildt (Neville-Jones, 1996, p. 50). The EU also took the lead in post-war economic reconstruction. Before 1995, EU assistance to Bosnia, although considerable, had been confined almost exclusively to humanitarian aid provided by the European Community Humanitarian Office (ECHO). Following Dayton, Brussels incorporated Bosnia into the PHARE programme, allocating €890.7 million for the 1996–2000 period. The EU as such did not participate in IFOR, but EU member states, led by France and Britain, provided about half of the 60,000-person force that entered Bosnia, with the USA and various non-NATO European countries contributing the rest. Even as troop deployments remained a NATO and national responsibility, the CFSP began to play a modest role in the Balkans, notably in Mostar, where the EU administration of the city, formally agreed upon by the Council of Ministers in May 1994, was one of the first Joint Actions carried out under the Second Pillar of the Maastricht Treaty.

Post-Dayton EU policy toward the Western Balkans was based on two general principles: regionalism and conditionality. In October 1996, the Council adopted a strategy document entitled *Future Contractual Relations with Some Countries of South-Eastern Europe* that outlined post-Dayton objectives for the region, including the promotion of political stability and economic prosperity, political and economic reforms, and respect for human rights, minority rights and democratic norms (Vukadinovic, 2001, pp. 447–9). The document linked progress in relations between the EU and the five Western Balkan countries with the strengthening of relations between these countries and their neighbours. The regional approach was resented by Croatia, which had hopes, based on its higher level of economic development, and cultural and geographic proximity to the EU, of relatively early accession, following the path blazed by neighbouring Slovenia. Conditionality was made a pillar of EU policy by a decision of the European Council in April 1997, when the EU declared that it would intensify relations with partner countries to the degree that those countries met both certain general policy principles and various country-specific conditions. Taken together, regionalism and conditionality were intended to stabilize the entire Western Balkan region by encouraging all of its component parts to work together in a way that had been completely absent since the collapse of Yugoslavia.

EU policy was only partly successful, however, in that it was unable to halt the drift towards yet another Balkan conflict, this time in Kosovo. The crisis first arose in March 1998 with the violent Serb crackdown on Kosovar resistance. Efforts by the Contact Group (comprising of EU member states France, Germany, Italy and Britain, along with Russia and the USA) to defuse the crisis through negotiation led to the convening in February 1999 of the Rambouillet conference under the formal chairmanship of the British and French foreign ministers. Negotiations with the Serbs and Kosovars were conducted by a triumvirate of the USA, Russia and the EU (represented by an Austrian, Wolfgang Petritsch). These negotiations were not successful, however, and their failure soon led to the NATO bombing campaign that compelled the Serbs to withdraw from Kosovo.

The EU played an important role in the negotiations that ended the war, and established a transitional post-war order for Kosovo. In May 1999, the EU designated Finnish president, Martii Ahtisaari, as the EU special envoy for Kosovo, and he worked with his US and Russian counterparts to broker the deal with Serbian president, Slobodan Milosevic, to end the war. The EU was also given a prominent and formally recognized role in the post-war reconstruction. UN Security Council Resolution 1244 established the United Nations Interim Administration in Kosovo (UNMIK), which in turn was divided into four 'pillars' with different functional responsibilities. The Humanitarian Assistance pillar was led by the UN High Commissioner for Refugees; the Civil Administration pillar by the UN itself; the Democracy and Institution pillar by the Organization for Security and Co-operation in Europe (OSCE); and the Reconstruction and Economic Development pillar by the EU. The EU quickly responded to the cessation of the NATO bombing campaign with a large package of aid intended to assist with the return of refugees and cope with the looming hardships of the approaching Balkan winter.

Along with the immediate response in Kosovo, the 1999 crisis gave a new impetus to broader EU regional policy toward the Western Balkans and prompted a new discussion about eventual accession. Hit by the economic costs of the war and the huge refugee flows from Kosovo, Albania and the FYROM sought an accelerated timetable for EU (and NATO) membership. The EU turned aside this request as unreasonable (given the low level of economic and political development in these countries), but responded by further developing its regional approach. In June 1999, the EU launched the Stability Pact for South-Eastern Europe and offered to negotiate Stabilization and Association Agreements (SAAs) with all the south-east European countries in the context of the pact. A kind of pre-pre-accession arrangement, the SAAs were to emphasize regional co-operation, democratization, capacity building and trade liberalization, both with the EU and intraregionally. The EU concluded a SAA with FYROM in April 2001, with Croatia in October 2001, and began negotiations with Albania in late 2002.

In December 2000, the Council established the Community Assistance for Reconstruction, Development and Stabilization (CARDS) programme as the primary means to implement the objectives of the Stabilization and Association Process. For the period 2000–2006, CARDS provided €4,650 million in grant aid for investment, institution building and other measures aimed at achieving four objectives: reconstruction, democratic stabilization and the return of refugees; institutional and legislative development, including harmonization with EU norms and approaches; structural reform and sustainable economic and social development; and promotion of closer regional co-operation among the SAP countries, and between *them* and the current and other prospective members of the EU. The Union also granted preferential access to its internal market for the SAP countries from late 2001.

As the EU's presence, and influence, in the region has grown, attention has shifted to forward-looking policies aimed at heading off crises, rather than responding after the fact, as happened in the 1990s. A case in point was the successful effort by CFSP High Representative Javier Solana in August 2001 to broker the Ohrid Framework Agreement to defuse escalating inter-ethnic conflict in FYROM. The EU used the offer of assistance under the Stability Pact and a long-term membership perspective to pressure and cajole all sides into accepting internal constitutional and political compromises. Solana also worked to head off a unilateral declaration of independence from Yugoslavia by Montenegro, and to reconstitute a loose Serbian–Montenegrin federation in which Montenegrin demands for autonomy and Serbian claims of sovereignty could be balanced, at least temporarily.

With the emphasis on crisis management and prevention, the Western Balkans has become the key laboratory and testing ground for the European Security and Defence (ESDP) component of CFSP. In 2002, EU member states were providing some 36,000 troops (or 80 per cent of the total number of peacekeeping forces) in the region, along with the largest number of civilian police, most of them under NATO command. The conclusion in December 2002 of the long-delayed agreement between the EU and NATO over the use of NATO assets for EU operations cleared the way for the EU to take over from NATO its first major out-of-area mission, Operation *Concordia*, in Macedonia, on 1 April 2003. The EU also signalled its willingness to assume responsibility for Bosnia. On 15 January 2003, the European Union Police Mission (EUPM) in Bosnia-Herzegovina was officially inaugurated, becoming the first civilian crisis management operation under the CFSP. Comprising 500 police officers and 300 international and local civilian staff, EUPM is charged with help-ing Bosnia-Herzegovina to develop its own police force to European standards. Taking responsibility for all peacekeeping in Bosnia, a far more ambitious task, was next on the list. In February 2003, the EU foreign ministers endorsed a UK–French position paper outlining a 'seamless transition' from NATO's Stabilization Force (SFOR) to an EU peacekeep-ing force by early 2004.

The EU faces daunting long-term challenges in the Balkans. The poten-tial for instability in the region was highlighted by the assassination, in March 2003, of the reform-minded prime minister of Serbia, Zoran Djinjic. Bosnia remains an international protectorate, making slow progress on such challenges as economic development, refugee return, and political and constitutional reform. In Kosovo, another protectorate, the question of final status cannot be deferred indefinitely. Independence for Montenegro will also return to the agenda as the interim agreement comes to an end. Meanwhile, Croatia formally submitted an application to join the EU in February 2003, thereby signalling its continued impa-tience with the regional approach and its desire, underpinned by its better economic performance and more central location, to separate itself from the rest of the region. Member states noted, however, that Croatia's economic performance was not matched by a willingness to hand over suspected war criminals for trial by International Criminal Tribunal for the former Yugoslavia (ICTY) in The Hague.

While unenthusiastic about the timing of the Croatian application, the EU has become increasingly clear in offering a longer-term membership perspective to all the countries of the Western Balkans. At the European Council session in Thessaloniki in June 2003, member states adopted the *Thessaloniki Agenda for the Western Balkans: Moving towards European Integration*, which reaffirmed the membership perspective for these countries and outlined steps needed to move them from their current pre-candidate status to the formal start of preparations for membership. With enlargement to most of the countries of Central and Eastern Europe complete, many of the financial and human resources that the EU has devoted since the early 1990s in helping to prepare these countries for membership will be freed up for assistance in the Balkans. In addition, the accession countries themselves will be well-positioned to share their own recent experiences in preparing for EU membership with the countries of the Western Balkans. Although much could yet go wrong, the long track record of enlargement suggests that over the long term the EU has a good chance of bringing these countries into the EU in a way that would help to ensure their stability and prosperity, and put an end once and for all to the crises that have plagued this region since the early 1990s.

The newly independent states

Enlargement also dramatically increased the level and scope of interaction between the EU and the NIS. The EU has had a common frontier with Russia since Finland's accession in 1995. With the 2004 enlargement, this expanded to include the Estonia–Russia and Latvia–Russia borders, and the potentially turbulent borders between Poland and Lithuania and the Kaliningrad exclave. The EU now also borders on Belarus (at the eastern frontiers of Latvia, Lithuania and Poland) and Ukraine (Poland, Slovakia and Hungary). Enlargement to Romania in 2007 will lengthen the EU border with Ukraine and create a new external border with Moldova. In addition to having an important stake in the stability of Kaliningrad, the EU has taken on direct responsibility for some 1.8 million ethnic Russians, Ukrainians and Belarusians living in the Baltic countries who have become EU citizens. Conversely, it has at least an indirect interest in the fate of thousands of ethnic Poles living in Russia, Ukraine, and Belarus; Hungarians in Ukraine; Lithuanians in Russia and Belarus; and other smaller cross-border minority populations (Berg and van Meurs, 2001, p. 142). Trade between the EU and the NIS is also expanding as a result of enlargement, as countries that traditionally have been important trading partners for Russia and the other NIS become part of the EU's single market.

Russia

Although formally there are many similarities between how the EU relates to Russia and its approach to other former communist countries, Russia represents a special case for EU external policy. As with other formerly communist countries, the overall thrust of EU policy towards Russia is integration: bringing Russia into a wider Europe with the EU at its core that in time will be part of a single economic space operating along market principles and dedicated to the same standards of democracy and good governance. At the same time, however, Russia is the only country in Europe outside the EU that has a tradition as a great power and that still has aspirations to be an important global actor as well as part of an integrated Europe. In forging its policies toward Russia, the EU thus has had to balance its efforts to integrate Russia into a wider Europe with a political need to respect Russia's continuing desire to be recognized as a great power, able to deal on an equal basis with the EU and its key member states.

The framework for EU–Russia relations is the Partnership and Cooperation Agreement (PCA) signed in July 1994. A mixed agreement between the Russian Federation on the one side and the EU and its

member states on the other, the PCA provides for the eventual establishment of a free trade area between Russia and the EU, economic convergence based on approximation of laws and regulations, joint
participation in industrial, scientific and cultural programmes and
projects, and regular political dialogue at various levels, including biannual meetings between the Council and Commission presidents and the
Russian president. Much of the co-operation called for under the PCA is
underwritten by the TACIS (Technical Assistance to the Commonwealth
of Independent States) programme, through which the EU has provided
more than €2.5 billion in aid to Moscow since 1991. Notwithstanding
these ambitious goals and the impressive institutional architecture of
bilateral relations, actual EU influence on the development of Russia in
the 1990s was limited. Because of delays in the ratification process partly
linked to the war in Chechnya, the PCA did not come into effect until
December 1997, just nine months before the August 1998 financial crash
in Moscow.

The Treaty of Amsterdam, signed in June 1997 and implemented in
May 1999, created a new foreign policy instrument, the Common
Strategy, which sets out aims for EU policy towards key regions and countries, and specifies the means by which the EU and the member states,
working together, are to achieve these aims. The first such strategy was
the Common Strategy for Russia, endorsed by European Council in
Cologne, in June 1999 (European Council, 1999). The quick adoption of
the Common Strategy reflected an effort to improve policy implementation on the EU side, and to give a visible signal of renewed urgency about
Russia following the financial crisis and the strain between Russia and the
West over the war in Kosovo. Hailed in Brussels as the basis for a new
'strategic partnership' with Russia, the launch of the Common Strategy
was followed by proposals for the creation of a 'common European
economic space' embracing Russia and the EU, a concept that was
endorsed bilaterally at the May 2001 EU–Russia summit. At their
October 2001 Brussels summit, Russia and the EU agreed to establish a
High-Level Group charged with elaborating a concept for closer
economic relations between the two sides, and specifically with defining
'the core elements which will need to be put in place in order to create a
Common European Economic Area'. The EU's Northern Dimension,
launched in 1997 and given new emphasis by the Finnish presidency in the
second half of 1999, provides an additional framework in which to tackle
the economic and environmental problems of north-western Russia as
well as the particular problem of Kaliningrad.

Despite the development of an impressive institutional architecture for
bilateral co-operation, EU–Russia relations have remained troubled in
many areas, with lingering differences over trade, managing the effects of

enlargement, human rights and Chechnya, and broader co-operation in Europe and the international system, including the fight against terrorism. Along with the USA, the EU has been an important player in Russia's World Trade Organization (WTO) accession negotiations which, most observers agreed, held the key to a full normalization of bilateral EU–Russia trade relations, and to progress on the eventual establishment of the free trade area called for in the PCA. The EU insisted on improved market access commitments in such areas as banking, financial services and telecommunications, and an end to the dual pricing of energy products that gives Russian industry an unfair subsidy in the contravention of WTO norms.

Russia ranks as the EU's sixth largest external market, accounting for €27.691 billion in exports in 2001. EU imports from Russia totalled €47.686 billion, with slightly over half – €27.728 billion – comprising of energy products. Russians complain about restrictions on their access to the EU market for non-energy products, which have been constrained by sectoral agreements in steel and textiles, and by Commission anti-dumping and anti-subsidy actions. Some of these Russian concerns were addressed by the EU decision of May 2002 to grant Russia full market economy status, a step that has implications for how anti-dumping actions are pursued. For their part, European officials and businesses complain about a poor, albeit in some respects improving, business environment in Russia that limits trade and investment, particularly in the energy sector. At the October 2000 EU–Russia summit in Paris, the two sides agreed to institute a regular energy dialogue leading to the establishment of an EU–Russian Energy Partnership. The Duma has not ratified the Energy Charter Treaty and its Transit Protocol, which the EU believes would enhance the legal basis for co-operation in this area.

Enlargement is both an opportunity and a challenge for Russia. EU officials argue that enlargement benefits Russia by enhancing stability on its western borders, creating a more affluent and growing market for its exports, and enhancing opportunities for cross-border co-operation in the contiguous regions of Kaliningrad and north-western Russia. Their Russian counterparts tend to emphasize the potential downsides. In its 'Medium-Term Strategy for the Development of Relations between the Russian Federation and the European Union (2000–2010)', presented to the EU at the EU–Russia summit in Helsinki in October 1999, Russia flagged up a number of concerns relating to enlargement, including the possible loss of export opportunities in Central and Eastern Europe, the impact of the Schengen visa regime on cross-border mobility, and above all the fate of Kaliningrad in the context of the adoption of Schengen restrictions by Poland and Lithuania. The latter issue was a source of bilateral tension throughout much of 2002, but ultimately was resolved in

November of that year with a compromise under which Russian citizens travelling by car between Kaliningrad and Russia will be issued with special multiple-transit documents to cross Lithuania, while those travelling by train will receive single-transit documents issued with their rail tickets. With Kaliningrad resolved, most of the other EU–Russia issues relating to enlargement are proving manageable. The accession countries of Central and Eastern Europe need to accede to the EU–Russia PCA, a step that Russia must approve. Many Russians, including members of the new business and commercial elites, are unhappy about the Schengen rules that complicate their movement to and from the new member states, but this situation may be ameliorated through faster and more efficient visa procedures and better-administered borders (the border between Russia and Finland is often cited as a model).

Chechnya and human rights in general remain irritants in Russia–EU relations, albeit ones in which the EU is able to shelter somewhat behind the more assertive posture of the Council of Europe and its Parliamentary Assembly. The sensitivity of these issues was highlighted in autumn 2002, when Russia requested that the EU–Russia summit scheduled to take place in Copenhagen in November be moved to Brussels to protest at the holding of the World Chechen Congress in Copenhagen the previous month. EU–Russian relations under the Danish presidency were further strained when Denmark refused to extradite the Chechen vice-premier, Ahmed Zakaev, who was in Denmark to attend the Chechen congress, and whom Russia accused of complicity in various crimes relating to the civil war in his homeland.

Beyond these specifically bilateral issues, the EU and Russia face the broader question of how they relate to each other, in Europe and globally, in the context of an evolving world order that officials on both sides like to characterize as being multi-polar. The EU and Russia have expressed their intention to co-operate on a broad range of issues, in what the EU calls a 'strategic partnership' between the two sides. In March 2000, the EU proposed a Common Action Plan for Russia on Combating Organized Crime, which became the basis for increased co-operation in this area. At the October 2000 summit, the EU and Russia signed a joint declaration concerning consultations and strategic dialogue on security issues, including disarmament, arms control, non-proliferation, and co-operation in operational crisis management. The following year it was agreed to hold monthly consultations between the Russian ambassador in Brussels and the troika of the EU Political and Security Committee. The EU is also keen to enlist Russian support for a number of initiatives designed at least in part to bolster the EU's international status and its standing relative to the USA. They include possible participation in the Galileo satellite navigation system, increased use of the euro (a trend already well under way among Russian businesses and consumers), and ratification of the Kyoto Protocol, a key EU environmental priority that, following the Bush Administration's rejection of it, could come into effect only with Russia's support.

The Iraq crisis of 2002–2003 highlighted both the potential for, and the more problematic aspects of, Russia's relations with the EU. In response to domestic political pressures, to protect Russian economic and political interests, and to advance a long-standing, if muted, Russian vision of a multi-polar world, President Vladimir Putin sided with French President Jacques Chirac and German Chancellor Gerhard Schröder against the USA and Britain over the use of force against Saddam Hussein in Iraq. But Putin was unable to translate his support for the diplomatic positions of the EU's two leading member states into concrete gains in dealing with the EU as such. At the height of the UN impasse over Iraq, Putin extended a hasty invitation to Commission President Romano Prodi to visit Moscow, and even loaned Prodi a Russian aircraft for the trip (Jack, 2003). Amid this high-profile effort to signal convergence between the Russian and EU positions on Iraq, Putin raised the issue of visa-free travel to the EU, and tried to advance Russia's cause in the WTO accession negotiations, but was unable to make significant progress in either area.

As this episode suggested, there continues to be a certain tension between Russia's status and role as a great power, able to act in the UN Security Council on a key global issue, and its position as a European power that has little choice but to adjust to rules – on trade, investment, energy, migration and many other issues – that increasingly are set by the EU. Russia can be expected to try to use its strength and status as a major power to try to shape these rules as best it can. For its part, the EU will have to balance the tension in its policy between its efforts to cultivate Russia as a strategic partner on the international scene (analogous in many respects to other key global actors such as Japan, India and China), and its declared interest in integrating Russia into the European economic space on terms that often imply a certain inequality between Russia and its by now much larger and wealthier western neighbour.

The new neighbourhood: Ukraine, Moldova and Belarus

Just as the press of events in recent years have caused the EU to modify its policies towards the Western Balkans, EU enlargement and developments in the western NIS are leading to changes in how the EU approaches relations with what have become Europe's new 'lands between' – that is, Ukraine, Belarus and Moldova. In the early 1990s, the EU and its member states drew a sharp distinction between the Central and East European countries and the former Soviet republics (Baltic countries excepted) of the Commonwealth of Independent States (CIS). The former were considered to be future member states and invited to negotiate Europe Agreements reflecting that aspiration, while the latter were not viewed as candidates and were offered Partnership and Co-operation Agreements that contained many of the elements of co-operation included in the Europe Agreements but without a prospect of membership. Ukraine was particularly unhappy with this distinction, which in its view implied exclusion from 'Europe' and potential consignment back to a Russian sphere of influence.

In recent years, the rigid Central and Eastern Europe-CIS, Europe Agreement–PCA dichotomies established in the early 1990s have begun to break down. EU officials continue to turn down requests by Ukraine and Moldova to discuss membership, but the EU has begun to accept, at least rhetorically, that it must take on more responsibility for these countries, as reflected in the proposal put forward by the Council of Ministers in 2002 for a New Neighbours Initiative that would define a new status for these countries somewhere between membership and exclusion.

In April 2002, the Council asked the Commission and CFSP High Representative Solana to develop a New Neighbours Initiative for relations with these countries, with the immediate goal of narrowing the gap in stability and prosperity between them and the EU. At their November 2002 session in Brussels, the EU foreign ministers reiterated the 'need for the EU to formulate an ambitious, long-term and integrated approach towards each of these countries, with the objective of promoting democratic and economic reforms, sustainable development and trade, thus helping to ensure greater stability and prosperity at and beyond the new borders of the Union' (Council of the European Union, 2002b). In March 2003, the Commission issued its *Wider Europe – Neighbourhood: A New Framework for Relations with our Eastern and Southern Neighbours*, which proposed that the EU 'should aim to develop a zone of prosperity and a friendly neighbourhood – a 'ring of friends' – with whom the EU enjoys close, peaceful and co-operative relations' (European Commission, 2003c, p. 4). The Convention on the Future of Europe further proposed embodying the new policy in Article 42 of the draft constitution, which states that 'The Union shall develop a special relationship with its neighbouring states, aiming to establish an area of prosperity and good neighbourliness characterized by close and peaceful relations based on co-operation'.

The key factor driving the search for a more effective policy toward the western NIS is enlargement, which has focused attention on the challenges for the EU of 'wider Europe' and which will bring into the EU new members with a direct stake in expanded relations with their eastern neighbours. Poland in particular has declared its intention to promote an 'eastern dimension' to CFSP, in much the same way that Finland and Sweden joined with Denmark to promote the Northern Dimension after their accession in 1995. Exactly how a New Neighbours Initiative will go beyond the existing pattern of relations with these countries remains unclear, however, as these relations are already highly institutionalized along lines established in the 1990s. The March 2003 Commission document was in fact greeted rather sceptically in Ukraine and Moldova, both because it did not come with offers of increased aid or trade benefits and, more importantly, because it seemed to place these countries in the same category as fellow 'neighbours' in North Africa, and thus deny their European aspirations.

EU policy towards Ukraine is pursued within the framework of the EU–Ukraine PCA, signed in June 1994 and implemented in March 1998, with additional guidance provided by the Common Strategy for Ukraine, adopted in December 1999. After Russia, Ukraine is also the largest recipient of EU aid in the NIS, with some € 1 billion allocated over the ten-year period to 2002, mainly within TACIS. The actual level of EU–Ukrainian integration remains uneven, however, with numerous barriers to further co-operation on both sides. Annual summits began in 1998, after the coming into force of the PCA, along with regular meetings of the ministerial-level Co-operation Council. At the June 2001 meeting of the Co-operation Council, the EU and Ukraine designated six areas as priorities for bilateral co-operation: approximation of Ukraine's legislation to that of the EU; energy; trade; Justice and Home Affairs; environmental protection; and transport and science and technology. A seventh area, investment and cross-border co-operation, was added later.

Progress in most of these areas has been modest. Bilateral trade relations remain troubled, with Ukraine lagging behind even Russia in its efforts to join the WTO. The EU, unconstrained by WTO obligations that do not apply to trade relations with non-members, has maintained a high level of protection against Ukrainian products, with the result that only 16 per cent of Ukraine's exports are directed towards the EU. While the PCA and the Common Strategy call for the eventual conclusion of a free trade agreement, for the present trade is constrained by a sectoral agreement on trade in textiles, a system of bilateral steel import quotas, and import quotas for grain. Unlike Russia, Ukraine has not been granted market economy status by the EU.

Energy has been a troublesome issue in EU–Ukraine relations. Kiev is concerned about what it sees as efforts by Russian gas suppliers and Western European importers to bypass Ukraine through the construction of pipelines across Belarus and Poland that could deprive Ukraine of a role in the energy trade, while EU officials and businesses complain about poor investment conditions in the Ukrainian energy industry. On the positive side, a major irritant in relations for much of the 1990s was removed in December 2000 when Ukraine finally shut down the last unit of the Chernobyl nuclear power station. The EU is working with other Western partners in helping Ukraine to meet the massive costs of decommissioning Chernobyl and developing alternative sources of power.

Justice and Home Affairs has become an increasingly important element in bilateral relations, as a result both of the enlargement process and the 2001 terrorist attacks on the USA. Concern about the impact on Ukraine of Schengen-mandated visa requirements by Poland, Slovakia, Hungary and Romania in the context of enlargement prompted discussions between Brussels and Kiev about an expedited visa system to facilitate border traffic. With the Russia–Ukraine border still largely open, Ukraine has become a major transit point for illegal migrants attempting to reach Western Europe from other parts of the NIS and from Asia. These matters and the related issues of organized crime, drugs, fraud, money laundering and co-operation in the fight against terrorism came under the purview of the December 2001 EU Action Plan on Justice and Home Affairs with Ukraine.

Over the longer term, the EU will have to confront the issue of a membership perspective for Ukraine. In June 1998, President Leonid Kuchma signed a decree adopting a policy document, 'The Strategy of Ukraine's Integration into the European Union', setting membership as a long-term goal. The EU has consistently rebuffed Kiev's efforts to have Ukraine recognized as a candidate country but, in line with the erosion of the sharp distinctions between candidate, pre-candidate and potential candidate countries, has begun to react more positively to such statements. The Common Strategy for the first time 'acknowledged' Ukraine's 'European aspirations' and welcomed its choice for Europe, without going so far as to conclude that 'Europe' necessarily meant full EU membership. Another indication of the shift was the decision by the June 2001 Göteborg European Council to invite Ukraine (and Moldova) to join the European Conference, a forum that previously had included only the member states, the twelve negotiating candidate countries, and Turkey.

Like Ukraine, Moldova has expressed its aspirations to join the EU and has been frustrated by not being accorded candidate status. The EU and Moldova signed a PCA in 1994, which came into effect in June 1998. Moldova became a member of the WTO in July 2001, but EU–Moldova trade relations remained troubled in a number of areas. Moldova benefits from certain EU preferences, but its chief exports – wine, fruit and other agricultural products – are politically sensitive and subject to strict EU quotas and tariffs. Less than a quarter of Moldovan exports are directed towards the EU, which suggests that Moldova has not made the fundamental redirection of trade towards the West that the accession countries made in the 1990s.

Transnistria, a separatist region that declared independence from Moldova when the latter became an independent country in 1991, is a major concern of EU policy towards Moldova. Brussels has continued to press Moscow to fulfil the commitments it made at the 1999 OSCE summit in Istanbul to withdraw all its forces from the region. As the Russian presence has receded, however, the separatist authorities in Transnistria have turned increasingly for survival to criminal activities, including the smuggling of arms, people and narcotics, a development with very negative implications for Romania, the Western Balkans and the EU itself. In a sign of how seriously these threats are taken, in early 2003 the EU and its member states joined with the USA in imposing a complete travel ban on officials from the breakaway republic.

Belarus remains the odd-country-out in the western NIS, in that it has reverted to authoritarianism and made almost no progress towards a market economy. The EU and Belarus signed a PCA in 1994, but the agreement was never implemented, because of displeasure on the EU side with the turn towards authoritarianism in Minsk, and in particular the undemocratic outcome of the 1996 referendum on the amendment to the constitution staged by President Lukashenko. EU–Belarus bilateral relations at the ministerial level were suspended, and EU technical assistance under TACIS frozen, except for humanitarian aid, regional programmes in which Belarus participates, and programmes aimed at promoting democracy. Relations reached a low point in the summer of 1998, when the EU and USA imposed diplomatic sanctions against Lukashenko and other high-ranking Belarusian officials following a dispute over the residences of Western ambassadors in Minsk.

With bilateral relations in a deep freeze, the EU has been forced to work primarily through the OSCE and the Council of Europe, both of which have had programmes in Belarus to monitor elections and promote human rights. The EU also provides limited TACIS funding to support non-governmental organizations and the development of civil society. Policy-makers in Brussels and the national capitals are well aware, however, that improved relations and expanded co-operation with Belarus are likely to be of increasing importance for the EU, particularly in the context of enlargement. Belarus is thus listed as a target country of the New Neighbours Initiative, even though its internal political situation continued to deteriorate.

The Caucasus and Central Asia

The Caucasus and Central Asia are peripheral regions for EU policy, where EU influence is limited. Other actors, including Russia, the USA, Iran, Turkey and China are major players in these regions, while the development of closer relations with the EU has been held hostage to a set of internal and cross-border conflicts that the EU has taken a supporting role in attempting to resolve. None the less, all these countries were recognized implicitly as being European by the decision to admit them to the OSCE following the breakup of the Soviet Union. Georgia (1999), Armenia (2001) and Azerbaijan (2001) have further bolstered their European credentials by becoming members of the Council of Europe. The EU also underlined the sense of a unified post-Soviet space linked to Europe by offering PCAs and TACIS aid to all these countries on the same basis as they were offered to the Slavic republics of the western NIS. PCAs with Armenia, Azerbaijan and Georgia came into force in July 1999, and provide for the usual mix of trade liberalization, alignment of standards, policy dialogue and TACIS aid. PCAs are in effect with Kazakhstan, Kyrgyzstan and Uzbekistan. A PCA was concluded with Turkmenistan, but has not come into effect. The EU and Tajikistan have not concluded a PCA.

The EU's flagship programmes for these region are TRACECA (Transport Corridor Europe Caucasus Asia), which aims to develop transport corridors across the Black Sea to the Caucasus and Central Asia, and INOGATE, which seeks to build or upgrade oil and gas networks. TRACECA began in May 1993 with a Brussels conference of donors and potential beneficiaries, and has since funded projects relating to transport infrastructure, legal and regulatory issues, and management training aimed at the long-term goal of linking TRACECA routes with the Trans-European Networks (TENs) in an enlarged EU. This will entail a major redirection of traffic from the north–south axes that developed in the Soviet period to an east–west dimension anchored on the EU. INOGATE was launched in 1995, and has funded approximately €50 million in projects in ten countries to assess the existing oil and gas networks, develop new transmission systems, and strengthen regulatory and management institutions. TRACECA and INOGATE both seek to catalyze much larger investments from the multilateral development banks and private industry.

Armenia, Georgia and Azerbaijan have declared their intention to work towards closer integration with the EU through increased trade and the approximation of regulations, with membership often mentioned as a long-term aspiration. But substantial progress along these lines has been hampered by the large number of internal and cross-border conflicts that have destabilized the region since the early 1990s. The EU supports international efforts to resolve these conflicts, including the OSCE-sponsored Minsk Group for the Nagorno–Karabakh conflict, and the OSCE mission for South Ossetia and the UN Special Representative for Abkhazia. In February 2001, the EU resolved to take a more active role in the region, aimed at preventing and resolving conflicts and supporting post-conflict rehabilitation. EU aid projects, such as assistance under a CFSP Joint Action to provide equipment to Georgian border guards, aimed at protecting OSCE monitors on the Chechen–Georgia border, are being tailored to support these efforts.

The Central Asian states are even more remote and less subject to EU influence than the Caucasus. None the less, Brussels has sought to carve out a role in the region through the PCAs and the provision of aid, which has totalled € 944 million since the early 1990s. Policy priorities are security promotion and conflict prevention, eliminating sources of political and social tension, and improving the climate for investment. Of particular concern is the narcotics trade, as 80 per cent of heroin on the Western European market is supplied from Afghanistan via Central Asia. After September 11, terrorism has become another major concern, alongside trafficking in arms and human beings. As EU sources readily acknowledge, however, this is an extremely challenging region in which to work. Aid programmes are hard to implement, and the conditionality that the EU wields toward other countries has a limited effect, given the modest resources available, the dictatorial nature of the regimes in power, and the absence of even a long-term membership perspective. Perhaps the most that can be said of the EU in Central Asia is that it is a positive force, but one that works alongside the USA, other bilateral donors, and actors such as the World Bank and the European Bank for Reconstruction and Development (EBRD), to address a very difficult set of circumstances.

Conclusion

Since the early 1990s, promoting peace and prosperity through all the former communist countries of Central and Eastern Europe and the Soviet Union has been a priority for the EU. In recent years, however, EU policy has been marked by increasing differentiation in both the form and the substance of its approaches to different countries and regions in the post-communist space whose prospects for membership are not immediate.

For all its difficulties, the Western Balkans has been set on a path seventual membership. The key questions for Brussels thus revolve around implementation: will the EU have the staying power and the financial and organizational resources to ensure that this region continues on a path toward stability and convergence with EU norms? Brussels tends to answer with an unequivocal yes, if only because there appears to be little alternative. The EU is too close to the Balkans and invested too deeply – with money, personnel, programmes and policy initiatives – to contemplate withdrawal and failure. The real question is how long integration of the Western Balkans will take, and whether engagement in this region will be so demanding that, along with the enlargements of 2004 and 2007, it diverts Europe from efforts to become a larger and more effective player on the global scene.

The situation with regard to the eastern periphery is less clear. Belarus may be headed for a de facto re-absorption by Russia, although new eastern initiatives led by Poland as a member state may succeed in heading off such an outcome. Moldova's fate is linked closely to a timely and successful EU accession process in Romania. Ukraine's future is more uncertain. It may succeed in its efforts to move closer to the EU and perhaps even achieve eventual membership. But other outcomes are possible. While reintegration with Russia is unlikely, Ukraine could emerge as one of those troubled middle powers (Iran, Pakistan, a future united Korea, and possibly Turkey, come to mind) that are too large to become part of any of the 'poles' in what many international relations theorists see as an emerging multi-polar global system, but too small to become poles in their own right. Ukraine thus would be a serious problem for the EU – too large to ignore, but also impossible to integrate.

Russia is yet another story. Like the EU, it has aspirations towards a larger and more influential role in the international system. It was precisely these aspirations that provided a basis for the alignment of Putin with Chirac and Schröder against the USA in the Iraq crisis of 2003, and that helps to underpin the EU–Russia 'strategic partnership'. At the same time, however, there is an inherent tension between proximity policy as practised by the EU and Russia's own striving to assert itself as a great power. However well intentioned it is, proximity policy involves the EU setting norms that Russia must accept, and launching projects in which Russia is then invited to participate. In that sense, proximity policy is inherently unequal and as such undercuts the very status that Russia seeks to achieve through ties with the EU (Van Oudenaren, 2003). Up to a point, Moscow and Brussels can paper over these differences while pursuing mutually beneficial economic and political ties. Fundamentally, however, there may be limits to an EU–Russia rapprochement, as Russia is likely to remain wary of an EU that increasingly makes the rules for Europe as a whole without giving Russia a full role in rule-making, while for its part the EU reacts cautiously to a Russia that claims to want integration with Europe but at the same time clings to a role as a great power with global interests that transcend its relations with Brussels.

While the overall outlines of EU policies towards the Balkans and the NIS are well established, these policies can be expected to evolve in the coming years as Brussels adjusts to successes and failures 'on the ground' in the target countries and as it absorbs the new Central and Eastern European member states. The accession countries are bringing their own ideas and resources to EU proximity policy, while in the Balkans and the NIS perceptions of the EU are inevitably changing as a result of more direct contact with the EU through the new member states. While particular policies can be expected to evolve as circumstances change, the overall challenge is likely to remain constant: that of helping to bring stability and prosperity to the regions to the east and south-east of an enlarged EU.

Chapter 15

Development Policy: Paradigm Shifts and the 'Normalization' of a Privileged Partnership?

MARTIN HOLLAND

Relations with the developing world are a long-established part of the European Union's external affairs. Yet at best they have been idiosyncratic and incomplete, reflecting the supremacy of incrementalism and pragmatism over consistency and coherence in policy formulation. Why is that so, and what are the origins, motivations and objectives of the EU's development policy? These simple questions need to be examined in order to understand the context in which the EU launched the latest stage of its development policy, in 2000.

First, the developing world has always had a specific meaning for the EU that does not correspond to other commonly held definitions of 'the South' or 'the Third World'. Levels of development and geography were largely abandoned as the guiding criteria for policy-making and the basis for policy implementation. Rather, the EU has preferred to define the developing world largely in terms of colonial, linguistic and historical ties, thereby focusing its attention on the so-called African, Caribbean and Pacific (ACP) countries. While relations with Latin America, the Indian subcontinent and South-East Asia have grown since the 1970s, from an EU perspective the developing world has been defined principally through the ACP prism.

Historically, the EU's policy towards the developing world has evolved through three distinct phases. The Yaoundé agreement of 1964 first established links between the then six member states and eighteen francophone former colonies (known as the Associated African States and Madagascar), thereby establishing heritage as the implicit motive behind European development policy. Subsequently, the first enlargement in 1973 raised the issue of British ties with Commonwealth developing countries, and helped to usher in the first of what were to be four Lomé Conventions, spanning a quarter of a century, involving forty-six states at the beginning (in 1975) and seventy-one at the end (in 2000) – see Table 15.1.

Table 15.1   *ACP–EU Conventions and Agreements 1958–2000*

Convention or Agreement	Date of implementation	No. EU member states	No. ACP states
Yaoundé Convention I	July 1964	6	18
Yaoundé Convention II	January 1971	6	19
Lomé Convention I	April 1976	9	46
Lomé Convention II	January 1981	10	57
Lomé Convention III	May 1986	12	66
Lomé Convention IV	March 1990	12	69
Lomé Convention IV (review)	November 1995	15	70
Cotonou Partnership Agreement	June 2000	15	78*

Note: *As of May 2003.

While Lomé may have symbolized Europe's imperfect definition of development co-operation, it was groundbreaking for its time. Its distinctive feature was a commitment to an equal partnership between Europe and the ACP. The preamble committed the signatory states 'to establish, on the basis of complete equality between partners, close and continuing co-operation in a spirit of international solidarity' and to 'seek a more just and more balanced economic order'. The major policy objectives of the Convention were as commendable as they were ambitious: the promotion of EU–ACP trade; agricultural and industrial development; special aid for the least developed states; and support for regional co-operation. Lomé's most substantive innovations were the adoption of non-reciprocity as the basis for trade policy with the ACP, and the introduction of export stabilization schemes.

Despite these benign and radical intentions, both the EU and the ACP came to regard the Lomé experiment as a policy failure. Radical reform was needed. Throughout the 1996–2000 period, both sides debated, negotiated and eventually ratified a new structure and mechanism for development policy, the so-called the Cotonou Partnership Agreement. This contemporary phase of EU–ACP relations links the EU (with the inclusion of East Timor in 2003) with seventy-eight countries. Like its predecessor, Lomé, Cotonou relies on the ACP as the framework for the relationship.

This chapter examines the Cotonou Partnership Agreement and discusses the major economic and political reforms that Cotonou introduced into EU development policy. Economically, the most fundamental change was the transition from non-reciprocity to free trade through regional Economic Partnership Agreements (EPAs) as the basis for future relations. The parallel introduction of the 'Everything But Arms' (EBA) initiative, which for the first time employs development status as an EU development policy criterion, is also examined, and its possible unintended policy contradictions analysed. Politically, Cotonou included a renewed emphasis on good governance and democratic conditionality. Above all else, Cotonou sought to facilitate the reintegration of developing countries into the global economy, thereby obviating the need for any special ACP privileges and protections. Whether such a normalization of the EU–ACP relationship can be achieved is the critical focus of this analysis.

The 2000 Cotonou Partnership Agreement

Constructing a new agreement acceptable to the ACP states and to the EU was, in itself, a significant achievement. The ACP was initially concerned by earlier proposals to redefine EU–ACP policy, such as those outlined in the 1996 Commission Green Paper, which threatened more drastic changes. For example, the EU appeared to exclude any specific concessions for the least developed countries (LDCs) and suggested that the ACP group itself be disbanded. Under the circumstances, as Poul Nielson, the Commissioner for Development and Humanitarian Aid, declared, the agreement was 'a major historical and political event'. Cotonou constituted 'a new era of a relationship based on a profound reform of the spirit, the objectives and the practice of our co-operation' (Nielson, 2000). For the Commission, it provided an important example of a successful and open process of policy debate and helped to redress the negative aspects of globalization on the developing world that had surfaced at the 1999 Seattle World Trade Organization (WTO) meeting. For their part, the ACP states recognized that a mutually acceptable agreement had finally been achieved, albeit one that was asymmetrical and involved concessions to reconcile significant differences in areas such as the political dimension, the new commercial framework and implementation of financial co-operation.

The broad objectives of the Partnership Agreement, as stated in Article 1, are:

> to promote and expedite the economic, cultural and social development of the ACP States, with a view to contributing to peace and security and to promoting a stable and democratic political environment.

> reducing and eventually eradicating poverty consistent with the objectives of sustainable development and the gradual integration of the ACP countries into the world economy. (Partnership Agreement, Art. 1)

EU support and encouragement to assist regional integration processes are expressly mentioned as mechanisms that can assist in realizing these primary EU–ACP objectives. In addition, Article 2 outlines four 'fundamental principles' that govern relations between the EU and the ACP. First is equality of the partners and local ownership of the development strategies. As the text states, 'The ACP States shall determine the development strategies for their economies and societies in all sovereignty'. Second, in order to foster the widest possible involvement and participation in political and economic affairs, the partnership is open to 'all sections of society, including the private sector, and civil society' as well as central government. Third, 'Dialogue and the fulfilment of mutual obligations' is pivotal to enacting the intent of the partnership. Finally, 'Differentiation' in the arrangements for ACP countries and for regions (reflecting different levels of development) is a fundamental principle, distinguishing between those more able to compete in the global economy and the least developed countries that are still in need of special protection. This last principle is the most significant departure from the uniform Lomé approach. It carries with it serious potential ramifications by paving the way for a multi-speed approach to future development that will inevitably differentiate between different regions of the ACP group. Collectively, these new principles signal three significant paradigm shifts in EU development policy that are economic, political and geographical in nature.

The new Partnership Agreement was the result of a lengthy negotiation process: much of the general experience and *acquis* of the previous twenty-five years of Lomé were retained (for example, the contractual nature and benefits of long-term agreements). But past policy failures were also seen as the motivation for reform. Historically, EU development policy focused on uniform preferential trade access and direct aid to each country. Less emphasis was placed on a country's development policy objectives or institutional capacity to deliver these development policy goals. The universally recognized result was that the EU's development policy failed to transform the ACP economies. Trade figures demonstrated that the ACP's share of the EU market declined markedly over the lifespan of Lomé (to just 2.8 per cent by 1999) and remained dependent on a narrow range of primary products depressingly reminiscent of a colonial economic structure (Holland, 2002).

Under the new Partnership Agreement, the EU sought to remedy its failure to address the economic policy objectives and political institutional contexts. The economic remedy proposed by the EU was straightforward and blunt: economic assistance would be extended to ACP countries based on their commitment to free trade. The rationale can be found in both the EU's own commitment to global trade liberalization, and in a deep-seated belief that only such economic reform could facilitate the integration of ACP into the global economy. Critics of this new policy argued that the liberal bias towards free trade was shortsighted, if not extreme (Holland, 2002). Transformation costs, the loss of customs revenue, the limited scope for trade expansion for most primary producer states, as well as the potential problem of agricultural access caused by the EU's Common Agricultural Policy (CAP) were indicative of the clear costs yet uncertain benefits promised by free trade. These radical proposals were partially moderated through concessions and safeguards, but the basic principle of ACP free trade areas was established, marking a paradigmatic departure from the spirit of Lomé.

The signs of a changing economic philosophy also began to emerge as the adaptation of the structural adjustment programmes of the Bretton Woods institutions became part of EU development policy for the first time. Similarly, Lomé IV tentatively promoted the role of the private sector in development, as well as that of regional co-operation. All these shifts in development policy were consistent with the global trends of the 1990s, which, for example, saw the market replace the state as the principle economic mechanism throughout Central and Eastern Europe.

The new Partnership Agreement also emphasized political conditionality as part of the institutional remedy to EU development policy. Here, the EU stressed the need for effective democratic institutions as a precondition for economic growth; the necessity for open and pluralistic models of civil society to emerge; respect for the rule of law; and the emergence of a culture of 'good governance'. Such overt political conditionality was largely absent from the early Lomé Conventions (I–III). However, the negotiation of Lomé IV coincided with the watershed of German reunification and the collapse of communism. Political conditionality was no longer taboo, but became an essential element of a new approach to development issues. Thus Lomé IV contained provisions that were expressly political and focused on human rights.

The third paradigm shift unveiled at Cotonou concerned the geographical focus of the dialogue with the EU. A fundamental characteristic of Lomé had been its group-to-group nature, which saw the EU negotiate and interact exclusively with the ACP as a single body. All ACP states were treated similarly, irrespective of their economic status or location. This uniformity was replaced by explicit differentiation under the Partnership Agreement. The ACP states are now divided into their regional parts as well as separated according to development status (distinguishing the LDC states from the 'other' ACP states). Separate A (African), C (Caribbean) and P (Pacific) regional agreements with the EU signifies a recognition of diversity that had been camouflaged in the original ACP grouping. It also reflected the need for the EU to develop dialogues that were more manageable in size and scope. The application of development status as a policy criterion was only adopted on the insistence of some member states, notably Britain. This 'concession' constitutes an important positive aspect of differentiation.

Tellingly, consensus had begun to emerge on all sides that the previous Lomé regime had failed to arrest, let alone reverse, the economic decline of the ACP: some went as far as to argue that it was in fact instrumental in accelerating the decline. This, together with the new WTO-based consensus and the economic development of the Central and Eastern European countries combined to overturn the economic philosophy that had underpinned Lomé for the previous quarter-century. Trade liberalization, accompanied by democratic institution building, was the new international context that the successor to Lomé was obliged to acknowledge and ultimately embrace. Consequently, the Partnership Agreement emphasized the political aspects of development, and not just the economic ones. The importance of institutional capacity, the support of civil society and the role of the non-state sector in promoting development underpinned this new philosophy and set the new context for EU development policy until at least the end of the Cotonou agreement in 2020.

Institutions

Cotonou largely retained the Lomé institutions. The three joint EU–ACP institutions – the Council of Ministers, the Committee of Ambassadors and the Joint Parliamentary Assembly – remained operational, with the Council involving all ninety-three governments – 103 after EU enlargement in 2004 – plus members of the Commission. The presidency of the Council and the Chairman of the Committee of Ambassadors alternates between the EU and ACP member states. Council decisions are taken 'by common agreement' (Art. 15.3). The Joint Assembly is composed of equal numbers of EU and ACP representatives (Euro-parliamentarians in the EU's case, and either members of national parliaments or their designates for the ACP). It meets twice a year, alternately in the EU and in an ACP state. While it may adopt resolutions and make recommendations, it is formally a 'consultative body' (Art. 17). A significant reform is the creation of a dispute settlement mechanism. Where the EU and ACP are in dispute, binding arbitration, normally using the procedures of the Permanent Court of Arbitration for International Organizations, now govern.

Financing

Like Lomé before it, Cotonou included a large development assistance

Table 15.2   *Financing of development co-operation, 1958–2000*

Legal basis	Fund	EIB* (ECUm)	EDF** (ECUm)	Total (ECUm)
Treaty of Rome	EDF 1	–	581	581
Yaoundé I	EDF 2	64	666	830
Yaoundé II	EDF 3	90	843	933
Lomé I	EDF 4	390	3,124	3,514
Lomé II	EDF 5	685	4,754	5,439
Lomé III	EDF 6	1,100	7,754	8,854
Lomé IV	EDF 7	1,200	10,800	12,000
Lomé IV (review)	EDF 8	1,658	12,967	14,625
Cotonou	EDF 9	1,700	13,500 (9,900)***	15,200 (25,100)***

Notes:
*Own resources, loans.
**Includes grants, special loans, STABEX, SYSMIN.
***Figures in parentheses include unspent EDF8 funds carried forward.
Sources: The Courier (1990) no. 120, p. 26 and (1996) no. 155, p. 12; *ACP-EU Partnership Agreement signed in Cotonou on 23 June 2000*, Special Issue, *The Courier*, European Commission, Brussels.

component. As Table 15.2 illustrates, the EU has used the European Development Fund (EDF), a special funding mechanism separate from the Community budget, to finance its development aid to the ACP. The ACP states were disappointed with the EDF allocation for the Cotonou agreement (the so-called EDF9), just as they were with previous EDF allocations. They pointed out that the size of the Cotonou allocation seemed inconsistent with the EU's supposed commitment to poverty eradication.

The final level of resources for EDF9 was set at €15.2 billion over a five-year period – €13.5 billion in the EDF and €1.7 billion from European Investment Bank's (EIB) own resources – a figure that was only marginally more than EDF8 (with no increase in real terms). To compromise, the EU agreed that unspent balances from earlier EDF allocations could be carried forward, making the total of new and old funds available over €25 billion. Nevertheless, disbursing the funds may prove to be more problematic than the size of the budget itself. The record of the EDF shows that disbursement faces serious obstacles, often because of insufficient institutional capacity in many ACP states, as well as within the Commission. At the time of the signing of the Cotonou Agreement, €9.9 billion remained uncommitted from previous EDFs. Critics have noted that no targets or timetable have been set for levels of disbursement, and predict that continued low levels of disbursement will also come to characterize Cotonou and undermine the main policy objective of poverty eradication (Laryea, 2000).

Financial co-operation must be consistent with the development objectives of the ACP states: this involves respecting their 'geographical, social and cultural characteristics' as well as emphasizing the 'importance of predictability and security' (Art. 56). While Cotonou stresses ACP ownership and responsibility for development programme priorities and objectives (for both state and non-state actors), the decision on funding any projects or programmes remains solely with the EU. Article 60 defines the scope of financing to include measures to reduce debt and balance of payments problems; macroeconomic and structural reforms; stabilisation of export earnings; institutional development and capacity-building; technical co-operation; and humanitarian and emergency assistance.

Cotonou hopes to promote greater efficiency by rationalizing the financial mechanisms available under the agreement. The complexity and diversity of instruments that operated independently, reducing overall coherence, was a major implementation problem under Lomé. The EDF now only provides for two financial instruments: one covering non-reimbursable aid such as long-term subsidies for development support; and the other providing risk capital and loans as a private-sector investment facility. Thus, rather than receiving a multitude of financial allocations, ACP states receive a single indicative total sum for all operations covering a five-year period. In addition, the new rolling programming system takes the performance of ACP economies into account when assessing financial support, and no longer makes decisions purely based on need. The criteria for assessment are based on EU–ACP negotiations, recognizing the different individual political, economic and social characteristics of each state. In this way it is hoped that resources will no longer be frozen in the indicative programme budgets of countries that are unable to use them effectively.

Cotonou also provides for three significant macroeconomic policies: debt relief; structural adjustment; and export earnings stabilization. The introduction of financial measures aimed at debt relief was a significant break with the past and reflected the success of global pressure, as well as of a change in member state positions on the issue during the late 1990s (especially in Germany and Britain). Resources covered by the Agreement can now be used for debt relief initiatives that have international approval: the EU has also given an undertaking to see if additional resources can be mobilized to reduce the debt burden. While welcoming the EU initiative on debt relief, the ACP continues to argue for greater EU involvement in support of a fully-funded international Highly Indebted Poor Countries programme, as well as the cancellation of unsustainable debt levels incurred by the ACP (Laryea, 2000).

Support for structural adjustments – particularly those that address regional integration issues – is also extended in the Partnership Agreement. Joint ACP–EU assessment of such macroeconomic programmes is envisaged to 'ensure that adjustment is economically viable and socially and politically bearable' (Art. 67). As long as the criteria employed by the principal multilateral donors (such as the IMF and World Bank) are met, EU financial support for structural adjustment programmes is 'automatic'. In this way it is hoped that disbursement of funds can be accelerated and fewer Commission staff resources committed to structural adjustment programme assessments. Finally, the spirit of both STABEX and SYSMIN are incorporated into the Agreement. Long-term support is provided 'in order to mitigate the adverse effects of any instability in export earnings, including in the agricultural and mining sectors' (Art. 68).

The paradigm shifts

Whether as a result of grand design or incremental change, Cotonou executed three significant policy paradigm shifts in EU development policy. First, it established an innovative economic paradigm. Second, it reinterpreted political conditionality. Third, it adopted the principle of differentiation as a new criterion. Each of these shifts is examined in more detail below.

Economic partnership agreements

Cotonou presents a blend of past practice and innovation. For example, the concept of partnership (irrespective of the actual content) was as much the defining characteristic of Lomé as of Cotonou. Similarly, while Cotonou's focus on poverty eradication, combined with sustainable development and the gradual integration of the ACP economies within the global economy, defined a more precise EU development role, such a focus was far from revolutionary. Poverty reduction has been part of the EU's formal treaty obligation since Maastricht, and informally for much longer. The renewed emphasis on poverty reduction – with the longer-term aim of eradication – does appear to promise that future EU policy may be more able to take into account the complexity and multi-dimensional nature of poverty. The former one-dimensional approach centring on preferential trade has been superseded by three priority areas of co-operation: economic development; social and human development; and regional integration and co-operation.

The one area where the Partnership Agreement can justifiably claim innovation concerns the context within which development occurs, emphasizing more trade and investment. As argued earlier, the EU's remedy for this has been to depart from Lomé's privileged trade preferences approach to embrace free trade as the better mechanism for economic growth. Transition periods notwithstanding, this constitutes a radical departure from the past uniform basis of economic relations between the EU and the ACP that had developed over twenty-five years.

In contrast to Lomé's uniformity, the Partnership Agreement now differentiates between levels of development for ACP states. The least developed countries remain governed principally by the traditional Lomé approach, while the EU applies new conditions for liberalized economic partnerships to the more economically able ACP states. Practically all LDC exports will benefit from non-reciprocal free access to the EU market by 2005 (the sugar and beef protocols being the only major exceptions to this). The EU's approach to the LDCs reflects a wider international assessment of the particular economic situation of these states. The EU's role is especially crucial as forty of the world's LDCs are signatories of the Cotonou Agreement.

The radical reform of trading relations, therefore, applies specifically to the non-LDC ACP states. A series of deadlines for the progressive abolition of trade barriers and the introduction of WTO compatible free trade has been promulgated in Article 37 of the Agreement. Negotiations on economic partnership agreements began in late 2002 with a view to their introduction no later than January 2008. During this interim period the Lomé IV trade regime is being maintained, although some commodity protocols are being reviewed. But agreements on trade liberalization seem far from inevitable with all the ACP states: consequently, Cotonou made provision for an assessment in 2004 to determine which of the non-LDC ACP states are not in a position to move towards free trade. For these states, alternative arrangements will be examined to provide them with 'a new framework for trade which is equivalent to their existing situation and in conformity with WTO rules'.

Even for those non-LDC states regarded as suitable, a further review in 2006 will assess whether a longer transition beyond 2008 is necessary. For those countries able to meet the original deadline, a transitional period will have to be agreed upon before all elements of the negotiated trade agreement are implemented fully. The wording of the Agreement is cautionary on this point, noting the need to take into account the socio-economic impact and variable capacity of ACP countries to adapt and adjust to liberalization. Consequently, negotiations will 'be as flexible as possible in establishing the duration of a sufficient transitional period . . . and the degree of asymmetry in terms of timetable for tariff dismantlement' (Art. 37). No timeframe for the transition is specified, but other agreements suggest that up to twelve years is possible.

In addition, Article 37 raises the issue of WTO compatibility in several places and calls on the EU and ACP to 'closely co-operate and collaborate in the WTO with a view to defending the arrangements reached'. Elsewhere the Agreement calls for identification of common ACP–EU interests and a more effective lobbying of the WTO agenda to promote a development perspective foreshadowed in the Doha round. Clearly conflict at the international level is widely anticipated. Given these intra-ACP–EU issues and the external challenges, the agreement signed in Cotonou in 2000 may be fully implemented only by 2020. Despite the hope that the new trade agreements will come into force in January 2008, there is ample opportunity for delay, intentional or not.

The precondition for these Economic Partnership Agreements is the development of regional groupings within the ACP. The template is for group-to-group economic relationships, not for a series of bilateral and *ad hoc* agreements between the EU and seventy-eight individual ACP actors. The assumptions and challenges this presents for the ACP are significant. Effective regional integration is a sensitive and often contentious economic and political issue between ACP states. It will require detailed and painstaking interstate negotiations over several years without any guarantee of success. Many of the anticipated regional groupings combine relatively developed ACP economies with those classified as LDCs. Any effective regional integration that combines these two groups will be especially difficult to achieve. At the same time, these ACP states will have to liberalize their economies in line with international standards and may face significant political and social upheaval. Under the circumstances, 2008 could prove to be an illusionary deadline for most of the eligible ACP states.

Trade liberalization is to go hand-in-hand with a wider range of co-operation across associated areas. For example, the Partnership Agreement covers competition policy, intellectual property rights, information and communication technologies, standardization, consumer protection, the environment and labour standards. On balance, Cotonou presents a more complete set of arrangements on which to construct the EU–ACP partnership than did its predecessor. And the overall aim remains ambitious and long-term in nature – 'sustainable development' that leads to the 'gradual integration of the ACP States into the world economy . . . implemented in full conformity' with WTO provisions (Art. 34).

Extending political conditionality

Negotiations on the political dimension of the agreement were among the most sensitive. Consequently, the most that was possible was to outline general principles and a limited number of specific issues, leaving their implementation and evaluation for future consideration. Article 8, for example, stipulates that the EU and ACP 'shall regularly engage in a comprehensive, balanced and deep political dialogue'. The purpose of the dialogue was similarly anodyne: to exchange information, foster mutual understanding and develop 'agreed priorities and shared agendas'. Areas of 'mutual concern or of general significance' that the dialogue specifically mentions are 'the arms trade, excessive military expenditure, drugs and organised crime, or ethnic, religious or racial discrimination' as well as 'respect for human rights, democratic principles, the rule of law and good governance' (Art. 8.4). Political dialogue was not confined to the formal institutional framework of the Agreement but could also take place informally and at regional or subregional levels as deemed appropriate.

For reasons of political expediency, yet somewhat confusingly, the Agreement distinguishes between 'essential elements' and a 'fundamental element' (Gomes, 2000). Duplicating Lomé IV, three 'essential elements' are identified: respect for human rights, democratic principles and the rule of law. These are expected to govern the behaviour of the EU and ACP both domestically and internationally. Article 9 describes these in the following terms. First, human rights are defined as 'universal, indivisible and inter-related': all fundamental freedoms and human rights, 'be they civil and political, or economic, social and cultural' must be protected and promoted under the Agreement. Second, universally recognized democratic principles must underpin the legitimacy and legality of state authority (reflected in its constitutional, legislative and regulatory system, and the existence of participatory mechanisms): on the basis of these universally recognized principles, each country develops its democratic culture. Third, the Agreement stipulates that the structure and authority of government 'shall be founded on the rule of law, which shall entail in particular effective and accessible means of legal redress, an independent legal system guaranteeing equality before the law and an executive that is fully subject to the law'. Breaches of any of these essential elements may ultimately lead to a country being suspended from the Agreement. Any party to the Agreement can bring such a breach to the EU-ACP Council of Ministers, which, within fifteen days, must engage in 'consultation' with the offending country on how best to remedy the situation. Where consultation proves unsuccessful or is refused, or in cases where immediate action is necessitated, 'appropriate measures' in accordance with international law and proportional to the violation, may be taken. Full suspension from the Agreement is seen only as a measure of last resort (Art. 96).

The text dealing with good governance and corruption is largely new and not simply duplicated from the earlier Lomé provisions. As such, it signifies the second paradigm shift identified in this chapter. The concept is defined in the following terms:

> good governance is the transparent and accountable management of human, natural, economic and financial resources for the purposes of equitable and sustainable development. It entails clear decision-making procedures at the level of public authorities, transparent and accountable institutions, the primacy of law in the management and distribution of resources and capacity building for elaborating and implementing measures aiming in particular at preventing and combating corruption. (Art. 9.3)

Achieving this broad definition was in itself considered to be a notable success (Gomes, 2000). Provisions for the regular assessment of good governance are built into the Agreement, taking into account 'each country's economic, social, cultural and historical context'. Because of ACP opposition, 'good governance' did not constitute an 'essential element' of the Agreement, but was given a somewhat different status – that of a 'fundamental element'. The consequence of this modification is that breaches of 'good governance' cannot lead to any sanctions or suspensions being invoked by the EU. The only exception is for cases of financial corruption, where suspension is again an option of last resort.

It remains to be seen whether this political conditionality will be substantive or cosmetic and selective. The greater involvement of civil society could prove a litmus test. For the EU, the involvement of non-governmental actors is essential to the consolidation of democracy, something that the EU regards as a pre-condition for economic development. Thus the promotion of democracy and democratic norms – bolstered through political dialogue – has become the core element in the EU's development policy towards the Third World in general. But 'good governance' can be viewed as a minimalist condition – the efficient management of public affairs – or as an inclusive one that involves pluralistic processes, norms and a rejection of corruption. Some commentators have argued that the democratic agenda of Cotonou is unrealizable and that, when coupled with poverty alleviation, Cotonou sets unrealistic and unobtainable goals (Holland, 2002). A framework for partnership may be able to contribute to these objectives, but it is an unreasonable expectation for Cotonou alone to achieve these outcomes.

The new agreement presents the ACP and the EU with a broader basis on which to engage in political dialogue. In principle, at least, any issue of mutual interest may be discussed. Explicit references to new topics, such as peace building and conflict prevention (Art. 11) and migration issues (Art. 13), have been incorporated, providing a legal basis for the development of

EU–ACP joint policy in these areas. The origins of violent conflict, mediation, negotiation and reconciliation processes may be examined, together with specific issues such as military spending, child soldiers and anti-personnel mines. On ACP insistence, migration is dealt with in some detail in the Agreement. This includes the 'fair treatment' of legally resident ACP nationals, the extension of rights comparable to those for EU citizens, as well as action to combat employment discrimination, racism and xenophobia. In response, the EU insisted on 'a prevention policy' on illegal immigration by normalizing migratory flows through improving social and economic conditions throughout the ACP. More pointedly, the Agreement now requires the ACP states to 'accept the return of any of its nationals' found illegally resident in the EU 'without further formalities' (Art. 13.5). The EU also wanted to extend this condition to non-nationals who used ACP states to enter the EU illegally, but the ACP was success in blocking it (Gomes, 2000).

These topics – peace, conflict and migration – are a logical consequence of the incorporation of development goals within the EU's Common Foreign and Security Policy (CFSP). Institutionally and in terms of EU competences, the Maastricht Treaty linked development policy across the three new pillars and gave greater legitimacy to political dialogue as an essential EU activity with third countries. It was no longer feasible to quarantine development policy as being purely economic in content; its association with CFSP made it undeniably political as well.

Differentiation: a Trojan horse?

The third paradigm shift promoted by Cotonou concerns geographical differentiation and regionalism. For impartial observers, the expression of ACP group solidarity has often been perplexing. What can micro Pacific Island states facing rising sea levels because of global warming really have in common with, say, the landlocked African state of Zambia, or a sub-Saharan giant such as Nigeria? And yet one of the principal objectives of the ACP states was to protect the integrity of the APC as a group. Maintaining recognition by the EU of the group collectively, rather than regionally or bilaterally, was paramount. The ACP was motivated by the view that a single voice for seventy-eight states would be the most effective negotiating position, and that twenty-five years of collective action had produced a degree of solidarity and commonality of views. The final outcome at Cotonou was an uneasy compromise. The ACP umbrella was retained, but the provisions for distinct and autonomous regional economic partnerships appeared to end the EU's uniform approach to the developing world of Africa, the Caribbean and the Pacific. Some have suggested that this compromise is tantamount to a

Trojan horse and will eventually succeed in dividing the ACP internally. Conversely, others have argued that any commonality expressed by the group was only superficial at best, and dismemberment of the group was long overdue.

The undeniable message from Cotonou is that the EU preference is to promote ACP regional integration and deal primarily on a region-to-region basis. Such a development corresponds to the EU's original philosophy and is consistent with a view of integration as a global process. However, the EU also regards regional integration as the most effective route by which the ACP states can re-enter the international economy. In the words of Article 35.2 of the Partnership Agreement, 'regional integration is a key instrument for the integration of the ACP countries into the world economy'. Articles 29 and 30, covering the promotion of single, unified regional markets, cross-border issues, and direct assistance for the institutionalization of regional integration, lend practical support to this. Furthermore, regional integration, if it does promote growth, is also seen as a means of realizing the EU's major development policy objective: the reduction of poverty. It may also help to bridge the gap between the LDCs and other developing countries within a particular region. All of these potential advantages are, of course, premised on the political requirement on which any form of regional integration is based: the promotion of democracy and good governance. The corresponding economic requirement – sound economic management, including the removal of intra-regional tariffs (and subsequent loss of revenue) – may prove to be problematic and require a revision in the Cotonou free trade timetable.

The special differentiation provisions for LDCs in the Partnership Agreement complement the emphasis on regional integration. Cotonou recognizes realistically the dichotomy that had always existed within the ACP but went largely unrecognized in Lomé: namely, that between the very least developed states and the other developing ACP countries. Cotonou uses the LDC category as a new organizing principle for its economic reforms: development status under the Partnership Agreement now determines the appropriate trade regime.

As is the case for LDCs in general, Cotonou's LDCs are located predominantly in Africa; there is only one LDC in the Caribbean and six in the Pacific (see Table 15.3). The predominance of LDCs in Africa – representing half of all African states – presents a serious challenge to the objective of integrating these countries into the global economy. Any regional integration arrangement inevitably must include a number of LDCs. Indeed, according to Article 29 of the Partnership Agreement, one of the objectives of regional economic integration is 'fostering participation of LDC ACP States in the establishment of regional markets and sharing the benefits'.

Table 15.3   *Least developed countries covered by 'Everything But Arms'*
(EBA)

The 49 EBA states	
ACP LDCs	*Non-ACP LDCs*
Africa: Sudan, Mauritania, Mali, Burkina Faso, Niger, Chad, Cape Verde, Gambia, Guinea-Bissau, Guinea, Sierra Leone, Liberia, Togo, Benin, Central African Republic, Equatorial Guinea, Sao Tomé and Principe, Democratic Republic of Congo, Rwanda, Burundi, Angola, Ethiopia, Eritrea, Djibouti, Somalia, Uganda, Tanzania, Mozambique, Madagascar, Comoros, Zambia, Malawi, Lesotho	Yemen, Afghanistan, Bangladesh, Maldives, Nepal, Bhutan, Myanmar, Laos, Cambodia
Caribbean: Haiti	
Pacific: Solomon Islands, Tuvalu, Kiribati, Vanuatu, Samoa, East Timor	

Note: There are 49 LDCs on the UN list: 40 of these are ACP countries. All GSP preferences for Myanmar have been suspended, and this also applies to EBA preferences.
Source: http://europa.eu.int/comm/trade/miti/devel/eba4_sum.htm

The Agreement does not require LDCs to adopt trade liberalization regimes. It recognises that LDCs need to be accorded 'special treatment in order to enable them to overcome the serious economic and social difficulties hindering their development' (Art. 85). Specifically, the provisions for the new economic and trade regime propose that, by 2005 at the latest, 'essentially all products' from the LDCs will have duty-free access 'building on the level of existing trade provisions of the Fourth ACP–EC Convention' (Art. 37).

But the broader policy issue remains problematic. How will future free trade agreements between any regional grouping and the EU accommodate the protectionist needs of LDCs? Detailed rules of origin and tariff controls needed by the LDCs would appear to conflict with any notion of trade liberalization and demand high compliance costs. Thus, for the core ACP countries and the vast majority of their impoverished citizens, notably in Africa, effective regional economic partnership agreements would seem a distant prospect at best. This position is further compounded by the separate 'Everything But Arms' initiative launched by the EU in 2001.

To summarize the effect of Cotonou: other than for the LDCs, the continuation of the Lomé framework has largely been abandoned, and the principle of trade liberalization replaced by that of non-reciprocal privileged access. While the shock of this change will be cushioned somewhat by lengthy negotiation and transition periods that retain some aspects of the Lomé *acquis*, there has been a paradigmatic shift in the focus and direction of EU–ACP relations. But ultimately, these reforms depend for their success on a wider global agenda and on improved institutional capacity to enhance policy implementation. Without better, quicker and more coordinated implementation (on the part of the ACP, but also the EU) the primary objective of the Partnership Agreement – poverty reduction – will remain impossible to attain. The challenges that confront the effective implementation of Cotonou and how this agreement meshes with the most recent EU development initiative – the 'Everything But Arms' proposal – are discussed in the following section.

Beyond the ACP: 'Everything But Arms'

Both the complexity as well as the dynamic pace of change that has come to characterize the EU's development policy at the start of the twenty-first century was reflected in the so-called 'Everything But Arms' proposal adopted by the EU Council of Ministers on 28 February 2001. 'Everything But Arms' provides all LDCs – including those in Asia – with duty-free non-reciprocal access to the EU for all products other than weapons. This new approach is consistent with the thrust of the Partnership Agreement, while none the less suggesting a fundamental break with the EU's previous approach to development policy. As has already been noted, Cotonou introduced the principle of differentiation according to development status and offered special treatment for ACP states classified as least developed countries (LDCs). The Agreement even foreshadowed the general application of this new principle. While being consistent with the Cotonou philosophy, the EBA has breached the long-established policy of offering the ACP preferential advantages over all other developing countries. To extend non-reciprocity to non-ACP LDCs implied, if not endorsed, a view that the ACP as a group was no longer the dominant organizing principle for EU–Third World relations. The EU initiative split the ACP into the thirty-eight non-LDCs and forty LDCs, which would in future be dealt with under an exclusive new 49-country LDC framework. This would appear to have vindicated critics who saw the Lomé renegotiation process as the forerunner of the fragmentation of the ACP group.

According to the Commission, EBA constitutes a ground-breaking plan to provide full access for the world's poorest countries to EU markets by granting them duty-free status. The proposal covered all goods apart from the arms trade: hence the slogan, 'Everything But Arms'. European Trade Commissioner, Pascal Lamy, was forthright in his advocacy of the new proposal:

> There has been plenty of talk about how market access for poor countries is critical if we are to tackle their growing marginalisation in the globalising economy . . . But talk is cheap. We now need to move beyond opt-out clauses. It's time to put access to our markets where our mouth is. That means opening up across the board, and for all the poorest countries. So we want to move to liberalise everything but the arms trade. (Lamy, 2001)

Given its implications, the proposal drew fire from two directions. First, a number of existing ACP beneficiaries feared that their interests would be affected by this more inclusive programme. Second, some of the more protectionist EU member states initially expressed opposition. To placate the ACP, concessions were made on transitional arrangements for significant products (specifically rice, sugar and bananas). None the less, the potential impact on ACP bananas was still regarded as problematic by several Caribbean states. And, of course, these concessions inevitably promoted continued LDC reliance on largely unprocessed raw products with little added value accruing. Member state concerns over the potential for fraud and the difficulties of monitoring rules-of-origin were addressed in the eventual regulation, and specific measures were established to safeguard the EU from a flood of fraudulent imports. A somewhat different criticism was also raised by some LDCs, who argued that greater benefits would result from ceasing European arms sales to the developing world rather than excluding the duty-free export of Third World arms to the EU.

The Council adopted 'Everything But Arms' as an amendment to the EU's Generalized Scheme of Preferences: as of March 2001, goods from the world's forty-nine LDCs have received tariff-free access to the EU market for all products other than arms and ammunition. This made the EU the first major trading power to commit itself to opening its market fully to the world's most impoverished countries. Duty and quota restrictions were eliminated immediately on all products apart from certain sensitive ACP items, where full liberalization is to be phased in over a lengthy transition period. 'Everything But Arms' complemented the LDC content of the Cotonou Agreement and triggered a process intended to ensure free access for 'essentially all' products from all LDCs by 2005 at the latest.

Possible impact

What will be the likely effect of the 'Everything But Arms' initiative? Does its economic content match the EU's rhetoric? According to Commission figures, the EU is the main destination for LDC exports. In 1998, LDCs exported goods worth € 15.5 billion; of this total, the EU took 56 per cent (worth € 8.7 billion) while the USA imported 36 per cent (worth € 5.6 billion) and Japan just 6 per cent. However, the previous regime excluded about 10 per cent of the 10,500 tariff lines in the EU's tariff schedule. The EBA regulation addressed this omission by granting duty-free and unrestricted quota access for a further 919 lines, covering products from all LDCs. The new list left out just twenty-five tariff lines, all of which were related to the arms trade. For the first time, all agricultural products were covered, including beef and other meat; dairy products; fresh and processed fruit and vegetables; maize and other cereals; starch; oils; processed sugar products; cocoa products; pasta; and alcoholic beverages. Only the three most sensitive products – bananas, rice and sugar – were not liberalised immediately. As the Commissioner for Trade, Pascal Lamy commented:

> We have been through this line-by-line, product-by-product, and have concluded that we should now take this important further step. Of course, some of the products are relatively sensitive, but there is no point in offering trade concessions on products, which LDCs cannot export . . . We of course recognise that duty free access alone is not enough to enable the poorest countries to benefit from liberalised trade. We need to help them build their capacity to supply goods of export quality, and we reaffirm the Commission's commitment to continued technical and financial assistance to this end. (Lamy, 2001)

This seeming European largesse has to be balanced against other provisions of the EBA regulations that seek to stabilize the effect of this liberalization, and in extreme circumstances protect EU producers and EU financial interests. Article 2.7 gives the Commission the authority to invoke if necessary the 'temporary suspension of the preferences'. Typically, the EU has designated itself judge and jury in any such cases. More generally, Article 4 provides for measures to combat fraud, including the failure to provide sufficient administrative co-operation to verify the precise country of origin of LDC goods, and 'massive increases' in the normal levels of LDC production and export capacity to the EU. Finally, Article 5 provides for the suspension of references by the Commission for a range of particularly sensitive products 'if the imports of these products cause serious disturbance to Community markets and their regulatory mechanisms'. A 25 per cent annual increase is sufficient to trigger this procedure. Through these mechanisms the EU will monitor carefully imports of rice, sugar and bananas, and apply safeguard measures where necessary.

It is hard not to suspect the EU of making a self-serving compromise in relation to these omnibus provisions. The Commission's case – that the reason for these safeguards is to ensure that trading benefits accrue only to the countries for which they are intended (the LDCs) – lacks a certain conviction. The scrupulous application of anti-fraud measures has at least as much to do with placating the interests of member states whose domestic production will be most effected by the new concessions. To clarify the issue, the Council has asked the Commission to report in 2005 on the extent to which the LDCs are really benefiting from EBA, and whether the EU's provisions on rules of origin, anti-fraud and safeguards are adequate. Therefore the Commission is examining the impact of such trade within the EU and on LDCs, as well as on the African, Caribbean and Pacific countries, to propose appropriate changes where necessary.

Conclusion: normalization of a partnership?

Both Cotonou and the EBA are potentially ground-breaking agreements: the EBA goes beyond any other WTO initiative, and Cotonou adopts a fresh approach to development. While the European initiative has been welcomed widely, developing countries would benefit further if America and Japan followed the EU's lead. Of course, neither agreement addresses the non-tariff barriers that often restrict developing country exports from entering the EU market, or the supply-side problems common in many developing countries that limit their trade potential.

Without undermining the benign intent of the EBA, there is growing concern among some developing countries that the EBA may conflict with the broader development strategies of Cotonou. In an ideal world, the reform process that led to the Cotonou Agreement would have developed simultaneously with the EBA discussions, ensuring a degree of coherence, co-ordination and complementarity. But the existence of two separate agreements, with overlapping but not identical membership, presents the ACP with a potential dilemma. The least developed ACP countries are party to both agreements and have a choice of frameworks: the non-LDC ACP states, however, are excluded from the benefits of the EBA and some are concerned that the market access guaranteed by Cotonou will, in practice, be undermined by the more generous EBA provisions provided for non-ACP LDCs.

More significantly, the tariff-free access offered to the least-developed

ACP states seems to obviate the necessity to enter into regional free trade agreements with the EU, as suggested in the Cotonou Agreement. All potential ACP regional free trade agreements include the least developed countries. Why should any ACP LDC exchange non-reciprocal unlimited access to the EU market for a regional free trade agreement that would give the EU free access to its markets and remove its ability to raise tariff revenue at its borders? Thus, unintentionally perhaps, the EBA could undermine the Cotonou Agreement's objective of creating regional free trade agreements. Once gain, the viability of the ACP as a coherent group can be questioned. And perhaps more worryingly, the complexity of orchestrating a global approach to development policy at the EU level that respects consistency and coherence, as well as complementarity, may inadvertently compromise the integrity of these new policy-making frameworks. Such unintended consequences could undermine the effectiveness of EU development policy in the twenty-first century.

To conclude, EU development policy has entered a new and radical phase. The three paradigmatic shifts identified here – free trade, good governance and differentiation – together signal an end to the Lomé framework that shaped EU–ACP relations for a quarter of a century. In addition, the extension of LDC non-reciprocal trading relations to non-ACP LDCs underlines the evolving change in the EU's conceptualization of the 'Third World'. Policy is now being driven by development criteria other than colonial pasts. Of course, such comprehensive revision always carries with it the risk of unintended consequences that could undermine policy coherence and complementarity. Irrespective of the benign intent, the EBA and the Partnership Agreement appear to present such a potential conflict.

Finally, has Cotonou led to a normalization of relations? The conclusion is mixed and as yet uncertain. The assumption that regional integration will result in the creation of six ACP regional partners for the EU is, at best, contentious. If the ACP states can reorganize themselves into effective regional groupings, then there is at least the potential for normal (liberalized) trading relations for the non-LDC states. But for the LDCs the 'abnormality' of Lomé-style non-reciprocal preferences continues to define their relationship with the EU. Although optimists see this as a transitionary phase to free trade, others conclude that it foreshadows dependency in perpetuity. Some critics even suggest that the EU's desire to normalize relations with the LDCs is inappropriate and that policy should recognize the reality of continued long-term marginalization. And, ultimately, it is difficult to talk of normalization when the EU–ACP relationship remains conditional on good governance, at the insistence of the EU.

Chapter 16

Developments in European Integration Theory: The EU as 'Other'

MARIA GREEN COWLES AND STEPHANIE CURTIS

This chapter examines how theoretical and methodological approaches to the study of the European Union (EU) have evolved in recent years, reflecting changes in European integration and in the nature of the European polity itself. Theoretical developments, after all, do not occur in a vacuum. Rather, scholars often re-examine existing theories and explore new theoretical approaches to help to explain the 'real world'. Thus the first theoretical accounts in the early years of European integration were helpful in describing the emergence of the European Coal and Steel Community in 1952. The same theories in the 2000s, however, fail to capture decision-making processes in the European Parliament or the dynamics of Central and Eastern enlargement. As Rosamond notes, 'Theoretical work on European integration is obviously bound up in complex ways with the unfolding story of the EU' (Rosamond, 2000, p. xi).

Theoretical developments also take place because of changes in the scholarly community. American international relations theorists such as Haas (1958), and Hoffman (1966), Lindberg (1963) and Schmitter (1970) dominated the study of the European Community for several decades. By the 1990s, European scholars such as Bulmer (1994), Kohler-Koch (1993), Héritier (1997) and Scharpf (1988) easily rivalled their American counterparts in developing public policy and comparative theoretical approaches to describe and explain EU policy-making. New EU scholars, particularly from the Nordic countries and from Central and Eastern Europe, are contributing to a field long dominated by academics from large Western European countries and the USA. No doubt their perspectives are transforming the EU theoretical debate.

How is the theoretical study of the EU evolving? What subject matter do EU scholars address? Which theories do they employ? Why? This chapter suggests that EU theory has gone through several different phases of development. The first phase highlighted the origins and development of European integration. The second examined the single market and day-to-day policy-making in the European Community (EC). The third identified the EU as a polity, not a supranational or intergovernmental organization *per se*, but a political organization with state-like qualities. During this phase, scholars focused on governance, often comparing the EU to other polities.

EU theoretical development is now in a fourth phase, in which scholars no longer look at the EU as a self-contained polity. Rather, they are grappling with the boundaries of the EU (geographic, legal, political and so on); with EU identity as understood by individuals as well as the outside world; and the larger meaning of the EU itself. For many scholars, the EU can no longer be studied solely as a Euro-polity to be compared to other systems of governance, but as something 'other' – a transforming presence in domestic structures, an international actor, a less-Western polity, a constitutional entity.

The first section of this chapter highlights the initial phases of EU theoretical development. The second examines the 'what, which and why' of the current phase. It looks at the subject matter ('what'), the theories used to examine these subjects ('which'), and some of the reasons for looking at these subjects ('why'). The chapter concludes by reflecting briefly on these changes, as well as on the future theoretical direction in EU studies.

Theoretical developments over time

What is theory, and in particular, EU theory? Scholars differ on the definition of social science theory. F.N. Kerlinger defines theory as 'as set of interrelated constructs (concepts), definitions, and propositions that presents a systematic view of phenomena by specifying relationships among variables, with the purpose of explaining and predicting phenomena' (Kerlinger, 1986, p. 9). King *et al.* (1994) expand on the definition of theory and carefully point out the difference between descriptive and causal inferences. Arguably theories that describe things or ascribe normative values to phenomena are not theories in the strict social scientific sense, but rather descriptive devices or methodological approaches.

Moravcsik (1993) has led the charge in positing that EU theory should follow this social scientific approach by specifying more carefully the variables and conditions under which European integration takes place. A number of European scholars have countered that American-influenced social scientific theory is just one means of explaining the dynamics of integration. Scholars point out that to define the 'proper' or appropriate way to theorize about the EU tends to bias one type of theory over another. T. Dietz and A. Wiener maintain that theories serve different purposes. While one type of theory may provide one approach to explaining the decisions made by heads of state and government, another may be better disposed to provide normative guidance: '[D]ifferent theoretical approaches to European integration are informed by different understandings of the meaning and purpose of theorizing' (Dietz and Wiener, 2003, p. 2). Broadly speaking, different theories *explain, describe,* and in certain cases *assess,* European integration in different ways and for different reasons (ibid.).

Of course, such a broad definition of theory can be problematical. None the less, the purpose of this chapter is not to champion one kind of theory over another, or to make distinctions between social scientific theory and methodological approaches. Rather it is to look at EU theory, as presented by scholars in various ways, and discuss its development.

Figure 16.1 identifies five phases of EU theoretical development. These are not discrete phases. After all, the focus in the first phase (the beginning), analysing European integration, remains an important aspect of EU theorizing in the fourth phase (the period since 2000). Nevertheless, the phases serve as heuristic tools to highlight EU theoretical development.

The first phase of theoretical development focused naturally on the origins and development of the EC. Neo-functionalist theories of Haas (1958), Lindberg (1963), Lindberg and Scheingold (1970) and Schmitter (1970) sought to explain the nascent EC. According to the neo-functionalists, European integration first took place because of the shifting loyalties of non-state actors – economic and political elites – who found their

Figure 16.1   *Five phases of theoretical development*

Theory phases	Explanatory foci	Key theories
1 The Beginning (1950s–1980s)	Origins and development of European integration	Neofunctionalism, intergovernmentalism, transactionalism
2 The Market (1989–mid 1990s)	Creation of single market, grand bargains versus everyday policy-making;	Neofunctionalism, Intergovernmentalism, regulation theory
3 The Polity (1990s)	EU as a polity, governance of the polity	Institutionalism, comparative politics, public policy
4 The 'Other' (2000s–)	Reconceptualization of the polity, reform of the polity, beyond the polity	Institutionalism, constructivism, Europeanization, networks, political economy
5 The Future?	– –	– –

demands were being met by the emerging supranational organization. This supranational body was the second focus of neo-functionalists. Run by technical experts, the supranational authority had the wherewithal to structure agendas, develop policies and address these societal concerns. Neo-functionalists also created the concept of spillover: the notion that technical expertise in one policy area would overlap with and flow into another area, thus allowing the supranational body to assume more political authority.

The infamous 'Empty Chair' crisis in the mid-1960s, when President Charles de Gaulle asserted the primacy of French national interests, pointed out the limits of neo-functionalist theory. European integration was not a smooth, linear process, but one that ebbed and flowed, and, at times, appeared not to advance at all. Hoffmann (1966) argued that societal elites and supranational institutions were not the primary actors of European integration. Offering an intergovernmentalist critique, Hoffmann maintained that it was nation-states who ultimately determined whether the European project would proceed or not. Haas (1975) himself later acknowledged the limits of societal demands and the role of supranational institutions in European integration.

The launch of the single market programme ushered in the second phase of EU theoretical development. Neo-functionalist theory (Sandholtz and Zysman, 1989) and intergovernmentalist theory (Moravcsik, 1991) emerged as the primary theoretical explanations for the programme and for the Single European Act of 1986 which, by extended qualified majority voting to most single market measures, made it possible to implement many of them before the stipulated deadline of 1992. Indeed, the lack of alternative theories ensured the resurgence of neo-functionalism and intergovernmentalism. Slowly, however, EU theory began to evolve. Moravcsik (1993), with his liberal intergovernmentalist theory, offered a more robust explanation of state action in European integration with a two-stage approach. During the first stage, Moravcsik opened up the 'blackbox' of the state. Hoffman's intergovernmentalist approach, for example, emphasized the important role of states but did little to explain why states would promote European integration – or prevent it from taking place. Moravcsik, however, argued that domestic societal groups expressed their preferences to state leaders, thus shaping member states' approaches to the EU. In the second stage, Moravcsik offered a power-bargaining approach to explain how governments would then negotiate among themselves over whether and how to advance European integration.

Simultaneously, scholars began to incorporate other theoretical frameworks. Majone (1989) raised and later elaborated upon (Majone, 1993) regulation theory and incorporated principle–agent theories to explain why states (the principles) would delegate regulatory policy-making to EU institutions (the agents). While scholars have argued that regulation and related policy analysis theories do not qualify as 'full theories of the integration process' (Caporaso, 1998, p. 8) such theories none the less paved the way for the development of different theoretical approaches to the EU. Whereas Moravcsik focused on the so-called 'grand bargains' and 'high politics' (key decisions made at European Council meetings), other scholars turned their attention to 'everyday policy-making'. European integration, they argued, resulted not merely from the decisions made by EU leaders, but from the cumulative effects of policies and policy-making that rarely made the headlines.

Ironically, the recognition of the 'everyday policy-making' and functioning of the EU helped to introduce an important third phase of EU theorizing in the 1990s. Scholars maintained that the EU was best conceptualized not as an intergovernmental organization but as a polity (Hix, 1994). Their focus was less on an evolving supranational entity and more on the integrated political entity itself. Building on numerous empirical studies of a decade earlier, scholarship in the 1990s brought in comparative politics and public policy perspectives (Richardson, 1996; Sbragia, 1992; Wallace and Wallace, 1996).

Scholars also sought to place this everyday EU policy-making in a larger historical context. Historical institutionalism emerged as an important new theory that focused on how institutions not only provide an arena for EU politics but also 'play an important role in shaping the norms, values and conventions shared by actors involved at the EU level' (Cram *et al.*, 1988, p. 16; see also Bulmer, 1994). Institutionalist scholars argued, for example, that the single market programme was more relevant in the 1990s than in 1985 because it transformed the political and legal contexts of EU capabilities and governance (Armstrong and Bulmer, 1998, p. 4). Institutionalist scholars also noted that government decision-making is shaped not only by the preferences of domestic societal actors but also by the governments' historical participation in the EU. After all, intergovernmental bargaining occurs between 'member states' – and not 'nation-states' – who have a vested interest in the EU. In short, 'membership matters' (Sandholtz, 1996).

Institutionalists also developed another important notion of European integration – that of path dependence (Pierson, 1996). Once governmental decisions are put in place, institutions created and/or policies developed, it is very difficult to reverse them. Because they expend considerable effort to forge these decisions, institutions and policies, governments may simply find it easier to continue working within the EU framework rather than creating new or outside mechanisms. Moreover, certain rules – for example, co-decision – make it difficult for governments to overturn processes. There is thus a built-in bias in favour of European institutional development.

The result of the third phase of EU theoretical development was a shift from 'classical integration theory (that asks which forces and actors account for the development of the Euro-polity)' to a 'governance approach', which takes the Euro-polity for granted (Jachtenfuchs, 2001, p. 255; see also Kohler-Koch, 1993; Kooiman 1993; Kohler-Koch and Eising, 1999; Marks *et al.*, 1996). Instead of asking why and how European integration takes place, scholars seek to understand what are the 'forms, outcomes, problems and development paths of governance in the Euro-polity' (Jachtenfuchs, 2001, p. 256). Put another way, scholars focus less on why governments agreed, for example, to the provisions of the Nice Treaty. Instead, they evaluate how these provisions will have an impact on the ways in which rules are created and policies developed, and will mesh with the existing patterns of day-to-day functioning in the EU.

Theoretical developments today

At the time of writing the EU theoretical debate has entered a fourth phase. Like the previous phase, scholars largely accept the EU as a 'Euro-polity'. At the same time, however, they are seeking to understand better the nature of this polity. Rather than focusing primarily on EU policies and processes and comparing them to other polities, scholars are wrestling with the boundaries, identity and meaning of the Euro-polity.

Boundaries are important determinants of how one governs the EU polity. In earlier phases of EU theoretical development, neo-functionalist and intergovernmentalist scholars alike tried to separate domestic and international boundaries. Intergovernmentalists, for example, argued that domestic groups shaped the negotiating positions of their government, which then bargained with other states at the international level. Multi-level governance approaches in the 1990s sought to make the linkage between domestic, European and international boundaries more explicit (Marks, 1992). In the current phase of European theoretical development, scholars further blur these boundaries. As discussed below, EU governance is no longer confined to Brussels, but also takes place at national and subnational levels. Governance of the EU therefore goes below the member-state.

EU governance also goes beyond the member-state. Indeed, in the current phase of EU theoretical development, scholars conceptualize that the EU has legal, transactional, geopolitical and cultural boundaries that do not necessarily correspond to its traditional institutional boundaries (Friis and Murphy, 1999). For example, EU legal boundaries move beyond the EU when non-EU member states such as Bulgaria accept the *acquis communautaire* in the hope of one day being offered EU membership. The EU thus wields considerable governing power in Bulgaria despite the fact that the country is outside EU geographical boundaries.

Scholars are also focusing on EU identity. Neo-functionalist scholars in the early phases of EU theoretical development focused on shifting loyalties and identity of various societal groups. Scholars in the 'polity' phase recognized that individuals could share multiple identities. An individual could be a Basque, a Spaniard and a European at the same time. Moreover, a person's identity mattered little in terms of the functioning of the European polity. Scholars in the current theoretical phase are again less interested in geographical identities and more concerned with the construction of a collective European identity. Rather, they are interested in understanding why certain groups identify themselves with 'Europeanness' and why others do not.

By addressing boundaries and identity, theorists are also wrestling with the larger meaning (or meanings) of the EU. As opposed to the third phase of theoretical development, the EU is more than a political entity – a polity that can be compared and contrasted to other forms of governance in the world today. The EU is at once an important player on the world economic scene, a transforming force in domestic politics, a promising future for Central and Eastern European governments, a major location for international investment, and a guarantor of human rights and freedoms, among other things.

The subject matter: what?

Figure 16.2 identifies the primary subject matter found in over 400 articles in the *Journal of Common Market Studies* (*JCMS*) and the *Journal of European Public Policy* (*JEPP*), the leading journals in EU scholarship, between 1999 and 2003 (see Cowles and Curtis, in progress). It shows that, in certain respects, the current phase continues to reflect key subject matter addressed in the third phase of theoretical development. The study of EU policies (141 articles) remains a primary focus for EU scholars. Figure 16.3 further breaks down the policy category, identifying specific categories also found in the chapters of this book. That EMU heads the list is not surprising, given the creation of the European Central Bank and the introduction of the euro during this period. Other policies include agriculture, cohesion, migration and asylum, trade, and the environment. Missing from the journals, yet present in this book, is the development of police and judicial co-operation within the framework of the so-called 'Third Pillar' (Justice and Home Affairs), an area too new to have been

Figure 16.2   *Primary subject matter*

EU policies*	141	IGCs and treaties	20
Institutions and reform	74	Non-state actors	20
Enlargement	36	Conceptualizing the EU	17
Europeanization (as subject)	28	European integration	16
Legitimacy and democracy (as subject)	28	Welfare state	11
External relations	21	Governance (as subject)	10
EU theory	22	Other	11

Notes: *Includes all EU policies except external relations. Some article had more than one primary subject matter and were coded for multiple topics; consequently, there are 440 instances of primary subject matter listed above for 414 articles.

Figure 16.3   *Breakdown of EU policies*

EMU	22	Trade	7
Regulatory policy (general)	12	Environmental	6
Agriculture/CAP	11	Standards	6
Migration/asylum/immigration	8	Competition	6
Social	8	Structural policy	4
Gender	7	JHA (general)	2

Note: Excluding external relations.

covered in *JCMS* or *JEPP* before mid-2003. John Occhipinti's contribution to this book (Chapter 10), and his ground-breaking monograph on the subject, underscores the quick and expansive transformation of this policy area in just two years (Occhipinti, 2003).

Given the implementation of the Amsterdam Treaty, and the negotiation and difficult ratification of the Nice Treaty during this period, it is not surprising that articles focusing on institutions and their reform are the second most important topic. The pending accession of the Central and Eastern European countries and its possible impact on the EU invariably contributed to enlargement as the third most important subject for discussion in these two journals. What is different, however, is the theoretical manner in which scholars address enlargement now.

The introduction of Europeanization as a primary subject matter in EU studies is a novel development in the fourth phase. Europeanization is defined in broad terms as the impact of EU structures of governance on domestic institutions – including programmes, policy styles, institutional culture and so on – and the resulting feedback on European institutions. In certain ways, the focus on Europeanization represents a new phase in EU studies (Cowles *et al.*, 2001). Studies on Europeanization emerged slowly (see Andersen and Eliassen, 1993; Cowles *et al.* 2001; Mény *et al.* 1996; Olsen, 1995 and Rometsch and Wessels). Indeed, many of the *JCMS* and *JEPP* journal articles during this period did not begin to use the term 'Europeanization' as a separate identified subject until 2000–2001. Europeanization is an important development in that it examines the EU as a deeper form of polity than that described in the 1990s. Arguably, Europeanization represents a more dynamic understanding of the EU and of European integration itself.

Another set of topics that has grown in importance during the fourth phase is legitimacy and democracy. Of course, scholars addressed the famed 'democratic deficit' in the 1990s, particularly in the aftermath of the Maastricht Treaty (Banchoff and Smith, 1999). In more recent years, practitioners and scholars have wrestled with the larger notion of how to address more profound concerns of legitimacy and democracy. The introduction of civil society groups in trade policy issues is one effort being made to address these concerns. The creation of a European constitution is arguably the most important. Leaders across Europe are actively engaged in constructing a European entity to govern and be accountable to the EU populace. Yet, as Paul Taggart and Aleks Szczerbiak point out in Chapter 4 of this volume, some of these efforts may be misguided. The point is that scholars are addressing not only what type of legitimacy and democracy exists or might exist, but also (as the discussion of constructivist theory below suggests) the type of polity they are defining in the first place.

Yet a third important area in recent scholarship focuses on external relations. Again, this might not be surprising given the war in Kosovo and the ensuing agreement between Britain and France in 1998 to strengthen security and defence co-operation in the EU (see Chapter 12). While some *JCMS* and *JEPP* articles focus on developments in the Common Foreign and Security Policy, and the European Security and Defence Policy, others explore the broader notion of the EU as an international actor, as a diplomatic entity, and as a leader in key international policy issues such as the campaign to eradicate landmines. In short, the scholarly emphasis is on the EU as a global player.

In sum, the 'what' of EU literature has changed as practitioners and scholars alike attempt to address the EU not merely as a polity, but also as something else: a transforming presence in domestic structures, a constitutional entity and an international actor. Not surprisingly, the use and choice of theories to explain the EU have also changed.

Theoretical approaches: which?

As Figure 16.4 highlights, EU scholars now use a variety of theoretical and methodological approaches. Institutionalist theory has clearly

Figure 16.4   *Primary theories and methodological approaches*

Institutionalist	95	Multi-level governance	12
State-centred	58	Governance (as theory)	10
Constructivist	55	Globalization	10
Europeanization (as theory)	26	Legal	9
Networks/movements	24	Legitimacy/democracy (as theory)	8
Policy-centred	19	Public opinion	7
Political economy	19	Partisan politics	7
Principle agent	17	The 'what'	6
Supranationalism/neofunctionalism	16	Critical approach	5
Pluralism/corporatism	15	Private governance	4
Comparative	14	Organizational	4

Note: Many articles examined more than one theory.

emerged as the leading theoretical approach in EU studies. Scholars have employed institutionalist accounts to explain, for example, the development of particular patterns of EU environmental policy-making and the perseverance of EU policies such as the Common Agricultural Policy. In the fourth phase, however, scholars have also expanded their application of historical institutionalism to governance both below and beyond the member state. Most recent articles on Europeanization, for example, use historical institutionalism to explain how EU-level policy-making transforms domestic institutions (Cowles *et al.*, 2001; Olsen, 1995). Whether there is a separate 'Europeanization theory' as suggested in Figure 16.2, or whether this is just a description of a larger institutionalist account remains to be seen. Historical institutionalism is also used as a theoretical means to explain the EU's growing role in international trade negotiations and related external policy matters. In short, the boundaries of EU governance and, therefore the application of institutionalist theory, have shifted during this EU theoretical phase.

It would appear from Figure 16.4 that state-centred approaches remain an important theoretical tool in EU studies. Such appearances, however, are misleading. In fact, scholars now often cite state-centred approaches in order to discuss their limits in explaining EU policies and decisions, and in conceptualizing the EU in terms other than nation-state preferences. In other words, while intergovernmentalist theory may have improved upon Hoffmann's original state-centred thesis, the theory is no longer touted as the 'grand theory' once envisioned. Indeed, scholars use intergovernmentalism increasingly as a 'straw man' – a weak theory that can easily be confuted – to discuss policy outcomes in what were once the 'grand bargains' of EU integration. The point is not that state-centred approaches are weak, but that they are increasingly inadequate in capturing the focus of scholarly inquiry.

The fact is that EU theory itself is changing. One of the most important developments in EU theorizing in recent years is the application of constructivist theory, including sociological institutionalist accounts of the EU. Constructivist theory provides an alternative means for understanding how rules, decisions, norms, discourses, government actions and the like are created. Indeed, constructivism is less a theory than what some call 'an ontological approach to social inquiry' – an approach focused on understanding the underlying nature of things. At its core, constructivism is based on two assumptions: '(1) the environment in which agents/states [act] is social as well as material; and (2) this setting can provide agents/states with understandings of their interests (it can "constitute" them)' (Checkel, 1998, pp. 325–6). Roughly stated, the social environment in which we find ourselves helps to create our understanding of reality. Reality is not something that 'is' but something we 'construct'. As such, constructivist approaches are far removed from traditional social scientific inquiry that recognizes reality as 'given'.

Constructivist approaches have been used to move beyond state-centred explanations of polity and law. For example, if one conceptualizes the EU as 'state-like' as opposed to being 'a state', then legal scholars are not confined to sovereign state interpretations of democracy and legitimacy, and can therefore discuss the democratic deficit in different ways (Shaw and Wiener, 2001). Rather than arguing that there can be one European identity and one European state, scholars can analyse the creation of multiple identities and different understandings of EU citizenship. Constructivism allows EU scholars to conceptualize the EU in different ways and to focus on 'the other'.

While some scholars have argued that the EU has taken a constructivist turn (Christiansen *et al.*, 1999) and that we are in a phase focused primarily on 'constructing the EU' (Dietz and Wiener, 2003), an undue focus on constructivist theory itself would be misplaced. As Figure 16.4 suggests, other theoretical approaches have also gained currency in EU studies. Policy network approaches (Börzel, 1998; Peterson, 2003), for example, examine the network of stable non-hierarchical relations among public and private actors that share common interests with regard to policy and co-operate to achieve policy goals. Policy networks have been used to explain the influence of sectoral networks in areas such as telecommunications technology and environmental policy. Policy networks across different levels of government and society have also been used to describe a new form of modern state in Europe (Héritier *et al.*, 1996; Kohler-Koch, 1996). At a minimum, policy networks enable scholars to conceptualize the EU as an emerging form of 'governance without government' (Rosenau, 1992). From the policy network perspective, scholars can also view the EU as 'other'.

Political economy approaches provide similar opportunities. For example, political economists now examine the EU as a primary locus of international investment. Scholars debate whether the EU can be characterized as an 'optimal currency area' for European monetary policy (Frieden *et al.*, 1998). Thus political economy approaches suggest there are a number of theoretical approaches at the time of writing that allow scholars to view the EU as something 'other' than a Euro-polity.

No single theory can account for the major theoretical trends in the EU at the start of the 2000s. Nor can any single theory explain developments in a specific subject matter. Enlargement illustrates this point. As H. Wallace notes, while past accounts of enlargement have focused primarily on descriptions of enlargement negotiations or the demands of the *acquis communautaire* on the candidate states, the current literature is much more varied and dynamic (Wallace, 2001). On the one hand, institutionalist accounts of enlargement focus on the impact of enlargement not only on candidate countries but also on the EU itself. Indeed, much of the institutionalist literature on Europeanization has benefited from recent scholarship on enlargement. Constructivist accounts of enlargement, on the other hand, examine the role of European integration in constructing the discourse of eastward expansion. Constructivism, therefore, can explain why member states agreed to support enlargement when liberal intergovernmentalist accounts focusing on domestic preferences would predict otherwise (see Sedelmeier, 2001). Constructivist accounts can also explore the changing identity of the EU as a 'Western European' power. This matters significantly in terms of the EU's relations with the outside world (see Chapters 14 and 15 in this volume). Finally, the literature on governance and boundaries can help to explain why enlargement poses tremendous challenges not only for the candidate countries, but also for the governance of the EU as a whole (Friis and Murphy, 1999).

Theoretical approaches: why?

There are several reasons why scholars chose to take these approaches in the current phase of theoretical development. One is that theory in general has evolved in political science in recent years. Constructivist approaches received more visibility in international relations theory, with key publications by Checkel (1998), Finnemore (1996), Katzenstein (1996) and Klotz (1995). The network literature (Florini, 2000; Haas, 1992; Keck and Sikkink, 1998) re-emerged during the same period, suggesting that EU theoretical developments are dovetailing broader theoretical developments in political science and international relations theory. A second reason for the prevalence of these theories is the introduction of new scholars to EU studies. Scandinavian-based scholars, for example, have made important contributions to the constructivist litera-ture. Central and Eastern European scholars have focused on Europeanization and have challenged American and Western European historical institutionalists to broaden their understanding of these processes.

Yet another reason governing the choice of theory is that as the EU itself continues to change, so does our understanding of it. The classical theories of European integration tell us very little about the transforma-tion of domestic structures in Europe in the 2000s. Multi-level gover-nance theories may provide only a modest insight into EU external activities, and comparative politics and public policy theories are limited in what they can explain about EU investment opportunities and mone-tary policies. As scholars seek to understand the EU, they have little choice but to explore new theories and expand upon existing ones.

Conclusion

The study of the EU remains dynamic. From the early years of European integration, through the development of the single market, to the recog-nition of the EU as a polity, scholars have developed different theoretical and methodological approaches. Developments in the EU, in turn, have prompted a new phase of theoretical inquiry in recent years. The empha-sis is less on the EU as a self-contained polity, and more on the evolving and expanding nature of the polity itself.

As discussed in the book's introduction, governance, legitimacy and identity have emerged as important themes in the EU in the 2000s. EU scholars continue to focus on governance of public policies and policy-making. Yet the recognition of Europeanization – governance structures that influence domestic structures within member states – expands our understanding of governance and requires new theoretical tools to address it. Similarly, changing external relations and enlargement have focused attention on EU governance issues beyond Brussels. European integration theory has pursued a similar path.

Legitimacy is also paramount. As the EU moves towards the adoption of a constitution, as new members join its ranks, as its impact continues to shape citizens' daily lives, the public's acceptance of the EU as a lawful, rightful entity is critical. Practitioners and scholars alike have examined and suggested ways in which such legitimacy might be construed. Yet public policy and comparative theories may be of limited value. EU theo-rists have recognized increasingly that the type of legitimacy required will depend on the type of polity that is being created.

Finally, there is identity. What is the EU today? In many respects, the discussion of EU identity no longer focuses on whether the EU is a polity, a state or an intergovernmental organization. Instead, scholars have recognized, as evidenced by their theories, that the EU remains something 'other' than those familiar constructs. It is at the same time an external actor, a transforming presence in domestic society, and a source of international investment. It is also an entity that is being constitutionally constructed. How one understands the EU depends, in part, on the theoretical approach embraced. For now, there can be no 'grand theory' of European integration. Instead, the theoretical literature on the EU will remain as rich and varied as the EU itself.

Guide to Further Reading

Chapter 1   The Road to Enlargement

There is a large and growing literature on the Central and Eastern European enlargement of the EU. Most relevant scholarly journals, notably the *Journal of Common Market Studies*, have at least one article per issue on the subject, and have devoted special issues to it. Although inevitably overtaken by events, Baun (2000) provides one of the best overviews of the road to enlargement. Avery and Cameron (1999), Dabrowski and Rostowski (2001), Gower and Redmond (2000), Grabbe (1998), Ingham and Ingham (2002), Mannin (1999), Maresceau (1997), Papadimitriou (2002) and Piazolo (2001) are essential background reading on enlargement. Charemza and Strzala (2002), Pellegrin (2001) and van Brabant (1999) provide in-depth economic analyses of the impact of enlargement on the Central and Eastern European Countries. Steunenberg (2002) examines the political and institutional implications of enlargement for the EU as a whole.

Chapter 2   Reconstituting Europe

Devuyst (1999), Mancini (2000) and Weiler (1999) provide excellent accounts of the constitutional challenges confronting the EU. Chryssochoou (1998) and Lord (1998) deal specifically with the question of democracy. Siedentop (2000) argues that the democratic deficit is deep and difficult to surmount; Moravcsik (2002) argues that it is overblown and not such a bad thing after all. Steunenberg (2002) examines the constitutional and institutional implications of EU enlargement.

Chapter 3   Europeanization and the Member States

For the Jospin government, see the special issue of *Modern & Contemporary France* (August 2002). On the impact of the EU and globalization on French distinctiveness, see Gordon and Meunier (2001). A good summary of British politics and the euro issue is offered by Hix (2002). For Germany, see the special issue of *German Politics* (2001) on Germany and Europe. On the emergence of domestic protest politics and the EU, see Imig and Tarrow (2001). General sources on Europeanization include Cowles *et al.* (2001); Olsen (2003), and Radaelli (2000).

Chapter 4   Supporting the Union? Euroscepticism and the Politics of European Integration

There has been very little published on Euroscepticism. Two articles worth looking at are Taggart (1998) and Kopecky and Mudde (2002), which deal with Western European and Central and Eastern Europe, respectively. The *Opposing Europe?* volumes (Szczerbiak and Taggart, forthcoming, 2004) provide the most comprehensive overview and bring together a range of country studies and comparative pieces. There is also a wealth of related material available online from the same project at the website of the European Parties, Referendums and Elections Network (www.sei.ac.uk). For the Central and Eastern European states, a useful volume is Henderson (1999). For public opinion on European integration in the member states, the best work is Gabel (1998). For material on the democratic deficit it is worth looking at Weiler (1999). For a general consideration of political parties see Hix and Lord (1997).

Chapter 5   The Euro and the European Central Bank

On the origins and development of Economic and Monetary Union, see Gros and Thygesen (1998), Heisenberg (1999), McNamara (1998), and Verdun (2002). For developments since the introduction of the euro, see Brunila and Franco (2001), Crouch (2000), Howarth and Loedel (2003). Jones and Torres (1998) and Walsh (2000) discuss the implications of EMU for particular member states. For information on the Stability and Growth Pact, see http://europa.eu.int/comm/economyfinance/about/activities/sgp/sgp_en.htm.

The Treaty on European Union can be found at http://europa.eu.int/en/record/mt/top.html.

More information on the European Central Bank can be found at http://www.ecb.int/index.html.

Chapter 6   Completing the Single Market: The Lisbon Strategy

Turner (2001) provides a provocative critique of EU economic policy. For a discussion of new methods of economic integration, see Devuyst (1999), Hodson and Maher (2001), Scharpf (2002) and Sisson and Marginson (2001). Wallace (2001) puts these methods and approaches in their political context. Fratzscher (2001) presents a comprehensive assessment of the impact of EMU on financial markets in the EU.

Chapter 7 The Common Agricultural Policy and Cohesion

Grant and Keeler (2000) provide an authoritative account of agricultural policy in Western Europe. Grant (1997) is the best account of the origins and development of the CAP, including the MacSharry reforms. Grant (2003) and Roederer-Rynning (2003b) bring the story of CAP reform up to date. Fernandez (2002) examines the possible impact of the CAP on Central and Eastern Europe. Rumford (2000) provides a comprehensive overview of cohesion policy in the EU. Danson *et al.* (2000); Hooghe (1996); Marks (2001); and Magone (2003) analyze the impact of cohesion policy on the EU political system.

Chapter 8 Environmental Policy: At a Crossroads?

Weale *et al.* (2000) provides a good overview of EU environmental governance. Jordan (2002a) is a useful collection of key articles on this topic published during the previous ten years. Knill (2002), Wurzel (2002) and Jordan (2002b) look at the interplay between (selected) member states and EU policy-making. On the EPI principle, see Lenschow (2002); on governance and implementation, Knill and Lenschow (2000), and a recent project by Wurzel, Jordan, Zito and Brückner (2003).

Chapter 9 Immigration and Asylum: A High Politics Agenda

Geddes (2000) and Kostakopoulou (2001) analyse the different aspects of the emerging EU immigration regime from its inception to the Amsterdam Treaty. Lavenex (2001) focuses on EU asylum policy. Lavenex and Uçarer (2002) examine the consequences of EU policy on candidate countries and the EU's external relations. Groenendijk *et al.* (2002) examine the implementation of Schengen border controls. For an analysis of the dynamics behind the shift of immigration-related policies to the EU, see Guiraudon (2000, 2003). Most documents pertaining to immigration and asylum are available through the EU web site (europa.eu.int) and the 'watchdog' NGO Statewatch (www.statewatch.org) puts on its web site EU documents not yet made available to the public. The *European Journal of Migration and Law* publishes articles on current EU immigration and asylum debates by social scientists and policy actors. The monthly *Migration News Sheet* covers policy developments in the member states and at EU level. Statistics on asylum are posted on the UNHCR website (www.unhcr.org). The OECD publishes an annual report on *Trends in International Migration*.

Chapter 10   Police and Judicial Co-operation

Occhipinti (2003) includes a detailed chronology and examines police co-operation and the evolution of JHA in the context of European integration, covering events from the Trevi Group to June 2002. Occhipinti (2004) elucidates the impact of enlargement on JHA. Mitsilegas *et al.* (2003) is a useful volume on internal security in Europe. See also the special issue of *Policing & Society* (2002) devoted to EU police co-operation. Uçarer (2001, 2002a, 2002b and 2003) writes authoritatively on JHA, dealing in particular with the Commission's role and immigration policy. Europa, the EU's website (http://europa.eu.int) includes a lot of information on police and judicial co-operation, and the website of the London-based civil liberties watchdog, Statewatch, has valuable links to official documents and critical analyses www.statewatch.org.

Chapter 11   The EU and World Trade: Doha and Beyond

Winters (2001) provides a critical but balanced assessment of the EU's trade policy. Woolcock and Hodges (1996) give an accessible account of the EU's participation in the Uruguay Round. Woolcock (2000) provides a useful overview of contemporary EU trade issues. Johnson with Rollo (2001) examine in depth the implications of enlargement for EU trade policy. Meunier and Nicolaïdis (2001) give a brief account of the negotiations on trade policy at Nice. Young (2002) charts the evolution of the EU's trade policy and explores co-operation among the member states in areas of mixed competence. Young (forthcoming) examines the interaction between the single European market and the WTO. Specifics of the EU's negotiating positions in the current multilateral trade round can be found on the European Commission's Directorate General for Trade's website (http://trade-info.cec.eu.int/europa/index_en.php).

Chapter 12   The Foreign and Security Policies of the European Union

By far the best regular surveys of the EU's foreign and security policies are the chapters by David Allen and Michael Smith in the Annual Review of the *Journal of Common Market Studies*. For a general survey, see Ginsberg (2001) and Nuttall (2000). The website of the European Commission's directorate-general for external relations (RELEX) provides regular updates on the latest news.

Chapter 13   The European Union, the United States, and Asia-Pacific: A New Trilateralism?

There is a plentiful literature on EU–US relations, covering both their broader development and current issues. See, for example, Guay (1999) Pollack and Shaffer (2001); McGuire and Smith (forthcoming, 2004). On EU–Asia Pacific relations, see in particular, Dent (1999); Gilson (2000); Maull *et al.* (eds) (1998); Wiessala (2002). The best general website for EU policies is the Europa site: http://www.europa.eu.int (a large amount of material can be found under external relations, trade and foreign and security policy); the European Commission Delegation in Washington DC has a website with very good links to other resources: http://www.eurunion.org; and on the ASEM and other EU–Asia processes a good source is the website of Asia House in Essen, Germany: http://www, asienhaus.org/englisch/eu-asia.htm. Both EU–US and EU–Asia relations are covered in the chapter on 'External Policy Developments' in the annual *European Union Review* published by Blackwell (Oxford): the current editor is Lee Miles.

Chapter 14   Policy Towards the Extended Frontier: The Balkans and the Newly Independent States

Information about EU policy towards the Balkans and the NIS can be found on the home page of the External Relations Directorate of the European Commission, europa.eu.int /comm/external_relations. In-depth treatments of EU policy towards the NIS are found in Kempe (2001), and towards the Western Balkans in Van Meurs (2001). For a general discussion of the EU as an 'extended empire' and of proximity policy in general, see Emerson (2001), Emerson (2002) and Kempe and Van Meurs (2002).

Chapter 15   Development Policy: Paradigm Shifts and the 'Normalization' of a Privileged Partnership?

For the contextual basis underpinning Europe's development policy, the early Lomé Convention agreements should be analysed. Here two key texts exist. Ravenhill (1985) provides a policy analysis of the earlier Conventions; and Grilli (1993) approaches the topic from a political economy perspective. To supplement these detailed analyses, a more general overview is offered by Lister (1997). The contemporary nature of the Cotonou Agreement means that very few recent publications are able to provide any in-depth analysis. The two notable exceptions are: van Reisen (1999) and Holland (2002). For informed but possibly less academically critical commentaries on Cotonou, the EU periodical publication *The Courier* is an invaluable source of current material. Similarly, the two most useful general websites that provide relevant information are: www.Europa.eu.int/comm./development and www.one-world.org/ euforic

Chapter 16   Developments in European Integration Theory: The EU as 'Other'

There are several excellent texts on EU theory. Rosamond (2000) provides a comprehensive overview. The edited volume by Dietz and Wiener (2003) includes chapters on particular theoretical approaches by leading scholars in the field. For an excellent account of early theoretical development, see Caporaso and Keeler (1995). Journal articles summarizing key theoretical debates include Hix (1994) on comparative politics; Caporaso (1998) on institutionalism; Hix (1998) and Jachtenfuchs (2001) on governance; and Christiansen *et al.* (1999) on constructivism.

Bibliography

Abramowitz, Morton and Hurlburt, Heather (2002) 'Can the EU Hack the Balkans?' *Foreign Affairs*, vol. 81, no. 5 (September/October).

Allen, D. and Smith, M. (since 1993) 'External Policy Developments', *Journal of Common Market Studies Annual Review*.

Allen, D. and Smith, M. (2001) 'External Policy Developments', *Journal of Common Market Studies*, Annual Review, vol. 39, pp. 97–114.

Allen, D. and Smith, M. (2002) 'External Policy Developments', *Journal of Common Market Studies*, Annual Review, vol. 40, pp. 97–115.

Andersen, S. and Eliassen, K. (eds) (2001) *Making Policy in Europe. 2nd edition.* Thousand Oaks, Calif.: Sage.

Andreas, Peter and Snyder, Tim (eds) (2000) *The Wall Around the West: State Borders and Immigration Control in North America and Europe.* New York: Rowman & Littlefield.

Armstrong, K. and Bulmer, S. (1998) *The Governance of the Single European Market.* Manchester University Press.

Artis, M. J. and Buti, M. (2000) 'Close-to-balance or in Surplus: A Policy-maker's Guide to the Implementation of the Stability and Growth Pact', *Journal of Common Market Studies*, vol. 38, no. 4, pp. 563–92.

Artis, M. and Winkler, B. (1997) 'The Stability Pact: Safeguarding the Credibility of the European Central Bank', Discussion Paper series 1688, London: CEPR.

Association of Private Client Investment Managers and Stockbrokers (APCIMS), Speech by Angela Knight, CEO to the 2001 Annual Meeting.

Atkinson, Tony (2002) 'Social Inclusion and the European Union', *Journal of Common Market Studies*, vol. 40, no. 4.

Avery, Graham and Cameron, Fraser (1999) *The Enlargement of the European Union.* Sheffield: Sheffield Academic Press.

Aylott, Nicholas (forthcoming, 2004) 'The Glacier Melts, Slowly: Euroscepticism and Party Politics in Sweden', in Aleks Szczerbiak and Paul Taggart (eds), *Opposing Europe? The Comparative Party Politics of Euroscepticism.* Oxford University Press.

Bachtler, J. and Yuill, D. (2001) 'Policies and Strategies for Regional Development: a Shift in Paradigm', University of Strathclyde, European Policy Research Papers, No. 46 (August).

Baker, D., Gamble, A., Ludlam, S. and Seawright, D. (1999) 'Backbenchers with Attitude: A Seismic Study of the Conservative Party and Dissent on Europe', in S. Bowler, D. Farrell and R. Katz (eds), *Party Discipline and Party Government.* Ohio State University Press, pp. 72–88.

Baker, David, Gamble, Andrew, Randall, Nick and Seawright, David (forthcoming, 2004) 'Elite Party Based Euroscepticism in the UK: A Case of Fractured Consensus and Asymmetrical Attitudes', in Aleks Szczerbiak and Paul Taggart (eds), *Opposing Europe? The Comparative Party Politics of Euroscepticism.* Oxford University Press.

Baker, S. (2000) 'Between the Devil and the Deep Blue Sea: International

Obligations, Eastern Enlargement and the Promotion of Sustainable Development in the European Union', *Journal of Environmental Policy and Planning*, no. 2, pp. 149–66.

Baker, S. and Jehlička, P. (1998) 'Dilemmas of Transition: The Environment, Democracy and Economic Reforms in East Central Europe: An Introduction', *Environmental Politics*. vol. 7, no. 1, pp. 1–25.

Banchoff, T. and Smith, M. (1999) *Legitimacy and the European Union: The Contested Polity*. London: Routledge.

Batory, Agnes (2002) 'Europe and the Hungarian Parliamentary Elections of 2002', *RIIA/OERN Election Briefing No. 2*. Brighton: Sussex European Institute. Website: http://www.sussex.ac.uk/Units/SEI/oern/ElectionBriefings/Paper1Hungary.pdf.

Batory, Agnes (forthcoming, 2004) 'Euroscepticism in the Hungarian Party System', in Aleks Szczerbiak and Paul Taggart (eds), *Opposing Europe? The Comparative Party Politics of Euroscepticism*. Oxford University Press.

Baun, Michael J. (2000) *A Wider Europe: The Process and Politics of European Union Enlargement*. Lanham, Md.: Rowman & Littlefield.

Benedetto, Giacomo (forthcoming, 2004) 'Explaining the Failure of Euroscepticism in the European Parliament', in Aleks Szczerbiak and Paul Taggart (eds), *Opposing Europe? The Comparative Party Politics of Euroscepticism*. Oxford University Press.

Bensahel, N. (2003) *The Counterterror Coalitions: Co-operation with Europe, NATO and the European Union*. Santa Monica, Calif.: Rand.

Bentel, Jorg (2002) 'The Economic Impact of Objective 1 Interventions for the Period 2000–2006', Final Report to the Directorate General for Regional Policies, European Commission. Website: europa.eu.int/ comm/regional policy/sources/docgener/studies/pdf/objective1/ final report. pdf.

Berg, Eiki and van Meurs, Wim (2001) 'Legacies of the Past, Ethnic and Territorial Conflict Potentials', in Iris Kempe, *Beyond EU Enlargement*. Gütersloh: Bertelsmann.

Blair, Tony (2002) 'A clear course for Europe', Speech at Cardiff, 28 November 2002.

Böcker, Anita and Havinga, Tetty (1997) *Asylum Migration to the European Union: Patterns of Origin and Destination*. Luxembourg: Office for Official Publications of the European Communities.

Börzel, T. (1998) 'Organizing Babylon: On the Different Conceptions of Policy Networks', *Public Administration*, 76, pp. 253–73.

Börzel, T. (1999) 'Towards Convergence in Europe? Institutional Adaptation to Europeanization in Germany and Spain', *Journal of Common Market Studies*, vol. 39, pp. 573–96.

Brunila, A. Buti, M. and Franco, D. (eds) (2001) *The Stability and Growth Pact: The Architecture of Fiscal Policy in EMU*. Basingstoke: Palgrave.

Bulmer, S. (1994) 'The Governance of the European Union: A New Institutionalist Approach', *Journal of Public Policy*, vol. 13, pp. 351–80.

Caporaso, J. (1998) 'Regional integration theory: understanding our past and anticipating our future', *Journal of European Public Policy*, 5(1) March, pp. 1–16.

Caporaso, James, C. and Keeler, J. (1995) 'The EU and Regional Integration Theory', in C. Rhodes and S. Mazey (eds), *State of the EU*, Vol. 3. Boulder: Col.: Lynne Rienner.

Cecchini, P. (1988) *The 1992 Challenge from Europe: The Benefits of a Single Market*. Aldershot: Gower House.

Charemza, Wojciech and Strzala, Krystyna (eds) (2002) *East European Transition and EU Enlargement: A Quantitative Approach*. Heidelberg: Physica-Verlag.

Checkel, J. T. (1998) 'The Constructivist Turn in International Relations Theory', *World Politics*, vol. 50, no. 2, pp. 324–48.

Christiansen, T., Jørgensen, K. E., and Wiener, A. (1999) 'The Social Construction of Europe', *Journal of European Public Policy*, vol. 6, no. 4, pp. 528–44.

Christiansen, Ulf (2002) 'Migration from the Central and Eastern European States into the 15 Countries of the EU: Status, Trends and Models'. Website: http://www2.ihh.hj.se/ersasise2002/papers/Christiansen. pdf.

Chryssochoou, Dimitris N. (1998) *Democracy in the European Union*. London: Tauris Academic Studies.

Cini, Michelle (2003a) 'The Maltese EU Accession Referendum', *OERN Referendum Briefing*, No. 2. Brighton: Sussex European Institute. Website:http://www.susx.ac.uk/Units/SEI/oern/ ElectionBriefings/ Referendum/ Maltese2.

Cini, Michelle (2003b) 'The Maltese Parliamentary Elections of April 2003', *OERN Election Briefing*, No.12. Brighton: Sussex European Institute. Website: http://www.susx.ac.uk/Units/SEI/oern/ElectionBriefings/ Paper12Malta.pdf.

Climate Change: for continuously updated information on the climate change regime, see the publications of the Wuppertal Institut on the website: http://www.wupperinst.org.

Cole, A. and Drake, H. (2000) 'The Europeanization of the French Polity: Continuity, Change and Adaptation', *Journal of European Public Policy*, vol. 7, pp. 26–43.

Corbett, Richard (2001) *The European Parliament's Role in Closer EU Integration*. Basingstoke and New York: Palgrave Macmillan.

Costello, D. (2001) 'The SGP: How Did We Get There?' *The Stability and Growth Pact: The Architecture of Fiscal Policy in EMU*. Basingstoke and New York: Palgrave Macmillan, pp. 106–36.

Council of the European Union, 'Homepage for Justice and Home Affairs'. Website: http://ue.eu.int/jai/home.asp?lang=en.

Council of the European Union (2001) 'Outcome of Proceedings of the Strategic Committee on Immigration, Frontiers and Asylum Meeting with the United States dated 26 October 2001', doc. 13803/01 ASIM 21 USA 24. Brussels, 12 November.

Council of the European Union (2002a) 'Council Framework Decision of 13 June 2002 on Combating Terrorism' *Official Journal*, L 164, 22 June, pp. 3–7.

Council of the European Union (2002b) General Affairs Council, 2463rd Council Meeting, Brussels, 18 November, 14183/02 (Presse 350).

Cowles, M. G. and Curtis, S. (in progress) 'Theorizing the Union: The State of the Theoretical Debate', unpublished manuscript.

Cowles, M. G., Caporaso, J. and Risse, T. (eds) (2001) *Transforming Europe: Europeanization and Domestic Change*. Ithaca, NY: Cornell University Press.

Cram, Laura, Dinan, Desmond and Nugent, Neill (1998), 'Reconciling Theory and Practice', in Cram, L., Dinan, D. and Nugent, N. *Developments in the European Union*. Basingstoke and New York: Palgrave Macmillan.

Crouch, Colin (ed.) (2000) *After the Euro: Shaping Institutions for Governance in the Wake of European Monetary Union*. Oxford University Press.

Curtin, Deirdre (1993) 'The Constitutional Structure of the Union: A Europe of Bits and Pieces', *Common Market Law Review*, 30/7, pp. 17–69.

Dabrowski, Marek and Rostowski, Jacek (2001) *The Eastern Enlargement of the European Union*. Boston, MA: Kluwer.

Danson, Mike, Halkier, Henrik and Cameron, Greta (eds) (2000) *Governance, Institutional Change and Regional Development*. Aldershot: Ashgate.

de la Hesa, G. (2003) 'The New Governing Rules of the ECB', 17 February 2003. Website:http://www.europarl.eu.int/comparl/econ/pdf/emu/speeches/200302 17/ deladehesa pdf.

Delors, J. (1985) *Bulletin des Communautes Européennes*, no. 9, p. 8.

Delors Report (1989) *Report on Economic and Monetary Union in the European Community*, Committee for the Study of Economic and Monetary Union. Luxembourg: Office for Official Publications of the EC.

Den Boer, M. (2001) 'Law-enforcement Co-operation and Transnational Organized Crime in Europe', in M. Berdal and S. Serrano (eds), *Transnational Organized Crime and International Security: Business as Usual?* Boulder, CO: Lynne Rienner.

Den Boer, M. and Monar, J. (2002) 'Keynote Article: 11 September and the Challenge of Global Terrorism to the EU as a Security Actor', *Journal of Common Market Studies*, vol. 40, pp. 11–28.

Dent, C. (1999) *The European Union and East Asia: An Economic Relationship*. London: Routledge.

Devuyst, Youri (1995) 'The European Community and the Conclusion of the Uruguay Round', in C. Rhodes and S. Mazey (eds), *The State of the European Community Vol. III, Building a European Polity?* Boulder, Col.: Lynne Rienner, pp. 449–67.

Devuyst, Youri (1999a) 'The Community-method after Amsterdam', *Journal of Common Market Studies*, vol. 37, no. 1.

Devuyst, Youri (1999b) 'The European Union's Constitutional Order? Between Community method and *Ad Hoc* Compromise', *Berkeley Journal of International Law*, vol. 18, no. 1, pp. 1–52.

Dietz, T. and Wiener, A. (2003) 'Introducing the Mosaic of Integration Theory', in T. Dietz and A. Wiener (eds), *European Integration Theory*. Oxford University Press.

Dinan, Desmond (2004) *Europe Recast: A History of European Union*, Basingstoke: Palgrave Macmillan.

Dyson, K. (ed) (2002) *European States and the Euro: Europeanization, Variation, and Convergence*. Oxford University Press.

Dyson, K. and Featherstone, Kevin (1999) *The Road to Maastricht: Negotiating Economic and Monetary Union*. Oxford University Press.

Emerson, Michael (2001) *The Elephant and the Bear*. Brussels: Centre for European Policy Studies.

Emerson, Michael (2002) *The Wider Europe as the European Union's Friendly Monroe Doctrine*, CEPS Policy Brief No. 27.

Environmental agreements: for a list of multilateral Environmental agreements to which the EU is a party, see website: http://europa.eu.int/comm/environment/international issues/agreements en.htm.

European Central Bank (2002) *Labour Market Mismatches in European Countries*. Frankfurt: ECB.

European Commission (1993) 'Growth, Competitiveness, Employment: The Challenges and Ways Forward into the 21st Century', *Bulletin of the European Community*, S-6/93, Brussels.

European Commission (1994–2003) *Eurobarometer*, 41–59 (Spring 1994–Spring 2003), Brussels.

European Commission (1997) *Agenda 2000*, COM(1997)2000, Brussels.

European Commission (1999a) Financial Services Action Plan, COM(1999)232, Brussels.

European Commission (1999b), A comparative analysis of the regulations for 1994–1999 and those for 2000–2006 (updated version, June 1999), Brussels.

European Commission (1999c) *Sixteenth Annual Report on Monitoring the Application of Community Law (1998)*, COM(1999)301 Final, Brussels.

European Commission (2000a), 'The Reform of Article 133 by the Nice Treaty: The Logic of Parallelism', Website: *http://europa.eu.int/comm/trade/faqs/rev133en.htm*.

European Commission (2000b) *Communication of the Commission to the Council and European Parliament on a Community Immigration Policy*, COM (2000)757 Final, Brussels.

European Commission (2000c) *A Review of the Auto-Oil II Programme. Communication from the Commission*, COM(2000)626 Final, Brussels.

European Commission (2000d) *Seventeenth Annual Report on Monitoring the Application of Community Law (1999)*, COM(2000)92 Final, Brussels.

European Commission (2001a), Making a European Area of Lifelong Learning a Reality, COM(2001)678 Final, Brussels.

European Commission (2001b), A Mobility Strategy for the European Research Area, COM(2001)331 Final, Brussels.

European Commission (2001c), Impact of the eEconomy on European Enterprises, COM(2001)711 Final, Brussels.

European Commission (2001d) Final Report of the Committee of Wise Men on the Regulation of the European Financial Services Market, February 2001, Brussels.

European Commission (2001e) '4th WTO Ministerial Conference, 9–14 November, Doha, Qatar – Assessment of Results for the EU', Website: http://trade-info.cec.eu.int/europa/2001newround/compas.htm.

European Commission (2001f) *Commission proposes new action programme for the environment*, Press Releases, IP/01/102, 24/01/2001, Brussels.

European Commission (2001g) *White Paper. Strategy for a Future Chemicals Policy* COM(2001)88 Final, Brussels.

European Commission (2001h) *European Governance. A White Paper*, COM(2001)428 Final, Brussels.

European Commission (2001i) *Eighteenth Annual Report on Monitoring the Application of Community Law (2000)*, COM(2001)309 Final, Brussels.

European Commission (2001j) *Communication of the Commission to the Council and European Parliament on an Open Method of Coordination for the Community Immigration Policy*, COM (2001) 387 Final, Brussels.

European Commission (2001k), Sixth Environmental Action programme. Environment 2010: Our Future, Our Choice, Brussels.

European Commission (2002a) *Action Plan for Skills and Mobility*, COM(2002)72, Brussels.

European Commission (2002b) 'Bilateral Trade Relations: Candidates (10)', DG Trade A2/CG/SG/WB, November, Website: http://europa.eu.int/comm/trade/bilateral/data.htm.

European Commission (2002c) *Nineteenth Annual Report on Monitoring the Application of Community Law (2001)*, COM(2002)324 Final. Brussels.

European Commission (2002d) *Enlargement of the European Union. Guide to the Negotiations Chapter by Chapter*, Brussels.

European Commission (2002e) *Green Paper on a Community Return Policy for Illegal residents*, COM(2002)175 Final, Brussels.

European Commission (2002f) *Third Annual Survey on the Implementation and Enforcement of Community Environmental Law*, Commission Staff Working Paper. SEC(2002)1041, Brussels.

European Commission (2003a), Second Progress Report on Economic and Social Cohesion, COM(2003)34 Final. Website: Europa.eu.int/comm/regionalpolicy/ sources/docoffic/official/regulation/pdf/irfoen.pdf.

European Commission (2003b), Proceedings of a Conference organized by the European Commission, 'Managing Structural Funds in the Future: Which Division of Responsibilities?, Brussels.

European Commission (2003c) *Wider Europe – Neighbourhood: A New Framework for Relations with our Eastern and Southern Neighbours*, Communication from the Commission to the Council and the European Parliament, COM(2003)104 Final, Brussels.

European Commission (2003d) *Eurobarometer*, 59 (Spring, 2003), Brussels.

European Commission (2003e), Candidate Countries Eurobarometer, 2003.2 (Spring 2003), Brussels.

European Council (1999a) *Presidency Conclusions: Cologne European Council*, June.

European Council (1999b) *Presidency Conclusions: Tampere European Council*, October.

European Council (1999c) *Presidency Conclusions: Helsinki European Council*, December.

European Council (2000) *Presidency Conclusions: Lisbon European Council*, March.

European Council (2001) *Presidency Conclusions: Laeken European Council*, December.

European Council (2002) *Presidency Conclusions: Seville European Council*, June.

European Convention (2002), *Final Report of Working Group X, 'Freedom, Security and Justice'*, Brussels: European Convention Secretariat.

European Environment Agency (1999) 'Environment in the European Union at the Turn of the Century', *Environmental Assessment Report*, No. 2, 1 December, Copenhagen.

European Parliament, *Area of Freedom, Security & Justice in the EU – An Agenda for Europe*, Newsletter of the Committee on Citizens' Freedoms and Rights, Justice and Home Affairs. Website: http://www.europarl.eu.int/comparl/libe/elsj/default_en.htm.

European Report (1998) 'Justice and Home Affairs: Crime-Fighting Cooperation Pact Signed up to by 25 States', 30 May.

European Report (2002) Agriculture: Fischler Says that Mid-term Review of CAP will Go Ahead', 30 October.

European Round Table of Industrialists (2002). *Kick Start Lisbon – Message to the European Council*, March.

Europol (2003) *2002 Organized Crime Report*. Website: http://www.europol.eu.int/index.asp?page=EUOrganisedCrimeSitRep2002.

Eurostat (2001) 'The EU Figures for the Doha Conference', New Release 117/2001, 8 November. Brussels: Eurostat.

Everts, Stephen (2003) 'The EU and the Middle East: A Call for Action', Working paper, Centre for European Reform, January.

Fallend, Franz (forthcoming 2004) 'Opposing Europe: Euroscepticism of Political Parties in Austria', in Aleks Szczerbiak and Paul Taggart (eds), *Opposing Europe? The Comparative Party Politics of Euroscepticism*. Oxford University Press.

Featherstone, Kevin (1988) *Socialist Parties and European Integration*. Manchester University Press.

Fernandez, Javier (2002) 'The Common Agricultural Policy and EU Enlargement: Implications for Agricultural Production in Central and Eastern European Countries', *Eastern European Economics*, vol. 40, no. 3 (May/June), p. 28.

Ferrer, Jorge Nunez and Emerson, Michael (2000) 'Goodbye, Agenda 2000; Hello, Agenda 2003: Effects of the Berlin Summit on Own Resources, Expenditures and Net EU Balances', Working Document No. 140. Brussels: CEPS.

Finnemore, M. (1996) *National Interests in International Society*. Ithaca, NY: Cornell University Press.

Florini, Ann M. (ed.) (2000) *The Third Force: The Rise of Transnational Civil Society*. Washington, DC: Carnegie Endowment for International Peace.

Forster, A. (2002) *Euroscepticism in Contemporary British Politics: Opposition to Europe in the British Conservative and Labour Parties since 1945*. London: Routledge.

Fowler, Brigid (2002) 'Hungary's 2002 Parliamentary Elections', Briefing Note 2/02. Brighton: Sussex European Institute.

Franklin, Mark N., van der Eijk, Cees and Marsh, Michael (1995) 'Referendum Outcomes and Trust in Government: Public Support for Europe in the Wake of Maastricht', *West European Politics,* vol. 18, no. 3, pp. 101–17.

Fratzscher, M. (2001) *Financial Market Integration in Europe,* Working Papers Series, No. 48. Frankfurt: European Central Bank.

Frieden, J.,Gros, D. and Jones, E. (eds) (1998) *The New Political Economy of EMU.* Lanham, MD: Rowman & Littlefield.

Friis, L. and Murphy, A. (1999) 'The European Union and Central and Eastern Europe: Governance and Boundaries', *Journal of European Public Policy,* vol. 37, no. 2, pp. 211–32.

Gabel, Matthew (1998) *Interests and Integration: Market Liberalization, Public Opinion and European Integration.* Ann Arbor, MI: University of Michigan Press.

Garret, G. (1993) 'The Politics of Maastricht', in B. J. Eichengreen and J. A. Frieden (eds), *The Political Economy of European Monetary Unification.* Boulder, CO: Westview Press, pp. 47–66.

Geddes, Andrew (2000) *Immigration and European Integration.* Manchester University Press.

George, S. (1998) *An Awkward Partner: Britain in the European Community.* Oxford University Press.

George, S. and Bache, I. (2001) *Politics in the European Union.* Oxford University Press.

Gilland, Karin (2002) 'Ireland's Second Referendum on the Treaty of Nice, October 2002', *Opposing Europe Research Network Referendum Briefing No. 1.* Brighton: Sussex European Institute. Website: http://www. susx.ac.uk/Units/SEI/oern/ElectionBriefings/Referendum/Irelandno1. pdf.

Gilson, J. (2000) *The European Union and Japan: A Partnership for the Twenty-first Century?* Basingstoke and New York: Palgrave Macmillan.

Ginsberg, Roy H. (2001) *The European Union in International Politics.* Lanham, MD: Rowman & Littlefield.

Golembe, C. and Holland, D. (1990) 'Banking and Securities' in Gary Clyde Hufbauer (ed.), *Europe 1992: An American Perspective.* Washington, DC: The Brookings Institution.

Gomes, S. (2000) 'The Political Dimension of the New ACP–EU Partnership', *The Courier,* issue 181. Brussels: European Commission.

Gompert, D. and Larrabee, S. (eds) (1998) *America and Europe: A Partnership for a New Era.* Cambridge University Press.

Gordon, P. and Meunier, S. (2001) *The French Challenge: Adapting to Globalization.* Washington, DC: Brookings Institution.

Gower, Jackie and Redmond, John (eds) (2000) *Enlarging the European Union: The Way Forward.* Aldershot: Ashgate.

Grabbe, Heather (1998) *Enlarging the European Union Eastwards.* London: Royal Institute of International Affairs.

Grant, C. (2002) 'The Eleventh of September and Beyond: The Impact on the European Union', in L. Freedman (ed.), *Superterrorism: Policy Responses.* London: Blackwell.

Grant, Wyn (1997) *The Common Agricultural Policy*. Basingstoke and New York: Palgrave Macmillan.

Grant, Wyn (2003) 'The Prospects for CAP Reform', *The Political Quarterly*, vol. 74, no. 1 (January–March), pp. 19–27.

Grant, Wyn and Keeler John T. S (eds.) (2000) *Agricultural Policy*, Vol. 1: *Agricultural Policy in Western Europe*. Cheltenham: Edward Elgar.

Gregory, F. (1998) 'Policing Transition in Europe: The Role of Europol and the Problem of Organized Crime', *Innovation*, vol. 11, no. 3, pp. 287–305.

Groenendijk, Kees, Guild, Elspeth and Minderhoud, Paul (eds) (2002) *In Search of Europe's* Borders. London and Amsterdam: Kluwer Law International.

Goilli, E. (1993) *The European Community and the Developing Countries*, Cambridge University Press.

Gros, D. (2003) 'Reforming the Composition of the ECB Governing Council in View of Enlargement. An Opportunity Missed!', *CEPS Policy Brief*, No. 32, April.

Gros, D. and N. Thygesen (1998) *European Monetary Integration*. New York: Longman.

Guay, T. (1999) *The United States and the European Union: The Political Economy of a Relationship*. Sheffield: Sheffield Academic Press.

Guiraudon, Virginie (2000) 'European Integration and Migration Policy: Vertical Policy-making as Venue Shopping', *Journal of Common Market Studies*, vol. 38, no. 2, pp. 249–69.

Guiraudon, Virginie (2003) 'The Constitution of a European Immigration Policy Domain: A Political Sociology Approach', *Journal of European Public Policy*, vol. 10, no. 2, pp. 263–82.

Haas, Ernst (1958) *The Uniting of Europe: Political, Social, Economic Forces, 1950–1957*. Stanford, CA: Stanford University Press.

Hass, E. (1975) 'The obsolescence of regional integration theory', Research Series No. 25, Berkeley, CA: Center for International Studies.

Haas, Peter M. (1992) 'Introduction: Epistemic Communities and International Policy Coordination', *International Organization*, vol. 46, no. 1, pp. 1–36.

Hanley, Sean (forthcoming, 2004) 'Embracing Europe, Opposing Europe', in Aleks Szczerbiak and Paul Taggart (eds) *Opposing Europe? The Comparative Party Politics of Euroscepticism*. Oxford University Press.

Harmsen, Robert (2002) 'Europe and the Dutch Parliamentary Election of May 2002', *OERN Election Briefing No.3*. Brighton: Sussex European Institute. Website: http://www.susx.ac.uk/Units/SEI/oern/ElectionBriefings/Paper3Dutch.pdf.

Heipertz, M. and Verdun, A. (2003) 'The Dog That Would Never Bite? The Past and Future of the Stability and Growth Pact', Working Paper, Max-Planck Institute, Cologne.

Heisenberg, Dorothee (1999) *The Mark of the Bundesbank: Germany's Role in European Monetary Co-operation*. Boulder, CO: Lynne Rienner.

Henderson, Karen (ed.) (1999) *Back to Europe: Central and Eastern Europe and the European Union*, London: UCL Press.

Héritier, A. (1997) 'Policy-making by subterfuge: interest accommodation, innovation and substitute democratic legitimization in Europe – perspectives from distinct policy areas', *Journal of European Public Policy*, 4: 171–89.

Héritier, A. (2001) 'Market Integration and Social Cohesion: The Politics of Public Services in European Regulation', *Journal of European Public Policy*, vol. 8, pp. 825–52.

Héritier, A. (2002) 'New Modes of Governance in Europe: Policy-making without Legislating?' in Héritier, A. (ed.), *The Provision of Common Goods: Governance Across Multiple Arenas*. Boulder, CO: Rowman & Littlefield, pp. 185–206.

Héritier, A., Knill, C. and Mingers, S. (1996) *Ringing the Changes in Europe. Regulatory Competition and the Transformation of the State*. Berlin: DeGruyter.

Hix, Simon (1994) 'The Study of the European Community: The Challenge to Comparative Politics', *West European Politics*, vol. 17, no. 4, pp. 1–30.

Hix, Simon (1998) 'The Study of the European Union II: The "New Governance" Agenda and Its Rival', *Journal of Common Market Studies* vol. 5, no. 1, 38–65.

Hix, Simon (2002) 'Britain, the EU and the Euro', in P. Dunleavy, G. Peele and I. Halliday (eds), *Developments in British Politics 6*. Basingstoke and New York: Palgrave Macmillan, pp. 47–68.

Hix, Simon and Lord, Christopher (1997) *Political Parties in the European Union*. Basingstoke and New York: Palgrave Macmillan.

Hocking, B. and Smith, M. (1997) *Beyond Foreign Economic Policy: The United States, the Single European Market and the Changing World Economy*. London: Pinter.

Hodson, Dermott and Maher, Imelda (2001) 'The Open Method as a New Mode of Governance: The Case of Soft Economic Policy Coordination', *Journal of Common Market Studies*, vol. 39, no. 4 (November), pp. 719–46.

Hoekman, B. M. (1996) 'Assessing the General Agreement on Trade in Services', in W. Martin and L. A. Winters (eds), *The Uruguay Round and Developing Countries*. Cambridge University Press, pp. 88–124.

Hoekman, B. M. and Kostecki, M. M. (2001) *The Political Economy of the World Trading System*, 2nd edn. Oxford University Press.

Hoffmann, S. (1966) 'Obstinate or Obsolete? The Fate of the Nation State and the Case of Western Europe', *Daedalus*, vol. 95, pp. 892–908.

Holland, M. (2002) *The European Union and the Third World*. Basingstoke and New York: Palgrave Macmillan.

Holmes, P. and Rollo, J. (2001) 'EU Commercial Policy after Nice', *Euroscope*, vol. 19. Falmer: Sussex European Institute.

Holzinger, K., Knill, C. and Schäfer, A. (2002) 'Steuerungswandel in der Europäischen Umweltpolitik?', *Preprints aus der Max-Planck-Projektgruppe. Recht der Gemeinschaftsgüter*, No. 9, Bonn.

Hooghe, Liesbet (ed.) (1996) *Cohesion Policy and European Integration: Building Multi-level Governance*. Oxford University Press.

Hooghe, Liesbet and Marks, Gary (eds) (2001) Multi-level Governance and European Integration. Lanham, MD: Rowman & Littlefield.

House of Lords Select Committee on European Union (2000) *Seventeenth Report on Enlargement and EU External Frontier Controls*. London: House of Lords, 24 October.

Howarth, D. (2002) 'The European Policy of the Jospin Government: A New Twist to Old French Games', *Modern & Contemporary France*, vol. 10, pp. 353–70.

Howarth, D. and Loedel, P. (2003) *The European Central Bank: The New European Leviathan?* Basingstoke and New York: Palgrave Macmillan.

Howorth, Jolyon (2000a) 'Britain, NATO and CESDP: Fixed Strategy, Changing Tactics', *European Foreign Affairs Review*, vol. 5, no. 3, pp. 1–20.

Howorth, Jolyon (2000b). European Defence and Integration: The Ultimate Challenge? Chaillot Papers, vol. 43. Paris. EU Institute for Security Studies.

Hueglin, Thomas O. (2000) 'From Constitutional to Treaty Federalism: A Comparative Perspective', *Publius*, vol. 30, no. 4, pp. 137–53.

Huntington, Samuel (1993) 'The Clash of Civilizations?', *Foreign Affairs*, vol. 72, no. 3, (Summer), pp. 22–41.

Huysmans, Jef (2000) 'The European Union and the Securitization of Migration', *Journal of Common Market Studies*, vol. 38, no. 5, pp. 751–77.

Imig, D. and Tarrow, S. (eds) (2001) *Contentious Europeans: Protest and Politics in an Emerging Policy*. Lanham, MD, and Oxford: Rowman & Littlefield.

Ingham, Hilary and Ingham, Mike (2002) *EU Expansion to the East: Prospects and Problems*. Cheltenham: Edward Elgar.

IOM (International Organization for Migration) (2000) *World Migration Report*. Geneva: IOM.

Jachtenfuchs, M. (2001) 'The Governance Approach to European Integration', *Journal of Common Market Studies*, vol. 39, no. 2, pp. 245–64.

Jachtenfuchs, M. and Kohler-Koch, B. (2003) 'Governance and Institutional Development', in T. Dietz and A. Wiener (eds), *European Integration Theory*. Oxford University Press.

Jack, Andrew (2003) 'Prodi Flies to Russia for Putin Meeting', *Financial Times*, 19 February.

Jehlička, P. (2002) 'Environmental Implications of Eastern Enlargement of the EU: The End of Progressive Environmental Policy?', *EUI Working Papers*, RSC No. 2002/23. Florence: European University Institute.

Johnson, M., with Rollo, J. (2001) 'Enlargement and the Making of Commercial Policy', SEI Working Paper 43. Falmer: Sussex European Institute.

Jones, E., Frieden, J. and Torres, F. (eds) (1998) *Joining Europe's Monetary Club. The Challenges for Smaller Member States*. Basingstoke and New York: Palgrave Macmillan.

Jordan, A. (1998) 'Step Change or Stasis? EU Environmental Policy after the Amsterdam Treaty', *Environmental Politics*, vol. 7, no. 1, pp. 227–36.

Jordan, A. (ed.) (2002a) *Environmental Policy in the European Union. Actors, Institutions & Processes*. London: Earthscan.

Jordan, A. (2002b) *The Europeanization of British Environmental Policy. A Departmental Perspective*. Basingstoke and New York: Palgrave Macmillan.

Jordan, A. and Fairbrass, J. (2002) 'EU Environmental Policy after the Nice Summit', *Environmental Politics*. vol. 10, no. 4, pp. 109–14.

Kagan, Robert (2003) *Paradise and Power: America and Europe in the New World Order*. London: Atlantic Books.

Kaldor, M. (2003) 'American Power', *International Affairs*, vol. 78, no. 1.

Katzenstein, P. J. (1996) *Cultural Norms and National Security: Police and Military in Postwar Japan*. Ithaca, NY: Cornell University Press.

Keck, Margaret and Sikkink, Kathryn (1998) *Activists Beyond Borders*. Ithaca, NY: Cornell University Press.

Keeler, John (1996) 'Agricultural Power in the European Community: Explaining the Fate of CAP and GATT Negotiations', *Comparative Politics*, 29 (January), pp. 127–49.

Kempe, Iris (ed.) (2001) *Beyond EU Enlargement; Vol. 1: The Agenda of Direct Neighbourhood for Eastern Europe*. Gütersloh: Bertelsmann Foundation.

Kempe, Iris and Van Meurs, Wim (2002) *Toward a Multi-layered Europe: Prospects and Risks Beyond EU Enlargement*, Centre for Applied Policy Research. Munich: Ludwig Maximilian University.

Kerlinger, F. N. (1986) *Foundation of Behavioural Research*, 3rd edn. New York: Holt, Rinehart & Winston.

King, G., Keohane, R. and Verba, S. (1994) *Designing Social Inquiry*. Princeton, NJ: Princeton University Press.

Kleinman, M. (2002) *A European Welfare State? European Social Policy in Context*. Basingstoke and New York: Palgrave Macmillan.

Klotz, A. (1995) *Protesting Prejudice: Apartheid and the Politics of Norms in International Relations*. Ithaca, NY: Cornell University Press.

Knill, C. (2002) *The Europeanisation of National Administrations. Patterns of Institutional Change and Persistence*. Cambridge University Press.

Knill, C. and Lenschow, A. (eds) (2000) *Implementing EU Environmental Policy. New directions and Old Problems*. Manchester University Press.

Knudsen, Ann-Christina Lauring (forthcoming, 2004) 'Euroscepticism in Denmark', in Aleks Szczerbiak and Paul Taggart (eds), *Opposing Europe? The Comparative Party Politics of Euroscepticism*, Oxford University Press.

Kohler-Koch, B. (1993) 'Germany', in M. P. C. M. Van Schendelen (ed.), *National Public and Private EC Lobbying*. Aldershot: Dartmouth.

Kohler-Koch, B. and Eising, R. (eds.) (1999) *The Transformation of Governance in the European Union*. London: Routledge.

Kooiman, J. (ed.) (1993) *Modern Governance: New Government–Society Interactions*. London: Sage.

Kopecky, Petr and Cas Mudde (2002) 'Two Sides of Euroscepticism: Party Positions on European Integration in East Central Europe', *European Union Politics,* vol. 3, no. 3, pp. 297–325.

Kostakopoulou, Dora (2001) *Citizenship, Identity and Immigration in the European Union: Between Past and Future*. Manchester University Press.

Krämer, L. (2002) 'Development of Environmental Policies in the United States and Europe: Convergence or Divergence', EUI Working Papers, RSC No. 2002/33. Florence: European University Institute.

Ladrech, R. (1994) 'Europeanization of Domestic Politics and Institutions: The Case of France', *Journal of Common Market Studies*, vol. 32, pp. 69–88.

Laffan, Brigid (1997) *The Finances of the European Union*. Basingstoke and New York: Macmillan.

Laffan, B. (1999) 'Democracy and the European Union', in L. Cram, D. Dinan and N. Nugent (eds), *Developments in the European Union*. Basingstoke and New York: Palgrave Macmillan, pp. 330–49.

Lamy, Pascal (2001). Press Release Website: www.europa.eu.int/comm/trade/miti/devel/eba1.htm.

Laryea, G. (2000) 'Effective Poverty Eradication', *The Courier*, issue 181. Brussels: European Commission.

La Spina, A. and Sciortino, G. (1993) 'Common Agenda, Southern Rules: European Integration and Environmental Change in the Mediterranean States', in D. Liefferink, Lowe, P. D. and A.P.J. Mol (eds) *European Integration and Environmental Policy*. London: Belhaven, pp. 217–36.

Lavenex, Sandra (2001) *The Europeanization of Refugee Policies: Between Human Rights and Internal Security*. Aldershot: Ashgate.

Lavenex, Sandra and Emek Uçarer (eds) (2002) *Migration and the Externalities of European Integration*. Lanham, MD: Lexington Books.

Lees, Charles (2002) 'Dark Matter: Institutional Constraints and the Failure of Party-based Euroscepticism in Germany', *Political Studies,* vol. 50, no. 2, pp. 244–67.

Lenschow, A. (1999) 'Transformation in European Environmental Governance', in B. Kohler-Koch and R. Eising (eds), *The Transformation of Governance in the European Union*. London and New York: Routledge, pp. 39–60.

Lenschow, A. (ed.) (2002) *Environmental Policy Integration. Greening Sectoral Policies in Europe*. London: Earthscan.

Lindberg, L. (1963) *The Political Dynamics of European Economic Integration*. Oxford University Press.

Lindberg, L. and Scheingold, S. (1970) *Europe's Would-Be Polity: Patterns of Change in the European Community*. Englewood Cliffs, NJ: Prentice-Hall.

Lister, M. (1997) *The European Union and the South*. London: Routledge.

Llewellyn, D. (1992) 'Banking and Financial Services', in D. Swann (ed.), *The Single European Market and Beyond*. London: Routledge.

Lord, Christopher (1998) *Democracy in the European Union*. Sheffield: Sheffield University Press.

Magone, José M. (ed.) (2003) *Regional Institutions and Governance in the European Union*. Westport, CT: Praeger.

Majone, G. (1989) 'Regulating Europe: Problems and Prospects', *Jahrbuch zur Staats-und Verwaltungswissenschaft,* vol. 3. Baden-Baden: Nomos Verlagsgesellschaft.

Majone, G. (1993) 'The European Community: Between Social Policy and Social Regulation', *Journal of Common Market Studies*, vol. 31, pp. 153–69.

Mair, P. (1995) 'Political Parties, Popular Legitimacy and Public Privilege', in J. Hayward (ed.), *The Crisis of Representation in Europe*. London: Frank Cass, pp. 41–57.

Mannin, Mike (1999) *Pushing Back the Boundaries: The European Union and Central and Eastern Europe*. Manchester University Press.

Marcussen, M. and Zølner, M. (2001) 'The Danish EMU Referendum 2000: Business as Usual', *Government and Opposition*, vol. 36, no. 3, pp. 379–402.

Maresceau, Marc (ed.) (1997) *Enlarging the European Union: Relations between the EU and Central and Eastern Europe*. London: Longman.

Marks, G. (1992) 'Structural Policy in the European Community', in A. Sbragia (ed.), *Euro-Politics: Institutions and Policy-Making in the 'New' European Union*. Washington, DC: Brookings Institution, pp. 191–224.

Marks, G., Scharpf, F. W., Schmitter, P. C., and Streeck, W. (1996) *Governance in the European Union*. London and Thousand Oaks, CA: Sage.

Marotta, E. (2001) 'Responding to Transnational Crime – the Role of Europol', in P. Williams and D. Vlassis (eds), *Combating Transnational Crime: Concepts, Activities and Responses*, London: Frank Cass, pp. 303–14.

Martin, W. and Winters, L. A. (1996) 'The Uruguay Round: A Milestone for the Developing Countries', in W. Martin and L. A. Winters (eds), *The Uruguay Round and Developing Countries*. Cambridge University Press, pp. 1–29.

Mancini, G. F. (2000) *Democracy and Constitutionalism in the European Union: Collected Essays*. Oxford: Hart.

Maull, H., Segal, G. and Wanandi, J. (eds) (1998) *Europe and the Asia Pacific*. London: Routledge.

Maurer, A. (2003) 'The European Parliament, The National Parliaments and the EU Conventions', *Politique Européenne*, no. 9, pp. 76–98.

McCormick, J. (1999) 'Environmental Policy', in: L. Cram, D. Dinan and N. Nugent, (eds), *Developments in the European Union*. Basingstoke and New York: Macmillan, pp. 193–210.

McGuire, S. and Smith, M. (forthcoming 2004) *The European Union and the United States: Competition and Convergence in the Global Arena*. Basingstoke and New York: Palgrave Macmillan.

McNamara, Kathleen R. (1998) *The Currency of Ideas: Monetary Politics in the European Union*. Ithaca, NY: Cornell University Press.

Menon, Anand (2001) 'Playing with Fire: The EU's Defence Policy', *Politique Européenne*, vol.8, pp. 32–45.

Menon, Anand and Lipken, Jonathen (2003) 'European Attitudes Towards Transatlantic Relations 2000–2003: An Analytical Survey', Paper prepared for the informal meeting of EU foreign ministers, Rhodes and Kastellorizo, 2–4 May. Available at http://www.eri.bham.ac.uk/ameupaper.htm.

Mény, Y., Muller, Pierre, and Quermonne, J.-L. (eds) (1996) *Adjusting to Europe: The Impact of the European Union on National Institutions and Policies*. London: Routledge.

Meunier, S. (1998), 'Divided but United: European Trade Policy Integration and EU–US Agricultural Negotiations in the Uruguay Round', in C. Rhodes (ed.), *The European Union in the World Community*. Boulder, Col.: Lynne Rienner, pp. 193–211.

Meunier, S. and Nicolaïdis, K. (2001), 'Trade Competence in the Nice Treaty', *ECSA Review* (Spring).

Milner, S. (2002) 'An Ambiguous Reform: The Jospin Government and the 35-Hour-Week Laws', *Modern & Contemporary France*, vol. 10, pp. 339–52.

Mitsilegas, V., Monar, J. and Rees W. (2003) *The European Union and Internal Security: Guardian of the People?*, Basingstoke and New York: Palgrave Macmillan.

Monar. J. (2000) 'Justice and Home Affairs', *Journal of Common Market Studies*, vol. 38 (Annual Review), pp. 125–42.

Moravcsik, Andrew (1991) 'Negotiating the Single European Act: National

Interests and Conventional Statecraft in the European Community', *International Organization,* vol. 45, pp. 19–56.

Moravcsik, Andrew (1993) 'Preferences and Power in the European Community: A Liberal Intergovernmentalist Approach', *Journal of Common Market Studies,* vol. 31, pp. 473–524.

Moravcsik, Andrew (2000) 'Democracy and Constitutionalism in the European Union', ECSA Forum. Website: http://www.eustudies.org/DemocracyForum.htm.

Moravcsik, Andrew (2002) 'In Defense of the "Democratic Deficit": Reassessing Legitimacy in the European Union', *Journal of Common Market Studies,* vol. 40, no. 4.

Moravcsik, Andrew and Nicolaïdis, Kalypso (1998) 'Federal Ideas and Constitutional Realities in the Treaty of Amsterdam', *Journal of Common Market Studies,* vol. 36 (Annual Review), pp. 13–38.

Moss, B. and Michie, J. (eds) (2000) *The Single Currency in National Perspective. A Community in Crisis?* Basingstoke and New York: Palgrave Macmillan.

Neville-Jones, Pauline (1996) 'Dayton, IFOR and Alliance Relations in Bosnia', *Survival,* vol. 38, no. 4.

Nickell, S. (1997) 'Unemployment and Labor Market Rigidities: Europe versus North America', *Journal of Economic Perspectives,* vol. 11, no. 3.

Nielson, P. (2000) 'The New Agreement Will Benefit the Poorest', ACP–EU Partnership Agreement signed in Cotonou, on 23 June 2000; supplement to *The Courier.* Brussels: European Commission.

Notermans, T. (ed.) (2001) *Social Democracy and Monetary Union.* New York and Oxford: Berghahn Books.

Nugent, N. (2003) *The Government and Politics of the European Union,* 5th edn. Basingstoke and New York: Palgrave Macmillan.

Nugent, N. (ed.) (2004) *European Union Enlargement.* Basingstoke and New York: Palgrave Macmillan.

Nuttall, Simon (2000) *European Foreign Policy.* Oxford: Clarendon Press.

Oberthür, S. and Ott, H. E. (2000) *Das Kyoto Protokoll. Internationale Klimapolitik für das 21. Jahrhundert.* Opladen: Leske & Budrich.

Occhipinti, J. D. (2003) *The Politics of EU Police Co-operation: Toward a European FBI?,* Boulder, CO: Lynne Rienner.

Occhipinti, J. D. (2004) 'Justice and Home Affairs', in N. Nugent (ed.), *European Union Enlargement.* New York: Palgrave Macmillan.

OECD (Organisation for Economic Co-operation and Development) (2001) *Economic Survey of the Euro Area.* Paris: OECD.

OECD (Organisation for Economic Co-operation and Development) (2002) *Economic Survey of the Euro Area.* Paris: OECD.

OECD (Organisation for Economic Co-operation and Development) (2003) *Trends in International Migration; Annual Report 2002.* Paris: OECD.

Olsen, J. (1995) *European Challenges to the Nation State.* Working Paper No. 9, March. Oslo: ARENA.

Olsen, J. (2003) 'Europeanization', in M. Cini (ed.), *European Union Politics.* Oxford University Press, pp. 333–48.

Papadimitriou, Dimitris (2002) *Negotiating the New Europe: The European Union and Eastern Europe*. Aldershot: Ashgate.

Panagariya, A. (2002), 'Developing Countries at Doha: A Political Economy Analysis', *World Economy*, vol. 25, no. 9, pp. 1205–33.

Partnership Agreement (2000) 'ACP-EU Partnership Agreement Signed in Cotonou on 23 June 2000', supplement to *The Courier*. Brussels: European Commission.

Pelkmans, J. (1997) *European Integration: Methods and Economic Analysis*. Heerlen, Netherlands: Longman.

Pellegrin, Julie (2001) *The Political Economy of Competitiveness in an Enlarged Europe*. Basingstoke and New York: Palgrave Macmillan.

Peterson, John (1996) *Europe and America in the 1990s: Problems of Partnership*. London: Routledge.

Peterson, John (2001) 'The Choice for EU Theorists: Establishing a Common Framework for Analysis', *European Journal of Political Research*, vol. 39, pp. 289–318.

Peterson, John (2003) 'Policy Networks' in T. Dietz and A. Wiener (eds), *European Integration Theory*. Oxford University Press.

Piazolo, Daniel (2001) *The Integration Process between Eastern and Western Europe*. Berlin: Springer.

Pierson, P. (1996) 'The Path to European Integration: A Historical Institutionalist Perspective', *Comparative Political Studies*, vol. 29, pp. 123–63.

Piris, Jean-Claude (1999) 'Does the European Union Have a Constitution? Does It Need One?', *European Law Review*, vol. 24, no. 6, pp. 557–85.

Policing & Society (2002), vol. 12, no. 4.

Pollack, M. and Shaffer, G. (2001) *Transatlantic Governance in the Global Economy*. New York: Rowman & Littlefield.

Prodi, Romano (2003) 'Report on the Spring European Council', Speech delivered to the European Parliament, 26 March.

Quaglia, Lucia (2003) 'Euroscepticism in Italy and Centre-Right and Right Wing Political Parties', OERN Working Paper No.10. Brighton: Sussex European Institute. Website: http://www.susx.ac.uk/Units/SEI/pdfs/wp60.pdf.

Radaelli, C. (2000) 'Whither Europeanisation? Concept Stretching and Substantive Change', *European Integration Online Papers*, vol. 4, no. 8.

Rauchs, G. and Koenig, D. J. (2001) 'Europol', in D. Koenig and D. K. Das (eds), *International Police Co-operation: A World Perspective*. Lanham, MD: Lexington Books, pp. 43–62.

Ravenhill, J. (1985) *Collective Clientism: The Lomé Conventions and North–South Relations*. New York: Columbia University Press.

Reif, Karlheinz and Schmitt, Hermann (1980) 'Nine Second Order National Elections: A Conceptual Framework for the Analysis of European Election Results', *European Journal of Political Research*, vol. 8, no. 1, pp. 3–44.

Reuters (2003), 'Save Our Subsidies' Farmers Tell EU Parliament', 11 June.

Richardson, J. (ed.) (1996) *Policy-making in the European Union*. London: Routledge.

Roederer-Rynning, Christilla (2003a) 'From 'Talking Shop' to 'Working Parliament'. The European Parliament and Agricultural Change', *Journal of Common Market Studies*, vol. 41, no.1, pp. 113–35.

Rome Treaty (1917) 'Treaty Establishing the European Economic Community (1957), http://europa.eu.int/abc/obj/treaties/en/entoc05.htm.

Roederer-Rynning, Christilla (2003b) 'Impregnable Citadel or Leaning Tower? Europe's Common Agricultural Policy at Forty', *SAIS Review*, vol. 23, no. 1 (Winter/ Spring), pp. 133–51.

Rometsch, D. and Wessels, W. (eds) (1996) *The European Union and the Member States: Towards Institutional Fusion?* New York: Manchester University Press.

Rosamond, B. (2000) *Theories of European Integration.* Basingstoke and New York: Palgrave Macmillan.

Rosenau, James (1992) 'Governance, Order, and Change in World Politics', in Jo Rosenau and E.-O. Czempiel (eds) *Governance Without Government: Order and Change in World Politics.* Cambridge University Press. pp. 169–210.

Rüdig, Wolfgang (1996) 'Green Parties and the European Union', in John Gaffney (ed.), *Political Parties and the European Union.* London: Routledge, pp. 254–72.

Rumford, Chris (2000) *European Cohesion?: Contradictions in EU Integration.* Basingstoke and New York: St. Martin's Press.

Rusconi, Gian Enrico (1998) 'The Difficulty of Building a European Identity', *International Spectator*, vol. 33, no. 1 (January–March), p. 1.

Sandholz, W. (1996) 'Membership Matters: Limits of the Functional Approach to European Institutions', *Journal of Common Market Studies*, 34 (3): 403–29.

Sandholtz, W. and Zysman, J. (1989) '1992: Recasting the European Bargain', *World Politics*, vol. 42, pp. 95–128.

Sandholtz, Wayne and Stone Sweet, Alex (eds) (1998) *European Integration and Supranational Governance.* Oxford University Press.

Sapir, André *et al.* (2003) *An Agenda for a Growing Europe.* Brussels: European Commission.

Sbragia, A. (ed.) (1992) *Euro-Politics: Institutions and Policy-Making in the 'New' European Union.* Washington, DC: Brookings Institution.

Sbragia, A. (1998) 'Institution-building from Below and Above: The European Community in Global Environmental Politics', in Stone Sweet, A. and Sandholtz, W. (eds), *European Integration and Supranational Governance.* Oxford University Press, pp. 283–303.

Scharpf, Fritz W. (2002) 'The European Social Model', *Journal of Common Market Studies*, vol. 40, no. 4 (November) pp. 645–70.

Scharpf, P. (1988) 'The joint decision trap: lessons from German federalism and European integration', *Public Administration*, 66: 239–78.

Schlesinger, P. and Kevin, D. (2000) 'Can the European Union Become a Sphere of Publics?', in E. O. Eriksen and J. E. Fossum (eds), *Democracy in the European Union: Integration through Deliberation?* London: Routledge, pp. 206–29.

Schmidt, V. (1997) 'European Integration and Democracy: The Differences Among Member States', *Journal of European Public Policy*, vol. 4, pp. 128–45.

Schmitter, P. (1970) 'A Revised Theory of Regional Integration', *International Organization*, vol. 24, pp. 836–68.

Sedelmeier, U. (1998) 'The European Union's Association Policy Towards the Countries of Central and Eastern Europe: Collective EU Identity and Policy Paradigms in a Composite Policy', Ph.D. thesis, University of Sussex, April.

Sedelmeier, Ulrich (2001) 'Eastern Enlargement: Risk, Rationality, and Role-Compliance', in Maria Green Cowles and Michael Smith (eds), *The State of the European Union: Risks, Reform, Resistance, and Revival.* Oxford University Press. pp. 164–85.

Shapiro, Jeremy (2002) *The Role of France in the War on Terrorism.* Washington, DC: Brookings Institute, May.

Shaw, J. and Wiener, A. (2001) 'The Paradox of the "European Polity" ', in Maria Green Cowles and Michael Smith, *The State of the European Union: Risks, Reform, Resistance, and Revival.* Oxford University Press.

Siedentop, Larry (2000) *Democracy in Europe.* London: Allen Lane.

Siedentop, Larry (2001) *Democracy in Europe.* New York: Columbia University Press.

Silvia, S. (2002) 'The Fall and Rise of Unemployment in Germany: Is the Red–Green Government Responsible?', *German Politics*, vol. 11, pp. 1–22.

Sisson, Keith and Marginson, Paul (2001) 'Benchmarking and the "Europeanization" of Social and Employment Policy', *ESRC Briefing Note*, vol. 3, no. 1 (April).

Sloan, S. (2003) *NATO, the European Union and the Atlantic Community: The Transatlantic Bargain Reconsidered.* Lanham, MD: Rowman & Littlefield.

Slocock, B. (1996) 'The Paradoxes of Environmental Policy in Eastern Europe: The Dynamics of Policy-Making in the Czech Republic', *Environmental Politics*, vol. 5, no. 3, pp. 501–21.

Smith, M. (1984) *Western Europe and the United States: The Uncertain Alliance.* London: George Allen & Unwin.

Smith, M. (1998a) 'The European Union and the Asia-Pacific', in A. McGrew and C. Brook (eds), *Asia-Pacific and the New World Order.* London: Routledge, pp. 289–315.

Smith, M. (1998b) 'Competitive Co-operation and EU–US Relations: Can the EU Be a Strategic Partner for the US in the World Political Economy?' *Journal of European Public Policy*, vol. 5, no. 4 (December), pp. 561–77.

Smith, M. (2001) 'Europe and the German Model: Growing Tension or Symbiosis?', *German Politics*, vol. 10, pp. 119–40.

Smith, M. and Woolcock, S. (1993) *The United States and the European Community in a Transformed World.* London: Pinter.

Soetendorp, B. (2002) 'The EU's Involvement in the Israeli–Palestinian Peace Process: The Building of a Visible International Identity', *European Foreign Affairs Review*, vol. 7, pp. 283–95.

Solana, Javier (2003) 'Mars And Venus Reconciled: A New Era For Transatlantic Relations', Albert H. Gordon Lecture at the Kennedy School of Government, Harvard University, 7 April.

Statewatch (2003) 'EU–Ecuador. Proposed addition of Ecuador to visa "blacklist" ', *February 2003 News Bulletin*. Website: http://www.statewatch.org/news/2003/feb/07ecuad.htm.

Stein, Eric (1981) 'Lawyers, Judges, and the Making of a Transnational Constitution', *American Journal of International Law*, vol. 75/1, pp. 1–27.

Steunenberg, Bernard (ed.) (2002) *Widening the European Union: The Politics of Institutional Change and Reform*. London: Routledge.

Sturm, Roland (1994) 'The Chancellor and the Executive', in Stephen Padgett (ed.), *Adenauer to Kohl: The Development of the German Chancellorship*. London: Hurst, pp. 74–92.

Sullivan, M. (2002) *'Protecting Consumers? Regulation of Financial Markets in Europe'*, in S. Hatt, S. and F. Gardner, *Europe, Policies and People*. Basingstoke and New York: Palgrave Macmillan.

Szczerbiak, Aleks (2003) 'The Polish EU Accession Referendum, 7–8 June 2003, *Opposing Europe Research Network Referendum Briefing No. 5*. Website: http://www.susx.ac.uk/Units/SEI/oern/ElectionBriefings/Referendum/Poland5.pdf.

Szczerbiak, Alexs and Paul Taggart (2000) 'Opposing Europe: Party, Systems and Opposition to the Union, the Euro and Europeanisation', Sussex European Institute Working Paper No. 36. Brighton: Sussex European Institute.

Szczerbiak, Aleks and Paul Taggart (eds) (forthcoming 2004) *Opposing Europe? The Comparative Party Politics of Euroscepticism*, 2 vols. Oxford University Press.

Taggart, Paul (1998) 'A Touchstone of Dissent: Euroscepticism in Contemporary Western European Party Systems', *European Journal of Political Research*, vol. 363–88.

The Courier (1990) No. 120. Brussels: European Commission.

The Courier (1996) No. 155. Brussels: European Commission.

Thielemann, Eiko (2003) 'Does Policy Harmonisation Work? The EU's Role in Regulating Unwanted Migration', Paper presented at the European Union Studies Association, Nashville, Tenn., USA, 27–29 March.

Thompson, R. (2001) 'Doha Diary', Website: www.freetradewritersgroup. org.

Thurow, L. (1992) *Head to Head: The Coming Economic Struggle among the US, Japan, and Europe*. New York: Morrow.

Trebilcock, M. J. and Howse, R. (1995) *The Regulation of International Trade*. London: Routledge.

Tsoukalis, L. (1977) *The Politics and Economics of European Monetary Integration*. London: George Allen & Unwin.

Turner A. (2001) *Just Capital: The Liberal Economy*. London: Macmillan.

Uçarer, Emek (2002a) 'From the Sidelines to Center Stage: Sidekick No More? The European Commission in Justice and Home Affairs', *European Integration Online Papers* (EIOP), vol. 5, no. 5.

Uçarer, E. M. (2002b) 'Justice and Home Affairs in the Aftermath of September 11: Opportunities and Challenges', *EUSA Review*, vol. 14, no. 2.

Uçarer, E. M. (2003) 'Justice and Home Affairs', in M. Cini. (ed.), *European Union Politics*. New York: Oxford University Press, pp. 294–311.

UNHCR (2002) 'Number of Asylum Applications in 30 Industrialized Countries, 1992–2001', *Statistics at a Glance*. 31 May. Geneva: UNHCR.

Van Brabant, Jozef M. (1999) *Remaking Europe: The European Union and the Transition Economics*. London: Rowman & Littlefield.

Van der Eijk, C. and Franklin, M. with Ackaert, J. (1996) *Choosing Europe? The European Electorate and National Politics in the Face of Union*. Ann Arbor, MI: University of Michigan.

Van Meurs, Wim (ed.) (2001) *Beyond EU Enlargement, Vol. 2: The Agenda of Stabilisation for Southeastern Europe*. Gütersloh: Bertelsmann Foundation.

Van Oudenaren, John (2003) 'Russia's Elusive Place in Europe', in Simon Serfaty (ed.), *The European Finality Debate and Its National Dimensions*. Washington, DC: CSIS Press.

Van Riesen, M. (1999) *EU 'Global Player': The North–South Policy of the European Union*. Utrecht: Eurostep International Books.

Verdun, A. (2000) *European Responses to Globalization and Financial Market Integration. Perceptions of Economic and Monetary Union in Britain, France and Germany*. Basingstoke and New York: Palgrave Macmillan.

Verdun, A. (ed.) (2002) *The Euro: European Integration Theory and Economic and Monetary Union*. Lanham, MD: Rowman & Littlefield.

Verney, Susannah (1996) 'The Greek Socialists in Union', in John Gaffney (ed.) *Political Parties and the European Union*. London: Routledge, pp. 170–88.

Vogel, D. (1995) *Trading Up: Consumer and Environmental Regulation in a Global Economy*. Cambridge, MA: Harvard University Press.

Vogel, D. (2002) 'The WTO, International Trade and Environmental Protection: European and American Perspective', *EUI Working Papers*, RSC No. 2002/34. Florence: European University Institute.

von Homeyer, I., Carius, A. and Bär, S. (2000) 'Flexibility or Renationalization: Effects of Enlargement on EC Environmental Policy', in M. Green Cowles and M. Smith (eds), *The State of the European Union, Risks, Reform, Resistance and Revival*. Oxford University Press, pp. 347–68.

Vukadinovic, Radovan (2001) 'Yugoslavia', in Jan Zielonka and Alex Pravda (eds), *Democratic Consolidation in Eastern Europe*, Vol. 2. Oxford University Press.

Wallace, H. (2001a). 'EU Enlargement: A Neglected Subject', in M. Green Cowles and M. Smith, *The State of the European Union: Risks, Reform, Resistance, and Revival*. Oxford University Press.

Wallace, H. (2001b) 'The Changing Politics of the European Union: An Overview', *Journal of Common Market Studies*, vol. 39, no. 4, pp. 581–94.

Wallace, H. and Wallace, W. (eds) (1996) *Policy-Making in the European Union*. Oxford University Press.

Walsh, James I. (2000) *European Monetary Integration and Domestic Politics: Britain, France and Italy*. Boulder, CO: Lynne Rienner.

Weale, A, Pridham, G., Cini, M., Constadakopulos, D., Porter, M. and Flynn, B. (2000) *Environmental Governance in Europe*. Oxford University Press.

Weiler, Joseph H. H. (1991) 'The Transformation of Europe', *Yale Law Journal*, vol. 100, no. 8, pp. 2403–83; reprinted in Joseph H. H. Weiler (1999) *The Constitution of Europe, 'Do the New Clothes Have an Emperor?' and Other Essays on European Integration*. Cambridge University Press.

Weiler, Joseph H. H. (1999a) *The Constitution of Europe*, Cambridge University Press.

Weiler, Joseph H. H. (1999) *The Constitution of Europe, 'Do the New Clothes Have an Emperor?' and Other Essays on European Integration.* Cambridge University Press.

Werner Report (1970) 'Report to the Council and the Commission on the Realization by Stages of Economic and Monetary Union in the Community'. Council and Commission of the EC, *Bulletin of the EC*, Supp. 11, Doc. 16. 956/11/70, 8 October.

Whitman, Richard (1999) 'Amsterdam's Unfinished Business? The Blair Government's Initiative and the Future of the Western European Union', *Occasional Papers*, vol. 7, Paris, Institute for Security Studies of the WEU, January.

Wiessala, G. (2002) *The European Union and Asian Countries.* Sheffield: Sheffield Academic Press/Continuum.

Winters, L. A. (2001) 'European Union Trade Policy: Actually or Just Nominally Liberal?' in H. Wallace (ed.), *Interlocking Dimensions of European Integration.* Basingstoke and New York: Palgrave Macmillan, pp. 25–44.

Woolcock, S. (2000) 'European Trade Policy: Global Pressures and Domestic Constraints', in H. Wallace and W. Wallace (eds), *Policy-Making in the European Union*, 4th edn. Oxford University Press, pp. 373–99.

Woolcock, S. and Hodges, M. (1996) 'EU Policy in the Uruguay Round', in H. Wallace and W. Wallace (eds), *Policy-Making in the European Union*, 3rd edn. Oxford University Press, pp. 301–24.

World Bank (2000) *Global Economic Prospects 2001.* Washington, DC: The World Bank.

World Commission on Environment and Development (1987) *Our Common Future.* Oxford University Press.

WTO (World Trade Organization) (1995), *Trade Policy Review: European Union 1995.* Geneva: World Trade Organization.

WTO (World Trade Organization) (2001) 'Ministerial Conference, Fourth Session, Doha, 9–14 November 2001: Ministerial Declaration', WT/MIN(01)/DEC/W/1. Website: www.wto.org.

WTO (World Trade Organization) (2002a), *Trade Policy Review: European Union*, WT/TPR/S/102, 26 June. Geneva: World Trade Organization.

WTO (World Trade Organization) (2002b) *International Trade Statistics 2002*, available at www.wto.org.

Wurzel, R. (2002) *Environmental Policy Making in Britain, Germany and the European Union.* Manchester University Press.

Wurzel, R., Jordan, A., Zito, A. and Brückner, L. (2003) European Governance and the Transfer of 'New' Environmental Policy Instruments. Public Administration, vol. 81 Part 3, pp. 555–74. Website: http://www.uea.ac.uk/env/cserge/ research/futgovernance/Home.htm.

Young, A. R. (2002) *Extending European Co-operation: The European Union and the 'New' International Trade Agenda.* Manchester University Press.

Young, A. R. and Wallace, H. (2000) *Regulatory Politics in the Enlarging European Union: Weighing Civic and Producer Interests.* Manchester University Press.

Index